# The Anxiety Toolbox Program

# The Anxiety Toolbox Program

**THE COMPREHENSIVE, INTEGRATIVE APPROACH TO OVERCOMING ANXIOUS EMOTIONS**

**James Conrad Gardner, MD**

© 2017 James Conrad Gardner, MD. All rights reserved.
No contents may be copied without express written permission from Dr. Gardner.

ISBN-13: 9780692893913
ISBN-10: 0692893911

## Disclaimer

The Anxiety Toolbox Program (ATP) contains information the author believes to be correct but may or may not apply to your unique situation. This program is not a substitute for the advice and care of a skilled medical or psychological health professional. Although general principles and practices of treatment are described here, no specific recommendation for any individual's therapy or medical care is intended, expressed, or implied. When it comes to health care, no reader should act on the basis of any printed information, including the contents of this book, without consultation with a health-care professional. Nothing in the ATP should be construed as an attempt to diagnose, prescribe, or recommend a treatment for any health condition. You should not try to treat yourself with any of the methods described in this program without the guidance of a qualified health-care professional who is thoroughly familiar with both the remedies and your medical and psychological status. Some of the herbs and alternative remedies listed are known to be poisonous if taken inappropriately; some can elicit allergic reactions. Do not attempt to self-diagnose or self-treat based on information in this program, including the comprehensive anxiety screening tool self-test and the quick-fix formula.

*The Anxiety Toolbox Program* provides various URLs as helpful resources. Although I have chosen sites that reflect our standards, we take no responsibility for their content or any product that you might purchase from them.

## Mission Statement

The Anxiety Toolbox Program (ATP) requires the reader to self-design a unique and individualized path to recovery. When I realized twenty years ago that some 40 percent of patients in my general medical practice struggled with anxiety and depression, I made it a priority to understand emotional health diagnoses and treatments and to stay on top of the latest advances. This book is for people who do not have access to quality care or to a practitioner who cares. So many people of all ages and backgrounds have no coverage or have limited access to care when they most need it. They may have to wait several weeks for a doctor to give a delayed and often inadequate response to their emotional pain.

As a Kindle download or print-on-demand book, *The Anxiety Toolbox Program* offers immediate help. It presents treatment possibilities from all disciplines—medical, behavioral, and alternative—going back to the beginning of human history. *The Anxiety Toolbox Program* allows readers to delve into their diagnostic possibilities through the comprehensive anxiety screening tool self-test, a unique feature of this book. Then, after reading and understanding the rationales of hundreds of strategies to reduce anxiety, readers are guided to organize their self-chosen combinations of those strategies and incorporate them into their everyday lives as sustainable, long-term lifestyles and routines.

After finishing this book, readers will feel empowered with a clear understanding of their emotional conditions and their best individualized treatment options. They will know more than many medical doctors, psychologists, or even psychiatrists about diagnosing and treating emotional conditions such as obsessive-compulsive disorder (OCD), panic disorder, posttraumatic stress disorder (PTSD), generalized anxiety disorder, situational anxiety, social phobia, agoraphobia, unipolar and bipolar depression, mania and hypomania, specific phobias, panic attacks, and more. They will no longer be frightened and misdirected by "Dr. Google." They will be educated and prepared to make clear decisions about their treatment without letting a practitioner employ some hit-or-miss strategy based on a hasty assessment.

Too many times, patients suffering from anxiety and depression are paralyzed with indecision and fear. They give the decision-making role to family, friends, significant others, a guru, a religious adviser, a cult leader, or doctors in an overwhelmed and inefficient health-care delivery system. Instead of taking responsibility and being a proactive component of the process of regaining their emotional strength, they become passive and needy victims. This does not lead to long-term health, strength, or wellness—only disappointment, despair, relapse, suffering, and a higher risk of suicide. The overall cost to the patient, to his or her family and career, and to society is enormous and growing. The medical system in the United States and elsewhere has failed those with emotional-health challenges miserably, and it is only getting worse with federal cuts to Medicare and Medicaid and decreased coverage for mental-health services by managed-care insurance providers.

*The Anxiety Toolbox Program* aspires to help relieve the mental-health-care crisis that is upon us by putting the power for healing in the hands of the patient while relieving the anxiety caused by misinformation, delayed intervention, and ineffective treatment strategies. There is no substitute for the confidence, sense of achievement, and self-pride that comes from being the lead decision maker and designer of your recovery from uncontrolled anxiety. The primary mission of *The Anxiety Toolbox Program* is to help you maintain your individuality, inner conscience, inner child, and the freedom from manipulation and coercion by finding your own solution to anxiety, rather than being spoon-fed a solution that serves someone else. There is an anxiety that arises from the realization that you are the sole architect of your future and fate. If you want the freedom of being fully anxiety-free and in control of your life, there is no room for blaming your parents, the "system," your boss, spouse, or past traumas or difficulties. You must take full responsibility for your decisions and resulting outcomes.

About an hour after I wrote this mission statement, while sorting through one of the dozens of boxes of his personal notes, I pulled out a scrap of paper at random written by my late father, T.F. Gardner, who died on April 18, 2017, and to whom this book is dedicated. His remark below, dated September 2012, sums it up best. How it surfaced in a sea of thousands of scraps of papers is so like T. F.'s flare for the dramatic:

> There are simple solutions to anxiety caused by the uncertainty of self-determinism; you can get these solutions from your Parents, Priest, Preacher, Politician, or Prince. But then you are preserved, provided for, and possessed.

James Gardner, MD

# Emergency Information

If you are presently suffering from uncontrolled anxiety and panic attacks, feel an overwhelming sense of doom and dread, or feel you are out of control and having a nervous breakdown, you belong in the nearest emergency room. If you feel suicidal and are contemplating a plan of action to harm yourself, please call 911 and explain this to the operator or have a friend drive you to the hospital. You will be surprised how fast you can get help and support. Sometimes a sedative shot or pill will abort the frightening symptoms that you are now experiencing. Even though you are feeling a sense of doom and may believe you are dying, you will feel better within minutes of being given the proper medical treatment. Do not hesitate out of fear of humiliation or judgment. This happens every day to ordinary and otherwise healthy people of all cultures, backgrounds, education levels, and socioeconomic status. The hospital staff has seen this many times before and will treat you with compassion and understanding. They will likely give you a few days' worth of medication until you can see your regular doctor or a specialist. If you are suicidal or have a substance-abuse concern, a specialist will be called in to talk to you and get you the support and help you need. You should never suffer due to lack of money. All hospitals are required to evaluate you regardless of your ability to pay if they believe you are a danger to yourself. It may save your life and spare your friends and family a lifetime of sorrow, pain, unanswered questions, and regret. Remember, everyone is here for a reason—even you. There is something meaningful and purposeful beyond the despair and hopelessness you are feeling. Once things are under control and you are under the care of a medical professional, you can start *The Anxiety Toolbox Program* and find long-term answers for overcoming your fears and being the master of your emotions.

# Dedication

This book is dedicated to my father, the Reverend Thomas Frank (T.F.) Gardner, who died April 18, 2017, two months before his ninety-seventh birthday, as I was finishing the last chapter of this book. His spirit and observations on anxiety are shared throughout The Anxiety Toolbox Program. Active and fully "in charge" until the last few hours of his life, T. F. lived an independent, self-reliant, engaged, and vigorous life. The day he collapsed of a heart attack and aortic dissection, he had cleaned and vacuumed his apartment, washed his car, shopped for groceries, washed and dried his clothes, and was looking forward to Easter weekend with his kids visiting from out of town. He died three days later surrounded by his family.

T. F. was born in 1920 in London to a family of eight boys and two girls. Besides serving as a Presbyterian minister for sixty-seven years, he was an army air force officer and the last living P-61 night fighter pilot of WW II, a general contractor, a chemist, a professional actor, an opera buff and classical music historian, a black diamond skier, and the devoted father of seven children, fifteen grandchildren, and three great-grandchildren. His wife, Naomi Mae Heinrichs, also died over Easter weekend forty-nine years earlier of stage IV cancer, and he never remarried. At his graduation from the San Francisco Theological Seminary at San Anselmo, he was dubbed "The Maverick Theologian" because of his liberal views and broad inclusiveness ("Whoever is not against us, is for us" Mark 9:40). Eschewing Western medicine, he overcame PTSD, anxiety, and depression throughout life with his steadfast spiritual beliefs and the solace he found in music, poetry, literature, and conversation. His wisdom, drawn from years of study and painful life experiences, is well documented in many sermons and copious notes and will be the subject of my last book on the subject of anxiety. Some of his favorite quotes and verses are shared at the end of this book.

I would like to thank my wife, Patty, and son, Jacob; my sisters, Connie, Kay, Sydney, Naomi, and Gayle; and my brother, Tom, who helped and encouraged me through this difficult time; and to the Reverend Kent Webber for the kindness he has shown our family since he was a boy in T.F.'s bible school class at the First Presbyterian Church in Santa Cruz and through the many years he served as T.F.'s pastor in Novato, California.

# How to Use the Anxiety Toolbox Program

There are six sections of the ATP:

1. *The Anxiety Toolbox Program* will give you all the information you need to understand anxiety disorders and discuss them with authority with your health-care practitioners.
2. The comprehensive anxiety screening tool self-test will help elucidate your possible multiple or overlapping diagnoses.
3. The quick-fix formula can help bring relief within days.
4. The combat relief brief is for returning veterans, trauma survivors, and athletes at all levels who are experiencing PTSD and/or TBI.
5. The personal anxiety assessment plan will help you make a personalized list and own your unique set of issues.
6. A personal daily planner will help you organize, design, and implement a plan that fits you and your individual sensitivities and preferences.

The journey is about to begin! Follow the steps below to determine how you should focus on applying this book to your situation:

**Step one.** If you want some immediate help in getting anxiety symptoms under control, first print out or read the quick-fix formula workbook in appendix 2. You should take this to your doctor to make sure you are medically cleared to do the one-week "quick fix," which is helpful with or without adding a prescription medication.

**Step two.** The next step is to fill out the comprehensive anxiety screening tool self-test in appendix 1 and circle those diagnoses that you may meet the diagnostic criteria for.

**Step three.** Next, read the entire *The Anxiety Toolbox Program*. This may take one day to one week, depending on your speed, focus, and energy. At each "**TOOL**" checkpoint, decide if this is an item you would like to add to your personal program. If so, circle or highlight this tool so you can later integrate it into your personal daily planner. Mark the appropriate boxes as you go through the program, and make notes on each chapter as you go, if you feel inspired.

**Step four.** Next, you need a frank and honest assessment of yourself before you can design a program that will work for you. I want you to really put it all on the table. Fill in the personal anxiety assessment plan questions in appendix 4. This will be used as a baseline to compare against as you progress in the ATP and will be a resource you refer to on a daily basis.

I recommend that anyone experiencing anxiety seriously consider healthy self-care and personal organization tools; adjust any faulty attitudes, perceptions, or beliefs; choose positive and uplifting activities; and cultivate spiritual beliefs. In addition, I especially recommend the following tools for specific anxiety disorders. If, after completing the comprehensive anxiety screening tool test, you feel you meet the criteria for any of these specific disorders, be sure to include the recommended tools in your own personal program:

- **General anxiety disorder, OCD, PTSD, TBI, panic disorder:** medication; hormone optimization; deep, restful sleep; deep breathing; meditation; aerobic exercise, yoga, or rhythmic exercise; changing anxious self-talk, stopping automatic negative thoughts, stress-resistant thinking tips; eye movement desensitization and reprocessing (EMDR) therapy
- **Social phobia:** medication therapy; correcting wrong thinking in social situations; assertiveness training; social anxiety and social skills training; graded desensitization/exposure therapy
- **Specific phobia:** wrong thinking in specific phobia; graded desensitization/exposure therapy
- **Agoraphobia:** medication therapy, wrong thinking in agoraphobia; graded desensitization/exposure therapy
- **Speaker's nerves:** medication therapy; public speaking skills, graded desensitization/exposure therapy
- **Bulimia/anorexia/binge eating:** medication treatment, low-anxiety diet, light therapy, vitamins and supplements, EMDR
- **Situational anxiety (sports, performance):** guided imagery, visualization, self-hypnosis, biofeedback, deep breathing

**Step five.** Lastly, you will be building your own personal program using the personal daily planner in appendix 5. Fill it out and follow the instructions.

You will find all five items (quick-fix formula, comprehensive anxiety screening tool, combat relief brief, personal anxiety assessment plan, personal daily planner) as appendixes at the end of *The Anxiety Toolbox Program* that you have either purchased in a downloadable Kindle or print-on-demand form. The download format makes it easy to print out any section in which you need to keep track of the elements of your individual program and stay organized. Do it in the order that feels most natural to you.

Relax. Let this be fun. There is no more exciting adventure than the journey to feeling well and completely in control of your health and emotions!

# Table of Contents

Disclaimer ......................................................................................... v

Mission Statement ............................................................................ vii

Emergency Information ...................................................................... ix

Dedication ......................................................................................... xi

How to Use the Anxiety Toolbox Program ........................................... xiii

Preface ............................................................................................. xxix

Introduction ..................................................................................... xxxiii

        Getting Started ................................................................... xxxiii

        Medical Choices .................................................................. xxxiii

        Considering Our Own Contribution to Anxiety ..................... xxxiv

        The Cycle of Life ................................................................... xxxiv

        Transformation: The Way Out .............................................. xxxv

Chapter 1    What Everyone Should Know about Anxiety ........................ 1

        Good Anxiety—Bad Anxiety .................................................. 2

        The Concept of Dread ........................................................... 2

|  |  |  |
|---|---|---|
|  | Anxiety to Help Us Relax | 3 |
|  | When Anxiety Goes Terribly Wrong | 3 |
|  | Success On and Off the Court | 4 |
|  | Anxiety in Its Infancy | 4 |
|  | When Your Brain Is Playing Tricks on You | 4 |
|  | Where Anxiety Lives | 5 |
|  | How We Learn Anxiety | 5 |
|  | Unlearning Anxiety | 6 |
|  | Eastern or Western? | 6 |
| Chapter 2 | Recognizing Anxiety Disorders | 8 |
|  | Generalized Anxiety Disorder | 8 |
|  | Panic Disorder | 9 |
|  | Obsessive-Compulsive Disorder | 9 |
|  | Posttraumatic Stress Disorder | 10 |
|  | Bulimia Nervosa, Anorexia Nervosa, and Binge-Eating Disorders | 10 |
|  | Anxiety as a Symptom of a Mood Disorder | 10 |
|  | Social Anxiety Disorder/Social Phobia | 11 |
|  | Specific Phobia | 11 |
|  | Recognizing Phobic Fears and Behaviors | 11 |
|  | Anxiety Caused by Attention Deficit Disorder in Children and Adults | 12 |
|  | Acute Situational Anxiety | 14 |

| | | |
|---|---|---|
| | Who Gets Anxiety Disorders? | 15 |
| | How Are Anxiety Disorders Diagnosed? | 15 |
| | How Are Anxiety Disorders Treated? | 15 |
| | Additional Sources of Information | 16 |
| Chapter 3 | The Rewards of Mastering Anxiety | 18 |
| | Recognizing Fear's Gifts | 18 |
| | Human Nature: Sheep and Shepherds | 19 |
| | Choose to Be a Shepherd | 20 |
| | Setting Your Sights Up and Away! | 21 |
| Chapter 4 | Toolbox Compartment Number One: The Medical Treatment of Anxiety | 22 |
| | Using the "Symptom" and "Brain Function" Models to Determine Your Medical Therapy Options | 23 |
| |     The Symptom Model for Choosing an Effective Medical Regimen | 23 |
| |     The Brain Function Model for Choosing an Effective Medical Regimen | 27 |
| | The Importance of Thyroid and Sex Hormone Optimization in Treating Anxiety | 30 |
| | The Office Treatment of Needle Phobias and Procedure Anxiety | 33 |
| | Transcranial Magnetic Stimulation for Depression | 33 |
| | Stem Cell IV and Intrathecal Infusions for Healing TBI-Related PTSD | 34 |
| Chapter 5 | Toolbox Compartment Number Two: Alternative Medical Therapy Tools for Anxiety | 36 |
| | Vitamins and Supplements | 36 |
| | Probiotics, the Gut Microbiome, and Brain Function | 37 |
| | Fermented Cellulose Antioxidant | 38 |

Oxytocin · · · · · · · · · · · · · · · · · · · · · · · · · · · · · · · · · · · · · · · · · · · · · · · · · · · · · · · · · · · · · · · · · · · · · · · · 40

Low-Dose Naltrexone for Anxiety, Depression, and Pain Reduction · · · · · · · · · · · · · · · · · · · · · 40

IV Vitamin Infusions · · · · · · · · · · · · · · · · · · · · · · · · · · · · · · · · · · · · · · · · · · · · · · · · · · · · · · · · · · · · 41

MSM · · · · · · · · · · · · · · · · · · · · · · · · · · · · · · · · · · · · · · · · · · · · · · · · · · · · · · · · · · · · · · · · · · · · · · · · · · · · 42

B-Complex IV · · · · · · · · · · · · · · · · · · · · · · · · · · · · · · · · · · · · · · · · · · · · · · · · · · · · · · · · · · · · · · · · · · 43

High-Dose Vitamin C IV Infusion · · · · · · · · · · · · · · · · · · · · · · · · · · · · · · · · · · · · · · · · · · · · · · · · · · 44

NAD Infusion Therapy for Rapid Detox and Brain Restoration · · · · · · · · · · · · · · · · · · · · · · · 44

Medical Marijuana · · · · · · · · · · · · · · · · · · · · · · · · · · · · · · · · · · · · · · · · · · · · · · · · · · · · · · · · · · · · · · · 45

Oral, Inhaled, and IV Hydrogen Therapy · · · · · · · · · · · · · · · · · · · · · · · · · · · · · · · · · · · · · · · · · · · · 46

Microdosing of LSD for Depression and Anxiety · · · · · · · · · · · · · · · · · · · · · · · · · · · · · · · · · · · · 47

Ketamine · · · · · · · · · · · · · · · · · · · · · · · · · · · · · · · · · · · · · · · · · · · · · · · · · · · · · · · · · · · · · · · · · · · · · · · · · 48

Botox · · · · · · · · · · · · · · · · · · · · · · · · · · · · · · · · · · · · · · · · · · · · · · · · · · · · · · · · · · · · · · · · · · · · · · · · · · · · 49

Homeopathic Anxiety Remedies · · · · · · · · · · · · · · · · · · · · · · · · · · · · · · · · · · · · · · · · · · · · · · · · · · · 49

Anxiety Remedies of Chinese Traditional/Herbal Medicine · · · · · · · · · · · · · · · · · · · · · · · · · · · 51

Ayurvedic Strategies to Reduce Anxiety · · · · · · · · · · · · · · · · · · · · · · · · · · · · · · · · · · · · · · · · · · · · 52

| Chapter 6 | Toolbox Compartment Number Three: Anxiety Caused by Pain Management and Addiction Problems · · · · · · · · · · · · · · · · · · · · · · · · · · · · · · · · · · · · · · · · · · · · · · · · · · · · · · · · · · · · · · · 54 |
|---|---|

A Word about Anxiety and Pain Management · · · · · · · · · · · · · · · · · · · · · · · · · · · · · · · · · · · · · · 54

A Word about Anxiety and Addiction · · · · · · · · · · · · · · · · · · · · · · · · · · · · · · · · · · · · · · · · · · · · · · 56

| Chapter 7 | Toolbox Compartment Number Four: Healthy Lifestyle, Self-Care, and Personal Organization Tools · · · · · · · · · · · · · · · · · · · · · · · · · · · · · · · · · · · · · · · · · · · · · · · · · · · · · · · · · · · · · · · · · · 58 |
|---|---|

Low-Anxiety Diet · · · · · · · · · · · · · · · · · · · · · · · · · · · · · · · · · · · · · · · · · · · · · · · · · · · · · · · · · · · · · · · · 58

    High-Anxiety Foods · · · · · · · · · · · · · · · · · · · · · · · · · · · · · · · · · · · · · · · · · · · · · · · · · · · · · · · · · · · · · · · · · · · · ·59

    Low-Anxiety Foods · · · · · · · · · · · · · · · · · · · · · · · · · · · · · · · · · · · · · · · · · · · · · · · · · · · · · · · · · · · · · · · · · · · · · ·59

    The Latest in Nutrition Research and Human Genetics · · · · · · · · · · · · · · · · · · · · · · · · · · ·60

    Calories, Exercise, and Weight · · · · · · · · · · · · · · · · · · · · · · · · · · · · · · · · · · · · · · · · · · · · · · · · · · · · · · · ·61

Vitamins and Supplements · · · · · · · · · · · · · · · · · · · · · · · · · · · · · · · · · · · · · · · · · · · · · · · · · · · · · · · · · · · · · · · · · · · ·62

Exercise · · · · · · · · · · · · · · · · · · · · · · · · · · · · · · · · · · · · · · · · · · · · · · · · · · · · · · · · · · · · · · · · · · · · · · · · · · · · · · · · · · · · · · · · · · ·63

    Overview · · · · · · · · · · · · · · · · · · · · · · · · · · · · · · · · · · · · · · · · · · · · · · · · · · · · · · · · · · · · · · · · · · · · · · · · · · · · · · · · · · · ·63

    Common Excuses for Not Exercising · · · · · · · · · · · · · · · · · · · · · · · · · · · · · · · · · · · · · · · · · · · · · · · · · · · · ·64

    Getting Started with an Exercise Program · · · · · · · · · · · · · · · · · · · · · · · · · · · · · · · · · · · · · · · · · · · · · ·65

    What Type of Exercise Is Right for Me? · · · · · · · · · · · · · · · · · · · · · · · · · · · · · · · · · · · · · · · · · · · · · · · · · · · ·66

Deep, Restful Sleep · · · · · · · · · · · · · · · · · · · · · · · · · · · · · · · · · · · · · · · · · · · · · · · · · · · · · · · · · · · · · · · · · · · · · · · · · · · · · · · · · ·67

    The Biophysiology of Sleep · · · · · · · · · · · · · · · · · · · · · · · · · · · · · · · · · · · · · · · · · · · · · · · · · · · · · · · · · · · · · · · · ·67

    Healthy Sleep Hygiene · · · · · · · · · · · · · · · · · · · · · · · · · · · · · · · · · · · · · · · · · · · · · · · · · · · · · · · · · · · · · · · · · · · · · · ·69

    Herbal Sedatives · · · · · · · · · · · · · · · · · · · · · · · · · · · · · · · · · · · · · · · · · · · · · · · · · · · · · · · · · · · · · · · · · · · · · · · · · · · · · ·70

    Homeopathic and Over-the-Counter Sleep Remedies · · · · · · · · · · · · · · · · · · · · · · · · · · · · · · · ·70

    Medical Treatment of Insomnia · · · · · · · · · · · · · · · · · · · · · · · · · · · · · · · · · · · · · · · · · · · · · · · · · · · · · · · · · · · · · ·71

Personal Hygiene · · · · · · · · · · · · · · · · · · · · · · · · · · · · · · · · · · · · · · · · · · · · · · · · · · · · · · · · · · · · · · · · · · · · · · · · · · · · · · · · · · · · · ·72

Personal Organization · · · · · · · · · · · · · · · · · · · · · · · · · · · · · · · · · · · · · · · · · · · · · · · · · · · · · · · · · · · · · · · · · · · · · · · · · · · · · · · ·73

    Daily Rhythm · · · · · · · · · · · · · · · · · · · · · · · · · · · · · · · · · · · · · · · · · · · · · · · · · · · · · · · · · · · · · · · · · · · · · · · · · · · · · · · · · ·73

    Common Sense · · · · · · · · · · · · · · · · · · · · · · · · · · · · · · · · · · · · · · · · · · · · · · · · · · · · · · · · · · · · · · · · · · · · · · · · · · · · · · · ·73

    Presence of Mind · · · · · · · · · · · · · · · · · · · · · · · · · · · · · · · · · · · · · · · · · · · · · · · · · · · · · · · · · · · · · · · · · · · · · · · · · · · · · ·74

|  |  |  |
|---|---|---|
|  | Financial Responsibility | 75 |
|  | Be Committed | 76 |
|  | Get Rid of Clutter | 77 |
|  | Time Management | 77 |
| Chapter 8 | Toolbox Compartment Number Five: Goals and Values; Attitudes and Beliefs | 83 |
|  | Goals and Values | 83 |
|  | Write Your Eulogy and Epitaph | 84 |
|  | Five Years to Live | 84 |
|  | Top Ten | 85 |
|  | My Favorite Things | 85 |
|  | Essay Questions | 86 |
|  | Moving toward Your True Goals and Values | 86 |
|  | Attitudes and Beliefs | 87 |
|  | The Gardner Girls | 87 |
|  | Attitudes and Beliefs about Life | 88 |
|  | Attitudes and Beliefs about Success, Work, and Money | 91 |
|  | Other Attitudes and Beliefs about Work and Money | 93 |
|  | Attitudes and Beliefs about Love and Relationships | 96 |
| Chapter 9 | Toolbox Compartment Number Six: Mind-Body Tools | 103 |
|  | Meditation | 103 |

        Imagery/Visualization/Self-Hypnosis ················································ 107

                The Basics of Imagery ··················································· 107

                Step-By-Step Imagery ··················································· 107

                Autogenic Exercises ···················································· 108

                Self-Hypnosis ························································· 109

        Positive Affirmations and Relaxation Exercises ································· 110

        Biofeedback ····························································· 111

        Aromatherapy ···························································· 112

        Light Therapy ···························································· 113

                Overview ····························································· 113

                Light Therapy for Bulimia ··············································· 114

                Full-Spectrum versus Broad-Spectrum Light ······························· 114

        Music/Sound Therapy ····················································· 114

                Overview ····························································· 114

                Conti Music ··························································· 116

                Music for Stress Reduction ·············································· 116

        Humor Therapy ·························································· 117

**Chapter 10**   Toolbox Compartment Number Seven: Body-Mind Tools ························· 119

        Eye Movement Desensitization and Reprocessing ····························· 119

        Sensory-Deprivation Flotation Tank ········································· 120

Deep Breathing ............................................................. 123

    Overview ............................................................. 123

    Practicing Deep Breathing ....................................... 124

    Controlled Breathing ............................................. 125

Progressive Relaxation Exercises ..................................... 126

    A Little History ..................................................... 126

    Basic Instructions .................................................. 126

    Progressive Relaxation ........................................... 127

    The Shortened Version .......................................... 128

Yoga ........................................................................... 129

Tai Chi ........................................................................ 130

Reflexology .................................................................. 132

Massage Therapy .......................................................... 132

Acupuncture/Chi Kung .................................................. 133

Emotional Freedom Techniques ...................................... 134

Psychodrama and Experiential Therapy ............................ 135

Hydrotherapy ............................................................... 136

**Chapter 11** Toolbox Compartment Number Eight: Cognitive-Behavioral Therapy Tools ........... 137

Cognitive Distortions ..................................................... 137

    Overview ............................................................. 137

    Cognitive Distortions in Specific Phobia ..................... 145

    Cognitive Distortions in Social Phobia · · · · · · · · · · · · · · · · · · · · · · · · · · · · · · · · · · 145

    Cognitive Distortions in Agoraphobia · · · · · · · · · · · · · · · · · · · · · · · · · · · · · · · · · · · 146

    Refuting False Beliefs · · · · · · · · · · · · · · · · · · · · · · · · · · · · · · · · · · · · · · · · · · · · · · · · · · 146

    Changing Anxious Self-Talk · · · · · · · · · · · · · · · · · · · · · · · · · · · · · · · · · · · · · · · · · · · · 147

    Stopping Automatic Negative Thoughts · · · · · · · · · · · · · · · · · · · · · · · · · · · · · · · · 148

    Stress-Resistant Thinking Tips · · · · · · · · · · · · · · · · · · · · · · · · · · · · · · · · · · · · · · · · · · 152

Identifying, Expressing, and Communicating Feelings · · · · · · · · · · · · · · · · · · · · · · · · · · · · · 155

    Identify Your Feelings · · · · · · · · · · · · · · · · · · · · · · · · · · · · · · · · · · · · · · · · · · · · · · · · · · · 155

    Express Your Feelings · · · · · · · · · · · · · · · · · · · · · · · · · · · · · · · · · · · · · · · · · · · · · · · · · · 157

    Communicate Your Feelings · · · · · · · · · · · · · · · · · · · · · · · · · · · · · · · · · · · · · · · · · · · · 157

Stress/Anger Management · · · · · · · · · · · · · · · · · · · · · · · · · · · · · · · · · · · · · · · · · · · · · · · · · · · · · · · 157

    Counseling for Stress Management · · · · · · · · · · · · · · · · · · · · · · · · · · · · · · · · · · · · · · · 158

    Counseling for Anger Management · · · · · · · · · · · · · · · · · · · · · · · · · · · · · · · · · · · · · · 158

Assertiveness Training · · · · · · · · · · · · · · · · · · · · · · · · · · · · · · · · · · · · · · · · · · · · · · · · · · · · · · · · · · · 159

    Overview · · · · · · · · · · · · · · · · · · · · · · · · · · · · · · · · · · · · · · · · · · · · · · · · · · · · · · · · · · · · · · · · · 159

    What Is Your Behavior Style? · · · · · · · · · · · · · · · · · · · · · · · · · · · · · · · · · · · · · · · · · · · · · · 161

    Recognizing and Exercising Your Basic Rights · · · · · · · · · · · · · · · · · · · · · · · · · · · · · 163

    Knowing Your Own Needs and Desires · · · · · · · · · · · · · · · · · · · · · · · · · · · · · · · · · · · · 164

    Practicing Assertive Responses · · · · · · · · · · · · · · · · · · · · · · · · · · · · · · · · · · · · · · · · · · · 166

    Sample Scenarios · · · · · · · · · · · · · · · · · · · · · · · · · · · · · · · · · · · · · · · · · · · · · · · · · · · · · · · · 168

    Saying "No" · · · · · · · · · · · · · · · · · · · · · · · · · · · · · · · · · · · · · · · · · · · · · · · · · · · · · · · · · · · · · · 170

    Avoiding Manipulation · · · · · · · · · · · · · · · · · · · · · · · · · · · · · · · · · · · · · · · · · 170

  Social Phobia and Social Skills Training · · · · · · · · · · · · · · · · · · · · · · · · · · · · · · · · · · · · · 172

    Overview · · · · · · · · · · · · · · · · · · · · · · · · · · · · · · · · · · · · · · · · · · · · · · · · · · · · · · 172

    Factors Contributing to Social Phobia · · · · · · · · · · · · · · · · · · · · · · · · · · · · · · · · · 174

    Overcoming Social Phobia · · · · · · · · · · · · · · · · · · · · · · · · · · · · · · · · · · · · · · · · · · 176

    Social Skills Training · · · · · · · · · · · · · · · · · · · · · · · · · · · · · · · · · · · · · · · · · · · · · · 177

    Conversational Skills · · · · · · · · · · · · · · · · · · · · · · · · · · · · · · · · · · · · · · · · · · · · · · 181

    Public-Speaking Skills · · · · · · · · · · · · · · · · · · · · · · · · · · · · · · · · · · · · · · · · · · · · · 184

    Interview Skills · · · · · · · · · · · · · · · · · · · · · · · · · · · · · · · · · · · · · · · · · · · · · · · · · · 190

    Dating Skills · · · · · · · · · · · · · · · · · · · · · · · · · · · · · · · · · · · · · · · · · · · · · · · · · · · · · 193

  Graded Desensitization and Exposure Therapy · · · · · · · · · · · · · · · · · · · · · · · · · · · · · · · 196

    Sensitization and Avoidance · · · · · · · · · · · · · · · · · · · · · · · · · · · · · · · · · · · · · · · · 196

    Understanding How Exposure Works · · · · · · · · · · · · · · · · · · · · · · · · · · · · · · · · · 198

    Exposure Checklist · · · · · · · · · · · · · · · · · · · · · · · · · · · · · · · · · · · · · · · · · · · · · · · 204

    Interoceptive Exposure · · · · · · · · · · · · · · · · · · · · · · · · · · · · · · · · · · · · · · · · · · · · 205

**Chapter 12** Toolbox Compartment Number Nine: Activity Tools · · · · · · · · · · · · · · · · · · · · · 208

  The Purpose of Activities · · · · · · · · · · · · · · · · · · · · · · · · · · · · · · · · · · · · · · · · · · · · · · · · · 208

  Indoor Individual Activities · · · · · · · · · · · · · · · · · · · · · · · · · · · · · · · · · · · · · · · · · · · · · · · 209

    Pet Ownership · · · · · · · · · · · · · · · · · · · · · · · · · · · · · · · · · · · · · · · · · · · · · · · · · · · 210

    Writing Books or Poetry · · · · · · · · · · · · · · · · · · · · · · · · · · · · · · · · · · · · · · · · · · · 210

    Playing and Composing Music · · · · · · · · · · · · · · · · · · · · · · · · · · · · · · · · · · · · · · 211

  Crafts and Indoor Hobbies······211

  Gym Activities······212

Outdoor Individual Activities······212

  Gardening······212

  Hiking······212

  Fishing and Camping······213

Indoor Social Participation Activities······213

  Indoor Games······213

  Book and Dining Clubs······213

  Dancing······214

  Indoor Sports······214

  Performing Arts······214

Outdoor Social Participation Activities······214

Appreciation/Educational Activities······215

  Music and Theater Performances······215

  Museum and Academy Exhibits······215

  Foreign Language/Adult Education Classes······215

  Travel Programs······215

Volunteer/Group Activities······216

  The Red Cross/United Way······216

  Church/Temple/Synagogue/Mosque······216

| | Advocacy Groups | 216 |
|---|---|---|
| | Teams and Activities that Promote a Cause | 217 |
| Chapter 13 | Toolbox Compartment Number Ten: Spiritual Tools | 218 |
| | Religion and Spirituality | 218 |
| | Seeking a Spiritual Framework | 221 |
| | The Power of Prayer | 228 |
| | How Does Prayer Work? | 230 |
| | Other Spiritual Tools | 231 |

Final Note and Best Wishes ............................................................. 235

T. F. Gardner's Favorite Quotes and Bible Verses ............................... 237

Appendix I ..................................................................................... 241

    Comprehensive Anxiety Screening Tool Self-Test ........................ 241

    Interpretation Instructions for the Comprehensive Anxiety Screening Tool Self-Test ... 246

Appendix II .................................................................................... 251

    Quick-Fix Formula Workbook: Getting Anxious Emotions under Control in the First Week ... 251

Appendix III ................................................................................... 273

    Combat Relief Brief: What Returning Veterans and Athletes with TBI and Postconcussion Syndrome Should Know about PTSD ... 273

Appendix IV · · · · · · · · · · · · · · · · · · · · · · · · · · · · · · · · · · · · · · · · · · · · · · · · · · · · · · · · · · · · · · · · · · · · · · · · · · · · · · · · 277

    Personal Anxiety Assessment List Workbook · · · · · · · · · · · · · · · · · · · · · · · · · · · · · · · · · · · · · · · · · 277

Appendix V · · · · · · · · · · · · · · · · · · · · · · · · · · · · · · · · · · · · · · · · · · · · · · · · · · · · · · · · · · · · · · · · · · · · · · · · · · · · · · · · · 325

    Personal Daily Planner Workbook · · · · · · · · · · · · · · · · · · · · · · · · · · · · · · · · · · · · · · · · · · · · · · · · · · · 325

# Preface

This program was designed to provide the reader with a basic education about emotions—how our lives are affected by our emotions and how our emotions are influenced by how we live, our genetics, our medical imbalances, and our life experiences. The medical, hormone-optimization, dietary, and common-sense advice comes from my thirty years of aggressively recognizing, treating, and counseling patients with mild to severe manifestations of anxiety and mood disorders. *The Anxiety Toolbox Program* is a continuation and expansion of my previous two books, coauthored by Art H. Bell, PhD, and published by Career Press: *Overcoming Anxiety, Panic, and Depression: New Ways to Regain Your Confidence* (2000), and *Phobias and How to Overcome Them: Understanding and Beating Your Fears* (2005). *The Anxiety Toolbox Program* was published online in 2010 and updated in 2013. This is its third edition.

Throughout the book, I may suddenly change writing styles, telling an anecdotal story from my own life experience or the experiences of my patients. This is not because I like talking about myself or feel my life experiences or those of my patients should be particularly meaningful or applicable to your situation. It's simply that these are the only experiences I can draw from in a way that is honest and authentic. In addition, this strategy of changing gears may help relieve the monotony of my prose and will hopefully convey my feeling that, as humans, we are all in the same boat and that no one is alone in anxiety, grief, or emotional suffering.

Animals also feel pain, grief, and suffering. What sets us apart is our ability to hurt and grieve for people we have never met. Through writing this book, my emotions are lifted by the hope that I am helping to reduce your emotional suffering.

In researching and compiling the material for this program, I learned much about myself and ways I could improve my own behaviors and alter my mistaken expectations, perceptions, and beliefs, thereby helping my career and relationships. Too often we judge others harshly rather than looking in the mirror at ourselves and applying the same level of scrutiny. After all, we have control only over our own thoughts and choices. Fighting fear and anxiety starts with taking responsibility for our dysfunctional patterns of behavior and being willing to change them.

Time for a joke: How many psychiatrists does it take to change a lightbulb?

Answer: One, but only if the bulb really *wants* to change…

## The unique features of this program include the following:

- The comprehensive anxiety screening tool for efficiently screening for all forms of anxiety conditions, disorders, and major contributing factors
- The quick-fix formula that can help relieve anxiety within one to seven days, with or without medication
- The ATP, which provides dozens of medical, hormonal, nutritional, supplemental, cognitive-behavioral, alternative-medicine, mind-body/body-mind, and spiritual tools to control and conquer your anxiety long term
- The personal anxiety assessment list to get a firm handle on your unique situation
- The personal daily planner for creating your own personalized anxiety-busting program
- An explanation of anxiety and its causes in the first part of the book
- An explanation of alternative, complementary, and medication regimens that are effective for treating all forms of anxiety in the second part of the book
- A discussion of PTSD and traumatic brain injury (TBI) for veterans who have served in combat, victims of assault or traumatic experiences, and athletes

The ATP aspires to provide the following benefits to those who overcome their anxiety by using a self-designed combination of its strategies—including diet, exercise, supplements, hormone replacement, cognitive-behavioral therapy, and alternative and mainstream medical interventions:

- Slowing of the internal and external aging processes, both of which are accelerated by the inflammatory imbalances caused by anxiety and stress
- Improved memory, focus, concentration, and learning ability
- Reduced risk of heart attack, stroke, cancer, diabetes, and hypertension
- The return of deep, regenerative sleep cycles to wake up feeling fully rested
- Improved ability to control eating disorders, substance abuse, and addictions of all kinds
- More success in romantic relationships with better sexual performance and libido
- Better immune system response with faster recovery from illness and improved ability to fight infectious diseases and protect against cancer
- Improved performance in sports that require calm mental focus and concentration, stamina, endurance, muscle strength, and speed (especially for those optimizing hormonal balance)
- Better career performance, success controlling speaker's nerves, more successful social skills, and overall stronger and more confident leadership in business/career goals
- More energy, optimism, enthusiasm, and appreciation of life
- The ability to be more fun and have more fun
- Spiritual growth that comes from rejecting a fear-based thought and belief system
- Inner peace and joy resulting from sound emotional, financial, physical, and spiritual health

Lastly, my heartfelt appreciation to all those who contributed to the creation of this program and all those whose consistent support and encouragement made it possible. Thanks to my personal support team in the clinic and at home—especially my wife, Patty, who does the heavy lifting so I can do the fun stuff. Much appreciation is also owed to my mother-in-law, Julien Lin, for her care and education of my fourteen-year-old son, Jacob. I'm grateful for his unabashed love and his contribution to the section on gratitude at the end of this book. Heartfelt thanks are due Jacob's stellar teachers, Patricia Garcia, Lanette Radomile, and Shawn Atencio; and his beloved Pentathlon coach Ted Eckersdorff, Polo coach Toto, and piano teacher Alla Artemova. I also appreciate the support of my good friends Gary and Valerie Testa, Dr. Tanya Atagi, Lee Beverly, John Truxaw, Drew Prinz, and John Mintz, as well as the dedication and loyalty of Christine Young, Norma Cruz, and Alex Velichko of my office staff. Fabian Mach has been invaluable as my tech support and has come to my rescue on many occasions. My favorite Stanford professor, Dr. Herant Katchadourian, must be acknowledged for his life and career-changing influence. His dynamic and passionate teaching style compelled me turn toward the study of the human condition through science and medicine. As a family, we are fortunate to be part of the hugely supportive communities of the Bay School of San Francisco and Stanford University.

Finally, thanks to all my patients over the years who have allowed me the privilege of being intimately involved in their personal lives and struggles. In truth, they were my greatest teachers.

James C. Gardner, MD
Greenbrae, California

# Introduction

## Getting Started

So, you have anxiety and you're not going to put up with it anymore! Congratulations for taking responsibility by reading this book and applying the tools to your life in a way that best fits your personality and sensibilities. As soon as possible, you should also make an appointment with a medical professional. I recommend a primary care physician (general practitioner, family medicine, or internal medicine specialist) or a psychiatrist.

These are medical doctors who can evaluate your condition, make a diagnosis, and start a medical regimen if needed. Sometimes a course of medication to help you sleep or to control your anxiety attacks is very helpful while you are learning ways to manage and reduce stress. Once you have learned the lessons in this book and have incorporated a variety of tools into your daily life, you will be much less vulnerable to anxious emotions, and you may find that you no longer need medical treatment. After reading the materials presented in this program, you will no longer be fearful of or intimidated by healthcare professionals. You will be empowered to be proactive in discussing your diagnosis and participating in all aspects of your treatment decisions.

I suggest that you first read the section "How to Use the Anxiety Toolbox Program." It will orient you on to how to organize your time and prioritize your efforts in a way that will be most useful for your particular situation.

## Medical Choices

In chapter 4, we will discuss the medical treatment of anxiety while emphasizing the need for a thorough medical history, physical, and laboratory evaluation to rule out the many medical causes of anxiety. Intervention with modern medications is helpful to quickly correct brain chemistry imbalances. This is especially true if you are treating one or more of the anxiety disorders discussed in chapter 2. For those with severe anxiety caused by one of these conditions, trying to prevail without medical help is like fighting a modern war on horseback with a shield and spear. Thanks to the work of neuropsychologists, the brain is well understood and can be analyzed with noninvasive tests to determine the areas of dysfunction. These special metabolic brain scans are helpful but usually unnecessary, as a careful history of your symptoms and a thoughtful medical evaluation by a physician will usually lead to a swift and successful medical intervention that will greatly speed you toward emotional stability. We will look at both the somatic-symptom model and brain dysfunction model of determining the appropriate medical intervention. We will also discuss the latest medical advances in helping the brain unlearn programmed fear responses seen in specific and social phobias.

## Considering Our Own Contribution to Anxiety

> *The keenest sorrow is to recognize ourselves as the sole cause of all our adversities. The greatest griefs are those we cause ourselves.*
> —Sophocles, *Oedipus Rex*

In my study of anxiety, one truth seems to stand out: we create much of our own stress. This is both good news and bad news. The good news is that the contributing factors to anxiety and stress are largely under our own control. The bad news is that we need to change, which takes thoughtful consideration and effort. We must change our attitudes, perceptions, thoughts, behaviors, expectations, actions, and reactions.

Our lives are made up of the choices that we make, both the big choices—like which philosophy or set of values guides our life, who we choose as friends and mates, what we study to prepare for a career, where we choose to live—and the small choices—like what to eat, when to go to bed, how much to exercise, whether to greet our neighbor or pretend we didn't see them, or what newspaper to read or TV program to watch. All of these choices have an effect on the state of our emotional health.

Many anxiety problems can be traced back a failure to cultivate an important aspect of our lives—like our career stability, relationship success, creative passions, emotional responsibility and maturity, self-care (health and hygiene), or spiritual outlook. We all age and mature physically whether we like it or not. We may spend lots of time attending to our outer appearance and clothing. We likely put significant effort and focus into our education and jobs out of the necessity to earn a living. We then expend large amounts of time pursuing activities we are passionate about, that are a distraction from the work-a-day world, or that are just for fun and entertainment. Unfortunately, we often forget to occasionally examine our values and the progress of our emotional and spiritual growth. This may cause a pattern of unhealthy and unfulfilling relationship choices. Seeking self-gratification without balancing this with effort and progress with work and emotional growth can eventually lead to stressful circumstances. As human beings, we are programmed from day one to grow, be curious, and reach new milestones. So, if we ever reach a point of stagnation in any area of our lives—education, career, relationships, emotional maturity, or spiritual understanding—anxiety is bound to set in. In fact, anxiety is the warning light that tells us to stop and evaluate all areas of our lives to see where we may be blocked or failing to move past areas of dysfunction or stagnation.

## The Cycle of Life

In the modern world, we are particularly vulnerable to anxiety and stress because of our lack of a daily regimen. We have forgotten that we are part of nature, and nature has a rhythm. There is a reason why the earth rotates on its axis every twenty-four hours, with day and night alternatively encouraging our activity and rest, and why the moon circles the earth every twenty-eight days (the average length of the female hormonal cycle). We have evolved under the influence of natural cycles. They are deeply imbedded in our genetics, to the point that our brain chemistry and all our hormone-secreting glands are dependent on information from our internal clock known as the *pineal gland*. Men also have a twenty-eight-day lunar cycle of testosterone production and have a low point analogous to the female period.

But few of us respect our dependence on these natural cycles. Without a daily circadian rhythm, our system cannot connect and function efficiently. Who among us has a regular bedtime, gets up at the same time each morning, exercises regularly, eats three meals consistently, and has a healthy balance of work, play, family, social, and downtime? Such a person would probably not need this book. Starting with the lightbulb, followed by TV and computers, and now reaching unprecedented levels of obsession with video games and social media connectivity through our cell phones and tablets, we can finally work, entertain ourselves, post, tweet, like, dislike, and otherwise comment around the clock without heeding our internal natural rhythms. This workbook will stress the importance of balance, predictability, and consistency in your daily life.

Don't dilute your life energy by trying to be everywhere for everybody. Don't try to please everyone or spend excessive time portraying a happy and successful life on Instagram. Focus on yourself, your talents and skills, your interests and passions. Don't be a slave to things. As my father said, "Have few needs and fewer wants." You don't need those things that Madison Avenue tells you that you "gotta have" to be sexy, successful, and satisfied. You don't have to be popular on Facebook, posting selfies to document your every experience and responding daily on each of your five hundred closest friends' boards. And don't stay up binge watching an addictive Netflix or Amazon Prime series. Learn and practice self-discipline. Save your money and live within your budget. Keeping a cycle and rhythm in your life is a quiet commitment you make and keep to yourself, and it is a powerful tool in staying healthy and financially and emotionally secure.

## Transformation: The Way Out

The ATP is not just about creating a rhythm and structure for daily life; it is also about changing the course of our lives by exercising control over our choices. It is about building a stable life foundation that we can always count on and fall back on in difficult times. The tools in the toolbox are designed to help us examine our thoughts, perceptions, priorities, and values. There are also tools that will teach us how to breathe, sleep, eat, and exercise in a regular, healthy, daily routine.

Our minds have physical needs, and just like your car, if you don't take care of it, it won't take care of you. Getting healthy physically; medically treating sex and thyroid hormone deficiencies and neurotransmitter imbalances in the brain; and living and eating in ways that support emotional strength and balance are at the core of defeating anxiety. Each of these plays a role in raising our threshold for triggering anxious emotions so that we rarely experience anxiety.

Probably the most fun and amazing tools in the toolbox are those that give us the power to control our body, mind, and emotions in ways that few ever achieve. Through modern techniques, we can learn in days how to quickly elicit our theta-wave relaxation response, a feat that once took years of focused work and solitude.

In the end, we will be changed from the inside out—literally becoming new, improved versions of ourselves. Many people fight or reject this notion of transformation. They are afraid of change and growth. But we are on this planet for exactly that purpose—change and growth. Consider the notorious 2002 case of the California fertilizer salesman, Scott Peterson, who was convicted of killing his wife, Laci, who was eight months pregnant. It seems incomprehensible because he had so many other possible choices. Everyone said he was such a nice guy. Was he really a monster and sociopath? Or was this simply a case of a person unwilling to make the transformation from a self-centered, free-swinging bachelor to loving husband and father? Did his *fear* of commitment, emotional growth, and transformation lead to a double murder that ruined the lives of two families?

Embracing transformation, on the other hand, allows life to fall into place almost effortlessly. If you are open to change—really learning and practicing and living the simple tools in this book—you will have control over your emotions and develop a stable, calm, and positive character. You will learn to like, admire, and, unexpectedly, love yourself. This is not only a gift to yourself but to your family and the world.

Finally, if you want to skip chapters 1–3 because you feel they are too preachy or are stuff that you already know from therapy or life experience, that's fine. I put Western medical tools and alternative medical tools before cognitive-behavioral therapy, mind-body/body-mind, and spiritual tools, not because they are more effective or should be tried first. Some may argue that this book should be read backward, starting from a spiritual mind-set approach and adding additional tools as needed from there. In fact, the most powerful tools for long-term resistance to anxiety and depression are spiritual, I believe. Attitudinal tools are often derived from spiritual truths that are hard wired into the human creation. These truths are revealed in all religious belief systems but will just as easily be experienced by those with no religious inclinations. Foremost among these is the daily and mindful practice of gratitude. I'm grateful if this book is in any way supportive or helpful to you, as I feel my journey in life has led to a place where I can offer real hope and sincere encouragement to those with the most severe suffering and hardship. This is because I have seen so many recover from the deepest despair, reclaim their lives and families, and find a new sense of calm and even joy. Every path was different, but all had the same commonality: the acceptance of responsibility for getting better and the proactive involvement in creating the game plan for recovery (with professional guidance). No one can fix you. You should not ask anyone else to solve your emotional health challenges. Only you can bring lasting peace and stability through actively participating in the process. But therein lies the rebuilding of your self-confidence and self-love. It takes time. One day at a time, one decision at a time. But it is all worth it and very doable. It's OK to voice frustration, but never be discouraged and never give up. This is a noble journey, worthy of your full commitment and effort. And remember that you are not alone.

# CHAPTER 1
## What Everyone Should Know about Anxiety

Ours has been called the *age of anxiety*. In popular speech, the term *anxiety* usually means nothing more than worry or concern. In medicine, it is defined specifically as a painful and disproportional apprehension or uneasiness about an impending or anticipated ill fortune. It is an emotional reaction that manifests itself in various physical symptoms of different degrees of intensity. In true anxiety disorders, the fear response is exaggerated and unreasonable. In everyday, normal anxiety, the fear reaction is understandable and in proportion to the stress or threat at hand. The ATP provides effective tools for controlling both normal anxiety as well as anxiety from diagnosable anxiety disorders.

Anxiety is feared for the myriad symptoms that take hold of our bodies and shake up our emotions to the core of our beings. Below is a list of commonly recognized anxiety symptoms:

- Heart palpitations
- Sense of impending doom
- Inability to focus and concentrate
- Muscle tension, muscle aches, twitching in the muscles
- Diarrhea, abdominal cramps
- Chest pain or heart palpitations
- Hot flashes or cold sweats
- Uncontrolled shaking and tremors
- Undereating or overeating
- Difficulty falling asleep or early-morning awakening
- Irritability, moodiness, depression
- Fatigue, headaches, mental fog
- Breathlessness, hyperventilation
- Loss of sex drive and performance
- Being easily startled

## Good Anxiety—Bad Anxiety

In anxiety, we find a duality that lies at the core of the human experience. On one side, anxiety is a great motivator, protector, and teacher. It motivates us to succeed out of fear of failure and protects us from danger by triggering our anxiety alarm when we are confronted by situations that threaten harm. It teaches us to reevaluate our lives, values, and priorities by refusing to let us ignore or distract ourselves from an unhealthy lifestyle. Some say that anxiety is also the catalyst for human spiritual growth.

On the other side, however, we see lives, careers, and families suffer from the effects of unrelenting anxiety. There comes a point when anxiety has gone beyond its positive benefits and no longer is helpful. When it is severe and unrelenting, anxiety degrades, demoralizes, and paralyzes us so that we can no longer move forward with confidence, optimism, and enthusiasm. This is pathologic anxiety, during which we can see only the hopeless side of the coin. We then no longer see the world in proper perspective and are unable to appreciate the good and positive truths about our lives. This level of anxiety causes us to move away from a life-affirming mind-set and into a realm of self-absorption and negativity.

For some, this state of negativity is a prison from which they cannot escape due to chemical and structural brain imbalances. They may look to self-medicate with drugs or alcohol for the brief relief that it brings. For them, the road to recovery will necessarily require medical intervention and psychotherapy. For others, the wisdom of the tried-and-true remedies discussed in this book will be all that is needed for recovery and long-term remission from anxiety.

## The Concept of Dread

We have all experienced the physical symptoms of anxiety throughout our lives. Some of the many common symptoms include physical sensations, such as shortness of breath, heart palpitations, sweats, nausea, tremors, dizziness, chest pains, numbness and tingling, and a general feeling that we might die or are on the verge of experiencing a major catastrophe, like a heart attack or stroke. Other symptoms involve cognitive impairments, such as inability to focus, concentrate, or make decisions.

These symptoms are caused by the "mind-body response." That is, when the mind experiences anxiety, certain areas deep within the primitive part of the human brain begin to react and activate. Although many areas of the brain are involved in allowing us to experience and process emotions, the amygdale, basal ganglia, and hypothalamus are the origins of the fear/anxiety response. When aroused, they send signals to other areas within the brain and the body as part of a natural and preprogrammed reaction known as *fight or flight*.

This brain reaction to stress can actually be seen on a SPECT scan. Those deep emotional centers of the brain "heat up" on the scan due to increased metabolic activity caused by stress. These centers, in turn, are in conversation with the rest of the body by both hormonal messengers and direct nerve connections. By stimulating our glands, especially the adrenal glands, a large amount of stress hormones, like adrenalin and cortisol, are released into the body.

Activation of these glands and organs is designed to protect us from the threat we are facing. Whether we need to flee or stay and fight, our body will be better able to react in a way that best ensures survival. The heart will need to beat faster and stronger, our muscles will need better circulation, our mind will need to be jolted into alertness, and we will need a sudden surge of energy. But imagine if there is really nothing that is seriously threatening us. This mind-body activation is still going to cause all the unpleasant symptoms of the fight-or-flight response. We will experience anxiety symptoms, including the rapid heart rate, chest pains, sweats, and nausea. At the same time, the higher centers of the brain are in a state of overload. Just as your computer slows down if too many programs are running, your brain can experience loss of focus and concentration during times of anxiety.

## Anxiety to Help Us Relax

Although we probably don't usually think of anxiety this way, it can be a vehicle to help us achieve relaxation. This is also a common technique in art, music, and literature: an intricate, cubist form causes our minds to struggle until we finally relax and view the simple pattern within; the chords become intense and dystonic before the emotional release is allowed through a convergence of harmonizing elements; the story's suspense needs to build before the final dénouement.

Similarly, with many activities we engage in, the unconscious purpose is to exhaust our minds and bodies so that they can return to a state of relaxation. I believe that we sometimes seek extreme activities—such as bungee jumping, rock climbing, parachute skiing, and triathlon competing—because they allow a deep sense of calm and psychic peace once accomplished. This sense of relief from stress is probably mediated by morphine-like endorphin compounds released in the brain, which can become nearly an addiction, explaining why some people become obsessed with a particular adrenalin-producing activity. Even scary movies are popular because of their ability to energize us emotionally, thereby exhausting our "nervous energy" and allowing the relaxation phase to follow. The appeal of sex could also be explained from this vantage point; it creates the building of muscular tension, which is ultimately released through the orgasmic response, followed by a period of relaxation.

There is a common truth in the human experience: you can't see black without white; you can't fully appreciate peace without experiencing war; love is more intense when mixed with negative emotions of jealousy and anger; and pleasure is experienced to the degree that we have known pain. The point is that we often seek stress, anxiety, and emotional upheaval for the heightened awareness and intensity they bring to our experience of life, as well as the relaxation that may follow. Unfortunately, we may leave a wake of regrets, hurt feelings, and unpleasant consequences of such behaviors. This program will suggest some alternate strategies for eliciting the relaxation response that are healthier and more conducive to positive growth.

## When Anxiety Goes Terribly Wrong

In anxiety disorders, the anxiety response is out of proportion to the level of actual threat we are facing. In other words, our mind is setting off false alarms. This inevitably leads to a very disrupted and unpleasant existence during which we are consumed by our fears and the fear of more fear! In this state, it is impossible to live productively and joyfully in the present moment. This is how anxiety can steal weeks, months, and even years away from our lives. Many of the techniques in the ATP have been scientifically shown to "cool down" and soothe those deep emotional centers, allowing the mind to relax and quiet itself. Once you know how to do this, you will no longer be at the mercy of your anxious emotions.

## Success On and Off the Court

Success in our everyday lives may well depend on whether we are in control of our fear and have learned to harness its positive benefits and tame its destructive side. This is necessary for improving our skills in relationships, our career life, sports, and anything we put our hearts and minds to. The skills learned in *The Anxiety Toolbox Program* will teach you to do just this, whether you are trying to stop a lifetime anxiety disorder or just improve your golf handicap or pitching ERA.

For example, many sports activities require extreme concentration and the absence of distraction. Think of that twenty-foot putt to clinch the Masters Tournament, pitching a fastball on the outside corner during the World Series, hitting that fastball out of the park, catching a punt return, throwing a football on target in the face of a blitz, hitting a jump shot at the buzzer in a tie game, hitting the target in skeet shooting or archery, and on and on. There is no room here for a fearful thought, a tremor of the hand, a cold sweat, a wave of nausea, or a mental block. Knowing how to turn on anxiety to get motivated and then being able to turn it off at the exact moment you need calm focus is a subtle but important quality that separates the amateurs from the superstars.

The same is true in the corporate world. Those who succeed and make it look easy have a sense of confidence, an easy smile, think quickly on their feet, do not falter when asked to speak in public, and don't let fear stop them. You never see them sweat. Think of any of your heroes in sports, business, politics, the performing arts, or any other area of life. What do they all have in common? I suggest that it is not the absence but the mastery of fear.

## Anxiety in Its Infancy

Even as infants and toddlers, we are programmed to be alert and vigilant to our new world. If we see that a parent is tense or reacts with fear in a dangerous situation, we may program our own anxiety response to trigger given that same situation in the future. As teenagers and young adults, it is common to fear social situations and worry about the scrutiny of others. Embarrassing or humiliating experiences at this impressionable age can sometimes cause a social anxiety disorder. The temperament we are born with also determines if we are likely to be overreactive in our anxiety responses. A baby that startles more easily is more likely to have a timid temperament. If the parent of a timid child does not counteract this with calm reassurance, the child will be highly vulnerable to developing anxiety disorders as they grow older.

## When Your Brain Is Playing Tricks on You

Most people with anxiety disorders have identifiable abnormalities on their brain SPECT scan. This is a scan that measures metabolic activity in the brain, showing areas of the brain that are not working properly. We will talk more of this and Dr. Daniel Amen's work in chapter 4. The SPECT scan can help diagnose those people who do not process information, intercommunicate, or integrate emotional response in a normal manner. This could be because of genetics, birth trauma, head injury (TBI), medical conditions, or emotional trauma. But the exciting news is that the brain (even an old one) can learn new tricks! By practicing the ATP tools, the brain actually develops new connections and pathways around previously damaged or dysfunctional areas. This is called *plasticity*, and it means that the brain is capable of growth and change throughout life. In other words, your brain is constantly a work in progress!

## Where Anxiety Lives

The fear response lives deep within the primitive part of the mammalian brain in a group of structures called the *amygdale, hippocampus,* and *basal ganglia*. The amygdale is the emotional gear shifter that decides whether to activate the entire mind-body fight-or-flight response. The amygdale is influenced mostly by previous memories of fear that have been recorded and stored in the hippocampus. In PTSD, the amygdale will fire off an anxiety response merely from the memory of a past traumatic experience, without any real present danger. These structures, along with the basal ganglia, organize the anxiety response and send a variety of neuronal and hormonal messages throughout the brain and body, causing all the varied symptoms of anxiety.

## How We Learn Anxiety

We all know how long it takes to learn from studying a book. If we had to learn lifesaving lessons about our environment in this didactic fashion during our formative years, we would likely not survive. An infant or toddler does not have the ability to read and can understand only basic grimaces or facial expressions or a few simple words. How, then, does this new creature adapt quickly enough to ensure its survival into childhood and adulthood?

Nature has created the most powerful method of learning, called *experiential learning*. When you touch a hot stove and burn your hand or fall off the bed and whack your chin as a toddler, you learn immediately to modify your behavior so as not to repeat the experience. These are powerful memories that are stored in the emotional centers of the brain.

When a toddler does something potentially dangerous, like sticking a finger in the electric outlet, experts advise a sharp tone of reprimand and a brisk slap on the back of the hand. Such a reaction is mildly traumatic and leaves an immediate impression on the emotional mind through experience that this behavior has uncomfortable consequences. The toddler is much less likely to repeat this behavior with only one such exposure.

Animals are also programmed to benefit from experiential learning, as was demonstrated by my five-pound Yorkshire terrier, Gizmo. Letting his curiosity get the best of him, he got on the wrong side of a skunk and received a direct hit to the face and eyes. Several baths later, along with household remedies of tomato juice, hydrogen peroxide with baking soda, and olive oil eye drops, he had recovered physically from the ordeal. But the traumatic experience was stored firmly in his emotional brain centers. A week later, even without seeing the beast itself, the scent of a skunk in the backyard sent him scurrying back to the front door for cover. I doubt he learned that watching his favorite cable TV channel, *Animal Planet*!

Traumatic experiences become emotional memories held deep within our primitive psyche. Imagine if you nearly drowned as a child. You were struggling to keep your head above water, choking on gulps of water while trying to catch your breath. This traumatic memory would immediately be stored in the emotional centers. Later, and possibly throughout your life, this memory could be awakened by the sight, smell, or sound of water. You may no longer actually remember the event that happened so long ago, but your emotional mind remembers just how you felt and will trigger the same set of symptoms. You may feel like you are struggling to catch your breath, your heart will pound rapidly as it did when you were fighting to stay alive, and you will feel dizzy and lightheaded with a sense of doom, like you have no control over what is happening.

The point here is that experiential learning has nothing to do with the rational, higher centers of the brain. Anxiety learned through the emotional mind cannot be unlearned with the rational mind—that is, through talk therapy or simply reading this book.

## Unlearning Anxiety

You cannot unlearn anxiety solely through the efforts of the higher brain centers, such as the prefrontal cortex. This rational, calculating part of the brain tries to put things into perspective, analyze the real risks and threats involved, and produce a reasoned and controlled response. It is certainly true that the rational brain can, with training, be taught to help quiet the deeper, more primitive emotional fear centers. Through SPECT scan brain imaging, it has been shown that cognitive-behavioral therapy that focuses on correcting misconceptions and misinterpretations, as well as meditation and prayer, are successful ways of decreasing metabolic activity in the amygdala and basal ganglia.

Telling your prefrontal cortex to "just say no" to anxiety reactions may help in some cases. But for most, anxiety must be unlearned through experiential desensitization therapy. Also known as *exposure therapy*, it involves real-life, visualized, or virtual-reality exposure to the feared object or situation. These experiences are fed into the memory center of the emotional mind, the hippocampus. Over time and repetition, the older, unnecessary phobic memory is diluted and replaced with new, less-anxious memories. The phobic memory will no longer stimulate the amygdale as forcefully, effectively reducing and eventually *extinguishing* the anxiety response. Several sessions are usually needed, but the beneficial effects are almost immediate. The drug D-cycloserine, when given intramuscularly during desensitization therapy, has been shown to increase NMDA proteins in the hippocampus and allow faster extinction of anxiety caused by phobias. That is, the brain unlearns anxiety faster in the presence of these proteins, and it takes fewer sessions of exposure therapy to extinguish the phobia. In essence, the hippocampus unlearns the previously programmed fear as the phobic individual learns that the feared object can be survived with less and less discomfort. In the end, exposure to the feared stimulus, whether it is spiders, elevators, tunnels, or airplanes, will cause no unreasonable or irrational fear reaction at all.

The Western medical and many alternative methods of treating underlying anxiety disorders, such as OCD, panic disorder, PTSD, generalized anxiety disorder, and social anxiety, will be discussed in chapters 4 and 5. Using these strategies will also help facilitate the unlearning of anxiety.

## Eastern or Western?

The right chemical balance is necessary for healthy brain functioning. Whether unlearning phobic reactions or coping with an anxiety disorder, your success might be enhanced by the addition of an appropriate medical regimen. Other times, the brain will balance itself given the right diet, sleep, rhythm and structure, physical exercise, brain exercise, group and individual psychotherapy, attitude and behavioral therapy, and spiritual support. Alternative and complementary medicine adds the options of herbal and Ayurvedic remedies, acupuncture, traditional Chinese medicine, body-work therapies, and several other helpful strategies. The ATP recognizes the value of modern advances in Western medicine, as well as ancient wisdom from Eastern philosophies and healing practices. I believe there is some truth and benefit to both Western and Eastern modalities and that the fastest road to complete health lies in an individualized synthesis of these healing arts. Creating an integrated plan that fits your unique needs, sensibilities, and wiring is the core goal of the ATP.

# CHAPTER 2
## Recognizing Anxiety Disorders

Anxiety disorders are more than those occasional butterflies in our stomach when giving a public speech or the nervousness of a first date. Anxiety disorders are medical illnesses that can last for years or a lifetime, often having a dramatic effect on everyday life. Many don't go away by themselves and can get worse over time if left untreated. Often, people suffering with anxiety will spend large amounts of time and money trying to figure out what's wrong with them because the symptoms of anxiety are similar to many other medical illnesses. For this reason, a thorough evaluation and examination by your health-care provider (not "Dr. Google") is a must.

A number of medical conditions are commonly the underlying cause of a person's anxiety symptoms. Problems like thyroid imbalances, female and male hormonal changes, the overuse of caffeine and other stimulants, sleep disorders, sleep apnea, heart arrhythmias, chronic pain, and alcohol and substance abuse are just a few of the potential medical conditions that should be investigated first. Many people have learned that their anxiety is temporarily relieved by a number of means, such as sedative drugs, alcohol, tobacco, and food (triggering eating disorders). In fact, anxiety plays a role in most addictive behaviors. We call these self-administered remedies *self-medication*. Unfortunately, people who use these crutches do not improve over time. They only become dependent on the substance or behavior to feel better and have no other tools in their toolboxes to cope with anxiety. They feel they cannot survive without their "safety behavior." We will discuss the connection between pain management, addiction, and anxiety in chapter 6.

The ATP allows you to add healthy tools to your personal toolbox, empowering you to remove dysfunctional addictions and safety behaviors. Below is a discussion of the signs and symptoms of the most common anxiety disorders. You will also find diagrams on the criteria for the different kinds of anxiety problems in my and Dr. Bell's book *Overcoming Anxiety, Panic, and Depression: New Ways to Regain Your Confidence* and on phobic disorders in *Phobias and How to Overcome Them: Understanding and Beating Your Fears*. In addition, you'll find sources of more information on anxiety disorders as well as helpful URLs at the end of this section.

### Generalized Anxiety Disorder

Constant worry lasting more than six months might be a condition known as *generalized anxiety disorder*. Of course, this assumes that there is really little or nothing to worry about. A person with generalized anxiety disorder may realize there is no real reason to be consumed by worry, but they just can't help it. Some people call them *worrywarts* or *uptight*, believing they choose to behave this way. But no one chooses to live with constant fear. Worry needs to have an object of focus. So even if people with generalized anxiety disorder have no problems, they will invent them. They will start to focus on their health, marriage, work, or family issues as the source of "what's wrong" rather than looking inside for the answer. Many will quit their jobs, get a divorce, or seek multiple medical evaluations—all in an effort to find out what is giving them anxiety. In the end, they finally learn that they themselves are the only source of this endless worry—it is a condition that originates in their own brains' emotional centers, and it has nothing to do with the outside world. As you can imagine, having generalized anxiety disorder can make you very tense, irritable, and self-consumed. You might have problems concentrating or sleeping. Symptoms like tension headaches, stomach problems, heart palpitations, sweating, dizziness, and chest pain are common. Others might find you uncomfortable to be around, and your condition can make you more and more isolated over time. Those with generalized anxiety disorder can often trace the origin of their problems back to childhood or adolescence.

## Panic Disorder

Those with panic disorder experience random, unpredictable anxiety attacks. During these sudden attacks of overwhelming fear, they often feel they are going to die. In addition to feeling a sense of doom and dread, they may also feel a sense of detachment or unreality. Any number of physical symptoms may occur during these panic attacks, including fast heartbeat, trembling, sweating, uncontrolled shaking, nausea and vomiting, and head-spinning dizziness (sounds like a scene from *The Exorcist!*). Quite understandably, experiencing a panic attack often makes one worry about having another one. The fear of having a panic attack in a situation in which escape or finding help would be difficult may lead to agoraphobia. Agoraphobia (which means "fear of the marketplace") may cause one to avoid going to crowded stores, theaters, trains, planes, or buses or crossing over bridges for fear of having an attack with no escape route. Agoraphobics worry that an attack will incapacitate, embarrass, or humiliate them. This leads to avoidance behaviors that may greatly limit a person's life, making him or her a prisoner of fear, even to the point of being house bound.

## Obsessive-Compulsive Disorder

OCD usually begins in childhood. People with OCD experience persistent thoughts or images, called *obsessions*, which make them very anxious. No matter how hard they try, they can't keep these recurring thoughts from invading their consciousness. These thoughts usually focus on danger or risk of harm. To relieve the severe and unrelenting anxiety that these obsessions cause, people with OCD perform rituals, which they feel they must do to control their fear symptoms. Common rituals include handwashing, counting, arranging, and checking things over and over again. A person with OCD may check that the door is locked ten times before they go to bed, or they may wash their hands dozens of times a day. They may be unable to function unless their environment is arranged in a very specific way. Performing these rituals can take hours a day and interfere significantly with the sufferer's work and social life.

## Posttraumatic Stress Disorder

PTSD can happen to people who have lived through or witnessed a life-threatening event, such as an accident, the trauma of war, or a physical or sexual attack. It can also occur after a prolonged exposure to unrelenting stressful situations, like an extended period of emotional abuse or domestic violence. Images and recurrent thoughts of the traumatic event may take the form of nightmares or flashbacks. This makes the person with PTSD "relive" the painful experience over and over. They often have trouble sleeping and relaxing, feeling the need to be constantly alert and vigilant to possible danger. People with PTSD may avoid places, people, and things that remind them of the event or period of emotional trauma. They may become emotionally numb and avoid other people altogether. Sometimes PTSD begins immediately after a life-threatening event; other times it is delayed. It may last from a few weeks to several years. In veterans returning from combat, TBI often coexists with PTSD and creates additional challenges (see appendix 3).

## Bulimia Nervosa, Anorexia Nervosa, and Binge-Eating Disorders

People with eating disorders have anxiety at the center of their dysfunctional relationship with food. All can be treated successfully and often dramatically with medical options and cognitive-behavioral therapy, so people should get help before it goes too far. In bulimia, bouts of extreme overeating are followed by guilt and shame with self-induced vomiting, purging with laxatives, or fasting. In anorexia, the person will eat very little or skip meals to the point of becoming dangerously thin. With binge eating, there will be occasions of excessive eating that, although perhaps infrequent, are all consuming. The person will eat until uncomfortably full but will not purge with vomiting or laxatives. The overeating is often followed by shame, depression, and periods of food restriction or fasting. It is thought that the binge episodes arise from feelings of anger, anxiety, worthlessness, or shame. Initiating the binge is a means of relieving tension or numbing negative feelings. This is the most common eating disorder in the United States, affecting 3.5 percent of women, 2 percent of men, and up to 1.6 percent of adolescents. A person with binge-eating disorder may be normal weight or overweight. Co-occurring conditions such as depression, social isolation, moodiness, and irritability may be present. Feeling disgust about one's body size is not uncommon, and those with binge-eating disorder may have a tendency to avoid conflict, be inflexible in their thinking, have a strong need to be in control, have difficulty expressing their feelings and needs, and be perfectionists who work hard to please others. The FDA recently approved the amphetamine drug Vyvanse to help reduce these patients' overwhelming urge to binge. The serotonin reuptake inhibitors (SSRI) family of medications has also been helpful in treating eating disorders.

## Anxiety as a Symptom of a Mood Disorder

Those with depression and bipolar disorder (also known as *manic-depression*) are especially prone to periods of anxiety and substance abuse. It has been said that depression is regret about the past while anxiety is worry about the future. But it's not that simple. Depression is a medical disorder that can lead to imbalances in the brain chemistry and a decrease in the connections between brain neurons. Depression can also lead directly to stimulation of those anxiety centers in the amygdale, basal ganglia, and hypothalamus. Or it can indirectly lead to anxiety from the loss of functioning that occurs with depression. Depressed people are often in the midst of job, financial, or relationship difficulties that seem overwhelming and lead to a great deal of stress. All the symptoms found in anxiety attacks are also common to people suffering from depressive mood disorders.

## Social Anxiety Disorder/Social Phobia

Social anxiety disorder is also called *social phobia*. This is the most common anxiety disorder. Symptoms usually begin in childhood or adolescence and can include stuttering; fast heartbeat; sweating from the hands, feet, and armpits; trembling; blushing; and a queasy "butterfly" feeling in the stomach when confronted by social interaction. People with social phobia may appear to just be shy, but underlying this they have a persistent fear of being watched and judged by others. This perceived scrutiny by others results in a fear and avoidance of social situations. Those with social phobia may avoid public speaking, parties, performing, meeting new people, and dating. They are afraid that the social interaction will lead to embarrassment or humiliation. In fact, social phobia may begin after a particularly embarrassing moment in early childhood. Although some people with social phobia are afraid of all social situations, others fear only specific situations, like public speaking or being called on in class. People with social phobia are more likely to live alone or with their parents in adulthood. Many never get married or are soon divorced. Most choose jobs that do not require much social interaction or collaboration with others. This places enormous limits on their lives and careers.

## Specific Phobia

Specific phobias are irrational fears of specific objects or situations. The diagnosis of specific phobia is made only after other anxiety disorders have been excluded. Interestingly, some specific phobias seem to be inherited, including the fear of spiders and needles. Others seem to be acquired early in life from traumatic experiences. Almost everything you can think of and name, including the color purple, has been identified as a specific phobia for someone at some time. The popular reality television show *Face Your Fears* played on the contestants' specific phobias to see how well they could suppress their fears if they had to. Those afflicted by specific phobias can usually hide them. They know that their anxiety reaction is unreasonable and irrational, but they cannot control themselves from, say, screaming at the sight of a bird. Therefore, it is kept a deep secret, and the person gets good at making excuses to avoid any situation in which a bird might show up, such as a park or the seashore. Often these people will live a reasonably normal life around their phobias, enduring them if they absolutely must. But sometimes it does affect their choices. For instance, a person with a specific phobia to water may not be able to go on a cruise or island vacation that the family had been looking forward to.

## Recognizing Phobic Fears and Behaviors

In agoraphobia, the individual fears external danger signals, internal danger signals, symptom attacks, and imagined catastrophes. Examples of external danger signals are places, activities, and situations in which the person feels an attack of anxiety symptoms is likely. Internal danger signals are the inner symptoms that you feel at the beginning of an anxiety attack, such as heart pounding, nausea, difficulty catching your breath, or the onset of a cold sweat. The symptom attack is when the internal danger signal reaches its climax. For instance, the inner danger signal of nausea may eventually cause vomiting; difficulty breathing may ultimately cause you to faint. Finally, the agoraphobic patient lives in the shadow of the feared or imagined worst-case scenario, or catastrophe. It does not matter how unlikely or implausible the catastrophe is in reality—it will still remain the focus of worry and cannot be reasoned away.

Those suffering from phobias typically adapt to their disorders by accumulating a variety of dysfunctional behaviors. Safety behaviors are those crutches that help people get through exposure to the object of their phobias. For instance, an agoraphobic who fears having an anxiety attack and vomiting in a public place might make a habit of (1) checking the location of all exits and bathrooms in any public building they visit in case he or she starts to feel nauseated; (2) bringing along bottled water and some saltine crackers to quiet his or her stomach in the case of a bout of nausea; (3) carrying an iPod and blasting favorite tunes when and if the nausea strikes in an attempt at distraction; and (4) carrying a vomit bag so that he or she can puke in a corner—hopefully without anyone noticing. Avoidance behaviors are any attempt to avoid the phobic stimulus. In the example above, the person might hire someone else to do the shopping or bank online to avoid having to show up in person. Unfortunately, safety and avoidance behaviors delay healing from phobias because they reinforce the false belief that you cannot deal with the phobia without these behaviors. Even medications are considered a form of safety behavior. The underlying thought is, "I can't handle this without my tranquilizer." The truth is, you can handle and overcome anxiety without any self-medication, prescription drug, herbal remedy, or any other treatment from an external source. On the other hand, taking one step at a time sometimes requires that we hold onto a few grab bars. As you learn more tools in the ATP, you'll eventually be able to let go of medication, as well as safety and avoidance behaviors.

## Anxiety Caused by Attention Deficit Disorder in Children and Adults

ADD seems to be getting more attention than ever in the press, and rightly so. ADD (which I use interchangeably with *ADHD*, or attention deficit hyperactivity disorder) can cause a significant vulnerability to anxiety and depression if not understood, accommodated, supported, and possibly treated medically. This is really a condition of not being able to regulate attention and stay focused, especially when you are tired or the material you are reading is boring. Other times, when engaged in an exciting activity or being taught by a talented educator, an ADD student will have periods of sharp or even hyperfocused attention. Because work strains the brain, requires sustained focus, and is repetitive and boring, and play is engaging, fun, stimulating, and emotionally activating, ADD kids will seek to do the things they are passionate about, often putting play before work.

Keeping kids with ADD on track requires constant effort by parents and educators to redirect the student to get work done efficiently by staying on task and by developing organizational strategies to get homework done on time and to not forget and lose personal belongings. This is more successful if incentives are offered (e.g., "You can have twenty minutes of playing video games if you sit for thirty minutes and finish this task with a quality effort.")

ADD will readily show up on neuropsychological testing. There may be a discrepancy between (higher) IQ in verbal and perceptual reasoning scores with disproportionally (lower) brain-processing speed. This is not a learning disorder. Learning specialists correctly have dropped the term *learning disorder* in favor of *learning difference*. Up to one third of any grade-school classroom is populated with students who have some diagnosable learning difference. These differences should be recognized and accommodated so that the student can succeed without being falsely labeled as slow, lazy, or uncooperative.

If supported properly, these students often excel in creativity, imagination, and outside-the-box solutions. They may also have unusual talents in music, art, design, and hands-on technology and computer skills. They may exhibit kindness, empathy, and compassion beyond their years due to their own struggles with being misunderstood and falsely blamed and labeled. It is not a matter of intelligence or will power or of oppositional behavior; it's just, at times, the brain cannot process at a speed that allows productivity and completion of tasks without getting overwhelmed and exhausted. This leads to frustration, anger, and arguing with parents. If the school demands are high and the child is not supported, anxiety and depression can result. That's the last thing a student should have to struggle with.

The processing-speed issue can be helped by using the computer keyboard to speed up output on written assignments. (ADD patients often have advanced computer keyboarding skills and gaming joystick controller skills. They excel at video games because it's fun and keeps their brains in the focused, beta-pattern brain-wave mode.) ADD students are not linear thinkers; they skip around and often will look from the end of a problem and work backward, rather than the other way around. They don't feel the need to show the steps of their work on a math problem, because that is not the way they think. When they have reached overload capacity and can no longer hold attention, they need to take a break and reset. Pushing them further only leads to frustration, yelling, drama, and, ultimately, an anxious mind-set.

ADD students need a vibrant experiential learning environment, with lots of engaging discussions and visual demonstrations combined with equal time for the activities they are passionate about. For instance, if an ADD student is a "maker" who stays focused for hours if working on computer-assisted product design, he or she will best learn the technological vocabulary and mathematics necessary to pursue the passion while engaged in that activity, rather than in a boring, didactic classroom. Unfortunately, there is a paucity of schools that understand and can proactively nurture and motivate students with an engaging curriculum while consistently providing clear instructions and teaching organization and time-management skills.

That doesn't mean kids with ADD should not be held responsible for their efforts and attitudes or be allowed to blame others and see themselves as impaired victims. Kids with ADD often see things as unfair because of a less-effective working memory, which keeps them from seeing the whole picture of what happened in the past that led to a decision or action in the present. They must be given an explanation that cites a previous behavior or lack of responsibility to correct the misperception that the discipline or "no" answer is an arbitrary "I'm the boss so do as I say" parental response.

The best home environment is one that is structured and requires the child to maintain a consistent daily schedule when it comes to their hygiene, cleaning up after themselves, and study practices. This consistent enforcement of a structured program at home, with tutors, and at school is the support scaffolding that these kids need to become successful, enthusiastic students and confident, resilient, nonanxious adults. If they learn better by hearing than reading, it's OK to read to them or allow them to listen to an audiobook and then discuss the material verbally rather than force them to read it over and over on their own, as this will not train the brain to process faster. Remember, a person with ADD may be able to process input very quickly and understand things right away. But taking that information and producing output that is organized and purposeful becomes problematic.

ADD kids are often designed to be specialists as adults. They are not designed to go through the academic grind of middle- and high-school programs that try to put everybody into the same learning mold. In fact, they will be more content when they are adults and can focus on the things that have meaning and command their attention. The long-held belief that book learning is necessary to acquire a successful adult career is being challenged by new, progressive thinking that ADD kids should focus on the strengths and passions through project- and experience-based learning programs.

Those with ADD have symptoms in one or more of three categories:

- Inattention: easily distracted, disorganized, has problems remembering appointments and obligations
- Impulsivity: frequently interrupts, takes risks, does not consider consequences of disruptive behavior
- Hyperactivity: never seems to slow down, constantly talks and fidgets, has difficulty staying on task

This disorder often leads to depression and anxiety because the person with ADD as a child might not meet expectations or as an adult might have difficulty holding his or her life together. The exceptions are people who have a support system, such as an executive secretary or well-organized spouse. Marital discord and divorce is more common with those who have ADD because it is frustrating trying to live with someone who can't stay focused and forgets to follow through. Spouses complain that it's like raising another child to be married to someone with untreated ADD. Likewise, bosses and coworkers are dissatisfied, leading to career failures. A person with ADD often will succeed and reach a high level of education due to trying extra hard and getting special tutoring. Sometimes they cover for their deficiencies by relying on their good looks or charming personalities to get ahead. But, sooner or later, the condition gets in the way of normal functioning. When ADD causes loss and failure, anxiety begins to take over.

## Acute Situational Anxiety

Often we can point to a specific trauma or situation that triggered our anxiety condition—a death in the family, getting a letter from the IRS, worry over unprotected sex with a new partner, filing for bankruptcy, or receiving final divorce papers and realizing the finality of a broken marriage. Even though they may not meet the criteria of an anxiety disorder, symptoms such as sleeplessness, nausea, chest pains, and crying can be overwhelming. Often those who don't adjust and improve after a few weeks will go on to develop an anxiety disorder, especially if they can't eat, sleep, or care for themselves. Many will be found to have underlying stressors and a lack of coping skills that should be recognized and addressed.

## Who Gets Anxiety Disorders?

Women experience anxiety disorders twice as frequently as men. The gender difference is most pronounced in social anxiety disorder, for which women are two to three times more likely to develop the disorder. Many people with an anxiety disorder also have another emotional health condition going on at the same time. Depression is the most common disorder to coexist with anxiety. About 50 percent of those with panic disorder also suffer from depression. People who are especially vulnerable to anxiety include those with significant life stressors, medical problems, drug or alcohol abuse, a family history of anxiety, personality disorders (especially histrionic, paranoid, avoidant, and borderline personality disorders), or those born with melancholy or timid temperaments (as opposed to bold or cheerful temperaments) or who lack a support system and are disconnected from family and friends. As you can see, a thorough evaluation of stress, medical problems, addictions, family history, and the social and financial situation are necessary to really address an anxiety condition.

## How Are Anxiety Disorders Diagnosed?

Anxiety disorders are sometimes difficult to diagnose because of all the contributing factors and dysfunctional behaviors that must be sorted out. But a trained professional, like your medical doctor, psychiatrist, or psychologist, is well equipped to diagnose your condition and get you started on the right course of treatment, be it medical, psychotherapeutic, or some alternative modality. You may be asked to fill out any number of questionnaires designed to more clearly understand your anxiety or to uncover a mood or personality disorder. Of course, you will likely need a full physical exam with labs ordered by your doctor. Often your doctors will need only to listen to your story to arrive at the correct diagnosis. The comprehensive anxiety screening tool self-test worksheet in this book will indicate the areas that you and your physician should consider when looking at the diagnostic possibilities.

## How Are Anxiety Disorders Treated?

First and foremost, I want to emphasize that the ATP in no way substitutes for the advice and care of a skilled medical or psychological professional. Although general principles and practices of treatment are described throughout this book, no specific recommendation for any individual's therapy or medical care is intended, expressed, or implied. When it comes to health care, no reader should act on the basis of any printed information, including the contents of this book, without consultation with a health-care professional.

My books on anxiety, panic, depression, and phobias give an overview of the medical treatments for these conditions. *The Anxiety Toolbox Program* will help you understand the medical treatment options and also suggest nonmedical tools for your toolbox so you can reset and repair yourself whenever you need to. I will summarize the pharmaceutical strategies used to treat anxiety and depression in chapter

4. The alternative medical strategies will be discussed in chapter 5. The first strategy for correctly choosing a medication to treat anxiety is what I call the "somatic-symptom strategy," which uses your physical and emotional symptoms as the basis for selecting the appropriate medication. The second strategy I call the "brain function model," which uses brain scans to determine how the brain is functioning and which deficits should be treated medically.

I believe that knowing the diagnosis is not as important as knowing the symptoms when determining the most successful medical regimen. Rather than getting bogged down by the list of overlapping diagnoses, it is best to make a list of symptoms or take a questionnaire that will elicit your symptoms. It is important, though, to determine if a depressed patient is unipolar or bipolar in their "wiring." This will greatly influence the treatment decisions, as you will learn.

If you feel your anxiety is so severe that you can't go on, especially if you are having panic attacks that are out of control or feel suicidal, you should call 911 or have a friend take you directly to the emergency room. This is considered a medical emergency, and you will be helped with compassion and understanding by the hospital medical team. Often, just a pill or shot of an anxiolytic or sedative will stop the attack immediately. Other times, a medical treatment is absolutely necessary to get anxiety under control so that you can continue to work and keep your family together. This may be appropriate for weeks, months, or longer term.

The ATP is also invested in enabling you to be independent from medications and expensive therapies in the future. I want you to gain control over anxiety and actually heal and recover from the disorder, rather than finding temporary relief in a prescription medication or through self-medication with drugs, alcohol, or food.

Even before you start a medical program, you may find immediate benefits from better understanding your anxiety and using the simple methods described in *The Anxiety Toolbox Program*. In short, lifestyle modification, medication, and psychotherapy are the traditional methods to combat anxiety. In addition, a wide array of alternative techniques and natural strategies that elicit the brain's "relaxation response" or heal brain dysfunction and improve brain interconnectivity are at the forefront of the successful treatment of anxiety.

## Additional Sources of Information
### Anxiety and Depression Association of America
240-485-1001
www.adaa.org

### National Institutes of Mental Health
301-443-8431 or 1-866-615-NIMH (6464)
www.nimh.nih.gov

### American Psychiatric Association
703-907-7300
www.psych.org

**Freedom from Fear**
888-442-2022
www.freedomfromfear.org

**Anxiety and Phobia Treatment Center**
914-681-1038
www.phobia-anxiety.org

# CHAPTER 3
## The Rewards of Mastering Anxiety

Proper management of anxiety is a primary factor in determining whether we succeed or fail in sports, careers, relationships, or whatever our personal goals may be. No one escapes fear and anxiety, but those who understand and use it to their advantage sense a limitless and abundant future. Those who avoid or make excuses for their fears, or who fail to recognize the valuable lessons they hold, will likely lead a life of unnecessary suffering and unfulfilled potential.

Whether to manage anxiety in a healthy way or allow it to control us in a dysfunctional way is a basic choice that we face. This book is not about eliminating anxiety but about understanding how to reap its benefits while sidestepping its burdens. Knowing how to put fear in its place is the most valuable skill you will learn on the road to success.

### Recognizing Fear's Gifts

Fear's main purpose is to keep us safe. Usually there is a reason that a fear response was triggered. Recognizing that we are apprehensive or emotionally pulling back from a situation is helpful in evaluating our predicament and considering our options. Are we taking an unnecessarily high risk for the potential benefits of a particular activity or action? Have we thought about our reasons for taking this risk and thought through the consequences and outcome scenarios? Have we done anything to minimize the risk or taken precautionary steps to make ourselves feel more secure? Listening to our fear can save us from disappointing decisions and injury.

Fear can also be useful as a stimulus for creativity and artistic inspiration. It can sharpen our senses, fuel our imagination, and get us in touch with our emotions. If we are able to take the energy supplied by fear and channel it into meaningful and positive outcomes, then we have reaped the benefits of fear. On the other hand, if we allow it to paralyze us with what-ifs and "worst-case scenarios," it could stall the accomplishment of our goals. It's OK to envision negative outcomes of, say, a career-change decision. But it is equally important to force yourself to see all the positive benefits and outcomes and to use these positive scenarios as guiding visions. Rather than becoming emotionally exhausted by allowing fear to be the center of your focus, you can learn to see opportunities as exciting and possible by examining and correcting misperceptions at the core of the fear. Anxiety makes us blind to our own potential for success because, deep down, we don't feel confident or competent to move ahead, compete, and get the job done. While many Americans did not support President Donald Trump, there are few who would deny that he is fearless. He has never let anxiety or self-doubt keep him from his vision for himself and what he thought possible.

Sometimes we unconsciously add a little fear to our lives when we feel in a predictable rut. We may create a risky situation as a stimulus to move ourselves forward and achieve growth. Getting creative and exploring new solutions takes on a sense of urgency when we are faced with an emergency situation, a deadline, or the possibility of failure. Fear can spark new insight, conviction, and passion, which can then ignite the courage we need to explore and challenge ourselves.

Courage is not the absence of fear; it is action in the face of fear. Or, as actress Dorothy Bernard said: "Courage is fear that has said its prayers." By harnessing the gifts of fear, we may find the strength to commit to an action or make a positive change that would otherwise not be possible.

## Human Nature: Sheep and Shepherds

We are all capable of exhibiting either the best or worst in our own nature. At each moment of the day—each decision, each conversation, and each choice for action or inaction—we choose which aspect of our nature will govern that moment. Will it be our calm, kind, thoughtful, and well-reasoned nature, or will it be our impatient, angry, irritable, and irrational nature? By recognizing these choices, we can program our minds to respond in a way that brings us the optimal results in a consistent manner. Below is a list of the qualities describing someone who has mastered the techniques found in this program. I call them "shepherds" because they stand out from the flock by going about life with a calm control, realizing their goals while acting responsibly and with respect for others. Because they practice self-control, they are in a position to help others and lead by example.

## Shepherds:

1. Take responsibility for themselves
2. Blame no one for disappointments and mistakes but seek to learn how to do better
3. Expect to succeed
4. Love a challenge
5. Embrace opportunity, even if it involves some risk
6. Embrace change and transformation, even if it involves some degree of work or pain
7. Are good stewards of the gifts and talents they have been given
8. Seek solutions rather than create problems
9. Have no difficulty saying "no" to addictive behaviors; codependent and enabling relationships; or negative, self-defeating thoughts
10. Use time wisely in productive and purposeful endeavors
11. Are upbeat, optimistic, grateful, and self-confident
12. Never step on others to achieve their goals
13. Are concerned about the health and welfare of others

14. Are respected and admired by others
15. Are healthy mentally, physically, and spiritually

Those who do not have control of anxiety and fear, especially if they reject change, likely fall into the category I call "sheep." This is because anxiety has stripped them of their strength to stand alone as self-directed, self-motivated individuals. You can often find them huddling together to commiserate about their unhappiness.

**Sheep:**

1. Don't like to think outside the box or take any risk
2. Look for excuses for their failures rather than recognizing problems and fixing them
3. Expect to lose or be cheated out of success
4. Deflect blame away from themselves
5. Waste time on items of low importance and low priority
6. Are easy prey for food, nicotine, drug, and alcohol addictions
7. Are easy prey for disrespectful and unworthy relationships
8. Are easy prey for Madison Avenue advertisers who play on the anxieties and fears of consumers
9. Are not highly regarded or admired by themselves or others
10. Are frequently dependent on others to help them through their problems
11. Do not take advantage of their talents, opportunities, or available resources
12. Can easily fall into negativity, self-loathing, ingratitude, and pessimism
13. Are more concerned about themselves than others
14. Are unable to live joyfully and fearlessly

## Choose to Be a Shepherd

Anyone who so chooses can move closer to being a shepherd. No matter your age, socioeconomic status, education level, or past mistakes, anyone can become respected and admired. It takes commitment and discipline and a willingness to be consistent. And it takes self-sacrifice. But this is so much easier than the alternative. Think how many problems and mistakes could be avoided by following a responsible and structured life program. Rather than taking one step forward and two steps back, you can experience the joy and rush of taking three steps forward. That is what living in control of fear is like. Those who choose to be sheep believe it will be less painful and less work. But that is a common deception. It is considerably more painful, difficult, and unpleasant work to be a sheep. Consider moving forward toward your destiny of being a shepherd. The truth is that life comes easier to shepherds. They will get whatever they want, the relationship they desire, financial security, the career or job situation they seek, and any purpose or endeavor they put their minds and hearts to.

## Setting Your Sights Up and Away!

Let's be real—before you can be successful in anything, you must first have faith in yourself and freedom from unhealthy anxiety. Anxiety is a condition that causes your world to turn inward and become self-focused. I call it a "black hole" because it sucks inwardly all of your attention and energy, not allowing any light or non-self-thought to escape. It's all about how you are feeling: "I don't feel good." "What's wrong with me?" "When will this improve?" "Am I going crazy and need to be admitted to the psych ward?" "What do these symptoms mean?"

Pathologic anxiety means you can see and feel only what's going on with *you*—how lousy *you* feel, how much stress *you're* under, how things aren't going well for *you*. There is no room in your life to care about others. You can't be a good listener, friend, partner, or parent if you are riddled with anxiety symptoms. And you can't be helpful to others if you cannot let go of yourself and live outwardly in the present moment. The ATP encourages you to change your life from the inside out. Anyone can learn the tools to conquer anxiety. And in doing so, a whole new world of possibilities will open to you. Never be controlled by an addiction, settle for a seriously flawed relationship, or be satisfied with an unhappy job or career path. Rediscover your self-confidence, strength, and true purpose. Create the future you desire by saying adios to anxiety. And escape the black hole to let your creativity, compassion, and light-hearted light shine outward with no inward gravity or weighty internal emotional concerns.

# CHAPTER 4

## Toolbox Compartment Number One: The Medical Treatment of Anxiety

In my previous books, I discuss the reasons why you should seek a medical evaluation as part of the initial assessment of your anxiety or mood disorder. This is because many medical problems, toxic exposures, medications, and supplements can play a role in the genesis or propagation of anxiety and depression. For instance, hormonal imbalances, diabetes, over- or underactive thyroid gland, heart arrhythmia, chronic pain, autoimmune disorders, and many neurological conditions can be the cause of anxious emotions. Stimulant medications, activating supplements, and certain habits (sugar, nicotine, caffeine) can exacerbate or trigger anxiety. These problems must be recognized and treated first to allow for successful resolution of anxiety. If no health problems are discovered, or if anxiety persists after correcting the medical problem, it is time to consider the medical treatment of anxiety.

For some, the medical treatment is needed only for a few months to a year to correct a transient imbalance and restore stability to the nervous system. For others, long-term medication is needed due to an underlying brain dysfunction caused by genetics, brain injury, or a chronic psychiatric illness. Unfortunately, many people who would do very well without medications never take the time to learn how, just as those who absolutely need medical intervention (as in bipolar disorder) never persevere and find the optimal drug for their condition. They may never learn that they can be the masters of their anxiety. We hope this program will inspire them to learn a variety of tools that eventually allow them to be anxiety free with or without a medical option.

Now comes the hard part. Even the best doctor or psychiatrist in the world may need some time to find the right medical regimen for you, if that is what you need. Often, the trial-and-error method is used, as there is no magical diagnostic tool that can see exactly what's going on in your brain. Even if the doctor gets the diagnosis right, you may have to try several drugs before finding the one that works best with your system, metabolism, and genetics. New genetic and metabolic blood tests have been developed to help determine which medications you will most likely tolerate and get a good response from. These tests can also determine if you have a MTHFR gene mutation, especially of the C677T or the A1298C genes, or worse, both. If so, you may need to take L-methylfolate as a supplement for your antidepressants to work! This vitamin is available in a prescription called Deplin. You should ask your doctor to order this panel of tests if you do not respond well to the first medication that is prescribed.

The process of finding the right medication is greatly helped by an accurate history and diagnosis. You are more likely to respond favorably to a particular medication if a close family member tolerated it well and got good results. My clinic has found that many individuals have a variety of diagnoses that overlap. For instance, it is not uncommon for a patient to have social phobia, panic disorder, depression, and ADD all at the same time. How can we make the simplest and most effective treatment plan to cover all the bases?

First, we need to understand that the brain uses different hormonal chemical messengers called *neurotransmitters* to carry impulses from one nerve to the next. By augmenting these chemicals, we can actually improve how the brain is functioning in certain key pathways. This, in turn, allows us to boost the pathways necessary for good emotional health. The main chemical pathways in the brain that support balanced emotions are called the *dopamine, norepinephrine, serotonin,* and *GABA pathways*. Drugs that influence the first three neurotransmitters are generally called *antidepressants*. Drugs that influence the GABA (Gamma-amino-butyric acid) system are called *anxiolytics* and *hypnotic agents*. In addition, many drugs work by stabilizing the neuronal brain cell membranes rather than by augmenting any particular neurotransmitter. These drugs fall into the categories of mood stabilizers, neuroleptics, and atypical antipsychotics. They can sometimes work even faster than antidepressants in blocking anxiety attacks and restoring restful sleep patterns.

## Using the "Symptom" and "Brain Function" Models to Determine Your Medical Therapy Options
### The Symptom Model for Choosing an Effective Medical Regimen

Knowing how the brain responds to the different chemical neurotransmitters and how this affects symptoms in our minds and bodies allows us to make a rational decision based in science as to which medical regimen is likely to work best. This way of addressing emotional disorders has been advocated by the preeminent neurobiologist Dr. Stephen Stahl. The detailed and thoughtful paradigm that we follow for determining the medical treatment that will best address your symptoms is a constant work in progress. Below is a summary and simplification of this model.

*Symptomatic Features that Respond to Serotonin Augmentation*

1. Significant obsessional thoughts and fears or behavioral compulsions
2. The tendency to think catastrophically (worst-case scenarios) with a high level of sensitivity to perceived external threats
3. Carbohydrate cravings or binge-eating patterns, during which the patient uses food to help improve his or her mood
4. Intense irritability or episodic rage attacks (such as road rage)
5. Anxiety and anxiety attacks due to underlying anxiety disorders, including OCD, panic disorder, PTSD, generalized anxiety disorder, and body dysmorphic disorder

6. Depressive mood or seasonal affective disorder and hormonal fluctuations (seen after childbirth, before the menstrual period, and during the perimenopausal and menopausal change of life)
7. Eating disorders (bulimia or binge eating) (specifically, high-dose Prozac, Celexa, or Lexapro)
8. Serotonin augmentation has also been found to be beneficial in treating the symptoms of fibromyalgia syndrome, chronic fatigue syndrome, and migraine headaches.

**Drugs with serotonin activity:** Prozac, Paxil, Zoloft, Celexa, Luvox, Lexapro, Cymbalta, Buspar, Anafranil, Serzone, Pristiq, Viibryd, Trintellix, Fetzima, Effexor, Remeron, Elavil, and Sinequan

**NOTE:** Buspar, or buspirone, is an anxiolytic (antianxiety drug) that is in a class by itself and has a mechanism of action that is not fully understood. Buspirone differs from typical benzodiazepine anxiolytics in that it does not exert anticonvulsant or muscle-relaxant effects and has very little sedative effect. Buspirone has a high affinity for serotonin (5-HT1A) receptors. Buspirone has no significant affinity for benzodiazepine receptors and does not affect GABA binding. It has moderate affinity for brain D2-dopamine receptors. Some studies suggest that buspirone may have indirect effects on other neurotransmitter systems. Trintellix is successful in treating anxiety because of its full agonist effect at the 5-HT1A receptor, and it has low risk of weight gain or sexual dysfunction.

*Symptomatic Features that Respond to Norepinephrine Augmentation*

1. Impairments in attention, focus, and concentration
2. Slowness in information processing and deficiencies in working memory
3. Psychomotor retardation (slowing of physical movement and response)
4. Diminished energy and easy fatigability
5. Melancholic depression
6. Bipolar depression (after treatment with mood stabilizer has been initiated to reduce risk of provoking mania)
7. Difficult, treatment-resistant depression
8. Cognitive symptoms of ADD (Strattera)
9. Binge-eating disorder (specifically Wellbutrin and Vyvanse)
10. Chronic pain syndromes (specifically Effexor, Cymbalta, Savella, and Remeron)
11. Hot flashes of perimenopause (specifically low-dose Effexor)

**Drugs with norepinephrine activity:** Effexor, Pristiq, Savella, Wellbutrin, Remeron, Trintellix, Fetzima, Cymbalta, Strattera, Desipramine, Nortryptiline, and amphetamines

*Symptomatic Features that Respond to Dopamine Augmentation*

1. Diminished capacity to experience pleasure and excitement (losing interest in sex, hobbies, spontaneous fun)

2. Impairments in attention and concentration
3. Diminished volitional capabilities, low motivation and initiative
4. Decreased energy, increased fatigability
5. Diminished libido and sexual responsiveness
6. Atypical and bipolar depression (specifically Wellbutrin and Parnate)
7. Cognitive impairments of ADD
8. Addictive behaviors involving nicotine, alcohol, opioids, marijuana, risk-taking behavior, compulsive gambling (specifically low-dose Naltrexone)
9. Dopamine is also helpful in treating obesity and chronic pain syndromes.

**Drugs with dopamine activity:** Wellbutrin, Parnate, high-dose Effexor, high-dose Zoloft, low-dose Naltrexone, Buspar, Dexedrine, Mirapex, and amphetamines (Adderall, Evekeo, Focalin, Vyvanse, and Concerta).

### *Symptomatic Features that Respond to Mood Stabilizers and Atypical Antipsychotics*

Terms like *mood stabilizers* and *antipsychotics* are scary and seemingly have no place in a book about anxiety. The drugs in this category do treat the more serious psychiatric conditions of bipolar mania, bipolar depression, psychosis, and schizophrenia and have been approved by the FDA for these purposes. However, as is true of many medications, these drugs have other off-label uses. This means that doctors have found them to be beneficial in other circumstances for which they have not been formally approved. In the case of mood stabilizers and atypical antipsychotics, we have found great benefit in quieting the irritable, hypersensitive, and hypervigilant nervous systems that are often fertile grounds for anxiety and phobic disorders. These types of drugs have been helpful in controlling the following symptoms:

1. Poor sleep architecture, not achieving restful sleep
2. Nighttime and early-morning anxiety attacks
3. Excessive rumination (thinking about the same thing over and over) and racing of the mind (not able to slow down your thoughts)
4. Feeling of too much energy seen in bipolar manic and hypomanic patients
5. Excessive paranoid ideation, thinking others are scrutinizing you in a negative way or are out to get you
6. Anger and oppositional behavior
7. General chronic anxiety or nervousness

**Drugs that are in the family of mood stabilizers and atypical antipsychotics:** Risperdal, Seroquel, Zyprexa, Abilify, Geodone, Lamictal, Depakote, Lithium, Neurontin, Topamax, Keppra, and Vraylar

### *Symptomatic Features that Respond to Benzodiazepines*

The GABA neuronal system in the brain suppresses neuronal excitement throughout the brain when activated. Benzodiazepines activate GABA receptors, thereby triggering the relaxation response both psychologically and physically, because GABA stimulation affects both our mind and our body's emotional response through the limbic system. High concentrations of GABA receptors are found in this area of the brain where personal feelings and emotional memories are generated and stored. When you feel a strong emotion, or are faced with a threatening challenge, it is the limbic system that interprets the ambiguous physiological responses of the autonomic nervous system that accompany these situations (i.e., change in heart rate, blood pressure, breathing, sweating, nausea, etc.) to determine exactly which emotion is being experienced. Is it fear? Excitement? Anxiety? Anger? By analyzing the particular situation and comparing it to any memories associated with similar experiences, the limbic system helps us to identify and name the emotions we feel. Well then, it seems like a no-brainer that these drugs would be the mainstay of therapy for anxiety and phobias. Unfortunately, they have the potential for overuse and addiction and are potentially fatal in overdose, especially if mixed with sleeping pills or alcohol (the Marilyn Monroe cocktail). Since many anxious patients also suffer from depression and insomnia, this is a real concern. Benzodiazepines are all related to Valium and have been modified to change how quickly they work (time to peak blood concentration), how quickly they wear off (half life of the drug), and which GABA receptors they bind to. Some benzodiazepines last a few hours, while others last a whole day. The symptoms we would expect to be helped with this class include the following:

1. Poor sleep patterns
2. Anxiety and panic attacks
3. All the somatic symptoms of anxiety (chest pain, heart palpitations, sweats, nausea, dizziness, and so on)
4. Phobic anxiety (occasional, situational use)
5. Benzodiazepines are also useful for muscle spasm, twitching muscles (fasciculations), and reducing the brain's vulnerability to seizure.
6. They can provide quick relief of irritable/aggressive mood.

**Drugs that are in the benzodiazepine family:** Valium, Xanax, Ativan, Librium, Tranxene, Serax, Xanax XR, and Klonopin (Clonazepam). Benzodiazepines that have been designed to work as sleeping pills (quick onset of action and wearing off by eight hours) include Restoril (Temazepam), Halcion (Triazolam), and Dalmane (Flurazepam). Some other sleeping pills, such as Ambien (Zolpidem), Sonata (Zaleplon), and Lunesta (Eszopiclone), also work by more selectively affecting the GABA system and may wear off with less morning sedation.

*Symptomatic Features that Respond to Beta-Blockers*
One of the oldest treatments for anxiety and phobia symptoms is the use of Propanolol, a short-acting beta-blocker helpful for those with anxiety attacks, speaker's nerves, or fear of public speaking. Beta-receptors are the places where our stress hormones bind when our sympathetic nervous system wants

to prepare the body for the flight-or-fight response. They are in our muscles, arteries, hearts, and glands and are responsible for the physical fear symptoms of rapid heart rate, tremors, sweats, dizziness, nausea, and just about any other symptom caused by sympathetic nervous system activation. Since beta-blockers bind to beta-receptors throughout the body, this fear response can be successfully blocked. Taken before a speech or presentation, this drug gives speakers the confidence that they won't embarrass themselves by having one or more of these symptoms. Since beta-blockers are primarily used to control blood pressure and heart rate in cardiac patients, they are especially appropriate for phobia patients who have these medical conditions. In this case, the longer-acting drugs in this category, like Atenolol or Toprol, would be preferred.

*TOOL: Using the somatic-symptom model, decide whether your symptoms might be helped by medical treatment. Circle the paragraphs above that apply to you, jot down possible medication choices that apply to your specific symptoms, and show it to your doctor. Ask if any of those options could be considered for your unique situation.

## The Brain Function Model for Choosing an Effective Medical Regimen

Although they are often not covered by insurance and therefore not affordable for many patients, determining treatment based on sophisticated, high-tech scans that look at how the brain is functioning—especially where it is over- or underactive—is rapidly gaining acceptance in mainstream psychiatry. Dr. Daniel Amen, author of *Change Your Brain, Change Your Life*, *Healing ADD*, *Healing Anxiety and Depression*, and other best-selling titles, has founded several clinics nationwide where treatment decisions are based largely on metabolic brain scans, known as *SPECT scans*. More and more, specialists are relying on scans as well as metabolic and genetic blood tests to help elucidate the type of brain dysfunction and which treatment choices are most likely to work and be well tolerated. You may want to check if your health savings or flex spending account money provided by your employer will help pay for these advanced diagnostic techniques.

At Amen Clinics, patients are given a detailed report of their SPECT scan findings, along with a review of their medication regimen and recommendations for any changes, if applicable. In addition, recommendations for nonmedical therapies, such as vitamins and supplements, psychotherapy, dietary adjustments, further education, group support, life skills/coaching, exercise, and self-relaxation techniques, are also given.

Below is a summary of the areas of the brain evaluated by the SPECT scan, the problems and conditions caused by dysfunction in these areas, the medications and supplements typically used to help correct the conditions, and other treatments and modalities that have proven helpful. Pay attention as you read about other treatments for each area of the brain. This will tell you the location in the brain where the tools in the ATP are exerting their effect.

The following paradigm was developed by Dr. Amen and is followed by his staff of specialists at the Amen Clinics. I have modified it to include the specific treatments and tools taught in this program. For more information and a list of Amen Clinics, visit the URLs that follow.

### Amygdala and Basal Ganglia

**Functions:** To set the "idle speed" of the brain, control anxiety levels, mediate pleasure signals, control smooth motor movement, and modulate motivation and enthusiasm

**Problems:** If metabolic activity is increased in these structures, the result may be an increase in anxiety, panic, irritability, tension, hypervigilance and apprehension, overactivity, avoidance of conflict, and pessimism. If activity is decreased in these structures, the result may be low motivation and ADD-like symptoms of poor focus and attention.

**Conditions:** Anxiety disorders, including OCD, PTSD, Tourette's/tics/movement disorders

**Medications:** Anxiolytics (Valium, Ativan, Klonopin, Xanax), Buspar, Inderal, antidepressants (SSRIs, tricyclics, MAOIs), anticonvulsants (Neurontin, Gabitril)

**Supplements:** Valerian Root, Kava Kava (this combination has been called *nature's Valium*)

**Other treatments:** Biofeedback, hypnosis/meditation, EMDR, cognitive behavioral therapy, assertiveness training, relaxing music, limit caffeine, nicotine, and alcohol

### Prefrontal Cortex

**Functions:** Focus, organization, planning, attention, forethought, judgment, empathy, impulse control, emotional control, insight, learning from mistakes

**Problems:** Short attention span, impulsivity, procrastination, disorganization, poor judgment, lack of insight, and lack of empathy.

**Conditions:** ADHD, depression, brain trauma, dementia, schizophrenia, antisocial personality disorder

**Medications:** Stimulants: Ritalin, Concerta, Vyvanse, Adderall, Dexadrine, Evekeo. Modified stimulants: Provigil, Nuvigil. Nonstimulants: Strattera

**Supplements:** L-tyrosine, probiotics

**Other treatments:** Neurobiofeedback, coaching/organizational help, intense aerobic exercise, relationship counseling, stimulating activities, and higher protein diet

### Anterior Cingulate Gyrus

**Functions:** The brain's "gear shifter," improving cooperation, ability to see options, cognitive flexibility, easily shifting from idea to idea, and able to go with the flow

**Problems:** Gets stuck frequently on one idea, thought, or option; holds grudges (can't get over and get on with it); worries; obsesses; inflexible; argumentative; compulsions; oppositional; trouble shifting attention; and addictions

**Conditions:** OCD, anxiety disorders, oppositional-defiant disorder, PTSD, premenstrual syndrome, addictions, eating disorders, chronic pain

**Medications:** Effexor, Pristiq, Cymbalta, SSRIs (Prozac, Paxil, Zoloft, Celexa, Luvox, Lexapro), atypical antipsychotics in difficult cases (Risperdal, Zyprexa, Abilify, Geodon, Vraylar, Seroquel)

**Supplements:** 5-hydroxytryptophan (5-HTP), Saint-John's-wort

**Other treatments:** Biofeedback, cognitive-behavioral therapy, intense aerobic exercise, relationship counseling, anger management, lower protein, higher complex carbohydrate diet

*Deep Limbic System*
**Functions:** Sets the emotional tone; stores charged memories; modulates motivation; allows emotional bonding; regulates appetite, sleep cycles, body temperature, fight-or-flight response, sense of smell, and sex drive
**Problems:** Negativity, guilt, blame, irritability, sadness, low self-esteem, low energy/motivation, social isolation, impaired sleep/appetite, and loss of sex drive
**Conditions:** Depression, many of the symptoms of hormone deficiency seen with premenstrual syndrome and perimenopausal syndrome, cyclic mood disorders, pain syndromes
**Medications:** Effexor, Wellbutrin, Tricyclic antidepressants (Imipramine/Desipramine), SSRIs, MAOIs (Marplan/Parnate)
**Supplements:** DL-Phenylalanine, L-Tyrosine, S-adrenosyl-methionine (SAM-e)
**Other treatments:** Biofeedback, cognitive-behavioral therapy, EMDR, relationship counseling, intense aerobic exercise, increased protein diet


*Parietal Lobes*
**Functions:** Processing sensory information, directing movements, spatial cognition
**Problems:** Impaired sensation/movement, denial or indifference to illness, dyslexia, acalculia, agraphia
**Conditions:** Trauma, toxic exposures, substance abuse, Alzheimer's dementia
**Treatments:** Prevention of brain injury, avoidance of toxic substances, occupational therapy, maximize brain nutrition, hyperbaric oxygen therapy


*Cerebellum*
**Functions:** Motor control, posture/gait, executive functioning (via connections to the prefrontal cortex), speed of cognitive integration
**Problems:** Impaired coordination/gait, slowed thinking and speech, impulsivity
**Conditions:** Trauma, alcohol abuse
**Treatments:** Prevention of brain injury, stop alcohol use, occupational therapy, maximize brain nutrition, hyperbaric oxygen therapy


*Temporal Lobes*
**Functions:** Understand/use of language, retrieval of words, auditory/visual learning, long-term memory, reading social cues/faces/voice intonation, emotional stability, music/rhythm
**Problems:** Anxiety, impaired memory, aggression (left temporal lobe), spaciness or confusion, religious preoccupation, dark thoughts, hypergraphia, unexplained headaches or abdominal pains
**Conditions:** Anxiety, depression, head injury, dissociation, temporal seizures, amnesia, dyslexia (left side), autistic spectrum disorders (right side)
**Medications:** Anticonvulsants, Neurontin, Gabitril, Depakote, Trileptal, Topamax, Lamictal; often a stimulant is added

**Supplements:** GABA, omega-3 fatty acids, probiotics
**Other treatments:** Biofeedback, improved sleep, relaxing music, recalling positive experiences, relationship counseling, anger management, increased protein diet

*****TOOL:** Consider finding the nearest Amen Clinics at www.amenclinic.com or www.danielamenmd.com. They can help with medication choices and have a number of other supportive programs to help optimize brain performance, including an online university which offers courses for college credit. They also have a line of nutraceutical products to improve brain function and emotional health; find more information at https://www.brainmdhealth.com.

## The Importance of Thyroid and Sex Hormone Optimization in Treating Anxiety

I always ask my patients, male and female, whether their symptoms of anxiety or depression started after age thirty-five. This is when testosterone starts dropping in both sexes, women faster than men. And ladies, don't let your gynecologist tell you that testosterone is a male hormone and you don't need it. If you have any doubts, read the book by Kathy Maupin, MD: *The Secret Female Hormone: How Testosterone Replacement Can Change Your Life.* A gynecologist herself, Dr. Maupin takes you through her own personal journey of dysfunction caused by hormone deficiency and how she found that the optimization of sex hormones through implanted natural hormone pellets was the best way to control emotional changes caused by estrogen and testosterone deficiency.

During the course of your regular checkup, your gynecologist may respond to your laundry list of complaints with the answer, "It's not your hormones because you're still having your period." But it *is* your hormones. Menopause comes in two parts. First comes testosterone menopause, which starts around age thirty-five. This does not affect your periods, as that is completely a product of the cycling of your ovarian estrogen production for fertility purposes. Testosterone menopause and cessation of your periods might come twenty years apart. Often, testosterone will not have even been checked before you are told, "It's not your hormones." If it is checked, and your level is zero to forty-five nanograms per deciliter (ng/dl), you may be told, "See, you're normal." Although zero to forty-five ng/dl might be in the normal range on the lab report form, this is the postmenopausal, older-than-fifty level—and you're thirty-five to forty-five! The normal perimenopausal level is twenty to seventy ng/dl for the forty- to fifty-year-old group. The youthful, optimal, twenty-year-old level is believed to be 80–120 ng/dl. That's when you felt your best, slept your best, and looked your best. So your eighteen-year-old level is your optimal level, even if you are ninety years old. It is a fault of nature, not the wisdom of nature, that we lose our sex hormones.

If a man comes in and has one-third of his youthful level of testosterone, we immediately replace him back to his eighteen-year-old levels because it would be a disaster if he couldn't have a full erection. But a woman who drops to one-tenth of her youthful level is told it's OK, it's a "male hormone," anyway, so what they're really saying is: "Men need their hormones for sexual interest and libido, but you can fake an orgasm!" And a woman with testosterone deficiency is having a lot more problems than just sexual dysfunction (see the list below). Another point is that women lose their testosterone and later their estrogen suddenly and dramatically over a few months, whereas men lose slowly and are able to adjust gradually over decades.

The link between hormone deficiency in midlife (yes, age thirty-five is hormonal midlife) and anxiety, depression, exhaustion, mental fog, insomnia, weight gain, and loss of sexual interest and performance (erections in men, loss of orgasm in women) is well documented. Even more frightening are emerging theories supported by numerous studies that loss of our sex hormones leads to a general breakdown in our health over time, causing higher risk of neurodegenerative disease like Alzheimer's and Parkinson's disease, higher rates of autoimmune disease, and immune system dysfunction, higher rates of all cancers, bone deterioration leading to osteoporosis and osteoarthritis, and insulin resistance leading to weight gain and type II adult-onset diabetes. That's a lot to be anxious and depressed about!

The truth is that natural hormones are good for you, with a few exceptions, such as active prostate and uterine, ovarian, or breast cancer. Misleading studies based on synthetic, man-made versions of sex hormones by the pharmaceutical industry have led influential groups like the American Congress of Obstetricians and Gynecologists advise restricted use of hormones in midlife and beyond due to concerns about cancer, heart disease, stroke, and blood clots. But the rest of the world, especially Europe and Japan, has been studying natural, plant-based estrogen and testosterone treatments for more than fifty years. The overwhelming consensus? Bioidentical hormones make you healthier and happier with *lower* risk of all cancers, including breast and prostate cancer; lower rates of heart disease, stroke and dementia; almost no risk of developing osteoporosis; and no increased risk of blood clots. Blood pressure improves, weight improves, cholesterol profile improves, bone density improves—all things that reduce risk of vascular and degenerative disease and would be expected to increase quality and quantity of life.

But to achieve all this, women must balance low-normal estrogen levels with high-normal testosterone levels and adequate progesterone if they still have their uteruses. Men should maintain testosterone in the 800–1,200 ng/dl range. In 2013, I got a call from a long-time friend and colleague Tanya Atagi, MD, a plastic surgeon and regenerative medicine specialist in Denver, Colorado. She had been implanting natural hormones for several years by implementing a program developed by Dr. Gary Donovitz, a gynecologist in Dallas, Texas. For twenty years he developed his clinic's protocol for using bioidentical hormone pellets for his peri- and postmenopausal women and their andropausal boyfriends and spouses, and he took his company, BioTE, nationwide in 2008.

Dr. Atagi told me how many of her patients' lives were being turned around within a matter of days or weeks by hormone implants; they started sleeping through the night; their anxiety and depression lifted; their strength, endurance, stamina, energy, and sex drive returned; and their body shape and weight improved. And when you feel better and look better, your confidence and motivation soar. You want to get out there, exercise, be more social, and connect with the things you're passionate about. You want to be healthy and take better care of yourself. Dr. Atagi felt very gratified that she was saving professional careers, giving a happy and functional mom or dad back to their children, or returning that "man or woman I married" back to their spouses. She confided that she often felt more gratified with her patients' satisfaction with her hormonal intervention than her personal satisfaction with a great cosmetic surgical outcome she had achieved.

My interest peaked when Dr. Donovitz told me that almost 80 percent of his patients were able to get off antidepressants within a cycle of starting implanted hormones, especially if their anxiety or depression came on with hormone loss after age thirty-five. He also said his patients were routinely getting off statin drugs for cholesterol, blood-pressure drugs, treatments for osteopenia and osteoporosis, and diabetes medication for the adult-onset insulin-resistance type. Dr. Donovitz's BioTE pellet program is nationwide, treats tens of thousands of patients in the United States, and uses the only bioidentical hormone pellets made by a licensed pharmaceutical company in the United States (Anazao Pharmaceuticals). This means the pellets are made to the same exacting specifications and come under the same scrutiny as name-brand drugs made in the United States. Each batch of each dose is independently, third-party tested for sterility, dosage, purity, and pellet rigidity (to make sure it can be implanted correctly in the fat layer under the skin in the upper, outer area of the butt). Pellets generally last three to six months, and the procedure is done under local anesthetic in about five minutes. No stitch is required to close the small, two- to three-millimeter opening, just a steri-strip covered by a waterproof patch, and you're reloaded and on your way. Dosage is determined by a proprietary formula that takes into account many variables, including weight, age, symptoms, past medical history, and extensive blood-work results. The labs are usually covered by insurance, whereas pellets, since they are not on insurance formularies (because they are naturally produced by plants and not synthesized and patented), usually need to be paid for out of pocket. Health savings and flex spending accounts through employers usually can be used to cover this expense.

In my clinic, I also offer patients hormone-replacement programs using natural, compounded creams and vaginal inserts, called *mini-inserts* or *sublingual oral torches*, or compounded BLA tablets that absorb into the lymphatic system. These have to be applied, inserted, or taken orally daily; often do not achieve optimal blood levels; are less convenient; and often cost more than hormone pellets. The symptoms we would expect to be helped by sex-hormone optimization include the following:

1. Difficulty falling or staying asleep
2. Poor mental focus, concentration, memory, or brain fog
3. Fatigue, exhaustion, low energy
4. Weight gain, weaker muscles, increased body fat
5. Mood swings, irritability, anxiety, depression
6. Poor sex drive (libido) and performance, reduced female orgasmic response
7. Thinning skin, hair, and nails and cosmetic aging appearance
8. Hot flashes and night sweats
9. Low motivation, reduced confidence, social anxiety
10. Urinary dribbling and vaginal dryness caused by estrogen deficiency

**\*TOOL:** If you are a woman and feel you may be having symptoms of testosterone deficiency due to genetic underproduction, perimenopause, or the use of birth control pills, get your doctor to order your blood level and discuss the natural, plant-based topical, intravaginal, or implanted testosterone options. If you can't find a sympathetic ear, search for someone offering bioidentical hormone replacement therapy treatments in your area. The website www.biotemedical.com has a physician finder tool; just supply your zip code to see if there is a provider near you. I have many patients who travel more than three hours to see me every four to six months to get their pellet implants, so they must be satisfied! Men should also get the blood test and have their total testosterone checked to see if there is a problem if they feel they are having symptoms of testosterone deficiency.

## The Office Treatment of Needle Phobias and Procedure Anxiety

One of the most common anxiety conditions I deal with daily in my office is the fear of needles and procedures. Also, many patients are claustrophobic about the closed-in MRI scanners, so I make sure they take Valium an hour before imaging procedures. I perform many (sometimes uncomfortable) cosmetic procedures, including body sculpting with laser-assisted liposuction, injectable fillers, Botox, NovaThread Lifts, intra-articular and IV stem cell treatments, platelet-rich plasma joint injections, platelet-rich plasma hair restoration, laser leg vein removal, laser skin rejuvenation and peels, Ultherapy skin tightening, VelaShape radio-frequency body-shaping, E-Matrix radio-frequency skin tightening, and internal hormonal pelleting with bioidentical estrogen and testosterone. I'm more likely to have repeat patients if I am careful with pain and anxiety management. For anxiety, I may give a benzodiazepine, like Xanax. For pain, I give five milligrams of Oxycodone. I also find that the topical refrigerant, Unfortunately, a patient is not allowed to drive home after taking an anxiolytic or pain medication. To get around this, I use nitrous oxide instead. Also called *laughing gas*, nitrous oxide is inhaled by the patient in a fifty-fifty mixture with pure oxygen. This is an extremely safe sedative that allows relaxation, pain, and anxiety control throughout the procedure. Best of all, it wears off very comfortably in about ten minutes. Patients can then drive themselves home feeling refreshed and relaxed instead of frazzled and tense. I recently used nitrous oxide on a male patient who comes in regularly for testosterone hormone pellet implants. The problem is that he has a needle phobia and starts screaming and freaking out at the sight of the needle I use to numb the treatment area. He has extreme fear in anticipation of pain, even though the real pain is minimal. He makes so many agonizing groans and moans before we even get started that he scares the other patients in the waiting room (who think I must be torturing him). So, I persuaded him to breathe the nitrous oxide mixture during pelleting. What a difference! He was very calm, and we talked off and on during the procedure. Several times he fell asleep. Afterward, he said that he could understand everything I was saying, but he had no procedure or needle anxiety. He felt like an observer with no emotional reactivity to what was going on. I moved through the procedure much more quickly and efficiently because he was calm and comfortable. He slept for ten minutes afterward and woke up feeling great. He then texted all his friends about how he didn't fear coming in for hormone pellets anymore and was actually looking forward to the next time! Let your doctor know if you have problems with procedure anxiety or needle phobia. He or she probably has a way to make the experience more tolerable.

## Transcranial Magnetic Stimulation for Depression

You've probably heard about electroconvulsive therapy for severe, refractory depression that is unresponsive to all medications. That scene from *One Flew Over the Cuckoo's Nest* seems barbaric and medieval to most people today. You'd think that something better would have come out by now for these most difficult cases. Well, yes and no. I still have a patient who feels that electroconvulsive treatments under general anesthesia are the only thing that pulls him out of a suicidal, deeply depressive state. Electrostimulation devices implanted in the brain with long-life batteries seem more humane and work in many cases. Similar devices also improve uncontrolled tremors in some Parkinson's disease patients. The frequency and amplitude of the electromagnetic energy being delivered to the selected area of the brain can be modulated by the patient with a remote-control device. But implantation requires a surgical procedure that has some inherent risks. What if you could provide electromagnetic stimulation through an external device that requires no surgery—that would be progress! Well, it's here: transcranial magnetic stimulation.

During a transcranial magnetic stimulation session, an electromagnetic coil is placed against your scalp near your forehead. The electromagnet painlessly delivers a magnetic pulse that stimulates nerve cells in the region of your brain involved in mood control and depression. And it may activate regions of the brain that have decreased activity in people with depression. The benefits of transcranial magnetic stimulation have been compared favorably to psychopharmacologic (medication) treatments with fewer side effects.

While still in early stages of investigation, this technology will become more and more widely used and will likely help those with anxiety related to depressive disorders. Rick Trautner, MD, of Bay Psychiatric Associates in Berkeley, California, is an expert in the use of transcranial magnetic stimulation and a member of the Clinical TMS Society. He treats adults and adolescents for depression, anxiety, OCD, PTSD, bipolar disorder, and psychotic spectrum disorders with a combination of transcranial magnetic stimulation, psychotherapy, and psychopharmacology. His contact information can be found at http://baypsychiatric.com/provider-r-trautner.php.

## Stem Cell IV and Intrathecal Infusions for Healing TBI-Related PTSD

In appendix 3, "Combat Relief," I talk about how anyone who has had a TBI, whether on the battlefield, the sports field, or the roadways, is vulnerable to anxiety, cognitive impairment (brain fog), and depression. It's hard enough for someone with TBI just to survive, much less succeed. This is especially true of a soldier trying to assimilate back into a normal life after returning from a tour of duty.

One big hope for the future is the use of stem-cell treatments to heal the brain and, in some cases, to completely reverse the effects of brain injury. Pluripotent stem cells can morph into any type of cell in the body, including brain neurons and their supporter cells, replacing those that have been injured or have died as the result of brain injury. In fact, one study on trained mice that were then brain injured showed that if stem cells were intravenously infused within two weeks of the trauma, the mouse recovered fully, with no signs of postconcussion syndrome or lingering cognitive impairment. In fact, the mice performed the tasks they were trained to do even faster and more accurately after the injury if they were given IV stem cells!

It appears that there is about a two-week window after injury during which stem cells can cross the blood-brain barrier and replace damaged or dead neurons. This is because the body opens the blood-brain barrier so that cells can cross over to help clean up damaged cells and reduce swelling and inflammation. Then the barrier closes and blocks the stem cells. That's because stem cells can cross over only when there is an inflammatory/injury signal being given off by the dying cells.

What if your TBI happened a few years ago, but you still have impairments? Scientists are working on ways to gently "injure" the brain by vibration and sound waves to cause the blood-brain barrier to open back up again and let IV stem cells through. This actually works, at least in the mice studies. Another way proven to get stem cells into the damaged brain is through the ventricles by intrathecal infusion of stem cells directly into the spinal cord, just like when an epidural is given to a woman in labor.

In addition to TBI cases, brain degeneration from inflammatory and autoimmune reactions, such as multiple sclerosis, Parkinson's disease, and Alzheimer's disease, improves with stem-cell infusions. I have used both autologous mesenchymal stem cells (liposuctioned from the patient's own fat) and umbilical-cord mesenchymal stem cells (from carefully screened mothers of full-term, healthy babies and collected by a reputable cord bank). Both are undifferentiated and can be injected or infused without significant risk of reaction or rejection. The best result is to infuse the IV after injecting some directly into the area of damage or degeneration. This gives real hope for those whose anxiety stems from TBI that has, up to now, been untreatable.

# CHAPTER 5

## Toolbox Compartment Number Two: Alternative Medical Therapy Tools for Anxiety

We will now open the door to the possibilities of alternative medicine in the treatment of your anxiety. Alternative-medicine therapies have been around for hundreds and even thousands of years and still have validity today. I discuss vitamins and supplements, homeopathy, Chinese traditional medicine, herbal, and Ayurvedic remedies in this section. In addition, some outside-the-box remedies that are being investigated and have validity will be discussed.

### Vitamins and Supplements

Vitamins and supplements generally work by helping support the brain and body in performing their natural functions. Many things can lead to depletion of basic nutrients, minerals, and cofactors, including stress, poor dietary intake, poor intestinal absorption, illness, and exposure to toxic elements in the environment. Those who smoke cigarettes, drink alcohol, are dehydrated, are hormone deficient, or are overexerting themselves physically are particularly vulnerable and may benefit from a reasonable supplement program.

Many physicians, including myself, do not recommend large doses of vitamins due to the possibility of toxic reactions and feel those supplements with hormonal activity should be approved by an endocrinologist first. Certain products, however, are mentioned repeatedly in the literature for improving the body's response to stress, as well as calming anxiety, insomnia, and irritability and relieving depression and fatigue. We also give IV vitamin support in our clinic, which will be discussed in another section below. Here is a brief list of oral-supplement options:

**Anxiety, irritability, and insomnia:** Niacin (vitamin B3), vitamin B6, vitamin B15, folic acid, choline, L-tryptophan, vitamin A, beta-carotene, chromium, inositol, B-complex, calcium, selenium, magnesium, silicon, and manganese. Natural Calm made by Natural Vitality includes magnesium and really works.

**Depression and fatigue:** Vitamin B12 (injection or under-the-tongue formula), high-dose vitamin D3 (5,000–10,000 IU), B complex, selenium, calcium and magnesium, flower essence, pyridoxine (B6), thiamine (B1), niacin (B3), choline, chromium, vanadium, zinc, potassium, lecithin, iodine, essential fatty acids, vitamin C, L-tyrosine, folic acid, and inositol.

**Stress:** B complex (especially B2, B5, B6, and B15), folic acid, vitamin C, bioflavonoids, vitamin E, calcium, magnesium, lecithin, phosphorous, Bach flower remedy, zinc, potassium, selenium, L-tyrosine, and fish oil (omega-3).

**5-HTP:** 5-HTP is formed in the body from the amino acid tryptophan. 5-HTP is then used to create the neurotransmitter serotonin. Because it can readily cross over the blood-brain barrier and enter the brain from the bloodstream, taking supplemental doses of 5-HTP ultimately works by increasing brain serotonin levels. The 5-HTP that is available in stores comes from the *Griffonia* seed, the product of an African tree grown mostly in Ghana and the Ivory Coast. Like many of the SSRIs, the list of disorders and ailments helped by 5-HTP is long and includes eating disorders, depression, anxiety, insomnia, fibromyalgia, premenstrual syndrome, and migraine headaches. The supplement is considered safe and generally well tolerated.

**DHEA:** Dihydroepiandrosterone was once at the center of controversy regarding Mark McGwire's 1998–1999 record-setting baseball season. It is an adrenal and gonadal hormone shown in some studies to have mood-elevating properties. It appears to reduce stress and improve sleep patterns and is thought to improve memory and cognition in the elderly, as well. It may enhance sexual performance and increase muscle bulk and strength because some of it is eventually converted into testosterone, the primary male sex hormone, in the body. As with all hormonally active supplements, we recommend you discuss taking DHEA with your physician first.

**SAM-e:** SAM-e is a dietary supplement whose antidepressant effects were first reported in 1973. Used for many years in Europe and especially Italy, SAM-e is now finding increasing popularity in the United States. The three monoamine brain neurotransmitters (serotonin, norepinephrine, and dopamine) are synthesized with the help of SAM-e by its donation of a methyl group to these brain chemicals. The daily dose range is from two hundred to eight hundred milligrams per day for anxiety and depression. I recommend four hundred milligrams twice a day.

**Phytochemicals:** Do you get enough vine-ripened fruits and vegetables? It is thought that early picking prevents the production of hundreds of phytochemicals (chemicals created in plants with the help of photosynthesis) that are manufactured in the plant during the final stages of ripening while still on the vine or tree. These chemicals may have antioxidant and disease-fighting properties more potent than vitamins and include limonenes in citrus fruits, indoles and isothiocynates in broccoli, flavones in beans, genistein in soybeans, and flavonoids in almost all fruits and vegetables. Juice Plus is a name-brand supplement designed to provide these naturally occurring phytochemicals to people whose diets may be weak in vine-ripened produce.

*TOOL: Create a daily vitamin/supplement program to complement your good dietary habits. You may simply want to take a multivitamin/mineral supplement along with B complex or take it even further with some of the other products mentioned. You can learn more at https://nccih.nih.gov/health/vitamins or shop online at www.vitaminshoppe.com.

## Probiotics, the Gut Microbiome, and Brain Function

Probiotics are beneficial bacteria that colonize our small and large intestines and provide us with many valuable products that are absolutely necessary for proper immune-system functioning, cancer protection and defense, liver detox and support, micronutrient absorption, and heart and brain support. When it comes to reducing anxiety, as well as promoting general health, probiotics play an important role in maintaining cellular function and the natural intelligence of our cells throughout the brain and body. Our gut is home to trillions of bacteria; in fact, there are more than ten times the number of bacteria in the human gut than total number of cells in the human body. This is called the *gut microbiome*. Healthy bacteria, using the process known as *fermentation*, digest cellulose and other fibers that we can't digest. In return, they give us enzymes that promote better absorption of the micronutrients in the diet and compounds known as *short-* and *medium-chain fatty acids*. Short-chain fatty acids have been extensively studied, and many of their actions are known. For instance, the short-chain fatty acid called *propionate* is helpful with liver function and detoxification, improving insulin resistance in type II diabetes, energy, and metabolism. Acetate is a short-chain fatty acid that improves heart strength and crosses the blood-brain barrier to get into brain cells and enhances neuronal mitochondrial production of adenosine triphosphate, the cell's energy molecule. Better energy in the brain cell means better mood and energy for you. Another short-chain fatty acid that we get only from the activity of good gut bacteria is butyrate, which reduces colon inflammation and the risk of colon cancer. Also, our immune system T-regulator cells undergo differentiation and training in the walls of the gut under the influence of butyrate. This T-cell activation reduces problems caused by vaginal bacteria and yeast overgrowth, reduces our vulnerability to urinary tract infections, makes us resistant to the development of cancer, and may help suppress the growth of existing cancer cells. Bad bacteria in the gut are happy when you eat more sugar and processed foods. They can then rise up and outcompete the good strains, especially when we take antibiotics or eat the wrong foods. The resulting gut microbiome imbalance can cause symptoms of bloating, gas, pain, diarrhea, and constipation and can weaken the immune system. We also lose the stimulation and support to the brain, heart, and liver that the good probiotic strains provide. The best way to feed your probiotic bacteria is with prebiotic fiber in the diet from high-fiber fruits, green vegetables, and whole/ancient grain sources. The stalks of broccoli and asparagus and especially leeks (delicious sautéed) are excellent prebiotic-fiber foods to support the good bacterial strains and give them the substrate they need to produce all the special compounds we need.

### **Fermented Cellulose Antioxidant**

Along the lines of probiotics is fermented cellulose antioxidant, a product that is available only in a private clinic in Japan at this time but will soon be produced in the United States and distributed as a dietary supplement. I mention it in this book because it improves brain cell mitochondrial function through the short-chain fatty acid acetate, which helps energy and sense of well being. It will also bring hope to those anxious about serious health problems and degenerative conditions such as severe Lyme disease (neuroborelliosis), stage 4 cancer, end-stage liver failure, and conditions that cause wasting of the body or "failure to thrive." While promoted as a powerful antioxidant because of its very high ORAC values, I have found there is more to fermented cellulose antioxidant than that.

Fermented cellulose antioxidant was developed some forty years ago in Japan by Kokichi Hanaoka, PhD, a membrane scientist and electrochemist who also invented Essentia functional electrolyzed water. His inventions are being brought to the United States by a devoted student and entrepreneur, Edward

Alexander, CEO of Innovative Designs and Technology, USA. Fermented cellulose antioxidant, which will be marketed in the United States under the name Esperer.fca, was created by Dr. Hanaoka after his observation that herbivorous animals can digest cellulose in their appendix, hindgut, or foregut through a fermentation process to extract additional energy. Humans have no enzymes for cellulose digestion, even though they belong to the herbivorous animal family. From studies showing a decrease in immune resistance in individuals who have had their appendixes removed, Dr. Hanaoka thought that there may be products of fermentation that are helpful in immune-system functioning, particularly enzyme products that are uniquely formed by intestinal bacteria during cellulose fermentation. He was ahead of his time!

The process of fermented cellulose antioxidant production involves the fermentation of cellulose from rice stalks and rice bran with lactobacillus bacteria, which is submerged in large, wooden trays for more than ten thousand hours in the sun. The end product is a thick paste that is processed and sterilized to produce a soft gel capsule that is sealed in foil packets.

With Dr. Hanaoka's encouragement, I have used fermented cellulose antioxidant for four years on my medical patients with serious health challenges who have very few treatment options. The first was a long-time patient who was suffering from neuroborelliosis (Lyme disease) that had invaded her brain and nervous system. She was failing fast and could no longer eat, sleep, or take care of herself due to mental fog and exhaustion, as well as understandable feelings of depression and anxiety. She had gone from 140 to 85 pounds, and I believed she was close to death. I sent her to the hospital to have one final evaluation. I did not want to be the last doctor to see her alive. Maybe I had missed something. She had already been seen by five different Lyme and infectious-disease specialists and had tried all standard and alternative remedies.

About six weeks later, she appeared in my office almost unrecognizable from the desperate state I just described. She had regained weight to 110 pounds, felt much better energy and appetite, was sleeping better, and felt her brain was starting to work again. The hospital had released her with no treatment as "nothing could be done." Then an old friend who had worked with Dr. Hanaoka in Japan gave her a supply of fermented cellulose antioxidant to try—five gel caps three times a day with meals and lots of water. I was intrigued and wrote to Dr. Hanaoka, telling him of this outcome. He had never treated a Lyme disease patient before but was not surprised.

Since that time, I have used fermented cellulose antioxidant on many stage IV cancer patients and an end-stage liver-failure patient. All are still alive and stable, and some even improved. The liver-failure patient was initially given less than a month to live by the liver-transplant teams at Stanford and UCSF Medical Centers, saying that he was too ill to be a liver-transplant candidate and would certainly not survive the six-month waiting period. He had all the end-stage complications: severe jaundice, ascites requiring eight liters of fluid to be taken out of his peritoneum every week, bleeding esophageal veins, periods of coma due to elevated blood ammonia levels, and spontaneous bacterial peritonitis with sepsis. After six months on full-strength fermented cellulose antioxidant, the patient went back to his liver specialist, who was shocked that his liver had recovered and he was now too healthy for a liver transplant. Since then, he is back to his life without treatment for his liver and continues to have completely normal liver tests.

My belief is that fermented cellulose antioxidant derives its benefits from the known fatty acids and digestive enzymes that are produced by bacterial fermentation of indigestible probiotic fibers in the gut. The problem is that very sick patients cannot successfully support bacterial colonization due to degraded health and poor dietary intake of fiber. Therefore, they do not get the support of these essential compounds when they most desperately need them. To test this theory, I asked Dr. Hanoaka to run an assay in his Kyoto lab to test for the presence of the most well-studied short-chain fatty acids: propionate, butyrate, and acetate. The results confirmed that all three are present in fermented cellulose antioxidant.

## Oxytocin

The pituitary hormone oxytocin has effects on both the peripheral and central nervous system. It is released naturally in large amounts in women during childbirth, as well as with the nipple stimulation of breastfeeding. In men and women, oxytocin is released during orgasm and is considered the primary hormone involved in desire, social recognition, and bonding between sexual partners and parent and child.

It is not surprising, then, that oxytocin has been found to reduce anxiety and promote a sense of well being emotionally. Oxytocin has been studied and used successfully in treating autism spectrum disorders, social anxiety, depression, sexual dysfunction (interest, orgasm, and erectile functioning), and phobias/situational anxiety. I have a patient who uses oxytocin to handle her social anxiety. She takes it under the tongue (sublingually) just before a challenging social situation, and it works well with no sedation or side effects. It has no adverse reactions with other medications or alcohol and can be taken sublingually fifteen minutes before sex to improve libido.

Traditionally, oxytocin has been administered by injection or by nasal spray because oral-dose forms would be destroyed by the gastrointestinal tract before ever getting to the bloodstream. To overcome this, Belmar Pharmacy in Colorado compounds an oral tablet of oxytocin using a system it developed called Bio-Available Lymphatic Absorption (BLA). The BLA System is designed to present the hormone directly to the lymphatic network in the gut, thereby bypassing first pass through the liver. The lymphatic system then drains directly into the bloodstream. This is great for daily use. The sublingual dose form is better for libido and social anxiety taken fifteen minutes before the activity as needed.

This provides an inexpensive, convenient, and readily available source of oxytocin to be taken either regularly (for chronic depression or generalized anxiety) or as needed for social anxiety and situational anxiety conditions. To get more information on the oral formulation, contact Belmar Pharmacy at BelmarPharmacy.com.

## Low-Dose Naltrexone for Anxiety, Depression, and Pain Reduction

Low-dose Naltrexone at one to five milligrams per day has some unexpected and unique benefits that are used to help fatigue, anxiety, OCD (especially with picking, cutting, and hair pulling), PTSD, anorexia and bulimia nervosa, depression, autoimmune disease pain, fibromyalgia pain, autism spectrum disorders, addictions and cravings (alcohol, gambling, sex, Internet, smoking), weight management, and sex drive. How could a drug that was developed to reverse opiate drug binding to brain receptors (at a dose of fifty to one hundred milligrams per day) actually improve important "happy" brain chemicals like dopamine and endorphins? It is counterintuitive that very low doses of this drug would stimulate brain dopamine and endorphin levels as well as brain-derived neurotrophic factor (BDNF), but this has been studied and shown to be true.

BDNF stimulates the growth of brain neurons. BDNF, endorphin, and dopamine enhancement is associated with a general sense of well being, contentment, increased interest in hedonistic (fun) activities, drop in pain levels, improved sexual interest, regulation of appetite, and enhanced immune-system functioning. Our endorphin levels are naturally secreted in response to exercise; orgasm; food (chocolate, spices, alcohol); pain; fear; sunshine; pleasant sensations, like touch and the smell of our favorite food or flower; and compulsive behaviors such as shopping, gambling, sex, and eating. So that's why the pain caused by cutting oneself is helpful in breaking an anxiety reaction, because cutting triggers a release of endorphins. It's also why we develop a craving for compulsive behaviors such as overeating, smoking, sex addiction, and gambling. Low-dose Naltrexone causes a release of endorphins that gives us the same benefit as the release of endorphins caused by destructive behaviors. This allows us to let go of that dysfunctional behavior—we don't need to do it anymore to get the endorphin benefit.

If our BDNF, dopamine, and endorphin levels are low, we are likely to cry more easily, avoid social situations because we lack confidence, have difficulties getting over setbacks, feel physical and emotional pain more acutely, and crave pleasures and rewards such as alcohol, tobacco, creature comforts, food, coffee, chocolate, or the temporary lift from sex or a shopping spree.

The pain-reduction benefit of low-dose Naltrexone is complicated but is thought to be accomplished by modulation of the immune response through increasing BDNF, as well as counteracting pain amplification in the brain by increasing the levels of endorphins and dopamine.

## IV Vitamin Infusions
### Myers's Cocktail
Myers's Cocktail is named after the late Baltimore physician John Myers and includes various B vitamins, vitamin C, magnesium, selenium, and calcium. He used this combination of vitamins and minerals through IV infusion on thousands of patients with consistent benefit for enhancing immune-system function, reducing fatigue, helping with seasonal allergies, and reducing the symptoms of fibromyalgia, asthma, migraines, muscle spasm, and respiratory tract infections. He also observed improvements in athletic performance with IV vitamins.

The Myers's Cocktail works by increasing the blood concentration of several essential vitamins and minerals beyond that which can be achieved when supplementing orally. For example, vitamin C given intravenously has been found to reach blood concentrations more than fifty times greater than what can be achieved when given orally.

The idea is that many illnesses and conditions are associated with digestive disturbances such as bloating, indigestion, and food sensitivities and that people with such conditions may not absorb many of the nutrients needed to return them to good health. Also, diseases and inflammatory processes cause the body to use nutrients at a faster rate or to require higher amounts for proper healing. When nutrients are given intravenously, digestive absorption is bypassed. The blood levels are temporarily increased so that the nutrients are "coaxed" into the cells, activating cellular mitochondria to improve cellular functioning. This temporary boost frequently kick-starts the cells. This is how the immune system becomes activated very soon after an infusion.

Some patients feel an energy boost lasting days or weeks. In the case of fibromyalgia, decreased pain can be observed in the trigger points. In other chronic conditions such as rheumatoid arthritis and ulcerative colitis, because of the leaky nature of the gut, the infusion helps get necessary nutrients into the cells. Chronic asthma and other lung diseases, congestive heart failure, and chronic allergic problems may respond with more energy and better symptom control in patients. Patients who get frequent viral illnesses may find an improved immune response with less susceptibility to infections.

The improved cellular energy through enhanced mitochondrial function also gives the brain a needed boost to make more neurotransmitters for brain communication and connectivity. This improves mood and decreases anxiety. Feeling better from fatigue, illness, and pain also reduces anxiety. Patients with chronic conditions can get infusions every one to four weeks until they are stable.

## Glutathione by IV Push

Glutathione is a potent antioxidant that works by promoting cellular repair from oxidative damage and promoting mitochondrial activation. We usually give it through IV push (injected through the IV line) after administering the Myers's Cocktail. The vitamin C in the Myers's Cocktail extends and enhances glutathione effect, or it can be given with high-dose IV vitamin C alone.

IV glutathione is used for treatment of fatigue and neurodegenerative disorders such as Parkinson's, in patients undergoing chemotherapy, and even reportedly for skin-lightening purposes. A side effect of glutathione is that it can decrease the skin melanin index by inhibiting certain enzymes in the body, essentially decreasing the concentration of dark pigments. Patients usually feel an enhanced calmness and sense of well being after glutathione and have better energy to be productive. Anxiety is often magnified if we are exhausted from emotional or physical trauma because we are too tired be proactive, make tough decisions, and get motivated to work on solutions. IV glutathione helps by improving our ability to cope.

## MSM

MSM supplements supply the body with extra sulfur for creating methionine, which helps in important bodily processes such as making other chemicals, forming connective tissue, synthesizing and metabolizing foods, and absorbing nutrients to be used for energy. It can be given as a dietary supplement or, for more immediate and aggressive benefit, be given through an IV. Most of the conditions listed below that respond to MSM IV cause anxiety because of disability and pain.

One of the most notable attributes of MSM supplements is that they help accelerate healing and detox the body by improving how chemicals enter and leave our cells. MSM essentially makes cells more permeable, releasing certain built-up minerals that can cause problems (like calcium, for example), heavy metals, and waste and toxins, while also helping usher in nutrients and water. This helps keep us hydrated and lowers inflammation, which is the root of most diseases. MSM also stabilizes cell membranes, improves the body's antioxidant abilities, slows or stops leakage from injured cells, and scavenges hydroxyl free radicals.

Using MSM supplements is tied to better immune function, accelerated healing, and reduced pain because it helps counteract certain byproducts (like lactic acid) that contribute to the feeling of soreness, stiffness, and inflexibility. This is one reason some athletes and very active people choose to use an MSM supplement to improve recovery time and performance and encourage the process of rebuilding new, healthy muscle and joint tissues. Also, MSM's sulfur plays an important role in the production of glutathione, discussed above.

IV MSM treatment is primarily used for muscle and joint disorders, including the following:

- Autoimmune diseases
- Rheumatoid arthritis
- Lupus
- Scleroderma
- Osteoarthritis
- Fibromyalgia/Chronic Fatigue Syndrome
- Neuropathic pain (Postherpetic neuralgia from shingles, pinched nerves, peripheral neuropathy)

## B-Complex IV

The B-complex IV infusion contains all of the essential water-soluble vitamins except for vitamin C. These include thiamine (vitamin B1), riboflavin (vitamin B2), niacin (vitamin B3), pantothenic acid (vitamin B5), pyridoxine (vitamin B6), biotin, folic acid, and the cobalamins (especially the Methylcobalamin form of vitamin B12). Each member of the B complex has a unique structure and performs unique functions in the human body. Vitamins B1, B2, and B3 and biotin participate in different aspects of energy production, vitamin B6 is essential for amino acid metabolism, and vitamin B12 and folic acid facilitate steps required for cell division. Each of these vitamins has many additional functions. Methylcobalamin is one of two coenzymes forms of B12. Cyanocobalamin, the second coenzyme, is the most common form of B12 provided in physician offices and over-the-counter supplements. Methylcobalamin is the more bioavailable of the two, meaning that Methylcobalamin is ready for the body to use once infused. Cyanocobalamin must be first broken down within the liver only to produce small amounts of Methylcobalamin for the body to use. Methylcobalamin is the only active form of B12 found within the central nervous system. Benefits of Methylcobalamin supplementation include the following:

- Alleviates depression and reduces anxiety. Methylcobalamin acts as a methyl donor and participates in the synthesis of SAM-e, a nutrient that has powerful mood-elevating properties
- Supports immune-system regulation
- Repairs damaged myelin sheath (myelin is essential for proper functioning of the nervous system)
- Increases metabolic function
- Supports healthy red blood cells

## High-Dose Vitamin C IV Infusion

So, Linus Pauling was not such a crackpot, after all. His contemporaries ridiculed his crusade for high-dose vitamin C, but the protective and regenerative effects when given by IV are well documented. As he predicted, our ability to fight and control cancer-cell growth is enhanced with vitamin C. My friend and colleague in Los Angeles, nationally known regenerative and antiaging clinical nutritionist Drew Prinz, was very encouraged after a case of biopsy-proven prostate cancer that he was treating completely resolved with vitamin C IV therapy every ten days and dietary intervention and vitamin K. The subsequent MRI showed that the patient's prostate mass had disappeared over just four months. As far as anxiety benefit, there is a general sense of improved energy, enhanced brain cognitive function, and stress reduction after vitamin C IV.

*TOOL: You may want to find a vitamin-infusion clinic and give this a try if you have fatigue, lethargy, depression, or brain fog or are challenged with a health problem, such as pneumonia, chronic obstructive pulmonary disease, chronic fatigue, Lyme disease, and so on. I have patients who are always going on stressful travel trips for work or who tour with a rock band or are exposed to the public and get viral illnesses that are hard to shake. Many have found that an IV vitamin infusion before a tour or trip makes them feel younger, sharper, more energetic, and less likely to get sick on the road. Those who are already sick claim that they feel better within hours and that the illness turns the corner and starts improving.

## NAD Infusion Therapy for Rapid Detox and Brain Restoration

Nicotinamide adenine dinucleotide (NAD) is a biological molecule that participates in many metabolic reactions. Recent studies show that NAD also plays important roles in transcriptional regulation, longevity, life-span extension, and age-associated diseases. It has been suggested that NAD affects longevity and transcriptional silencing through the regulation of the Sir2p enzyme family, which are NAD-dependent deacetylases. More surprising has been the use of NAD for anxiety, depression, chronic fatigue, and quick addiction detox and withdrawal prevention.

Dr. Richard Mestayer, whose clinic and research center is in Springfield, Louisiana, is an international expert and the most experienced practitioner of IV NAD therapy that I know of. He has treated anxiety, depression, PTSD, and addiction with IV NAD since 1978. He remains active in NAD research and trains physicians nationwide in the use and benefits of NAD therapy. I first contacted Dr. Mestayer a few years ago at the request of a patient who had been treated at his clinic with IV NAD for dependence on and overuse of sleeping pills. She would take up to three different sleeping pills every night and could not sleep at all without them. And now they weren't even working any more. After the first IV dose of NAD in his clinic, she slept fine with no sleeping pills that night. She finished a three-day regimen and went home free of sleeping pills for the next two years. Then she gradually got hooked on them again and wanted me to give her the same treatment. I gave Dr. Mestayer a call, and he very graciously answered while on vacation in a wilderness retreat.

He responded in detail to all my questions and e-mailed me many articles and research studies on NAD, some going back sixty years! It became apparent to me that IV NAD was very effective in quickly activating cellular mitochondria and providing cellular detoxification, as well as rebooting the brain within days to clear chemical dependence (without withdrawal) while restoring mental clarity, energy, and a positive mood. What I could not believe is that a patient dependent on alcohol or heroin would lose all cravings with a single treatment and would not need any medical support or supervision for withdrawal symptoms or relapse. They could just stop alcohol or drugs cold turkey and come in daily for up to twelve days for IV infusions. They were allowed to go home at night or back to their hotels without any worry that they would have any desire to drink or get a fix while on the NAD protocol. The patients described how great they felt off alcohol and narcotics, with no more depressed mood, anxiety, exhaustion, shakiness, or insomnia. They suddenly felt renewed physically and emotionally, and their brains were functioning better than in years. Why mess that up with a drinking alcohol or using? Even sedative and sleeping pill (benzodiazepine) addiction was successfully being treated with NAD infusions, on an outpatient basis, with minimal medical support and daytime group and individual therapy programs.

Ken Starr, MD, in Arroyo Grande, near San Luis Obispo, California, is the founder and medical director of a very successful drug and alcohol detox and rehabilitation clinic that uses IV NAD treatments as the main component of the medical program. Patients come in daily for up to twelve days for treatments and therapy, as well as medical monitoring, but they stay in local hotels or with friends at night with no oversight. Seems much more civilized than traditional inpatient detox programs!

Patients must be medically monitored while on IV NAD for side effects such as flushing or itchy skin. This is treated by slowing the IV infusion rate until the patient's symptoms go away.

**\*TOOL:** If you are burdened with TBI, post-concussion syndrome, PTSD, anxiety, or depression; if you suffer from addiction that is recurrent and difficult to control, and you don't have the time or money for an extended inpatient program; or if you feel you need a total brain rejuvenation for mood, sleep, energy, and focus—IV vitamins and NAD infusions may be worth looking into. You can find more information at these websites:

Dr. Starr specializes in wellness group, addiction medicine, and NAD therapies: http://www.kenstarrmd.com/

Dr. Richard Mestayer discusses brain restoration with NAD on Vimeo: https://vimeo.com/70905141

## Medical Marijuana

I live and practice in California, where voters approved the legalization of marijuana in 2016 for recreational use. Before this, only medical marijuana was allowed, and its use required a physician's attestation that the patient was being treated for a medical condition and marijuana was being recommended for symptom control. The symptoms that were appropriate to treat with marijuana included anxiety, depression, nausea and vomiting, migraine headaches, insomnia, loss of appetite and weight loss (often in cancer patients), and muscle spasm or physical pain (especially cancer related). If patients intended to take their supplies of medical marijuana across state lines or into an airport, they were required to be registered by the state and carry an up-to-date state identification card with them. As medical marijuana became more widely used, the study and science of various strains and delivery mechanism widely expanded to give patients a much more tailor-made experience with fewer unwanted side effects. There are strains specific for anxiety that don't promote paranoia; strains for pain that don't cause sedation;

strains specific for appetite and nausea control; strains more helpful for headache disorders or insomnia, and so on. I have always been amazed at the knowledge and scientific expertise that is required in making fine wines, described to me by my patients who are vintners in Napa Valley. But recently I talked to a patient about his family's medical and recreational marijuana production business. The family owns several greenhouses in the San Francisco Bay Area that produce all the varieties of plants needed for medical marijuana applications, and the complexity is every bit as fascinating as wine production.

In my experience with patient care over thirty years, medical marijuana has been very helpful and rarely harmful to control mood, anxiety, and sleep problems in patients who tolerate it well. With the newer, more specific cannabis and flexible delivery options (vaping, topical gels, gelcaps, brownies or cookies, suppositories), patients will likely be able to find even more helpful support from medical marijuana.

*TOOL: First, get a complete assessment from your physician and see if he or she agrees with this treatment possibility. Then check with your state requirements and talk to a local cannabis club to see if this is something you might want to try. Get a knowledgeable practitioner to explain to you the various options and learn your symptoms so the best treatment can be recommend.

## Oral, Inhaled, and IV Hydrogen Therapy

You will begin to hear more and more about the safety and efficacy of various hydrogen therapies delivered by drinking hydrogen water, breathing hydrogen air, or getting hydrogen through an IV infusion. Scientists in Japan, though their veterans administration, are currently conducting a study on hydrogen therapy for PTSD in soldiers. The MIZ Group in Japan has conducted decades of rigorous research and development and is the leader in hydrogen therapy, having patents on many different delivery techniques. There are over 400 published scientific studies attesting to the health benefits of hydrogen therapy.

I am working with Ed Alexander, CEO of Innovative Designs and Technology, USA, to help make the MIZ Group's hydrogen therapy treatments available to patients here. The thought that we could use a completely natural and innocuous substance to help restore brain function is along the lines of alternative medicine's view that we should try to reactivate the natural intelligence of our body through natural means. This is also the belief in naturopathic medicine and functional medicine schools of thought. I think they all have validity and will work for many people, often better than pharmaceutical drug options. So far, inhalation of hydrogen gas, oral ingestion by drinking hydrogen water, hydrogen baths (because hydrogen easily penetrates the skin and distributes throughout the body via blood flow), IV infusion of hydrogen saline, and treatments that promote the increased production of hydrogen by gut bacteria are being actively studied for many conditions, including anxiety and depression.

Hydrogen therapy for the prevention and treatment of a variety of diseases—particularly those associated with reactive oxygen species and inflammation—has become a hot research subject. Many reports in peer-reviewed scientific and medical journals, including in vitro and animal studies and some clinical trials in humans, have already been published. Hydrogen therapy may help other conditions, including atherosclerosis and recovery from heart attack and stroke, diabetes, stress-induced cognitive impairments (mental fog), Parkinson's disease, multiple sclerosis, and Alzheimer's disease.

Colonic bacteria releases hydrogen, carbon dioxide, and methane gases in the fermentation of carbohydrates that reach the lower digestive tract. Hydrogen has been known to have antioxidant properties for a long time, but its recognition as having some advantages over conventional antioxidants and its potential use as a therapeutic agent have only recently been explored.

One of the most interesting findings concerning hydrogen is the discovery that it is a novel antioxidant because it scavenges hydroxyl radical (the strongest of the oxidant species) and the oxidant peroxynitrite (formed by the reaction of superoxide and nitric oxide), but it is far less effective in scavenging physiological radicals such as superoxide and nitric oxide, important (at low concentrations) as signaling molecules. Moreover, hydrogen is able to diffuse extremely rapidly into tissue and effectively reaches the nucleus and mitochondria, suggesting preventive effects on lifestyle-related diseases, cancer, and the aging process. Hydrogen also passes through the blood-brain barrier, while most other antioxidant compounds cannot do this.

Hydrogen is reported to have no cellular toxicity, even at high concentrations. The safety of H2 for humans is demonstrated by its application in Hydreliox, a breathing gas mixture of 49 percent hydrogen, 50 percent helium, and 1 percent oxygen, which is used to prevent decompression sickness and nitrogen narcosis during very deep technical diving.

**\*TOOL:** Hydrogen therapy will become more available as an inhalation therapy and as hydrogen-rich water for daily home use. Inhaler hydrogen delivered while sitting in a hyperbaric chamber seems to be highly effective and well-tolerated. IV hydrogen therapy in holistic centers that provide IV-infusion therapies will also proliferate, but these will be more expensive and harder to find. There is a clear benefit of hydrogen treatments in TBI and PTSD patients, and I expect this to be supported as more information comes in.

## Microdosing of LSD for Depression and Anxiety

Another outside-the-box alternative option being investigated is the microdosing of psychedelic drugs, including LSD (lysergic acid diethylamide, or "acid"), MDMA (Ecstasy), and psilocybin (magic mushrooms) in patients with depression, anxiety, PTSD, and emotional hardship due to life-threatening conditions such as advanced cancer. The studies focus on patients who are unresponsive to traditional medications. I have long maintained that we really don't know why SSRIs, SNRIs, dopamine stimulation, electroconvulsive therapy, or any medical treatment works. The mechanisms of action of these drugs and procedures do not always explain why they fail or succeed. They may work for a while, then the dose needs to be increased. Then, the side effects outweigh the benefits. So we switch to a different medication and it works for a while, and then that also fails to give relief. So guess what? We change back to the first drug, and it works again! My belief is that all treatments for anxiety and depression, medical or alternative options alike, work by throwing the brain a curveball. That's right; when the brain sees a different configuration of chemistry, has to figure out a new chemical challenge, or is exposed to a new experience like electric shock, it has to wake up and react to achieve homeostasis. It is this natural adaptability and plasticity of the brain that achieves connectivity and healing. And it is this corrective reaction that leads to emotional stabilization. Why do medications that were previously successful "poop out"? Perhaps it's because the brain has figured it out and is no longer surprised and feeling obligated to adjust. That's when we need to change strategies because it isn't working anymore. What if all traditional medications and treatments were no longer effective in bringing relief from anxiety or depression? Do we give up? No, we mix it up a bit to make the brain react and reboot itself. That may be what is happening with the microdosing of psychedelics. Another possible mechanism proposed by scientists is that disparate regions of the brain are activated and communicate with each other, freeing the mind to deal with suppressed trauma and release it.

**\*TOOL:** Although it seems counterintuitive to take a hallucinogen to reduce the symptoms of anxiety and depression, it might be reasonable to consider this if you have a condition that is refractory to all other accepted options or if you have a terminal condition and are not expected to survive it. As these substances are illegal to possess or use in the United States, you would need to qualify for a trial study by a licensed group or institution. Several of the current studies have been conducted in Marin County and San Francisco, California, and initial outcomes are promising. The dose of LSD used in one study was ten to twenty micrograms (one tenth the usual dose for illicit use) every four days. Based on limited information, this dose did not cause hallucinations or adversely affect mental clarity. James Fadiman, PhD, has initiated much of this discussion by his own initiative and investigation. You may read more at microdosingpsychedelics.com.

## Ketamine

This year, a patient of mine who is a psychologist at a Bay Area Kaiser Permanente hospital told me of the great success they were having using the sedative and anesthetic drug ketamine in treating refractory anxiety, depression, and PTSD. Although ketamine has been used as a recreational drug, it is recognized by the World Health Organization as an essential medicine, which includes the most effective and safe medicines in the healthcare system.

Ketamine has been classified as an NMDA receptor antagonist but its mechanism was not well understood as of 2017. It is a legal prescription medication used for a variety of purposes, but it's use as a treatment for depression and PTSD is off label yet growing very quickly as research studies are showing benefit. All you need to do is search online on *ketamine* to find doctors actively prescribing it in your area. As the BBC wrote in a 2014 article about ketamine, "Some patients who have faced incurable depression for decades have had symptoms disappear within hours of taking low doses of the drug."

What makes ketamine so remarkable for treating depression is that its positive effects begin almost immediately, within 1 - 12 hours, compared to SSRIs that may take weeks to start working, if they work at all. Ketamine also seems to have much fewer side effects than SSRIs (although it hasn't been studied for long term safety and efficacy) and is incredibly useful for people who don't respond well to SSRIs and other anti-depressants. If you've had limited success with other treatments, you may respond to ketamine.

Dosage for ketamine varies depending on whether it's taken intranasally, intravenously (IV), orally, or sublingually. Taking ketamine orally or sublingually is considered safe and convenient. Some doctors and treatment centers will give ketamine in an IV. Treatment with a doctor or specialty center can be expensive.

The anti-depressant effect of ketamine typically wears off after a few days to a month, though the relief that is felt while it is active can often lead to lasting improvements. There are various protocols for using ketamine to treat depression. Some people take small amounts of ketamine daily, others weekly, and others monthly. Starting with a moderate dose once a week and adjusting based on how it feels seems prudent.

Sublingual ketamine it thought to be more potent than oral ketamine. Starting with a very small "microdose" and trying a little more each session until you find the minimum amount that works for you is a suggested dosing strategy. According to one internet source, most patients see results using .3mg of ketamine per pound of body weight (or .75mg per kg of body weight). This works out to about 50mg for someone who weighs 160lbs (72kg). But starting at a much lower dose is advised.

## Botox

The use of Botox for anxiety and depression is off label (not FDA approved) but is well documented. In *Time* magazine dated January 16, 2017, the cover story by Alexandra Sifferlin is, "How Botox Became the Drug That's Treating Everything." I have known for years that my cosmetic patients getting facial Botox injections often feel a calming or even mood-elevating effect of the treatment. I thought it was either because they were so happy with the cosmetic result that the elation over their improved appearance accounted for the improved emotions—or the reduced frowning and tensing of the forehead during emotional stress had a body-mind benefit: as the face feels relaxed, the mind feels relaxed. This is called the *facial feedback hypothesis* that arose from research by Charles Darwin and was further explored by American psychologist William James. But now the thinking is that a very different, more complex mechanism of action may be at play. In a study from Italy in 2008, rats injected intramuscularly with Botox were subsequently found to have Botox in the brain stem, suggesting that Botox may actually migrate to the central nervous system and the brain. This was confirmed in 2016 by Edwin Chapman, professor of neuroscience at the University of Wisconsin–Madison. One thought is that Botox may influence endorphin neuropeptide modulation in the brain, but it is anyone's guess what is really going on. If Allergan, the maker of Botox, can prove through a double-blind, placebo-controlled study that Botox works for anxiety and depression, then insurance companies may be required to pay for it, as they now do for its use as a migraine treatment.

## Homeopathic Anxiety Remedies

Homeopathy is a system of alternative medicine created in 1796 by Samuel Hahnemann based on the belief that "like cures like." Homeopathy claims that a substance that causes the symptoms of a disease in a healthy person would cure similar symptoms in a sick person. Those with phobias, as well as chronic anxiety conditions, may consider trying a homeopathic remedy, especially if they are apprehensive about medical treatments or find they cause side effects.

Be aware that homeopathy operates from different assumptions and methods from mainstream medical science. The following homeopathic preparations have not, as a general rule, had the benefit of empirical testing. Their efficacy is largely anecdotal. I have never seen a problem with tolerability of these products, so I believe it is completely safe to try them. For homeopaths, Aconite is the remedy of choice for panic attacks, as well as anxiety that is the result of a sudden fright or shock. If you are grief stricken, the homeopathic practitioner may prescribe Ignatia. In situations such as stage fright, speaker's nerves, and other anticipatory and performance anxiety circumstances, Gelsemium is often recommended.

The homeopath will usually instruct you to begin the remedy with six times potency and take two tablets every four to six hours, depending on the severity of the condition. Once you begin to notice an improvement, you probably will be instructed to take the medication less often, and when you see significant improvement, you will likely discontinue the treatment entirely. In homeopathy, if you use a remedy longer than necessary, it may cause the symptoms to recur. You will also be instructed to take your remedy with a clean mouth free from drink, food, tobacco, or mouthwash.

Homeopathic physicians have found the following remedies useful in the treatment of anxiety:

**Aconite** (Aconitum napellus) is indicated for panic attacks that come on suddenly and unpredictably. The symptoms of panic may include heart palpitations, shortness of breath, a sense of doom with a fear of dying, and cold sweats.

**Argentum nitricum** is indicated when anxiety develops before a big event, such as a job interview, exam, public speech, social engagement, your wedding, and so forth.

**Ignatia album** is for hypochondriacs (those who are deeply anxious about their health) and those who are extremely concerned with order and security (perhaps leaning toward OCD).

**Ignatia carbonica** has been used for symptoms of claustrophobia and fear of heights. It is also used for those who have a problem keeping warm, are easily fatigued, have a craving for sweets, worry too much, have a nagging dread of some impending disaster, and are easily agitated by bad news.

**Gelsemium** is indicated for feelings of weakness and trembling and for those paralyzed by fear or complaining of mental dullness. Many phobias have been treated with this remedy, including fear of crowds, fear of falling, and fear the heart might stop beating. It is most commonly used for anticipatory anxiety, such as a public performance, impending visit to the dentist, or anxiety before a test.

**Ignatia amara** is used in sensitive individuals who are anxious because of grief, loss, disappointment, criticism, loneliness, or any emotional stress. Other indications are a defensive attitude, frequent sighing, and mood swings. It has also been used for the sensation of a lump in the throat (globus hystericus).

**Kali phophoricum** is for the person who is exhausted by overwork or illness. Those who are jumpy and oversensitive, feel deep anxiety and an inability to cope, or are startled by ordinary sounds may also benefit.

**Lycopodium** patients attempt to cover an inner sense of inadequacy by putting up fronts, pretending to be something they are not. They are self-conscious and easily intimated. They have a deep fear of failure but usually do well once they focus on a task. This remedy is thought to reduce anxiety from mental stressors and increase self-confidence.

**Silicea muriaticum** is primarily used for those who hide their emotions and have a self-protective shyness that makes them seem aloof, reserved, and private. Easily hurt and offended, they often become isolated and are known to brood, bear grudges, and dwell on unhappy feelings. Phobias that have been treated with this compound include fear of the night, fear of robbers or intruders, and claustrophobia.

**Phosphorus** is indicated when the patient is "openhearted, imaginative, excitable, easily startled, and full of intense and vivid fears. Strong anxiety can be triggered by thinking of almost everything." This description certainly includes features of mania and hypomania.

**Pulsatilla** is used in patients who are anxious and insecure and exhibit clinginess with a need for constant support and reassurance. They fear being alone and are easily discouraged, moody, tearful, whiny, and even emotionally childish. Pulsatilla is also used for anxiety caused by hormonal changes around the time of puberty, menstrual period, or menopause.

**Silicea** is indicated for individuals who are competent and serious in what they do, yet exhibit shyness, lack of confidence, and nervousness, especially when faced with a task or job that involves scrutiny by others. Anxiety caused by public appearances, interviews, and examinations is common in these perfectionists. Silicea is used to calm this anxiety while reducing exhaustion and increasing mental focus and concentration.

**Coffea cruda** is used for jittery nerves, racing thoughts, and mental exhaustion.

*TOOL: To find out more about homeopathic remedies, make an appointment with a homeopathic physician or visit these websites:
   www.abchomeopathy.com
   www.homeopathic.org
   http://homeopathyplus.com/anxiety-and-panic-attacks-tamed-by-homeopathy/
   http://www.calmclinic.com/anxiety/treatment/homeopathic-remedies

## Anxiety Remedies of Chinese Traditional/Herbal Medicine

Traditional Chinese medicine is one of the oldest written medicinal systems, using herbs in conjunction with a dualistic Taoist philosophy of yin and yang. Yin (the cool, dim, yielding, and feminine component) and yang (the warm, bright, dominant, and masculine component) are viewed as the two opposing forces in all living things. To enjoy good health and physical and emotional harmony, every human being in the traditional Chinese medicine perspective must maintain a balance of yin and yang. Stress and anxiety can lead to a depletion of the yin component, which can be restored with a combination of herbs, dietary adjustments, qigong exercises (incorporating deep breathing, stretching, and balancing), massage, and acupuncture. The many combinations of herbs used in traditional Chinese medicine are designed to maintain the proper balance necessary to promote health by preventing illness.

### Herbal Remedies

Although many herbal remedies have not been studied scientifically, they claim validity from wide use over many centuries by many cultures. We will focus on their use to alleviate various forms of emotional suffering. In many cases, herbs are strong chemicals that should be monitored by a medical professional. Among the most common herbal remedies for anxiety, depression, and insomnia symptoms are the following:

- Kava kava has calming effects without the depressed mood sometimes associated with tranquilizers. It is used for sleep as well.
- Hyperium (Saint-John's-wort) is a folk remedy used for anxiety, worry, depression, and sleeping problems.
- Valerian has been used for thousands of years in India and China as a sedative and sleep inducer.
- Chamomile is widely used in tea form for anxiety, nervous stomach, and relaxation.
- Ginsengs is a group of herbal medicines, called *adaptogens*, reputedly used to strengthen the body's ability to adapt to stress and stimulate the immune system. Ginsengs come in Asian, American, and Siberian varieties, each with a somewhat different strength and application.

Other popular herbal remedies for anxiety include the following:

- Polygonum root
- Jujube date
- Rehmannia root
- Polyrachis ant
- Duanwood reishi

*TOOL:** Visit your local herbal/Chinese medicine doctor to see what he or she recommends for your complaints. You might also learn more about these products and supplements through your local health food store. If you feel comfortable, go ahead and follow the advice of the herbalist, Chinese medicine practitioner, or store representative. You can always stop if it doesn't help or causes a side effect you don't like (or if you just hate the taste). Don't take two or more new products at once; start with one and wait several days before trying another so you'll know what the effects (good and bad) of each are. To learn more or shop online, visit the following websites:
www.chineseherbsdirect.com
https://agelessherbs.com/anxiety/natural-alternative-herbs/

## Ayurvedic Strategies to Reduce Anxiety

Ayurveda means the *science of life* and espouses the natural intelligence of all living things and the universe (which is also considered a living thing). The basic Ayurvedic philosophy is that health is our natural state, and ill health is unnatural. Nature has given our bodies the intelligence to be perfectly healthy. But when stress, inadequate nutrition, or poor sleep weakens our immune systems, we then allow disease an opportunity to make us ill. The body knows how to restore balance during these illnesses, no matter what came along to disturb this balance. Ayurveda provides insights into how to live one's life in harmony with nature and natural laws and rhythms. It provides guidelines for an intelligently regulated diet and daily routine, as well as stress management and exercises for increased fitness and alertness.

**Ashwagandha:** This is one of the most powerful herbs in Ayurvedic healing, has been used since ancient times for a wide variety of conditions, and is most well known for its restorative benefits. In Sanskrit, Ashwagandha means "the smell of a horse," indicating that the herb imparts the vigor and strength of a stallion and has traditionally been prescribed to help people strengthen their immune systems after an illness.

Belonging to the same family as the tomato, Ashwagandha is a plump shrub with oval leaves and yellow flowers. It bears red fruit about the size of a raisin. The herb is native to the dry regions of India, northern Africa, and the Middle East, and today it is also grown in more mild climates, including the United States. Ashwagandha is commonly used for the following symptoms:

- Stress
- Fatigue
- Lack of energy
- Difficulty concentrating

Ashwagandha contains many useful medicinal chemicals, including steroidal lactones, alkaloids, choline, fatty acids, amino acids, and a variety of sugars. While the leaves and fruit have valuable therapeutic properties, the root of the Ashwagandha plant is the part most commonly used in Western herbal remedies. Medical researchers have been studying Ashwagandha for years with great interest and have completed more than two hundred studies on the healing benefits of this botanical. Some claims under investigation include the following:

- Protects the immune system
- Helps combat the effects of stress
- Improves learning, memory, and reaction time
- Reduces anxiety and depression without causing drowsiness
- Helps reduce brain-cell degeneration
- Stabilizes blood sugar
- Helps lower cholesterol
- Offers anti-inflammatory benefits
- Contains antimalarial properties
- Enhances sexual potency for both men and women

Ashwagandha is typically ingested in capsule form. It is included in the single Ayurvedic herb collection at the Chopra Center Marketplace. The typical recommended dose is six hundred to one thousand milligrams twice daily. For people who suffer from insomnia and anxiety, having a cup of hot milk that contains a teaspoon of powdered Ashwagandha before bedtime is beneficial.

*TOOL: For those who want to learn more about this ancient and natural program for reducing anxiety, we recommend the Chopra Center at www.chopra.com and specifically Brent Becvar, Vedic counselor and program director at the Chopra Center. You can e-mail him at Brent@chopra.com. You can also find Ayurvedic supplements at the following websites:
www.eswayamvaram.com
www.bayanbotanicals.com

# CHAPTER 6

## Toolbox Compartment Number Three: Anxiety Caused by Pain Management and Addiction Problems

### A Word about Anxiety and Pain Management

Pain management has swung to both sides of the pendulum since I started practicing some thirty years ago. Back then, narcotics were used very sparingly postsurgically and for end-stage cancer patients. Addicts were given their daily Methadone at the Methadone clinic. They mostly had become hooked through illicit drug use, especially heroin. But some had become addicted from appropriate use of their postsurgical pain medications and had then fallen into aberrant, drug-seeking behaviors to get more pills due to tolerance and to prevent withdrawal symptoms caused by dependence.

Over time, especially with the development of newer and longer-acting narcotic options by the pharmaceutical industry, the belief about the use of narcotics for chronic pain changed. It became more accepted to keep patients on narcotics long term for chronic pain. Doctors were successfully sued for failing to prescribe adequate pain control by withholding narcotic prescriptions. I remember a doctor luncheon sponsored by a narcotic drug company in 2005 during which the speaker, a well-known pain-management specialist in my area, explained the need for wider use of narcotics for a variety of chronic pain syndromes. A colleague in attendance asked, "Don't you think that we're just going to create a new generation of addicts?" The answer was, "Frankly, that way of thinking is simply archaic and out of touch."

As it turns out, widespread dependence on and tolerance of narcotic medications resulted from years of overprescribing by physicians. Some doctors would give narcotics to anyone willing to pay for the office visit, with almost no documentation of the underlying disorder. These doctors were labeled "Dr. Feel Good." Patients learned to complain about something that could not be proven, such as terrible migraines or pinched-nerve pain, just to get pain pills to sustain their addictions. Some visited several doctors and made it a full-time business to procure prescription narcotics for their addictions or for diversion to be sold on the black market for large profits. Highly addictive drugs like Oxycontin became part of a dark drug trade that challenged law enforcement and encouraged gang activity and organized crime. Many (often young) people died from accidental overdoses thinking they could handle their addictions.

As the cost to society soared, the medical boards and federal and state agencies started cracking down on physicians who were overprescribing. Databases keeping track of doctors who were prescribing narcotics and their patients started proliferating, and the penalties for doctors causing harm by their lax prescribing habits became stiffer. Now, with the CURES system, doctors are required to be enrolled in a federal database program in which new patients being placed on narcotics must be screened to show they do not have a history of drug-seeking behaviors. Pharmacists must also check this system to see if the patient is using more that one doctor or pharmacy to get pain medication. There are now limits to the maximum doses and recommendations to taper all patients down to these levels. State medical board scrutiny has prompted many physicians to give up prescribing narcotics altogether, while the specialty of pain management has grown exponentially.

Pain management is expensive because you must see the specialist or nurse practitioner every month. The cost can be as much as $300 a visit and is often not covered by insurance. Pain-management physicians, especially anesthesiologists, may require that you undergo several procedures (epidural steroid injections, spinal blocks, or implanted stimulators that they perform and are well compensated for by insurance) to get your pain medication. And they will label you as "noncompliant" and stop prescribing narcotics if you don't do these procedures to prove you are trying to get well. Random urine drug screens are required, sometimes every month, as well as a daily patient log of pain levels to confirm that the treatment is doing more good than harm.

Extensive imaging, specialty consults, and documentation of the failure of conservative care for pain (like physical therapy, Tylenol, Advil, rest, ice, muscle relaxants, steroids, and so on) must be done before narcotics are prescribed. The cost and hassle of being on a narcotic pain-management regimen is certainly anxiety provoking! But consider also the cost in terms of the new problems you may face. Many people develop tolerance and addiction and spend lots of money and time getting off these drugs. There are several health problems that are far more likely in the pain-management population, such as poor dental health and loss of teeth, weight gain, loss of sexual functioning, mental fog, chronic fatigue, aspiration pneumonia, overdose, and death.

In the end, I believe it is very difficult for many people to have stable emotional and physical health while on chronic pain medications. It is best to never start them or to find a way to get off of them. In addition, narcotic medications do not work well for many types of neuropathic nerve pain, such as shingles neuralgia, herniated discs, headaches, and fibromyalgia. These are better treated with Gabapentin or Lyrica, along with the SNRI Cymbalta. Also, newer neurostimulation devices, such as ATI (http://www.ati-spg.com/us/en/) and Quell Relief (www.quellrelief.com), may be more beneficial than medications for migraine and cluster headaches and neuropathy pain. There are new trials under way showing great benefit for a narcotic blocker that has been out for many years. Naltrexone (Narcan) is used at a high dose (fifty to one hundred milligrams) to block narcotic receptors in overdose cases, and it also reduces cravings for drugs and alcohol and prevents misuse of narcotic prescriptions. But in a low dose of one to five milligrams, it has a paradoxical benefit in reducing pain and inflammation in lupus and other autoimmune diseases, as well as fibromyalgia neuropathic pain. It is completely nonaddictive.

I need to give a shout-out for regenerative medicine here. By partnering with Bruce Bertman of the Zizion Group based in Boca Raton, Florida, I have been able to get phenomenal results using patient-derived platelet-rich plasma injections, as well as using umbilical cord allograft products (CoreCyte, PolyCyte, and AmnioCyte) with stem cells (from healthy, full-term babies delivered by cesarean section) for both IV infusions and intra-articulate injections (find out more about regenerative allograft products at predbiotech.com). I have also used autologous (your own stem cells) harvested by liposuction, but these are not as viable and effective as those we harvest from the umbilical cord of the newborn baby. These regenerative technologies allow us to heal conditions that were treated only with pain medications or surgery in the past. One man with terrible shoulder pain due to a torn rotator cuff and severe degenerative arthritis was on six tablets of high-dose Oxycodone a day for pain control, which made him constipated and irritable. Even with this, he could not sleep on that shoulder, was unable to work (at a keyboarding desk job) or exercise, and was facing a full replacement surgery with all the downtime, expense, and rehabilitation. After one injection of stem cells with platelet-rich plasma, he had no pain whatsoever one week later. He canceled surgery and was back to full activities a month later, with no physical therapy. I have similar success stories on a weekly basis with these options. Although not usually covered by insurance, regenerative medicine may keep you off pain medications and save you lots of money and hardship.

Over the years I have seen it all when it comes to the benefits and risks of narcotic use for pain. There are clearly situations in which nothing else works and there is no quality of life without narcotic pain medications. But, many times, it only leads to a gradual worsening of the overall situation. I prescribe pain medication only to those who can show me that they are more functional on them. But narcotics are not good for you. They cause weight gain, loss of teeth over time, loss of normal sexual functioning, and depression. Like cocaine and amphetamines, they stimulate brain chemistry release, especially dopamine, and burn out the brain's ability to make normal amounts of these "feel-good" hormones in the future. This can lead to chronic anxiety and depression that does not respond to anything except more pain pills. This is a road that can lead to overuse and overdose.

Many pain syndromes can be managed with so many things in this book that are far better than narcotics: other medical options, flotation tank, cognitive-behavioral therapy, group therapy, activity modification, a good body worker, meditation, and so on. Don't have the mind-set that only a pill can help your pain and that when you have more pain, it is because you need more pills. The simple truth is that we cannot take away all pain all the time. Try to tolerate some level of pain. Keep your doses low and get off if and when you can. Be responsible for the things you can do to control pain and get better, and don't rely on doctors to do it all with medications. The people who have been able to turn away from pain medications (often with inpatient detox programs or NAD infusions) have had much better outcomes with the treatment of their anxiety and depression.

## A Word about Anxiety and Addiction

Substance abuse and addiction can be defined different ways. There is physiologic addiction in which you would go into a withdrawal syndrome if you stopped taking the substance (nausea, vomiting, sweats, diarrhea, abdominal pain, muscle cramps, shakes, and even hallucinations), and psychological addiction in which it would be extremely uncomfortable emotionally to stop or reduce the dose of the substance you're addicted to. Neither of these definitions should label an individual as an addict. For instance, it is normal when taking narcotics for a bona fide pain condition to develop tolerance and dependence. Tolerance means you are used to it, and you will need a higher dose to get the same result as when you first started taking the substance. Dependence means you will go into withdrawal if you stop taking the substance abruptly. These are expected outcomes of taking an addictive drug or substance over time.

Most physicians diagnose addiction from more of a social, functional, and behavioral standpoint. In this sense, a gambling addiction can be just as severe and harmful as heroin. An addict, for instance, is someone who does the drug instead of taking care of the kids and going to work. An addict is someone who lies or manipulates to get the drug or spends an inordinate amount of time obtaining it. An addict, as was said of Jerry Garcia of the Grateful Dead, is someone who "loved the drugs more than his friends or the music."

So addiction is a real tragedy that steals away the heart and soul of the addict. The addict has no higher purpose than to find and take the drug at any cost. It takes over the mind and makes it a slave to the drug, forsaking everything else that used to define that person. Often, anxiety comes before addiction and leads to self-medication with drugs or alcohol to bring temporary relief. This always backfires, and the anxiety gets worse as losses start to pile up: loss of family support structure; loss of job and financial security; medical and legal problems, including incarceration, with loss of health or freedom; and, ultimately, loss of self-esteem and self-worth. The ATP is another option and can be used as a road map away from giving in to addiction and having to spend years picking up the broken pieces and rebuilding a life worth living. It's not easy. As President John F. Kennedy said about going to the moon, "We don't do it because it is easy—we do it because it is hard." Everything worth doing is hard. Life is hard. But we are designed to be resilient and tough. Don't tell yourself you're too weak and don't have the will power. We all have a powerful will within us to change our lives and even the world.

**\*TOOL:** I believe all patients with addiction problems should try low-dose Naltrexone once they are off narcotics as described in the section on alternative treatments for anxiety above. If you are serious about getting off addictive drugs and/or alcohol, seek the help of a medical professional. Find out from your health insurance if an inpatient or outpatient drug rehabilitation program is covered in your area. Get away from people who also use drugs or who enable you to continue your addiction. Get into a twelve-step program and go every day, even if you are not ready to quit. Start the conversation with others who care about you and may be part of your support system in the future, once they see you are earnestly trying to be well. Tell them you are reading this book and are going to start designing your own strategy for success once you have detoxed off drugs and alcohol. Consider an NAD-infusion center like Dr. Ken Starr's clinic in Arroyo Grande, California, if you really need to reboot your brain. Whatever you do, don't give up!

# CHAPTER 7

## Toolbox Compartment Number Four: Healthy Lifestyle, Self-Care, and Personal Organization Tools

This section focuses on diet/supplements, exercise, personal hygiene, personal organization, and time-management skills. In addition, the medical and alternative methods you may need to get deep, restful sleep will be reviewed in this chapter. It will also stress the importance of proactively choosing a healthy and positive lifestyle. You may have some or none of these skills, but all of them are useful for accomplishing a successful, balanced life. These are tools you may have resisted in the past. They remind you of all the lectures from your mother or the rantings of your ex-spouse: "Don't stay up so late! You're hanging out with the wrong friends! Don't drink so much! Brush your teeth! You're always late! Your desk is a mess! You eat junk! You're out of shape! Stop losing and forgetting everything!

Well, guess what? They were right. It's difficult to live with someone who doesn't take responsibility for his or her own basic housekeeping or who has poor judgment when it comes to important issues. It's like trying to take care of a child rather than living with an adult who pulls his or her own weight. Therefore, review the material below honestly and assess your own performance in these areas. If you come across a recommendation or tool that might be helpful, then circle it and list it in your personal daily journal under the section on self-care tools.

Every choice we make should be informed by the answer to a simple question: which response will best serve my emotional health? If faced with a bottle of scotch while feeling anxious or depressed, the decision that best serves our emotional health, as we will explain in a moment, is to just say no. Being mindful about our choices at each moment and consistently opting for the positive, health-affirming direction is a chore at first. Later, after much practice, the right choices will come without effort because we are thinking from a well and balanced mind that recognizes the benefit of making the right lifestyle decisions. The fact that our choices and decisions influence our stress level is summarized by this truism, author unknown: "There is good and bad news about stress. The good news is: We create our own stress. The bad news is: We create our own stress."

### Low-Anxiety Diet

A well-balanced, nontoxic diet is essential for reducing the stress and anxiety that fuels anxiety. First we must eliminate the inflammatory and anxiety-provoking foods from the diet so that our nervous system has a chance to calm down.

## High-Anxiety Foods

**Caffeine**: Found in many products such as coffee, chocolate, tea, and soda, caffeine causes the release of adrenalin, which in turn increases anxiety and tension. Try gradually reducing or even eliminating caffeine from your diet. Abrupt discontinuation can cause withdrawal symptoms such as headaches, nausea, and tremors. If you don't feel anxiety with caffeine consumption, or if it helps your anxiety because it helps your attention, focus, and productivity, then disregard this advice.

**Alcohol**: Alcohol is one of the most common forms of self-medication for anxious individuals. But there is a huge downside. Alcohol stimulates the release of adrenalin and insulin. This sets off a cascade of metabolic changes that are toxic to our nervous system, especially the emotional centers of the brain. The short-term effect of elation from dopamine and endorphin stimulation, or sedation from overuse, is eventually replaced by increased nervous tension, irritability, mood swings, and insomnia (early-morning awakening). Excess alcohol increases the fat deposits in the heart and liver and suppresses the activity of the immune system. Because of its effects on liver metabolism, alcohol allows stress hormones produced by the adrenal glands to circulate longer in the bloodstream, increasing the level of damage to the nervous and cardiovascular systems.

**Sugar**: Sugars are also called *simple carbohydrates*, so named because their simple structure allows quick absorption and metabolism. Being calorie-dense foods, simple sugars are thought to be at the core of the current obesity epidemic in the United States. Sugars are often used as a quick energy or mood booster, but research shows there is a heavy price to be paid. As the most potent stimulator of pancreatic insulin production, sugar levels initially peak about an hour after ingestion and then crash as pancreatic insulin is released. These insulin and sugar "roller coasters" are responsible for the release of stress hormones from the adrenal glands and an unhealthy balance of prostaglandin proteins that contribute to lowered immune resistance, as well as negative mood and anxiety states. These foods include sugar itself, as well as anything made from processed flour (bread, pasta, pastries, baked goods) and fruit juice.

**Fat**: We've all heard about good fats and bad fats. Bad fats are usually termed *saturated fats* or *trans fats*, whereas good fats are called *mono-* or *polyunsaturated*. The good fats are mostly plant based, such as avocados, olives, vegetable oils, and peanut butter, but also include fatty fish. Bad fats generally come from animal products such as butter, milk, and meat. Good fats help our brain function better and help us lose fat if we are dieting (your body will hold onto fat and remain in "fat-storage mode" if you avoid fats while dieting). Because fat is a calorie-dense food that can lower metabolism if overeaten, it is a primary player in the development of obesity and cardiovascular disease. Saturated- and trans-fat consumption is also known for its damaging effects on the liver, where it interferes with the metabolic activities of that organ. Bad fats are believed to increase the likelihood of developing a variety of malignancies, including cancer of the colon, breast, and prostate.

## Low-Anxiety Foods

**Complex carbohydrates**: Increasing complex carbohydrates will help stabilize blood-sugar levels and will trigger brain serotonin release, promoting a sense of relaxation. Complex carbohydrates include brown rice, wild rice (actually not a true rice grain), whole grains (oats, wheat, etc.), and ancient grains, such as quinoa, spelt, and buckwheat.

**Fruits and high-fiber vegetables**: Eating the whole fruit, rather than just drinking the juice, especially if vine-ripened, will supply important antioxidant phytochemicals. Enjoy seasonal fresh fruits every day. Green, yellow, and orange vegetables are all rich in minerals, vitamins, and phytochemicals, which boost the immune response and help protect against disease. Vegetables also enhance the absorption of the amino acid L-tryptophan, the precursor of serotonin, thereby increasing serotonin production.

**Healthy Fats**: Healthy fats include the fatty fishes, like mackerel, lake trout, herring, sardines, albacore tuna, salmon, and halibut, as well as plant-based fats, like avocado, peanut butter, olive, rapeseed, and sunflower seed oils, ground flaxseed, almonds, walnuts, and peanuts, and nut butters.

**Lean proteins**: Legumes (beans) are good sources of protein, which help to stabilize blood-sugar levels. Soy beans can be found in a wide variety of products, from miso soup to tofu to soy milk. Peas, nuts, and seeds should also be included in the diet. Lean dairy and meats (lean red meats, fish, chicken/foul without the skin) are also good sources of protein.

## The Latest in Nutrition Research and Human Genetics

- Garlic contains nutrients that slow down proteins in the body known as *phase 1 enzymes*. These enzymes metabolize toxins to form carcinogens, or chemicals that are known to cause cancer. This is especially important for Japanese Americans, because 70 percent have a genetic vulnerability that speeds up phase 1 enzymes, which puts them at high risk for stomach cancer.
- Green tea helps silence genes that fuel breast cancer in some women.
- Broccoli boosts genes that protect against heart disease.
- Soybeans influence 123 genes involved in the development of prostate cancer. Specifically, the activity of gene p53, which helps the body kill mutant cells and block tumor formation, is enhanced by soybean proteins.
- Turmeric suppresses genes that increase inflammation, which helps decrease the risk of colon cancer and Alzheimer's disease.

**\*TOOL:** Change to a healthy, reasonable dietary program. Get the advice of a nutritionist, especially if you would like to lose or gain weight. Cut back on sugar and simple carbohydrates and boost up the green vegetables. Try gluten-free eating for two weeks to see if you feel (and look) much better.

## Ask Drew

Drew Prinz, my good friend since our college days at Stanford University, is a nationally recognized and esteemed clinical nutritionist in Woodland Hills, California. My patients ask Drew how they can achieve their personal weight, health, and fitness goals. At the forefront of anti-aging medicine, Drew analyzes the raw data from your 23 *and Me* profile and gives you a heads-up on potential health problems and how to avoid them with dietary adjustments, specific supplements, and careful monitoring for your vulnerabilities. Drew's clinic utilizes everything from hormonal treatments, vitamin infusions, stem cell therapies, specially prepared and individualized supplement packs, and clear nutritional recommendations to help their patients successfully meet their goals. You can contact Drew and his staff at his office phone or email address below:

(818) 887-2720

drewprinz@sbcglobal.net

## Calories, Exercise, and Weight

Like Warren Wiley, DO (www.getwell3.com), I believe weight is 100 percent a hormonal issue. It has nothing to do with calories in vs. calories out. It has nothing to do with exercise, except that exercise stimulates hormones that improve our metabolism. Testosterone, thyroid, and dozens of brain neurotransmitter hormones and gut incretin hormones regulate our weight. If we want to change weight, we need to change our hormone balance through eating the right foods (high fiber, good fats, and lean proteins) and avoiding sugar and simple carbs. It is also good to exercise but not excessively. Short bursts of high-intensity interval exercise (jumping rope or spinning on a stationary bicycle for ten minutes) is better than plodding along on a stair master machine for an hour. Overexercising or avoiding good fats in the diet will promote a fat-storage rather than fat-release mode. Look for foods that are nutrient dense, not calorie dense. One of the easiest ways to lose weight is to limit the portion size or amount that you eat. This, in turn, is made easier by choosing nutrition-dense foods. Try not to eat more than what would fit comfortably on the *inner circle* of a standard dinner plate, with no overlapping foods or second helpings. Women ages thirty-one to fifty should shoot for a maximum of 2,000 calories per day, while men in the same age group should limit themselves to 2,500 calories. It may take the counsel of a registered dietician or nutritionist to find a dietary program that fits your tastes, style, and culture and still follows the guidelines below:

## Include in your diet:

- Lean proteins: lean meats, nonfat dairy products, eggs, beans, soy/tofu, nuts, seeds, peas, whey protein powder
- Complex carbohydrates: brown rice, wild rice, oats, bran, whole/ancient grain cereals/bread. Take in three one-ounce servings of fiber-filled whole grains per day, which should account for 50 percent of your total daily carb intake.
- Limited fresh fruits, no or limited fruit juices. Eat up to two cups of fresh fruit daily.
- Nonstarchy vegetables (peas, carrots, string beans, broccoli, etc.)
- Calcium: If not dairy sensitive or allergic, drink two cups of milk daily or eat an equivalent amount of yogurt or other dairy foods.
- Potassium: Include foods high in potassium, such as bananas, which can counteract some of sodium's effects on blood pressure.
- Good fats: Eat healthy fats found in fatty fish and plants (like avocado and nut butters).

## Avoid in your diet:

- Caffeinated beverages if you are sensitive (anxious) with consumption. If this is hard, substitute black tea for coffee, as it has one-third the caffeine and none of the harmful oils.
- Sugar and other simple carbohydrates, including anything made from flour, white rice, fruit juices, and candy.
- Alcohol
- Fatty and fried foods cause fatigue, obesity, and lower immune system functioning. Avoid trans fats in favor of poly- and monounsaturated fats.
- Sodium: Eat less than 2,300 mg of sodium daily (about one teaspoon of salt!).

## ALCAT Testing

At this juncture, I should mention ALCAT testing. What if you are eating healthy food but still feel bloated, gassy, and crampy in your gut and can't lose weight? This is often because you have a food sensitivity, or a food intolerance. This means your body is having an immunologic activation in response to the foreign proteins in the food and has decided to attack. The result is inflammation, poor nutrient absorption, fatigue, weight gain, irritability, and anxiety. This is not a food allergy, and won't show up on blood IgE food allergy testing. But it will show up on the ALCAT test, which tests your blood against two hundred and thirty-seven different foods. There is more than an 80 percent chance that you are sensitive or intolerant to foods you eat every day. Usually, you will be found to be reactive to several seemingly unrelated foods. Knowing the list of things that you should avoid or reduce in the diet is a powerful way to improve your overall physical and emotional health. Within days, patients have seen an improvement in mood, anxiety, sleep, weight, arthritis pain, asthma, energy, autoimmune disease flares, cognitive alertness and focus by avoiding foods on the ALCAT list. To get your own ALCAT test, talk to your doctor or nutritionist, or order online at www.whatsmyfoodintolerance.com.

## Vitamins and Supplements

Although most vitamins and supplements are unnecessary if you have a healthy, well-balanced diet, some over-the-counter regimens have been shown to be helpful for those with anxiety or excessive stress. Most of these are included in standard multivitamin/mineral supplements widely available. Others may take some looking on the Internet or a visit to your local vitamin shop or health-food store.

A more detailed review of the vitamins and supplements can be found in chapter 5.

**Anxiety-reducing vitamins and minerals**: B complex (especially B1, B2, B3, B5, B6, B12, and B15), folic acid, choline, vitamin C with bioflavonoids, vitamin E, vitamin A, beta-carotene, calcium, chromium, magnesium, manganese, silicon, lecithin, phosphorus, zinc, potassium

**Antianxiety supplements**: 5-HTP, SAM-e, Saint-John's-wort, phytochemical nutrients, L-tyrosine, L-tryptophan, Bach flower remedy

Other sedating, antianxiety supplements will be described in an upcoming section on sleep in this chapter. I do not believe in megadoses of vitamins or active adrenal hormone supplements (DHEA, pregnenolone) unless recommended by an endocrinologist. Often, adrenal hormones are stressed because of deficient sex hormones and will rebound to normal levels when estrogen and testosterone are optimized. Bioidentical sex hormone replacement is safe and effective for women in peri- and postmenopause and men in andropause, as discussed in chapter 4.

*TOOL: With the help of a nutritionist/supplement counselor, create a reasonable program of a healthy diet and daily vitamin/supplemental therapy.

*TOOL: Reduce caffeine consumption if it helps. Try switching to black tea and tapering down from there. When you are more stabilized with other tools, you can add back in the caffeine. In defense of coffee, there is no health risk to moderate consumption. It may trigger a heart palpitation or a wave of anxiety, but it is otherwise safe and may even have health benefits. Your 23 *and* Me genetic profile will tell you if you will likely be a big caffeine consumer and metabolize it well or shy away due to poor production of the enzyme that breaks it down. In any case, they recommend keeping coffee under three 12oz cups per day, or less than 400 mg of caffeine per day. To finish this book, I relied on a steady intake of caffeine in the form of café mochas. I should give a shout out of appreciation to Bret and Matthew at Muffin Mania in San Rafael, May and the gang at Starbucks in Novato, and my father's favorite as well, Joey Wiessler and his team at Peet's in The Village at Corte Madera.

*TOOL: Stop alcohol. If you are really serious about this and think it will be too difficult for you, ask your doctor if he or she recommends a medical treatment to help you quit. Taken daily, these can be helpful in stopping the craving for alcohol.

*TOOL: Stop smoking. Those who smoke do so for a reason: to self-medicate or for boredom, anxiety, habit, or due to the addictive effects of the drug. Unfortunately, the benefits are transient, while the dangers and risks are great and long lasting. A third of all cancers are related to smoking, while another third of cancer deaths are related to other lifestyle choices, namely obesity, lack of exercise, and poor diet. Those who quit smoking, eat healthfully, exercise, and lose weight as recommended in this compartment of the toolbox, can expect nearly a 70 percent reduction in their lifetime cancer risk, as well as a similar reduction in the risk of cardiovascular disease, including heart attack and stroke. If you think you have enough things to worry about now, you won't want to add to that a serious health problem. Remember, nicotine is really a stimulant that may only perpetuate your anxious nervous system.

# Exercise
## Overview

One of the fastest and most powerful ways to reduce stress and anxiety is to start a program of regular, rain-or-shine, daily vigorous exercise. Exercise is nature's way of burning off nervous energy, which is really the body's state of fight-or-flight arousal. Those who participate in regular exercise report fewer and less severe panic attacks. Exercise has also been shown to decrease the anticipatory anxiety seen in phobic conditions. Those who spend time and energy worrying about what might happen will find that these anxious thoughts are greatly reduced after exercise.

According to recent government guidelines, all physically able adults should engage in regular physical exercise—at least thirty minutes on most days to reduce the risk of chronic disease (cardiovascular disease, diabetes). I recommend brief five- to ten-minute spurts of high-intensity activity up to three times a day (running in place, jumping rope, or cycling), as it may benefit weight control and help relieve stress and anxiety. Several studies from Northern Ireland and the University of Pittsburg have found that short bursts of two to ten minutes of exercise several times a day are preferable to traditional forty- to sixty-minute workouts for weight loss and provide equal benefits for lowering blood pressure and decreasing fats in the bloodstream.

Exercise reduces anxiety by directly affecting the physiology of anxiety in the following ways:

- Reduced muscular tension, which is partly responsible for feelings of being tense or uptight. Muscular tension, through the body-mind connection, sends tense signals to the emotional centers of the brain that you are stressed and nervous, causing those centers to become aggravated and inflamed, which makes the anxiety even worse. Exercise and stretching sends signals to the brain that you are relaxing, which quiets down the emotional centers.
- Increased metabolism of stress hormones, such as adrenalin, norepinephrine, cortisol, and excess thyroid hormones. Getting these stress-inducing chemicals out of the bloodstream faster ensures a sooner return of your nervous system to a state of calm.
  Release of emotions of anger and frustration. Exercise has been shown to cause endorphin release in the brain. These positive, stress-relieving chemicals go a long way in diffusing angry and irritable moods that fuel your stress and anxiety, improving oxygen flow to the brain and increasing alertness and concentration. In addition, the function of many other organ systems improves, including the digestive, respiratory, skin, and cardiovascular systems. Reduction of blood pressure is another important benefit. Exercise has been shown to reduce the risk of many cancers, as well as heart attacks and strokes.
- Improved metabolism of sugar, reducing hypoglycemia, diabetes, and helping weight loss.

Those who commit to regular exercise report increased self-esteem, a greater sense of well being, improved concentration and memory, better sleep, reduced depression, less anxiety, fewer panic attacks, and less dependence on self-medication (drugs and alcohol).

## Common Excuses for Not Exercising

**No time.** The most common excuse for lack of exercise is, "When will I find the time?" In truth, we all have time if we make exercise a priority. Are you wasting time watching TV, playing video games, or gabbing on the phone? If you feel there really are not enough hours in the day, you can at least change the way you go about your day. If you live close to work, sometimes walking or biking is nearly as fast as driving in traffic and finding parking. Take the steps rather than the elevator or escalator; run with the dog around the block a few times before and after work; play soccer in the yard for ten minutes with your kids in the evening; run up and down the stairs at work for three minutes before lunch; jump on the exercise bike for a few minutes while watching TV or talking on your cell phone (multitasking at its healthiest). And who doesn't have five minutes to jump rope or run in place? You see, you don't need that ninety-minute chunk of time to get to and from a gym!

**Too tired.** You could try exercising when you first get up in the morning. Go to bed thirty minutes earlier so you can get up thirty minutes earlier and exercise. Or, see if you can work out on your lunch break. And remember, fatigue is often relieved by brisk exercise.

**It's boring.** Then do something you enjoy with someone you enjoy. What about a sport like tennis or kayaking? Surely you don't find all physical activities boring. Even jogging may become more interesting over time as you feel the benefits to your sense of well being and settle into the daily rhythm of the things to see and people to greet along your route. You may also want to cross-train and shift among a variety of sports/activities to keep things lively.

**It's too much of a hassle.** Remember, you don't need the gym or even good weather. You don't need special equipment or a personal trainer. A home exercise bike, a jump rope, a video of aerobic exercise, even just the floor and gravity are enough to get a vigorous workout by running in place.

**I'm too out of shape/old/overweight.** First get medical clearance from your doctor before starting any exercise program. Perhaps you will need to start slow with low-impact activities, such as swimming or brisk walking. An exercise bike on low resistance might be a good way to ease into an exercise program. Remember, you are trying to start a lifetime habit. You are doing this for yourself, not to impress or keep up with anyone else. There is no race to achieve a specific goal by a certain date. Just be consistent and don't make excuses.

## Getting Started with an Exercise Program

- If you are unsure of your health, are older than forty, or have known health problems, consult with your doctor before initiating any exercise program.
- Always start slowly. Set limits at the beginning, such as no more than ten minutes/day of aerobic activity for the first few weeks. Very gradually build up to thirty minutes. If you are starting to get back into a favorite sport, like tennis, take lessons for the first few months and do some light aerobics and strength training before trying to get too competitive. The point is to not burn yourself out or get injured in the first few weeks from a surge of motivation.
- Warm up. Ease into your exercise program with five to ten minutes of stretches and calisthenics beforehand. Some initial soreness is normal and will gradually fade as your strength increases.
- Commit to your new exercise program for a minimum of one month, and don't let anything or any excuse deter you from your commitment. The benefits of exercise take a while to become clear. Once they do, you'll be hooked. The benefits you will see and feel become the motivation and reward for continuing and making it a long-term habit.
- Exercise first thing in the morning. This helps your metabolism all day long and is especially useful if you are trying to lose weight. Also, you get it out of the way when you are most fresh and energetic. Take a quick shower with eucalyptus body wash if you need to perk up first.
- Eat at least one hour before or after exercise.
- Skip exercise if you are sick or feel run down.
- Stop exercise if you feel any sudden, unexplained physical discomfort.

- If you feel low motivation or get bored without company, find a partner to go with you. Think about joining a local walking or hiking club. Or join a gym program that is structured around an exercise circuit that has timed stations arranged in a circle. Every few minutes the timer sounds, and you move to the next activity station. These fast-paced, multiexercise programs are done with a small group so you don't feel bored or alone! In my area, Curves gym for women has many locations and opens early.

## What Type of Exercise Is Right for Me?
There are three basic types of exercise—aerobic, strength training, and calisthenics:

- Aerobic exercise is sustained activity involving the major muscle groups, such as swimming, running, or brisk walking. Additional aerobic activities include sports such as tennis, volleyball, soccer, and some forms of martial arts. This kind of exercise strengthens your cardiovascular system and increases overall strength and stamina. The goal of aerobic exercise is for your pulse to reach a training rate that is appropriate for your age. Start out with five minutes three times a week, and try to gradually work up to a twenty- to thirty-minute session.
- Strength training can be accomplished through isotonic or isometric exercises. Isotonic exercise occurs when your muscles contract against a resistance with movement, as in weight lifting. Weight lifting causes tiny tears in the muscle being exercised that take several days to repair and rebuild. This process builds strength with increased muscle mass and causes our body metabolism to increase, thereby burning off fat, even on the days we are not lifting. Isometrics involves contracting your muscles against a resistance without movement. Isometrics increases muscle strength and tone without increasing muscle bulk.
- Calisthenics are stretching exercises such as sit-ups, toe touches, and knee bends. These exercises help increase flexibility and joint mobility.

The kind of exercises you choose depends on your personal preferences and your physical ability. Isotonic exercises should be limited to two times a week, as the body needs time to recover. Isometrics and calisthenics can be done every day, if time allows. Always get a complete physical exam from your physician before embarking on a new or vigorous exercise program.

***TOOL:** Choose to start an **aerobic exercise**, such as running, brisk walking, cycling, exercise machine (bike, treadmill, stair master, elliptical cross-trainer, etc.), swimming, rowing, aerobic dancing, or any other exercise that requires sustained activity of your large muscle groups. This type of exercise reduces stress and anxiety while building stamina.

***TOOL:** Choose to start a **strength exercise**, such as an isotonic activity like weight lifting, rigorous hiking, or rock climbing. This type of exercise builds muscle tissue as it firms and tones the body. Many feel emotionally more confident and secure when they feel good physical strength and power. This is because our minds, emotions, and bodies are one integrated unit, and a positive change in one aspect will invariably affect the other two. Those with social phobia will likely feel improved success with social interaction when they get positive feedback on their physical looks. Unfortunately, some people believe that their inner worth depends on the circumference of their biceps. It is important to realize that many factors define who we are.

*TOOL: Choose to start a **competitive or team sport**, such as golf, tennis, bocce ball, baseball, basketball, bowling, or volleyball. These activities are helpful to those who feel the need to discharge aggression and frustration (although golf has been known to add a degree of both these emotions). They also fill the need for those who enjoy socializing and working with others. Those with social phobia should force themselves to become involved in these kinds of informal social interaction as part of their training in social skills.

*TOOL: Choose to start a **rhythmic exercise**. I am saving yoga and rhythmic exercises, like tai chi, to discuss more thoroughly under body-mind tools.

NOTE: Regular exercise is always more enjoyable and sustainable when you have the encouragement and support of a dedicated work-out or activity partner. Try to pair up with someone who is motivated and serious about an exercise program.

## Deep, Restful Sleep
### The Biophysiology of Sleep

I am frequently surprised at how many patients' anxiety symptoms improve or resolve altogether with just a few nights of deep, restful, restorative sleep. The reason for this is that our mind recharges its neurochemistry hormones primarily when we are in states of relaxation or deep sleep. This means that, given the proper amount of sleep, our anxious minds can often correct themselves. Those who follow basic Aruvedic principles have known this for thousands of years.

Sleep and wakefulness are produced by the complex interaction of internal biological clocks, environmental influences, and activities that either stimulate arousal or induce sleep. Humans wake and sleep in twenty-four-hour cycles—usual sixteen hours of wakefulness followed by eight hours of sleep. These cycles are under the influence of the circadian pacemaker, also known as the *suprachiasmatic nucleus* in the brain. The suprachiasmatic nucleus is affected by several factors, including sunlight, the production of melatonin and certain neurotransmitters, and the brain receptors that provide feedback from the internal environment.

The primary element that sets our biological clocks is light. Special photoreceptors in the retina of the eye are stimulated by outdoor light levels, which reach one hundred thousand lux (a unit of light energy) as opposed to office room light at two hundred to four hundred lux. When you spend just a few minutes outdoors, your circadian clock is set. Spending the whole day in office room light levels will not set your circadian clock. It seems the worst idea of the industrial age was the invention of the lightbulb!

The special photoreceptors in the retina send signals directly to the suprachiasmatic nucleus (one on each side of the brain). The suprachiasmatic nucleus also receives wakeful signals in the morning from the adrenal glands in the form of adrenal corticoid hormones. The great mystery is what happens in the brain that permits us to fall asleep? One component of the answer is melatonin. During the day, the suprachiasmatic nucleus inhibits melatonin production. Later in the day, melatonin production begins to ramp up due to the release of the neurotransmitter norepinephrine in the pineal gland. Melatonin quiets and suppresses the wakeful signal from the suprachiasmatic nucleus, allowing us to fall asleep. Recent research and drug development has focused on melatonin receptors in an attempt to find a safe and effective way to induce sleep.

Melatonin helps us adapt to basic environmental rhythms, such as night and day. As night falls, melatonin increases and becomes a key player in signaling the start of various mental and physical restorative processes. It also accounts for much of the body's temperature rhythm, allowing the nighttime temperature drop that is required for sleep. Unlike serotonin, melatonin passes through the blood-brain barrier and can therefore be taken as a supplement.

Most of the brain's melatonin is generated in the pineal gland through the conversion of serotonin. The pineal gland has a particularly elaborate blood-vessel system and serves as a key modulator of the entire neurohormonal system. It is the gearshift that allows us to adapt to changing environmental conditions. Because the pineal gland is light sensitive due to connections with the optic nerves, it allows the brain to perceive the time of day.

Like serotonin, melatonin helps the nervous system adapt to a changing environment with the least amount of stress. Melatonin and serotonin inhibit the sympathetic nervous system (fight-or-flight response) and stimulate the parasympathetic system, which is associated with calming. Melatonin increases GABA, another important neurochemical in mood regulation. Like serotonin, melatonin affects prostaglandins, which seem to play a critical role in depression. Melatonin deficiency has been linked to depressed mood, sleep disruption, disturbed body rhythms, agitation, and higher body temperature. Melatonin levels have been found to be high during the manic phase of bipolar illness and low during the depressive phase.

Like with serotonin, melatonin levels are low with premenstrual syndrome. Alcoholics (even if recovered) have lower melatonin levels. In seasonal affective disorder, too much melatonin is released during the day with a drop-off at night. Light therapy suppresses daytime melatonin, allowing for a nighttime surge, which is the normal fluctuation of the circadian rhythm. Treating sleep disturbances with melatonin is well established. One-half to ten milligrams may be needed to affect the brain's clock. It should be taken near bedtime, unless you are trying to reset your clock (e.g., taking the dose several hours before bedtime if traveling east against time zones or in the morning if traveling west).

Another recent drug development focuses on facilitating the brain's ability to shift gears from the wakefulness circuit of neurochemicals to the sleep circuit. A new sleep medication, Belsomra, is a highly selective antagonist for brain orexin receptors OX1R and OX2R. The mechanism by which Belsomra counteracts insomnia is through blocking orexin receptors. The orexin neuropeptide signaling system is a central promoter of wakefulness, so Belsomra shuts off the wakefulness circuit so the sleep circuit can take over. This transfer of activation from one circuit to another takes all of five seconds when it occurs. Belsomra is non–habit forming and takes several days to reach maximum benefit. It should be taken thirty minutes before your desired bedtime.

The level of our relaxation, restfulness, and sleep can be determined by examining brain-wave patterns on an electroencephalogram (EEG) machine. During wakefulness when focus and concentration are required, our brain waves are in a beta pattern, which is short and stimulating. While daydreaming, we fall into an alpha pattern, which is also true when we are meditating or in REM sleep (known as *rapid eye movement sleep*, light sleep when most dreams occur). Delta and theta patterns are seen at the deeper, restorative levels of sleep and in certain deep meditation, or in trancelike states experienced in a flotation sensory-deprivation tank. These patterns are necessary for feeling well rested. In fact, you should go into these levels of deeper sleep two to three times a night for up to an hour each time.

This school-book account of the biophysiology of sleep is not itself meant to be a sleep aid, but it's just to point out how complex and multifactorial the processes of sleep and wakefulness are. If we don't respect this and acknowledge our physical limitations and needs, we are doomed to take a pill for every bodily function. I have patients who need to take a pill to go to sleep, then one to wake up, then one to calm down, and one to stay alert. They need one to have a bowel movement, one to allow their urine to flow comfortably, and one to calm their stomachs so they can eat. Then they need one to have an erection because they are too tired and not in balance.

The causes of insomnia are many. About 90 percent of those with anxiety or depression report difficulty sleeping. Conversely, insomnia is also thought to be a possible cause of depression, not just a symptom. Many medical problems can be contributing factors to insomnia, such as chronic pain, osteoarthritis, gastroesophageal reflux disease, asthma, emphysema, snoring with sleep apnea, alcoholism, and restless leg syndrome. Several prescription and over-the-counter medications and supplements have a stimulatory effect that could result in sleep disturbance. In addition, more than seven million Americans regularly work at night or have a rotating shift schedule. Constant changes in the time you go to bed, eat meals, and do certain activities can produce disruption in natural circadian rhythms, which leads to insomnia.

## Healthy Sleep Hygiene

Before considering a medical treatment or over-the-counter remedy for insomnia, you should first look at your sleep hygiene practices. Recent studies show that meditation and behavioral-therapy techniques are more effective at restoring normal sleep architecture than any medication! Basic guidelines for overcoming insomnia and achieving restful, healthy sleep include the following:

- Keep a regular schedule of when you go to bed and when you get up.
- Avoid afternoon naps that keep you from falling asleep at night.
- Do your exercise in the morning, not late in the day.
- Avoid alcohol and caffeine within six hours of bedtime.
- Use the bedroom for sleep and sex. Don't read, watch TV, do paperwork, answer the phone, have arguments, or do anything stressful in the sleep environment.
- Make sure the bedroom is quiet, dark, and comfortable. If you live in a noisy area, buy a device to create white noise, such as a fan, or use earplugs, if needed. Get blackout drapes for the window if too much light is shining through.
- Go to bed in a relaxed mood. If you're not relaxed, consider eating a snack high in carbohydrates, such as grains, legumes, pasta, bread, vegetables, fruits, or cereal.
- Don't lie in bed awake, thinking and worrying. Get up and leave the bedroom, go to the bathroom, eat a snack, or watch part of the late-night movie. When you feel sleepy and relaxed, go back to the bedroom.

## Herbal Sedatives

Often, a sedative is helpful to induce sleep and restore normal sleep architecture, especially in those whose sleep patterns have been disrupted by illness, international travel, or anxiety. You should be following all the above advice on proper sleep hygiene before turning to a supplement or medication. You should also not mix alcohol or drugs with any sleep remedy. Those with addictive personalities should stay away from sedative medications unless prescribed by a physician who knows you well.

For centuries, man has used herbal remedies to promote sleep. Unfortunately, there are only a few placebo-controlled studies to demonstrate their efficacy. The neuropharmacologic properties of these compounds are not always known, and their mechanism of action, active ingredients, and effective dose are sometimes uncertain. These remedies include the following:

- Kava kava: Although helpful for anxiety and insomnia, this herb has been associated with liver toxicity and withdrawal side effects. It should not be mixed with alcohol or sedative drugs or taken more than twenty-five weeks straight.
- Valerian root: From the plant *Valeriana officinalis*, this herb has shown benefit in the treatment of insomnia in some studies. It has been used for thousands of years in India and China as a sleep enhancer.
- Chamomile: This herb is widely used in the Western world as a treatment for anxiety, nervous stomach, and relaxation. It can be found in small amounts in a tea form or more effectively dosed through a standardized extract. The active ingredient, apigenin, works on GABA receptors much like the benzodiazepine medications.
- Hops: *Humulus lupulus*, the hops plant, has scaly, cone-like fruits known to have medicinal properties. Besides their use in flavoring and preserving beer, they contain a chemical (dimethylvinyl) that causes the tranquilizing effects of this plant. It is available as an extract or essential oil.
- Passion flower: *Passiflora incarnate*, or the passion flower, is native to North America and is used for nervousness, restlessness, anxiety, insomnia, and irritability. As a sleeping aid, it is known for having no hangover sedation in the morning.
- California poppy: This flower (*Eschscholtzia californica*) is gaining in popularity as a sleep aid and stress reducer. The active ingredients are alkaloids, just like the opium poppy, but without the addictive properties.
- Lavender aromatherapy: Insomniacs have been shown to sleep better if their rooms are scented with lavender. A hot lavender bath, in which several drops of the oil are placed in a tub full of comfortably hot water, may be better than a sedative for calming your nerves, relaxing your muscles, and preparing your mind for rest.

## Homeopathic and Over-the-Counter Sleep Remedies

Homeopathic remedies include the following:

- Ignatia is used for worry, insomnia, anxiety, and emotional stress.
- Pulsatilla is used for insomnia and anxiety.

- Sleep Ease, made by Lehning Laboratories in France, is a nonaddictive sleep aid first available in Europe and now being distributed in the United States.
- Natural Calm is a magnesium supplement made by Natural Vitality in ionic form to increase bioavailability. Magnesium relaxes the muscles and reduces anxiety, headaches, irritability, and heart irregularities. Take at bedside to see if you naturally fall and stay asleep better.
- Kavinace Ultra PM is 650 mg of a proprietary blend with 3 mg of melatonin that is made by NeuroScience. It claims to act by helping the brain maintain good levels of calming neurotransmitters, such as GABA, melatonin, and serotonin. I have had patients recommend this, so that's how I know about it.
- 5-HTP is created in the body from the amino acid tryptophan. It is then used in the synthesis of serotonin, the brain neurotransmitter most responsible for healthy sleep cycles. Because 5-HTP crosses easily into the brain across the blood-brain barrier, it ultimately causes an increase in the brain's serotonin levels. The supplement is considered safe and is generally well tolerated.
- Melatonin is marketed as a dietary supplement and has been shown to improve sleep. It is available in a number of forms (tablets, time-release capsules, under-the-tongue lozenges, liquid extract, and tea). Of course, you should cooperate with the melatonin in trying to regulate your circadian rhythms by going to bed at a regular time and following the other sleep hygiene recommendations. Doses of three to six milligrams thirty minutes before bedtime are most common, but I have seen patients who need up to fifteen milligrams to get the benefit.

Two over-the-counter antihistamines that do not require a prescription have been approved by the FDA for use as sleeping aids. They are diphenhydramine and doxylamine. These are the drugs most commonly found in "PM" products, such as Tylenol PM, Unisom, and Sominex. Although the drugs are available over the counter and are generally safe and nonaddictive, it is illegal to drive a motor vehicle while under the influence of these drugs if you are drowsy and impaired by them!

## Medical Treatment of Insomnia

Your doctor, if it is medically indicated, may prescribe antidepressants, benzodiazepines, or newer sedative hypnotics, especially if other methods have failed. Cognitive-behavioral therapy and music-therapy tools have been shown in several studies to be as effective as medical treatment, more sustainable, and far safer than the prescription medical options. I send all patients with insomnia to a behavioral therapist first. Antidepressants are usually tried next, as they do not have the habit-forming potential of the other two categories:

- Sedating antidepressants: These drugs have no potential for abuse/addiction. Some have generic equivalents that are more affordable.
    - Tricyclics (Amitriptyline, Nortriptyline)
    - Trazodone (Desyrel)
    - Mirtazapine (Remeron)

- Benzodiazepines: These drugs exert their effect on the GABA receptors in the brain. When stimulated, they trigger a decrease in brain-cell excitability. With regular use, these drugs are habit forming and cause rebound insomnia if you try to stop them suddenly.
    o Temazepam (Restoril)
    o Dalmane (Flurazepam)
    o Triazolam (Halcion)
    o Clonazepam (Klonopin)
    o Alprazolam (Xanax)
    o Lorazepam (Ativan)
    o Diazepam (Valium)
- Newer benzodiazepine receptor agonists: These drugs bind selectively to one or more of the GABA receptors, improving tolerability and safety. They are still habit forming and are difficult to get off of with chronic use. Sonata is a three-hour drug that helps initiate sleep or combat early morning awakening. Ambien is my least favorite due to following-day memory impairment, and some patients do things at night (such as sleepwalk, raid the refrigerator, or call friends on the phone) with no recollection of any of it the next day. This is called *retrograde amnesia*. I prefer Lunesta, which, at three milligrams, helps initiate and maintain sleep throughout the night.
    o Ambien (Zolpidem)
    o Sonata (Zaleplon)
    o Lunesta (eszopiclone): The first sedative approved for long-term use by the FDA.
- Newer agents take advantage of the melatonin release mechanism of action or help the brain shift gears between wakeful brain neurotransmitters and sleep neurotransmitters.
    o Ramelteon: A melatonin 1 and 2 receptor stimulator
    o Belsomra: A brain chemical that helps the brain shift into the cycle of neurotransmitters that induce and maintain sleep
    o Silenor: A low dose of the tricyclic drug Doxepin (three to six milligrams) helps maintain sleep through suppressing the wakefulness cycle with H1 receptor activation in the brain.

**\*TOOL:** One of your first priorities in overcoming anxiety will be to work on an effective sleep program. No tool or strategy to reduce anxiety has a chance of working if you are chronically sleep deprived. Start with the sleep hygiene recommendations. Once your physician has cleared you of any medical problems causing or contributing to your insomnia, you can consider the herbal, supplemental, or over-the-counter sleep aids. If these are not effective or not tolerated, and if your physician feels it is medically indicated, you may try a medical treatment for getting a good night's rest.

## Personal Hygiene

One of the first things to go when we feel anxious, overwhelmed, or depressed is our personal care. Especially if we are tired or feel hopeless, we may find it difficult to get the motivation to do just the basics, like showering, brushing our teeth, doing the dishes and the laundry, combing our hair, or dressing appropriately.

As we look and feel more disheveled and unpresentable, we send a clear message to ourselves that we are outcasts, isolated, and not worthy to be around others or fit for the outside world. This message becomes self-fulfilling and will be a barrier to the healthy interaction needed to maintain our support network, positive experiences and activities, and work or job hunting. In addition, as we become sloppy with our personal care, we become sloppy with our medication regimens and nonmedical program to overcome anxiety.

Rule number one for a business person is to "dress for success." If you don't treat yourself with respect and show confidence in yourself, others will not respect or have faith in you. Much of the key to success in life has to do with being ready when the opportunity presents itself. Those with anxiety usually experience a dramatic drop in their personal success because they lose sight of this basic truth. The consequence is that their health and financial situation begin to deteriorate.

*TOOL: Don't let your personal appearance deteriorate when you have anxiety or depression. In fact, make the extra effort to always be ready, as if you have an important meeting or job interview, even though your calendar is blank. Keep yourself on a schedule, even if you don't have a job to get up for. Set the alarm, get up on time, shower, dress, clean your room, wash your clothes and dishes, and read the morning paper. Always keep up your exercise or at least go for a morning walk. Be social and say "hi" to a stranger or two. Have faith that you will soon be well, and show this positive attitude in how you take care of yourself.

## Personal Organization
### Daily Rhythm

Don't forget that our bodily functions and brain chemistry are under the influence of our circadian rhythms directed by the chemical and neurological output of our suprachiasmatic nucleus and pineal glands. This means we are designed to run on a cycle and that we will perform better emotionally and physically if we adhere to our natural, cyclical rhythms. An easy way to do this is to make sure you get to bed and wake up at the same times, seven days a week. Eat at roughly the same time each day, and don't vary your diet widely from day to day so your gut can effectively prepare the enzymes it needs to digest the food. Exercise at about the same time each day as well. Even meditation is best done at a consistent time daily. Respecting the "rhythm of life" can go a long way in providing emotional stability and a sense of physical well being.

*TOOL: The personal daily planner is designed to make you commit to a daily program and "stay in rhythm" with your sleeping, eating, exercising, working, showering, meditating, etc. Many tools from the toolbox can be inserted into your daily program within this repeating framework and structure.

### Common Sense

The term *common sense* implies a certain basic understanding that is common to all of us. However, it is surprising to find that the practice of common sense is relatively uncommon. The result is that we end up spending extra effort and time redoing a task or dealing with a problem after not doing it right the first time.

Many years ago, I dated a woman who grew up on a farm, where common sense is a necessity for survival. I remember her questioning my practice of filling my gas tank only halfway because I got bored waiting. "Even though it costs more now and takes a little extra time," she reasoned, "it's better than spending more time and money looking for gas more frequently because you'll run out twice as fast." It made so much sense I felt embarrassed that I had never thought of this.

Now I use every opportunity to ask a simple question: "Could this be done more effectively another way?" Last week in my garden, I was trying to level a large, heavy clay pot, as the winter rains had eroded some soil and caused it to tilt. I was leaning into the pot while trying to kick some gravel underneath to fill the deficit, risking injury to my back. Sensing that I was not using common sense, I stopped and went to get a crowbar, which made the job more efficient without blowing out a lumbar disc.

Another common sense question is, "What is the priority of this task?" Often I will be all wound up about wanting to complete a certain project, so everything else in life must take a back seat. But when common sense is employed, I realize that other matters are more pressing and deserve my attention first. Stopping to prioritize our tasks makes sure that the important things will get done first. There is no more relaxing feeling than having the big issues in life under control.

*TOOL: Practice common sense. With any task you are attempting to complete, ask yourself these two questions: Could this be done more effectively another way? What is the priority of this task, and should I finish a more important task first?

## Presence of Mind

The phrase I remember most as a boy from many father-son lectures is "presence of mind." At first, the lecture would run on and on about how I should have been paying attention to the whereabouts of my belongings so as not to lose any more jackets or sweaters because they were expensive to replace and I would have to shiver in the cold until another could be acquired. It would always end with, "Jamie, you've got to have presence of mind!" Later, upon learning of another missing item of clothing, there was only an exasperated look and the utterance, "Presence of Mind!" As a person who likes to let my mind wander and daydream rather than focus on the mundane details of everyday life, I can appreciate how difficult it is to stay focused on the present moment.

But if we are not focused and alert, we miss the conversation/instructions/lecture that is important for our organization and success in school/relationships/business. We weren't paying attention, so the information was not stored in our memory and cannot be recalled at a later date. Those with ADD have a more difficult time holding focus and concentration even with great effort. They may need a medical treatment to get their brain waves up to speed. For others, it simply requires a choice to be aware and make it a priority to pay attention when it's really needed.

Presence of mind is necessary to avoid making the same mistakes over and over, to stop losing and forgetting things, and generally to stop annoying those who live or work with us on a daily basis. Some people spend an extreme amount of time and energy correcting problems caused by their lapses in concentration: "Where did I leave the keys? Honey, do you have the bills we were supposed to send out?

Has anyone seen my briefcase? You mean *I* was supposed to pick up the kids/dry cleaning/groceries? I don't remember us discussing that."

*TOOL: Practice presence of mind. Here are a few suggestions you can work on in your daily life to improve in this area:

- Listen. Don't make others repeat themselves.
- Ask for and remember names of people you meet.
- When someone is giving you instructions, act as if there is going to be a test on the material later and you will need to repeat what you have learned.
- Always pay attention to the location of all your personal items and effects, including your jewelry, watch, folders, briefcase, coat/scarf/purse, and, yes, car. Constantly make mental notes, especially if you lay something down. I count the number of items I am responsible for and recount them at each opportunity.
- Pretend as if you're on a vacation in a place where you will be immediately ripped off if you leave a piece of baggage, camera, or backpack unattended. Count all the items in your possession and keep checking to see if they are all accounted for, especially when transferring between car/taxi/bus/plane.
- Stop every morning before leaving for work and make sure you have everything you need. Make a checklist if you still forget things, and go over it every day just like a pilot goes through the preflight check of the plane.

## Financial Responsibility

Another piece of advice from my father was that I should always recognize the difference between wants and needs. He felt that people got into financial difficulty by not distinguishing between the two, ending up with things they really didn't need, including credit-card debt. Whenever we make a purchase, we must realize that we have simultaneously rejected the purchase of something else that might have been a wiser choice. We often want something that we don't really need, buy it, and then not have money for something we really need later.

We humans are hunters and gatherers by nature. It is therefore no big surprise that, in the modern world, we choose Macy's over the primal forest when it comes to the hunt. Scientists can even pinpoint clear physiological responses when we shop. An enticing array of cleverly displayed merchandise can kick our emotional centers into overdrive, increasing neurotransmitter release and causing adrenalin to surge through our arteries. Our hearts palpitate at a great bargain. And we experience a sense of well being, even elation, at the point of purchase: the thrill of the hunt, the ecstasy of the capture.

The only problem is that we get suckered into buying something we don't really need, have no place to put, and will use only once or twice before sending it to the storage room we're renting at $200 per month. Of course Madison Avenue is well versed in this human vulnerability and sends us all kinds of subliminal messages that we can never feel truly fulfilled until we have what they are selling.

So how are we so easily manipulated? According to Juliet Shor, director of women's studies at Harvard University, "Millions of Americans use consuming as a way to fight the blues, to savor a happy moment, to reward themselves, to enhance self-esteem, or to escape from boredom. 'Retail Therapy' is a response to just about any mood, state, or psychological problem."

Especially during anxiety, we have the tendency to distract ourselves from our problems at the mall. But often, one of our stressors is financial problems. The last thing we should do is spend money we don't have on things we don't need.

Financial responsibility is really about self-responsibility and about being honest. Why should we insist on keeping up with the Joneses when we can't afford to? The answer is dishonesty, arrogance, insecurity, and low self-esteem. It takes humility to live within your means and not owe anyone anything.

For a moment, imagine that you have no debt. How would that change your feeling about yourself, and how far would that go in reducing your anxiety and stress? Now imagine that you have $300,000 in cash in the bank because of a long-term pattern of saving rather than spending. Feel the anxiety level dropping yet?

And what about those sales people who gushed all over you and told you how you deserved the best and were worth every penny of that expensive purchase? Are they there to console you when the creditors are calling and threatening to report you to the collection agency? Why pay for false admiration and momentary companionship? Remember that all that matters is your family and good friends, the people who ask for nothing but your wellness and happiness. Save and protect your financial resources for yourself and the people you care about.

*TOOL: Live humbly within your means. Choose to stop unnecessary spending. Cut your credit cards in half, if need be. Follow a carefully prepared budget and don't give into a sudden craving for the outlet discount store. Save money as a regular discipline with each paycheck. Get professional advice if you are behind on payments before it ruins your credit. Talk to creditors immediately if you will be late or need an extension on a payment—they may be more than willing to work with you.

## Be Committed

Good things happen when you choose a path of commitment to your future, whether it's your school program, a long-term relationship, your career goals, your sports ambitions, or your spiritual growth. Your commitment to just one thing will often set off a chain reaction of positive events that guarantee success. I thought that dedication to my medical studies and becoming a doctor would guarantee my success. But it was only after committing to a long-term, stable relationship by marrying my wife that I realized the difference that commitment could make. Within a few short years, I owned my own medical practice, bought a home, found the focus to write books, fathered a beautiful son, and became financially secure.

Many of the friends I was hanging out with before I got married are in exactly the same place in their lives—in and out of jobs, renting their apartments, going from relationship to relationship looking for the elusive "perfect match," all the time treading water and not moving in any direction. Then I look at the people who made firm commitments earlier in their lives—stayed in school, got married, had families, focused on building their careers and businesses, saved money—and some my age are now able to retire early, while I still need to keep my day job.

**\*TOOL:** Choose at least one thing or goal and be absolutely committed to it coming to successful fruition. Make it a high priority in your life, and don't be diverted or distracted from this goal. Place it above shopping, going out with friends, or other fun activities. You must budget a significant and adequate amount of time to promote and cultivate this commitment, be it your investing in your marriage or a career, raising a child, learning a musical instrument or foreign language, or starting a new business venture.

## Get Rid of Clutter

Suzy Orman, in her best-selling book *The Courage to be Rich*, as well as in her popular seminars, persistently harps against the damaging effects of clutter to our financial success. Those who practice the art of fêng shui are really reducing clutter to improve the flow of creative energy and thought. It is an ancient concept that holds even more merit in the modern world of confusion, imbalance, and overcrowding. Read and take notes on *The Life-Changing Magic of Tidying Up: The Japanese Art of Decluttering and Organizing* by Marie Kondo.

Think of all the corners of clutter in your life. Start with your closets and drawers, and then go to the garage and storage rooms. Look at your desk and under your desk and in the trunk of your car. How about your briefcase or purse? Did you find anything you don't need, will likely never use, or had completely forgotten about? Maybe it's time to throw it away, sell it at a garage sale, or donate it to charity.

Just start with one small space and see how addictive it becomes to see that space transformed from turmoil to tidiness. You'll be surprised how liberating it is to clean the clutter out of your life. Now you have space to breathe, think, and relax.

**\*TOOL:** Take the time to identify areas of clutter. Then make a schedule with specific goals to purge each area one at a time on a reasonable-yet-firm timetable.

## Time Management

When considering how you spend your time, you should keep in mind that there are three basic categories that all activities fall into: things that you want to do, things that you do not want to do, and things that you'd better do. Time management is about identifying those things that, like it or not, you'd better do, and making those things a priority.

In looking at how you spend your time, it is a good idea to keep a time log for a few days. Starting with the moment you wake up, document how much time you spend on each task or activity of the day. Include time spent grooming (showers, hair, makeup), eating meals or snacks, commuting, working, talking on the phone or visiting with your friends, reading the newspaper, paying your bills or other paperwork, surfing the Internet, watching TV, and finally, sleeping.

Next, you should think about your goals and priorities. How much time do you actually spend on these items? Effective time management is finding out what is important to you and figuring out ways to spend more time doing those things. Time management does not mean trying to cram a lot of activities into a short period of time or trying to do things more quickly. Anything worth doing is worth doing right.

Be aware that not all things you do in life have the same value or worth. Some things mean more and matter more in the long run than others. Spending time with your child might have a higher value, for instance, than spending time in the gym or watching TV.

Make a checklist of those things that hold high value for you. An example of such a list might include some of these items:

- Spending time with spouse and children
- Spending time on a hobby or other passion
- Spending time on your career goals
- Reading more
- Exercising more
- Getting back into community or church activities
- Traveling
- Sleeping
- Spending time with friends

Now make a list of items you feel you are currently spending too much time on, like the following:

- Too much time at the office
- Too much time watching TV
- Too much time with certain friends or activities that you really don't enjoy
- Too much time surfing the Internet
- Too much time taking care of other people and their problems

The next step is to decide which type of time-management system you want to use. Most people are well versed in modern electronic gadgetry, such as tablets, smartphones, and iPads. And most people have access to the Internet or a free Wi-Fi signal. Learn how to use your device to keep track of appointments, tasks, and activities.

Once you are familiar with your time-management system, start defining your priorities. Going back to your record of daily activities, place a value code next to each item: 1 equals high priority and highly important to you; 2 equals medium priority; 3 equals low priority and you could take it or leave it without much consequence; X equals total loss/waste of time and it would take time away from other things that could be more helpful or meaningful to your life and health. Now your goal is to fill your daily planner with 1 items first, followed by items with the designation 2. Items coded as 3 can be inserted if there is time, and X items should be eliminated.

Remember that we all have a finite amount of time to make our lives what we desire, a finite number of breaths and heartbeats, a fixed number of hours to generate an income to support our families and our retirement, a limited amount of time to be with the ones we love and to tell them how we feel.

Think about that the next time you are watching a mindless television program or sitting at a sports bar staring at a game that really isn't that interesting while smelling the same old stale beer.

Below are some basic rules to consider when thinking about how to best spend your time:

- The 20/80 rule. One principle of time management is that successfully completing only the high-priority items on your list will give nearly as much overall satisfaction as completing all of the items on your list. Simply stated, the rule declares: Of all the things you have to do, doing the top 20 percent of the most valued items will provide you with 80 percent of the satisfaction of having done them all. In other words, prioritize tasks by value. It's OK if you don't get around to many of the lower-value, less-important items, so don't get distracted or fixated on these activities.
- Unload low-priority tasks. After prioritizing your activities and tasks, identify those things you could easily do without. Trim out of your life the nonproductive or meaningless activities so you'll have time for the things you'd really like to do. Resign from those clubs, boards, and organizations that you've lost interest in and are doing only because of a sense of obligation. Next, cut back on meetings that take you away from personal and family matters. You don't have to go to every meeting of the church, temple, school, or professional society. Give yourself permission to politely decline any number of invitations that might come your way if you are not truly interested in attending.
- Save time. Saving time is often about using common sense. As in the example I used when discussing common sense, it's best to fill up your tank each time you get gas so that you won't waste time going more frequently in search of a gas station.

Other ways to save time include the following:

- Pay your bills on time. Designate a time every two weeks to sit down with your bills that you have neatly placed in your "to pay" box. Make sure you are sending out the checks well in advance. Paying late results in more work later to explain and correct the issue. Also, it's inconvenient if the power or water is shut off because of a late payment. Your payment history is used to create your credit rating, so protect your credit by paying on time. You'll be more stressed out and spend more money later trying to fix your credit after being turned down for a loan you really needed.
- Batch your errands and tasks. As with paying your bills, there are many activities that are done more efficiently when batched. Organize a shopping trip every week or two and get everything you need at once. Save all your return phone calls and e-mails until a specified time and do them all at once. Prepare food for the whole week by cooking ahead and using Tupperware to keep it fresh.
- Get the most out of technology by putting it in its place. Many items that you need may be procured though mail-order catalogs or the Internet more efficiently. Your favorite stores usually have an online shopping option for the same merchandise with the same warranties and guarantees. Just don't give in to the temptation to buy things you don't need because it's so

easy to add it to the shopping cart. Also, much of your banking, business billing, travel planning, and research (e.g., what kind of car to buy) can be done faster and more effectively on the Internet, if you know how to get the information you need. Just have your kids teach you how to do it! Also, it's often faster to e-mail the whole family a message or send them all a digital photo of little Johnny. The problem is that you may start a wave of chattiness that takes even more of your time in returning correspondence from those with more time on their hands than you. If this happens, keep your responses to one or two words, and it will gradually die down. Stay off Facebook, Instagram, Twitter, or any social/dating/networking site that is designed to suck away your time and energy while providing your personal profile information to people who want to suck away your bank account as well!

- Realize when you are dillydallying. You may start out on the Internet with the intention of being efficient and on point but end up researching that power boat or custom light saber you always wanted but can't yet afford. Schedule your productive time on the Internet and limit your surfing time. When you are at work and there is suddenly a lull in the action, think about things you could do to use this time wisely, such as returning a call, getting to some unfinished paper work, taking a quick exercise break to run up and down the stairs, or taking a ten-minute meditation break. "Don't drag!" is a common admonition in our house when our fourteen-year-old son is not staying on task. His pattern is to waste time on low-priority items (that are fun) and then go into warp speed (with sloppy results) on the important items (like brushing teeth, doing homework, and cleaning his work space). We are looking forward to the day when his executive, supervisorial brain will develop to the point of understanding the value of "work before play." But be patient with kids, especially boys, as this can take time (the executive brain completes development around age thirty!).

- Minimize TV time. Limit yourself to one to two hours no more than five days a week. Choose programs you really want to watch, rather than randomly channel surfing. (That's right, two days a week with no passively absorbed entertainment!) Use your electronics-free nights to do something you really enjoy, like go on a date with your spouse, take a trip to the gym followed by the Jacuzzi and steam room, make a dish you love to cook, read, or just go to bed early.

- Minimize interruptions and distractions. Make sure your work space is private and quiet. Have your secretary hold your calls when you need to concentrate. Screen your calls, answering only those from people you want to talk to. Block e-mails from people or companies you no longer wish to be in contact with. Get caller ID to help with identifying who's calling. Let calls go unanswered and listen to the voice message later when you are not busy or driving a car. Call and leave a message on voice mail at a time you know the person won't pick up if you don't enjoy talking in person or he or she tends to keep you on the phone a long time. Ask solicitors to take you off their e-mail, fax, or phone lists. If you are interested in something they are selling but feel you are getting a hard-sell pitch over the phone, tell them you will consider their offer only if they send it to you in writing. Use a cordless phone around the house or office with an earpiece if this allows you to move around and do other mundane tasks. Be less available.

- Get up a little earlier. This usually means going to bed a little earlier as well. Late night is a nonproductive time if you are tired. For night owls, however, it may be a very productive time if you are alert because you wake up late or nap during the day. The most productive time is when you are awake, focused, energetic, and have peace and quiet (the kids have gone to sleep or they haven't awakened yet). If your brain has reached overload and you're tired, then your time will be more productively spent sleeping. Getting up fifteen to thirty minutes earlier a day may make your commute faster, allow you to get a few things done and organized before the workday starts, or get in a quick burst of exercise and an invigorating shower.

- Get hired help. Often, your time is more wisely spent on the things that generate income and promote your overall program. What is your time worth, and how much would it cost to hire someone to do the tasks you are always avoiding, like yard work, housecleaning, house repairs, washing the car, doing the laundry, catering a special event, or taking care of the pets? Give the job to someone you like who will appreciate the extra money, such as a family member, neighborhood kid, college student, or a client who supports your business.

- Do they deliver? Use a delivery service whenever possible. Find a deli that delivers sandwiches for a lunch meeting, a dry cleaner that comes to your door to pick up and deliver, and a pharmacy that delivers at no extra charge. Have movies delivered via pay-per-view or through the Internet, rather than spending the time picking up and returning DVDs.

- Learn to delegate. Perhaps it is true that no one is as competent as you, understands a particular situation better, is as motivated and dedicated as you are, or is as honest and trustworthy. These are common barriers many people face when considering asking someone else to complete a task for us. Even if the job might not get done just as perfectly as you would want, it may be better for overall time management and stress reduction to delegate it to others. This is especially true if the task is or should be someone else's to begin with. Often, we take over others' tasks because we feel it is just faster and easier for us to do it ourselves. Remember when you told your kids they would be responsible to feed, water, and bathe the puppy if they wanted one? But now who's doing it all? Share tasks with your spouse, depending on what makes the most sense. Let your coworkers hold up their own weight. Give the kids chores and responsibilities that are appropriate for their ages.

- Stop procrastinating. Without you realizing it, procrastination may be the main factor contributing to lost time and elevated stress levels. This is because you cannot see how your life would have gone more smoothly and efficiently if you had not put off and avoided important tasks. Most people procrastinate because it's too much effort to overcome inertia and get going on something you don't want to do but know you should. You may be an expert on how to distract yourself from the high-priority tasks in front of you, but you are only fooling and hurting yourself. Often, when you wait too long to act, an opportunity passes you by. This is also an unseen price you pay that will ultimately lead to a less-fulfilled and less-successful life.

There are many ways to face and overcome your tendency to procrastinate, including the following:

- Just do it! Remember when you were young and someone dared you to jump into the freezing-cold lake or ocean? You couldn't "just say no" because there was too much peer pressure from the other kids goading you on. So you said, "What the heck?" let out a war cry, and took the plunge. Sometimes you need to recall that life-force and fearlessness that allowed you to jump, as well as the sudden surge of energy and strength that allowed you to survive it! Turn that force loose on your garage-cleaning project sometime.

- Rewards or penalties. To effectively motivate yourself, you may want to give yourself a nice reward for completing a task on time. This could be a meal at your favorite restaurant, a cold brew, or going to a movie. If rewards don't work, try penalizing yourself for not finishing on time. The penalty would have to be something you'd really hate to do, like giving up all vices (alcohol, cigarettes, desserts) for one week, getting up half an hour early and running on the treadmill for thirty minutes every morning for a week (again, only if this sounds like torture), or giving up all entertainment (TV, movies, going out) for a week.
- Avoid being a perfectionist. Realize that being a perfectionist usually either causes you to spend too much time on a given task or avoid doing it altogether out of fear that you won't do it well enough.
- Keep a "to do" list. Document the tasks you would like to complete each day, when and how you plan to complete the tasks, and the results. At the end of the day, go over the list and see what happened. Now make a sheet for the next day, bringing forward any items that were not successfully accomplished but still have high value and importance to you. Here is an example:

|   | TO DO | WHEN AND HOW | RESULT |
|---|---|---|---|
| 1. | Call the real estate agent | 8:00 a.m. from car phone | Called |
| 2. | Get an estimate on car repair | 9:00 a.m. from office | Got it |
| 3. | E-mail Joe about the party | Anytime during work | Forgot |
| 4. | Read chapter of book | After work on the subway | Done |
| 5. | Pick up office supplies | On my walk home | Done |

The next day's list, of course, would again include getting that e-mail to Joe.

- Don't commute! When I first started practicing medicine, I was single and wanted to live in the big city. My job was an hour and fifteen minutes each way, and my girlfriend lived 360 miles north. I drove to see her almost every weekend. So, no surprise that I put fifty-four thousand miles on my car in the first year. Now, my office is a mere eight-minute drive away, and my wife lives in the same house that I do! I put about five thousand miles on my car annually. Just think how much time you'll have to sleep, unwind, catch up, or make some extra money by working another hour or two instead of wasting time and energy in a stressful commute!

**\*TOOL:** When it comes to time, simplify and get organized. Look at how you spend time. Place a value on the things you have to do, keep lists, use an electronic planner, and discipline yourself to do things on time. In your personal daily planner, under the section "Time Management," list the ideas you have read here that you actually plan to apply to your daily life; for example, "I will keep a daily to do list and review it every night before I go to bed." Think seriously about getting an apartment or home close to work or school, where you can even walk instead of driving to get the essentials of life. You will be able to afford a more expensive home or apartment near work because of the money you will make by working more hours and the money you will save in transportation costs by not commuting.

# CHAPTER 8

## Toolbox Compartment Number Five: Goals and Values; Attitudes and Beliefs

> *I love the man that can smile in trouble, that can gather strength from distress, and grow brave by reflection. 'Tis the business of little minds to shrink, but he whose heart is firm, and whose conscience approves his conduct, will pursue his principles unto death.*
> —Thomas Paine

## Goals and Values

One of the best ways to increase your resilience against stress is to be clear and consistent about your goals and values. This allows you to have purpose and direction, which prevents the alternative of stagnation and aimlessness that invariably lead to anxiety. Being true to your core values also allows a clear conscience. Spiritual beliefs and values are discussed in the last chapter of this book. But what about your personal values?

Your values and overall philosophy of life play a large role in determining your stress level. Who are you, and what are your aspirations and dreams? What do you believe in? What truths and beliefs do you hold sacred and would never forsake? Maybe you believe in the golden rule of treating others as you would like them to treat you. Or maybe you believe that it is "every man for himself" and that the end justifies the means.

Often we are not even consciously aware of our goals and values, yet these subconscious forces influence and inform every decision, from what we put in our mouths to whom we cultivate as friends or what we choose as our careers. If there is agreement between our actions and decisions and our goals and values, our stress level drops. Think of your goals and values as the road map of your life. If you stay true to this map and recognize when you've made a wrong turn, you'll be better able to turn things around and get to where you want and need to go.

Also realize that you may have inherited values and goals (becoming a doctor or a lawyer) thrust upon you by your parents. Other forces may also have influenced your goals and values without you fully participating in the decision. Your peers, religious upbringing, teachers, community, or things you have read in magazines or seen on TV or in movies may have all contributed to your present set of goals and values. But as you think more about it, you may find that you have changed and are going against what you truly believe. This is because goals and values often need to be reevaluated and reconsidered. Here are some exercises to allow you to examine your core goals and values.

## Write Your Eulogy and Epitaph

Imagine you just died unexpectedly. Someone has the job of planning your funeral. It might be your parents, children, a sibling, your spouse, or a long-time friend. This person has many details to consider. Among these are what to say to those who attend the funeral. This is called the *eulogy*. The other detail to consider is the epitaph.

The eulogy tells something about who you were as a person, what made you unique or special and how you viewed yourself, your life, and the world. In the end, people want to know not only what you accomplished but what you believed. They want to know your core beliefs and values, because that is most intimately who you are.

The epitaph is what should be inscribed on your tombstone or gravestone. Usually this is short and simple: "Loving father and husband" or "Precious son and brother." But on a large tombstone or mausoleum, there is more space to spell out the description of the deceased. Get out a piece of paper and write down your answers to the following questions:

1. What would you say about yourself if you had to write the eulogy for your own funeral? Keep it honest and simple, not more than 250 words.
2. How would you want your tombstone to read? Assume you have enough room for a few phrases.

Now look at your work and answer these questions:

1. Is there anything you wish were different about how you will be remembered?
2. Is there anything you wish were different about what you accomplished in life?

This exercise is designed to help you step back and look at the big picture of your life, both where you think you are and where you would like to be. It forces you to consider what you really value as worthwhile and important.

## Five Years to Live

What if you were told that you have five years to live? What would you do with the rest of your remaining time? Would you change anything? Ask yourself the following questions:

1. Would you stay at your present job?
2. Would you treat your spouse or family members differently?
3. What would your priorities be?

4. Which friends would you spend more time with and which friends less time?
5. What would you say to those you care about?
6. What would you still want to accomplish?

## Top Ten

An easy way to reveal your values and goals is to take a look at the top-ten list and rate each item according to its importance to you personally. Use a scale of 1–10, 1 meaning "not at all important" and 10 meaning "extremely important."

_____ Achieving wealth and financial success
_____ Being clever and smart
_____ Being powerful
_____ Being a leader
_____ Being a winner
_____ Helping others
_____ Being admired for good looks and sexual prowess
_____ Being admired as a role model
_____ Being recognized for honesty and integrity
_____ Having close family bonds
_____ Having close friends
_____ Achieving fame
_____ Being highly respected in your career field
_____ Being loved by family and friends
_____ Having a strong spiritual foundation

Finally, look closely at each item that you rated 7 or higher. Clarify what that value or goal means to you. For instance, if you want to be a leader, are you aspiring to be a leader of a country or a leader of a local community organization? If wealth is important, what do you want money and financial success to buy for you? One or two sentences should do for each item. The purpose of this exercise is to help you uncover what is important to you and whether you are focusing your energy on those things that are most meaningful.

## My Favorite Things

Write down a list of ten to twenty things you love to do. What would you rather be doing right now? Sailing, fishing, salsa dancing, playing the banjo, rock climbing, fossil hunting, gardening, traveling, or any other thing you wish you had more time or money to indulge in. As you try to forge a more anxiety-free life, you will want to strike a balance between what you have to do and what you would like to do. Building activities into your busy life that remind you of your core self-identity is an important step in taking control over anxious emotions.

## Essay Questions

Remember those pesky essay assignments on the college-admission applications? Each college had a different and usually nebulous question requesting a one-page answer. Now you realize that the admissions department was trying to tease out your goals and core values. You don't have to write an entire essay, but reflect on the following essay questions from actual college applications and write a short response for each.

1. If you were asked to write a book, what subject would you choose and why?
2. If you won $1 million in the lottery, what would you do differently?
3. Describe your life five years and ten years from now.
4. If you could be another person, either from past history or still living, who would you choose to be and why?
5. If you knew you had one hour to live and were allowed to make only three calls, who would you call and what would you say?
6. If you were made king or queen of the country, what laws would you change and why?
7. If you could start over at twelve years old, knowing everything you know now, what would you do differently?

## Moving toward Your True Goals and Values

Do you ever say to yourself, "I'll be more spiritual when I…" or "I'll spend more time with my family once I…" or "I would do the things I want if only I could …?" There is nothing wrong with occasionally delaying gratification to focus on getting the job done. Often we tell ourselves that we'll someday live by the goals and values that are deep within us. But, for now, we decide that we can't afford those "luxuries." We have to get a little dirty on our way to the top, or we have to focus on career before family, or we will finally get to the things we really love once we retire. The problem is that we then go through life ignoring what is really important to us. Life rarely accommodates our procrastination, and we may end up living a life that we regret. No one lying on a deathbed wishes he or she had spent more time at the office. Many would make a pledge to live their lives very differently if they had a second chance. But there are no second chances. Life goes by, and living apart from our inner values while losing sight of our goals increases our vulnerability to stress and anxiety.

***TOOL:** To make sure this doesn't happen to you, make a list of your top ten goals and values. Hopefully, the preceding exercises have helped you realize what these are. Consider the categories of job/career, family, friends, health, money, hobbies, interests, travel, and spirituality. Next to each item, rank your present success in how well you have achieved or actualized this goal or value (10 means "completely" and 0 means "not at all"). Your personal anxiety assessment plan has a section specifically for this purpose.

Now make a list of the ten ways you would like to change your life to include these goals and values. Begin each sentence with, "I would like to spend more time…" (e.g., with my family, on my boat, keeping in shape, drinking imported beer, growing spiritually, traveling, reading, advancing my career, looking for the Holy Grail, or with my spouse). Then write down how you could make time for this change in your busy schedule.

Again, your personal anxiety assessment plan has a place to keep and organize these thoughts and considerations. In your personal daily planner, you will allot time every day to review your goals and values and reinforce your new priorities.

## Attitudes and Beliefs

In this section, we want to examine our perceptions and attitudes while examining our core beliefs. Changing an attitude can be as simple as just choosing to do so. The attitude changes suggested below, if implemented, will help you become a happier and less anxious person.

Understanding the direction of your life, building a successful career or keeping a job you love, creating a connected and loving family life and circle of close friends, and finding a sense of meaning and purpose all start with your attitude on the subject. Some people have had their attitudes hijacked by an emotional disorder. For instance, someone who has dysphoric mania due to bipolar disorder may have an attitude tainted by irritability and agitation. Everyone around the person is an incompetent idiot who is getting in the way. For someone who has an anxiety disorder with a little paranoia, the attitude will always be one of distrust and suspicion.

For these reasons, it is critical that any possible emotional disorder be diagnosed and treated (usually with traditional Western medication) before attempting to work seriously on attitude adjustments.

Below, read each thought or attitude, which are divided into three main sections. If you run across anything that has special meaning for you, make a check mark to the left of the statement and list it in your personal anxiety assessment plan in the section provided. Then read and remind yourself on a daily basis that you are going to reinforce a healthier, more truthful, and more realistic alternative view. These changes of attitudes and beliefs will help reduce stress and allow a higher level of fulfillment.

We cannot change our mistaken attitudes and beliefs unless we have the courage to confront them, and we cannot be true to our attitudes and beliefs unless we identify and embrace them.

## The Gardner Girls

I grew up with five loving, smart, confident, and headstrong sisters. They eventually all got married, and their husbands quickly experienced the fortitude and resolve of "the Gardner girls." They would swap stories at family reunions about how the Gardner girls would relentlessly defend their positions without budging. One brother-in-law made the mistake of complaining to my father, "Your daughter is just plain stubborn." My father's response was, "No, she's not stubborn; she's steadfast." He knew that their unwavering strength in standing by their beliefs and values would someday be appreciated after they supported and defended their husbands through thick and thin. Often, those who have the conviction of their values and beliefs are also consistent with their attitudes and goals. They can be relied upon to stick with it until it's done, to never give up or get discouraged, and to be the same day in and day out, year in and year out. I saw this firsthand when my father died and my sisters quickly stepped in to help out and support me. Knowing your values and beliefs, keeping an attitude of self-reliance, and being focused on your goals is not being stubborn; it's being steadfast. And the world could use more daughters, wives, and sisters like the Gardner girls.

## Attitudes and Beliefs about Life
### *Life is all about me.*
One on the quickest ways to put life problems into perspective is to take yourself out of the equation. The formative years of our lives are all about us—what we need and want. Then there comes a time when we have taken in enough from the world and it is time to give something back. Letting go of ourselves and putting the needs of others first is a basic principle of many philosophies and religious thought. In losing ourselves, we find ourselves. By stripping away the layers of pretension and false image, we are able to find the calm, happy, and contented inner-self that has been waiting patiently for us to be quiet and listen. Stop demanding that the world, your work, and your family exist to serve your needs. Have faith that your needs will be met if you surrender your life to the service of others. A person trying to get out of a marriage will often use the explanation, "My needs are not being met." A person in a successful marriage says, "I have everything I need. Thank you for putting up with me. What can I do for you, honey?"

### *Life should conform to my expectations.*
Get it straight right now that you're not going to get life the way you wanted it or the way you expected it. Life is messy and largely tragic. The fairy-tale dreams of never-never land we have as children never come true, not even for Michael Jackson. Life is often unpredictable and uncontrollable. Then shit happens: taxes, illnesses, breakups, divorces, business failures or job losses, IRS audits, bankruptcies, DUIs, foreclosures, more taxes, and deaths. If you expect the unexpected and learn to roll with the punches and not take yourself or life too seriously, you might survive the wild ride of being human.

### *Extreme is cool.*
The movement toward extreme seems to be gaining momentum: extreme sports, extreme body building, extreme body piercing, extreme makeovers—and even extreme home remodeling! Whenever someone accomplishes something extreme on Ripley's *Believe It or Not*, there is another person right behind him or her ready to take it to the next level. People trying to make a video go viral on YouTube will often do extreme (and often extremely dangerous and stupid) pranks or stunts.

The need to be extreme probably has its origin in our basic human need to stand out from the crowd, to matter, to be different, and to push the envelope and boundaries of what it is to be alive. But where should the line be drawn? Have you gone too far if your health suffers or if your family suffers because you spend more time on your attention-getting obsession than on them? Or should you stay extreme until it injures or kills you?

Take, for instance, the use of anabolic steroids in sports. We as fans demand that our heroes be bigger than life, that they are puffed up like cartoon action figures. We want to see a home run every time we go to the ballpark. We want to see records shattered every year. The need to be extreme is driven by the demand to have and view extreme experiences. To satisfy readers and moviegoers, writers are compelled to create sensational characters and write stories that are increasingly outrageous. Notice how the movies have given more and more time to the action scenes, and these scenes have become increasingly fantastic, violent, and unbelievable. We are no longer satisfied by Steve McQueen's car chase through San

Francisco. Now there must be a horrendous explosion, mayhem with decapitations (a la Mel Gibson), alien ingestion, or an encounter with a gang of zombies with chainsaws to get our attention.

The problem with the extreme is that it is usually not real or authentic. Moreover, it tends to shorten our attention spans and desensitize us to violence and other sensory input. The outrageous behavior of extreme characters has become accepted and even admired. Some people actually adopt the mannerisms and actions of the characters they see on the screen as alter egos because they don't believe it is cool to be moderate and reasonable. Extreme experiences become addictive, but the bar has to be continually raised to get the same high.

Rather than looking for entertainment, validation, distraction, or attention through extreme experiences and behaviors, our time and money would be better spent inwardly focused on our own positive attributes and qualities that make us valuable and unique as individuals. By carefully selecting activities and experiences that bring out our positive attributes, strengths, and personal skills, we can keep on the path of a grounded and authentic life. And we will be less vulnerable to manipulation by peers, relationships, or advertisers if we choose to ignore the hyped-up world of the extreme. If more people were selective and discriminating in their behavior and choices, maybe screenwriters and authors would create characters that reflect real and powerful human experiences of triumph, tragedy, and sacrifice.

*My problems can wait until tomorrow since I don't want to face them now.*
Life and joy exist in the here and now, but so do pain and sorrow. Many people find ways to distract themselves from pressing matters at hand because it's too much work and too stressful to stay on task and take care of problems in the present moment.

Some of you may bluntly counter that this is because "the present sucks." Why engage in the present moment if you are in an unhappy marriage, just lost your job, have a family member who is ill or dying, or feel hopeless with anxiety and depression? It's easier to drown the present in alcohol or blur it with drugs or divert ourselves with escapist activities, such as intense exercise, endless home remodeling projects, or excessive sexual gratification. The problem is that the real world is still there when you get back from your detours and diversions, and real problems still have to be dealt with. And your energy and money have not been spent addressing the important issues at hand. You only have an effect on your future by living fully and being engaged entirely in the present moment, no matter how difficult that seems. Disappointment and loss are a part of life. We cannot grieve, heal, move on, learn new skills, or improve our lots in life unless we take full advantage of our time in the here and now. "Be grateful and take care of now; the future will take care of itself." (That's my dad, again.)

*I'm weak because of my fear and anxiety.*
Admitting fear is one of the most courageous things we can do. Most people who are recognized for courageous acts "above and beyond the call of duty" admit that they were frightened and just acted instinctively. Facing anxiety, or any emotional problem, takes tremendous courage, and anxiety and fear are signs that you have a normal, healthy emotional reaction to facing the unknown.

*I need to be in control.*
The need for an excessive amount of control in life may have its roots in a traumatic personal history. If you lived through experiences of abuse or neglect or divorce of your parents at a young age, when you felt powerless over your situation, you may develop a controlling personality. You may find that, to maintain control over everything and everybody, you need to develop an aggressive and unilateral form of communication. This, in turn, may lead to you being labeled a control freak who always has to have things your way. Survivors of traumatic personal events may also give up entirely, feeling it is hopeless to try to control anything in life. This state of discouragement is known as *learned helplessness*.

Those who need to control usually like everything to be predictable and planned in advance. They are unable to make spontaneous and carefree changes to their schedules and are unable to trust that things will "work themselves out." Check below any statements that apply to you and then read the alternative view. Consider adopting the alternative view; it's your choice.

*I am uncomfortable with anything unpredictable or unexpected.*
*Alternative view*: I can learn to be more accepting of the fact that life is unpredictable. There are many variables in life that cannot and should not be controlled. Unexpected changes are a part of everyday life. I am being unrealistic about my expectations of life if I continue to resist and fight them. How other people choose to behave, the weather, and the economic or political climate are all things that may change unexpectedly from one moment to the next. Other people have a right to change their minds, and I can be flexible and adjust my plans accordingly. I will stay relaxed, let go of unrealistic and perfectionist expectations of myself, and keep my mood on the positive, light side when faced with an unexpected change. In fact, I will use the opportunity to see if I can use humor and say something funny (not sarcastic) to lessen the discomfort others may feel. I will let go, not take myself and my schedule so seriously, and learn to trust that things will turn out OK. I do not always have to be the "general manager of the universe."

*I want to know now.*
*Alternative view*: People who are overly controlling want to know everything now so that they can be prepared for anything and have everything figured out in advance. If you're a boy scout headed into the wilderness for a month, this is a valuable quality. In everyday life, it is not practical. Often, situations do not have an immediate answer or solution. A difficult problem may have a solution that comes together over time and with much patience. Pushing others for an answer or commitment may lead to a result that is unsatisfactory and creates more problems. I will develop patience and be willing to wait for an answer or resolution to unfold, rather than forcing my own timetable on the problem. As Thomas Paine wrote in the introduction to *Common Sense*, "Time makes more converts than reason." Just as relevant are the words of Oedipus Rex, the king of Athens in the play written by Sophocles around 420 BC: "All things become clear in time." Trust that the answers will become clear when the time is right.

*Problems don't work themselves out; they need to be actively analyzed and fixed.*
*Alternative view*: If I think about it, my life problems have eventually worked themselves out. Even seemingly big problems with no forthcoming solutions were eventually seen far in the rearview mirror. I can sleep on it and not seek some clear and immediate response. I may feel very differently about the whole situation tomorrow.

*The final burden and responsibility to make sure things turn out right is on my shoulders.*
*Alternative view*: It is not my place to take responsibility for things in life that I realistically have no control over. I can seek a spiritual frame of reference and see my place in the universe from a different perspective. I can present my problems to my creator or a power greater than myself, asking for guidance and wisdom, understanding and accepting that the answer will come in its own time. Perhaps the things that are happening to us, including stress and anxiety, are for a purpose I do not quite understand. I will have faith and trust. I will focus on being a good person.

*Problems are to be dreaded and avoided. When faced with a problem, turn and run the other way.*
*Alternative view*: Problems are sometimes specifically designed for me to get my attention and point me in the direction I need to go. I should face my problems with open eyes, heart, and mind. We are largely defined by how we perceive, face, and manage our problems. Seeing problems as obstacles that we should skirt around may deprive us of learning valuable lessons about ourselves. Self-respect and self-confidence are promoted by accepting and facing our problems. Actively working on a solution may include waiting for time to give an answer, as well as working to resolve the problem through our own efforts, when possible.

## Attitudes and Beliefs about Success, Work, and Money
*I need to be perfect.*
You may think that perfectionism is a trait that would guarantee success and reduced anxiety. It is, in fact, this belief that drives those who insist on perfectionism. But there are two reasons that this theory proves false. First, perfectionists carry with them expectations of life, other people, and themselves that are unrealistic. This means that, eventually, they are doomed to fall short of their expectations and be disappointed and distraught. Second, perfectionists get bogged down with small flaws and mistakes, seeing only what went wrong instead of focusing on the positive gains and accomplishments. Because of this, they begin to feel that their efforts are never worthy or good enough. This leads to trying harder with even more attention to performing perfectly, which eventually causes undue stress, exhaustion, and emotional burnout.

To stop the vicious cycle of perfectionism, stop believing that your worth is determined by your accomplishments or whether you please others. Because of values pushed upon us by society, we often fall into the belief that our worth is measured by academic, social, competitive, or financial success. We do not put such pressure on our pets but instead bestow worth on them by virtue of their very existence and adorableness. Why don't we feel the same way about ourselves? After all, what is our true value? Do we really think we are more valuable people if we have a bigger bank account, are physically attractive, or have fancier jewelry or clothes? What about kindness, love, wisdom, and compassion? Have these things not more worth? Try measuring yourself by these standards rather than society's definitions of value and worth.

Perfectionists share certain flaws in their belief systems that should be confronted with an alternative view. Consider the following adjustments:

**I "should" or "must" perform perfectly.**
*Alternative view*: It's OK to do the best I can.

**If any part of a task is done wrong, then it's all wrong.**
*Alternative view*: This belief must be countered with the assertion that, while one part is flawed and needs attention, other parts may be fine and deserve praise.

**Failure is unacceptable.**
*Alternative view*: Winston Churchill once said, "Success is the ability to go from failure to failure without loss of enthusiasm." There can be no real learning without mistakes and setbacks.

**I can do more things and do them better than others.**
*Alternative view*: Since perfectionists tend to overshoot their abilities and disrespect the restrictions of reality, they may have lofty goals and visions of great accomplishments that are unlikely to be attainable. This would not be a problem, except that the perfectionist is often attached to this grandiose outcome. Again, they are setting themselves up for disappointment and self-inflicted stress. If you want to love yourself, start by accepting your personal limitations.

**Any activity that is not goal oriented is a waste of time.**
*Alternative view*: Perfectionists often feel they are wasting time if they are not fervently working toward their goals. They tend to take themselves seriously, becoming rigid and self-denying. The best way to counteract this is to allow time each day to relax, play, rest, or do something fun and self-indulgent.

**Winning is everything.**
*Alternative view*: Perfectionists often do not see the meaning and value in the process of doing things. They have no appreciation for the journey of life but are focused only on the destination and the end result. If they don't reach a certain outcome, then they see the journey as an entire waste. Such thinking can only invite regret and a sense of failure.

## Other Attitudes and Beliefs about Work and Money

In the workplace, there are many traps that are self-created by our attitudes that can get us into trouble. Consider an alternative outlook:

### *It's OK as long as I don't get caught.*

Many employees have no sense of loyalty to the person who has given them a job and no sense of integrity or responsibility when it comes to their work or interaction with their coworkers. It's like every person is out for their own self-interest, with no concern for each other or the expectations of their employer. The attitude of "I've got to look out for number one" is so prevalent that it is hard to find a dedicated, hard-working, honest worker. I've heard of or seen all the problem behaviors first hand:

- Refusing to learn new skills because you fear you will be asked to do more
- Clocking in earlier or clocking out later than your agreed-upon time so that you get hours better for your situation, even if it inconveniences the boss or other workers
- Hiding out in the bathroom, copy room, or lunchroom so others will have to answer phones or otherwise cover for you
- Calling in at the last-minute sick or claiming a family emergency when you really want to get back at the boss or a coworker for criticizing you
- Pretending you're busy with one task that you like doing so that someone else will be left with a task you don't like but should have done
- Stealing money because you feel you deserve it and the boss is rich anyway
- Texting, e-mailing, and doing your personal business when you are being paid to work

These are examples of willful misconduct that show an attitude of ingratitude, selfishness, and arrogance. Sometimes, those who demonstrate these types of attitudes are acting out of their own sense of low self-esteem and feelings of inadequacy. If they felt capable and had high self-esteem, they would start their own businesses and make the rules. Their bosses will eventually fire them, and they'll find that they can't get a good recommendation for their next jobs. Stress and anxiety are the prices one pays for not putting in an honest and dependable effort at work.

*Alternative view*: I will strive to be a loyal and valued employee and make myself indispensable to the success of this business, even if I don't see this as my long-term career.

### *Work comes first.*

The converse of the above example is the person who insists on losing themselves in their work. They devote themselves to their "duty," bringing home their work at night and using the weekend to catch up on the previous week's unfinished business and prepare for the next week's workload. They tell themselves they are just being responsible and dedicated, but sometimes it is a sign of a deeper problem. Are they hiding behind their work to avoid some other aspect of their lives? Are they allowing their bosses or supervisors to overload them? Do they fear social interaction and want an excuse to avoid it? Putting work first at all times means that you value work above all else. What message does that send to your spouse or child? Just as important, what message does that send to you? Are you not worthy of a balanced and happy life? Do you deserve to work like a plow horse? Even workhorses are required by law to be given time off every year to relax. I was surprised when my website designer informed me that she would not be available to discuss business over the weekend because that was "her time." I was so used to having those who help me be available whenever I needed them, just as I have always been available to my patients. But then I realized that she was right, and I admired her for carving out a more sensible and responsible balance.

*Alternative view*: Give work your all. Then give your family your undivided attention when you are home in the evenings and on the weekends. Give yourself some time to enjoy your passions unrelated to work. This will shift life to a happier and healthier perspective.

### *I'm unfairly picked on and blamed for everything at work.*
Ask yourself if you frequently feel you are the victim in your workplace environment. Do others tend to dump on you, blame you, complain about your work, write you up for disciplinary reasons, or tell you that your performance is "not satisfactory"?

While some people just happen to be working for a real jerk, others fail to see themselves as a possible reason for complaints from supervisors and coworkers. They cannot believe that they might be lazy, slow, not smart enough, or not teachable. But this may actually be the truth. Rather than looking at ways to improve, they disregard the criticism and see it as jealousy or the meanness of others. For example, many people with ADD find it very difficult to complete a task and stay organized. It is no surprise that they then fall behind and fail to live up to expectations at work. Many are not even aware that they have this condition and may choose to explain their shortcomings by blaming others.

*Alternative view*: Remember that there is a reason for everything. Ask yourself if there is a pattern in your life that might be explained by some learning difference or emotional health condition. Don't believe that others are out to screw you over. Is there something you could work on and take responsibility for? Everyone will want to help and support a person who wants to improve and who makes an honest effort—which is what you are doing right now!

### *I'll feel better when I finally "make it."*
As we achieve a certain measure of success in life, it is natural that we start thinking about how we compare and measure up to others around us. Alain de Botton, in his book *Status Anxiety* (Pantheon, 2004), notes that anxiety about our status in life is a relatively modern phenomenon: "For most of history...very few among the masses had ever aspired to wealth or fulfillment; the rest knew well enough that they were condemned to exploitation and resignation." The great movements toward democracy "altered forever the basis upon which status was accorded." As Alex de Tocqueville observed as early as 1835, "In America, I never met a citizen too poor to cast a glance of hope and envy toward the pleasures of the rich." De Botton says that status anxiety is a worry "so pernicious as to be capable of ruining extended

stretches of our lives." Keeping up with, or better yet, outdoing the Joneses is using up more of our emotional energy and generating more stress than ever before. Do we really need the biggest house, best car, or most fashionable clothes? And what is the real cost to our lives and emotional well being? It can't be calculated merely from the sticker price.

What about the time away from our spouses and children because of the extra work hours required to maintain our elevated status? What about the loss of our hobbies and leisure activities we are passionate about? We risk losing touch with who we are and what matters most to us in a senseless attempt to make others envy and respect us because of our material success. The best strategy to overcome anxiety over status is to learn to accept ourselves as we are, and to have faith in ourselves while retaining our humility.

*Alternative view*: Practicing humility and expressing gratitude for all we have goes a long way in relieving the anxiety caused by what we don't have when compared to our friends and neighbors. After all, status is ultimately measured by the quality of our soul, not our pocketbook.

### I'd be happier if I didn't have to work.

Have you ever thought that paradise is the absence of a time clock? Imagine never needing to set your alarm clock, sit through a supervisor's review, or reach a quota! Many people spend their lives with the aspiration that they will one day be able to sit on a private beach sipping a cool drink under an umbrella and not have anyone to answer to.

But the reality is that idleness often brings an increase in our anxiety. Many people retire only to find that they are without structure or direction. They are bored and more isolated. And worse, they are stressing out their spouses, who used to have peace during the day and now have to deal with the chronic whining of a malcontent. In fact, retiring should be considered hazardous to your health, as there is a higher rate of suicide and heart attacks in the newly retired. The secret is to find work that you enjoy and that makes you feel challenged and appreciated.

*Alternative view*: Think of reducing your workload but not retiring!

### I can buy security.

Many spend a great deal of time and energy building a fortress around themselves as insulation from the perceived threats and ugliness of the outside world. They build up reserve funds in multiple accounts in case there is a disaster and invest in elaborate schemes with the aim of self-preservation. The problem is, after all is in place, they still have an overwhelming sense of fear and apprehension. That's because they have only fortified without and not within.

*Alternative view*: I will cultivate the tools needed for my inner self to be truly fearless, confident, and comfortable in the world. Security is often an illusion. Deepak Chopra, a physician and leader in the field of mind-body medicine, explained in *The Seven Spiritual Laws of Success*:

> Attachment to money is a sign of insecurity. You might say, "When I have X million dollars, then I'll be secure. Then I'll be financially independent and I will retire. Then I will do all the things I

really want to do." But it never happens—**never** happens. Those who seek security chase it for a lifetime without ever finding it. It remains elusive and ephemeral, because security can never come from money alone. Attachment to money will always create insecurity no matter how much money you have in the bank. If fact, some of the people who have the most money are the most insecure.

**I hate work.**
Your attitude toward work may be something you have never sat down and thought about. Of course, everybody thinks about work, even to the point of losing sleep over it. But what about the meaning of work in your life? Is it just a paycheck? Is it a necessary evil between weekends? Does your work define you, or do you see your work as a small fraction of who you are?

There are generally two ways to put meaning and purpose into your work. Ask yourself this question: does work give meaning to my life, or does my life give meaning to my work? For some, work is a reflection of who they are. Their work is their passion or is such a big part of their lives that they cannot think of themselves as being separate from what they do. If you ask them to explain who they are, they'll say, "I'm a dentist," "I'm a lawyer," "I'm a model," or "I'm a conductor." What they do is who they are, and their work gives their lives purpose and meaning.

Others do not define themselves by their work but rather see their work as a means of fulfilling themselves in other ways. They may see their kids as the focus of who they are and work as a means of supporting their families. Or maybe they live to surf and their day job supports this passion. To them, work is given meaning and purpose because of the life it allows them to live.

But what matters more than whether you work to live or live to work is whether your work connects you to life, keeps you socially engaged, and allows you to shape your own future. It also helps if you feel your work is valued and provides a useful and helpful service to others. This is why most rehabilitation work programs for the imprisoned or homeless populations fail. The chores and odd jobs they are given do not reflect their individual talents and gifts. They do not see themselves as being an integral part of the product and do not see others benefiting from their efforts.

Work is your gift to others and your community. It is your way of giving back and taking responsibility for yourself. No matter how mundane, boring, unheralded, or simple, it has meaning if it serves others and allows you to support yourself. Those who try to get out of an honest day's work are denying themselves purpose and meaning. They will eventually question the reason for their existence and will feel a deep and pervasive sense of anxiety.

## Attitudes and Beliefs about Love and Relationships
*I need approval.*
Everyone desires the approval of others, especially those they respect or admire. With many anxiety conditions, however, the need for approval and acceptance can be excessive. By seeking the approval of others, we are looking for our own validation. Needing validation is based on a false belief that we are unacceptable just the way we are. Those who are overly concerned with approval are overly disapproving

of themselves. They have an inner sense of being flawed or unworthy. Because they are bent on being pleasing to others, those who need approval will often accommodate the needs and desires of others while being afraid that saying "no" and setting boundaries will lead to rejection. The problem is that you may end up in an abusive or manipulative relationship, subordinating your needs to the needs of others, leading to frustration and resentment. The end result is increased stress and more anxiety. Here are some beliefs often held by those who need approval, along with a more balanced alternative view:

- If someone isn't friendly toward me, there must be something wrong with me.
  *Alternative view*: There may be many reasons why some people are not able to accept or show interest in me that have nothing to do with me. They may be distracted by their own problems, be too tired to be friendly, or I'm just not their "type."
- When others criticize me, it shows how truly unworthy I really am.
  *Alternative view*: I may be oversensitive toward constructive criticism. Even though it seemed harsh, it was meant to help me. Accepting and learning from the observations of others will help me assess my strengths and weaknesses, and will eventually make me a stronger and more capable person.
- I go out of my way to be nice. Why do some people not like me?
  *Alternative view*: I cannot expect everyone to like me, no matter how hard I try. Why some people do or don't have good chemistry is a mystery that arises from human complexity, and emotions of attraction or repulsion are often irrational. (One thing I love about my son is his broad acceptance of the full rainbow of humanity. He gets along with all ages, races, sexual orientations, and personal styles of dress and self-expression and embraces each friend's passion, be it sports, technology, music and the arts, or intellectual pursuits. He believes there is good in everyone and is willing to let his friends be themselves so they can reveal the best that is within. Most people are not like this. They are looking for fault in others or seek to devalue others to feel better about themselves.) Don't hang out with narrow-minded, small-hearted people. Life is too short.
- Having others approve and accept me is very important to my emotional well being.
  *Alternative view*: The purpose and meaning of my life does not depend on the approval of others but on my own convictions and faith. Happiness comes from loving and respecting myself, not from demanding or craving affection or approval from others.
- Love is a riddle that requires years of patience and effort to solve.
  *Alternative view*: Love is a mystery that can never be solved. We can only embrace our relationships with open hearts in an attempt to learn and grow. We should not ask for assurances or guarantees, only the opportunity to experience life in all its complexity.
- Even though opposites attract, it is best not to plan a long-term relationship with someone you have little in common with.
  *Alternative view*: While it may be true that many successful long-term relationships are built on the foundation of shared values and beliefs, don't discount the value of the heart in helping us make relationship decisions. When we are drawn to another person by romantic feelings, it is because our minds yearn for growth and adventure. We choose partners from our hearts based

on the unfinished business of the heart. The ultimate goal of our relationships is not clear to us at the time. It is, ultimately, to find an intimate and loving connection with another individual to share life's joys and burdens. Who we are attracted to is a mystery that cannot be rationally explained. Trusting our heart may bring greater insight and growth than taking the predictable and expected path. Often, I see individuals limiting their choices of a mate because they want someone who will allow their dysfunctional behaviors. The converse is also true: our dysfunctional behaviors limit our choices for a successful partner. That is why I believe we should put off romantic relationships until we are clean, sober, and of sound mind and body. Why not go into a relationship with stable emotions and good health and expect the same in return?

- Love is a temporary high that eventually brings pain and dissolution. It is highly overrated and best avoided.

  *Alternative view*: The feelings of romantic love are an infrequent opportunity to discover the mystery that lies at the core of each of us. Falling in love causes us to experience life with more intensity; see new possibility and meaning; and feel grateful, humble, and elated at the same time. We usually go about our day-to-day existence along a horizontal path. We go to work and get things done while time passes quickly and we see ourselves getting older. But occasionally, this routine is broken by the experience of falling in love, when we see our vertical dimension that is eternal and timeless and is aware of the possibility of all things. Allow yourself to dwell for a moment in this experience and remember it later when you doubt your higher potential. Remember that the barriers we create around ourselves to keep from getting hurt are more effective in fencing us in than keeping others out.

### *Committing to a relationship will keep me from finding myself.*

How many of us think of marriage as bondage ("the old ball and chain") rather than a time of bonding? We even use terms like "tying the knot" and "getting hitched." Alternatively, we could view commitment as a mutual journey of growth toward healing and wholeness. Learning the qualities that make us wholly human—like compassion, inner strength, patience, courage, tenderness, generosity, and humor in the face of adversity—requires an environment conducive to growth. This is provided by a stable and committed relationship. Therefore, think of commitment as a journey to find our inner selves rather than a hindrance to this discovery. We can never achieve this enlightenment by going our own ways in the world and creating lives that serve only our own needs, with no one to bounce things off of or get feedback from.

### *I only pursue relationships if the other person plays "hard to get."*

Have you ever wanted someone just because you thought you couldn't get him or her? This implies that you thought you were not equal or as valuable as that person. In other words, you had less belief in yourself than the object of your affections. To have a balanced and sustainable courtship, two forces must be present in equal measure: the desire for the other person and the respect for and belief in one's self. If we want the other person more than we believe in ourselves, all of our energy is pulled away as the other person realizes he or she doesn't have to work much to keep things going. Eventually, there is not enough energy to pull the person to us, and he or she drifts away, making us feel that we loved and gave too much. If we don't respect ourselves and set boundaries that show this, we cannot expect another to value or cherish us.

*My jealousy/abuse means I care.*
If you grow up seeing your father or mother physically and emotionally abusing your other parent, you may get the message that this a normal way to show intense emotions that love can cause. Of course, this is far from a healthy or correct view, but you might come to this conclusion if your parental role model was abusive. Violence, threats, or coercion of any kind toward another really means you either don't have respect for that person or you are insecure about your own self-worth and want to frighten and bully your partner into staying with you. It is all about controlling another to feel more powerful and to boost your weak self-esteem. It has nothing to do with love for another.

Have you ever heard of a case in which a man kills his ex-spouse or lover and says, "I loved her so much I couldn't share her with anyone else. If I can't have her, then no one can." Does this sound like the kind of long-suffering, self-sacrificing love that is spoken of in scriptures, music, poetry, and great literature? If you grew up with this viewpoint and it has influenced your treatment of the people with whom you have relationships, talk to a counselor to gain new insight. Teaching your sons and daughters how to value a partner or spouse is one of the most important jobs you have as a father or mother. And this is done best by loving and respecting their other parent.

*By allowing this abuse, I show my love. I don't deserve better anyway.*
The purpose of a relationship—be it romantic or platonic—is for people to open up their hearts and to let others influence their thoughts and feelings. We all need the input of others to correct our misperceptions, inform our behaviors, and help us grow in a positive direction. By ourselves, we might choose a path that is self-serving, unhealthy, and destructive. A relationship that allows abuse and disrespect is not a relationship at all but a dysfunctional codependency. The person who needs control finds the person who feels he or she deserves punishment. Neither attitude is healthy. If you don't stand up for your right to be respected, you will not find respect; it's that simple. Just as bad, people who believe it is OK to abuse you will feel justified and may intensify their behaviors, encouraged by your fear and submission. No one deserves disrespect or abuse. Not even an animal deserves or should be treated with physical or emotional cruelty. Saying "NO" to abuse is saying "YES" to your divine nature, to your right to be loved by yourself and others, and to your respect for all life.

*When the fire is out, it's time to move on.*
Too many believe that passion is the purpose of a romantic relationship, and that, if the chemistry is right and things are "meant to be," the fire of passion will be self-sustaining. The truth is that waning sexual passion does not parallel the course of romantic love. In fact, romantic love may intensify as

sexual desire decreases. One of the critical tasks in primitive human tribes was to make sure the source of their fire stayed lit. Only those who could be trusted with responsibility would be allowed to attend the precious embers. This is true about relationships: the fire is the responsibility of both parties. If it goes out, it is because someone failed in this responsibility; don't blame it on the chemistry being wrong. "Moving on" is not a guarantee of finding love elsewhere. When you are in a committed marriage or relationship, think about whether you were fair, reasonable, and giving and put your all into it. Consider couple's therapy. Even if it doesn't lead to reconciliation, it may lead to self-awareness.

### I can't let go of a relationship that has ended.

Literature and poetry is replete with accounts of unrequited love, of those who pine away their lives in regret and a sense of loss for what they could not have or keep as a romantic relationship. It is our nature to try to find explanations, to try to make things right, to turn the clock back and change our mistakes, to yearn for second chances, and to dwell on who said what, when. There is a natural grieving process when someone you care about is no longer in your life, and it is appropriate to feel sad, cry, and miss that which you have lost. It may be appropriate to acknowledge that some of those feelings may persist deep in your heart throughout your life, even though you have moved on and are happily married to someone else.

It is important to recognize that this experience and the regret you feel is a powerful teacher. Perhaps you needed this breakup to grow as a person, and the person who has rejected you has given you a very precious gift. Some therapists may encourage you to be angry or to blame the other person to break the emotional bonds you have developed with him or her and move on. But ignoring the lesson to make things easier is not the point, and you may be doomed to repeat your mistakes in the future and go through the same painful experience again.

Finally, such heartache may be a test of your ability to love. If the love you feel for another is not returned, then you must give the other person back his or her life, including the right to move on without harassment or feeling guilty. Remember, there are no guarantees in human relationships, and people have the right to change their minds without having to explain or justify their decisions. We can never fully understand the complex chemistry, thoughts, beliefs, and emotions that go into being in love, and we must learn to accept when this has ended. Letting go is the most appropriate act of love in this case.

### I'm looking for the right formula for love.

There is so much information these days in books, magazines, and online dating sites about finding the perfect mate. They will give a checklist of compatibility items to make the process seem very well thought out and logical. Computer dating services are based on the assumption that a machine can more accurately determine what is right for us than our own hearts. After all, think of all the times your heart has been wrong!

The reality is that your heart was never wrong; it just needed to make certain mistakes to learn the truth. Read the personal ads in the paper sometime. See how many people list their perceived qualities as well as the qualities they are looking for/expect in a serious, long-term relationship. What if they get exactly what they ask for? Do they think the sparks will start flying?

Remember that a formula for romantic success will often fail to include individual biases, misconceptions, personal baggage, and past experiences. So many variables exist that the formula will likely result in an incorrect and irreproducible answer. Only the human heart and mind are designed to make decisions where human emotions are involved. This takes time and patience really getting to know the other person. And there should be a "gut feeling" of attraction, admiration, and excitement that is organic and drives you toward getting closer. I once asked Nobel-prize-winning scientist Dr. Linus Pauling what he thought about the new (at the time) advances in in vitro fertilization at a seminar when I was a student at Stanford. He said, "I still prefer the old-fashioned way of doing it." Funny guy, but he recognized the value of sex and human bonding. Don't look for a formula. Go out and live the best life you can. Make yourself available to the possibility of a romantic encounter. The old-fashioned way of meeting and courting is still the most fun.

*Saying I'm sorry means I've lost the argument and hurt my pride.*
Many human problems and relationships could be fixed with the simple words, "I'm sorry; I was wrong." But many, because of a sense of pride or concern about "losing face," will stubbornly stick by their mistakes and refuse to accept fault. They will insist they are right, even if it means a close friend or family member will no longer talk to them. If you are like this, you should stop to examine the advantages of not being the one to say "I'm sorry." Sure, maybe your pride was protected, and you may even be convinced that you are totally in the right. But, as James Taylor sings, "Whatchya gonna do with your foolish pride when you're all by yourself alone?" Or even more pointedly, as radio's Tony Grant asks, "Would you rather be right or loved?"

What good comes from insisting that your pride be spared at any expense? Saying you're sorry does not mean you have lost the argument; it means you have adjusted your position and changed your standpoint. It means that you take responsibility for your part of the misunderstanding or conflict. That's called being a mature grown-up, and people will only love and admire you more for acting like one.

How many of Dr. Phil's shows are really about two people who refuse to say they're sorry? After a common-sense lecture about "just getting along," they're sobbing and hugging and forgiving. What happened there? Dr. Phil gave them permission to say "I'm sorry," which is something that neither was willing to give themselves. This shows the power of a respected therapist in negotiating a truce and finding the common ground so that a relationship can get back on a healthy footing.

*I'll eventually find happiness if I keep looking for it.*
The problem with happiness is that it disappears every time you start looking for it. In truth, happiness is both a choice and a way of life. Happiness is truly an inside job. It is not something that is delivered to your door or even given to the winning lottery ticket holder. It is something that must be developed over time through consistently healthy life choices. Choosing friends and relationships wisely is

of primary importance. After this, we should strive to better ourselves, not only in our work and professional careers but also how we behave in our personal and family lives. By making healthy, positive choices in all aspects of our lives, we are preparing ourselves for a life of contentment—free from anxiety, worry, frustration, resentment, regret, and disappointment.

### *I'm unforgivable.*

A basic misconception of many anxiety sufferers is that others view them harshly and scrutinize them with the hope of finding some fault or defect. In reality, most people want to stand up for the underdog and give those who have failed or fallen a second chance. On the one hand, we all tend to feel better about our own lives when we focus on the problems of others. But, at the same time, we also want to give others a break, because we know we could easily be in the same boat. People want to forgive and accommodate, but you must be open and trusting enough to let them.

***TOOL:** Again, look at the items you checked above in the three sections on life, success/work/money, and love and relationships. What attitude or beliefs do you identify that could or should be changed to a healthier, alternative view? Enter these answers into the section provided in your personal anxiety assessment plan. You will be allotting time every day in your personal daily planner to review these attitudes and reinforce your corrected viewpoints.

# CHAPTER 9

## Toolbox Compartment Number Six: Mind-Body Tools

These are tools that work through the brain and central nervous system to trigger the relaxation response, including biofeedback, hypnotherapy, guided imagery/visualization, and meditation. It also includes tools that influence the senses that are integral parts of the mind, such as aromatherapy, light therapy, music and sound therapy.

## Meditation

Meditation has deep roots in spiritual expression and prayer. Meditative practices are taught as a path to self-realization and a deeper understanding of God in most religions. In meditative prayer, the goal is to be still and know God or to become cognizant of the eternal truths and the interconnectedness of all life. To do this, the individual must find a point of inner calm and quiet that allows him or her to let go of the awareness of the physical being and internal psychic dialogues.

Practitioners of many faiths around the world believe that only through meditation do we clear our minds of the clutter that keeps us from experiencing peace, comfort, and joy. However, the techniques of meditation do not require religious beliefs or spiritual aspirations. Through meditation, we become naturally inclined to treat ourselves and each other with greater compassion, whether or not it is set within a religious context.

Most of the people who learn meditation do so because of the beneficial effects on stress and anxiety. Stress hormones have been shown to decrease during meditation and remain stabilized for some time afterward. This translates directly into a reduction of anxiety and a nervous system that is not as vulnerable to the fear response that is triggered by anxiety. Other psychological benefits attributed to meditation include decreased depression, irritability, and moodiness; improved learning and memory; increased self-actualization; increased energy and sense of vitality; increased happiness; and overall emotional stability.

By simple definition, meditation is engagement in contemplation. The mind is trained to focus inward on a single form or idea, to the exclusion of all other forms, thoughts and ideas. The aspirant attempts to minimize perceptions through the senses—such as feeling, seeing, and hearing.

The goal of meditation is to quiet the mind and disconnect it from the constant barrage of external and internal stimulation. In studies on yoga, Zen Buddhism, and Transcendental Meditation, scientists have come to the conclusion that meditation is a "wakeful, hypo-metabolic state." They found that, during meditation, both the heart rate and the rate of respiration are slowed; the rate of metabolism is slowed as confirmed by decreased oxygen consumption and carbon dioxide output; there is an increase in the calm "alpha rhythm" brain waves as seen on EEG recordings; and the skin resistance to electrical stimulation is increased (indicating increased tolerance to external stimuli).

Recall for a moment our natural fight-or-flight mechanism of dealing with stressful situations. Brain neurotransmitters, like norepinephrine and dopamine, are activated, as well as our adrenal gland output of adrenalin and cortisol, all due to input from the sympathetic nervous system. This activation causes a decrease in brain alpha waves and an increase in the stimulating beta waves as the brain prepares to flee on foot or stand and fight. In our modern lives, such a fearful or violent reaction is rarely helpful or necessary. These instinctive defense-alarm reactions often do not serve our cause well and would be best replaced by more calm and serene reactions of equanimity and tolerance. Such desirable reactions of nonaggression and peaceful attitude are generated through meditation.

There are four components of the relaxation response that are also common to most practices of meditation and prayer:

1. The first component is a *quiet environment*. There is a reason why monasteries are located in desolate, far-away places, why nature mystics meditate in tranquil outdoor settings, and why many Hindu saints and Buddhist monks live a solitary life high in the mountains. Meditation involves both quieting our internal noise as well as external distractions.
2. The second component is an *object on which to focus our thoughts*. It may be a thinking of a word, listening to the tone of a bell or repeated chant, or gazing at a symbol. These are to help us block out other thoughts that might distract us.
3. The third component is a *passive attitude*. This means you do not care about how well you are doing with your meditation session. Moreover, you should ignore and not try to analyze any thoughts or perceptions; just let them pass in and out of your consciousness. Just as when you are falling asleep, let you mind relax and not have to work at anything.
4. The fourth component is a *comfortable position*. You should find a position you can hold comfortably for at least twenty minutes. A sitting position is recommended. At first, it may seem to take effort to maintain this posture, but if you continue to practice on a daily basis, the position will become easier to maintain as your body strengthens. Although lying down is most comfortable, it may lead you to fall asleep, which is not the desired state of mind.

Dr. Herbert Benson of Harvard University developed some recommendations based on his studies of meditation and the relaxation response. He suggests you choose a technique that you feel comfortable with, and he reminds us that the relaxation response can be elicited by many different techniques, all of which (and more) are covered in this book. They include the following:

- Meditation
- Meditative prayer

- Autogenic training
- Sensory deprivation flotation tank
- Progressive muscular relaxation
- Jogging
- Swimming
- Lamaze breathing exercises
- Yoga
- Tai chi
- Chi kung
- Knitting, crocheting, and other repetitive, relaxing activities

Evoking the relaxation response is no mystery. We have already experienced this trancelike state many times, such as when we are engrossed in our favorite TV show or movie. In this state, we may forget what time it is or fail to hear our spouse calling our names for the tenth time. Remember, these are the two basic steps required:

Step one. Focus on a chosen word, phrase, object, or sound. The repeated word could be from nature, humanity, or religion, such as "one," "ocean," "earth," "moon," "love," "peace," "calm," and so on. The sound could be a fountain, a gong, or the repetition of a sung tone or chant. The object could be a symbol, a plant, a cross, or some other item of special meaning.

Step two. Maintain a passive attitude, ignoring everyday intrusive thoughts without irritability or concern. Recognize them and let them go, turning your attention back to your meditative focus point in step one.

In performing the above, Dr. Benson reminds us to relax our muscles, close our eyes, sit quietly in a comfortable position, breathe slowly and naturally from the diaphragm, continue for ten to twenty minutes, and practice this technique once or twice every day.

*TOOL:* Practice daily meditation. Even if you have only ten minutes first thing in the morning before you exercise, on your lunch break, or when you get home in the evening, meditation will have significant benefit to your emotional outlook if you make it a part of your daily life. Below is a simple meditation technique that can be done just about anywhere:

- First, dedicate a room in your house or a deck or garden in your yard (if the weather cooperates) to practice your daily meditation. If a room is not available, then use a corner of the room; if that is not possible, then designate at least a special chair or cushion used only for meditation. You may also want to create a meditative space by wrapping yourself in a comfortable cloth garment. Turn off all phones, electronic devises, and any other possible distractions.
- Choose a specific time of day to meditate and be consistent with this time.
- Sit in a relaxed position with a straight back to help avoid slouching. This may seem uncomfortable at first, but as your muscles strengthen over time, you'll be able to hold this position longer and avoid back problems.

- Begin your meditation with the awareness of a single breath. Think of nothing but the sensation of the air slowly and completely filling your lungs, then experience your chest wall relaxing as the air is released in a slow and controlled expiration.
- Now take several slow "awareness breaths," letting go of past problems and future worries, moving yourself closer and closer to the present moment. Be aware of how your body feels and let go of any muscle tension except for that which allows good posture.
- If you find your attention wandering, it may be helpful to focus on a single word, phrase, or name repeated over and over. Choose one word or name for the inhalation and another for the exhalation phase. For instance, for those with religious beliefs, it may be helpful to choose words that reflect your faith. Those of the Jewish faith may, for instance, say "Sh'ma" during the inhalation and "Yisrael" during the exhalation. Similarly, "God" and "love" or "Jesus" and "Savior" may be meaningful to a Christian, "Allah" and "great" to a Muslim, "Hare" and "Krishna" to a Hindu, and so on. In truth, any name or word that holds meaning for you is equally useful to focus your concentration and attention. Some people prefer a tone during the exhalation, sung softly or hummed, using the utterance: "Ommm."
- Continue this practice over and over, letting your focus shift away from your breathing and body to your tone, word, or name.
- Remember, the purpose of the practice of meditation is to let go of our own thoughts and awareness by letting the conscious mind relax and take a break. It is not a "trying" but an "allowing." As the mind and body are encouraged to relaxed, our deeper self is free to experience a natural awakening.
- When you are ready to conclude your meditation session, release your focus on the word, name, or tone and end the process just as you began, by noticing each breath and how your body feels. Then take a deep breath and slowly open your eyes. Take a few moments to gently stretch your arms and legs.

I recommend that people memorize the above script and know beforehand how they are going to approach their meditations. With practice, there is less and less to remember, and the steps will proceed as natural stages in a single meditative process.

A regular, daily practice of even five or ten minutes is better than no meditation at all. Over time, you will enjoy longer sessions of twenty to thirty minutes. Don't worry if you find your distracting thoughts are sometimes intruding into your meditation. This does not mean you are doing anything wrong. Recognize the thought, let it go, and return your focus back to the meditation. As Ted Falcon, a Jewish rabbi, wrote, "Meditation is not a competition; it is a learning process and a practice—you will learn more about how your mind works, and you will experience the quiet spaces behind your thoughts. You will find the meaning in the doing."

*TOOL: To learn more about meditation options that fit your situation, you may want to visit these websites:
www.tm.org
www.learningmeditation.com

## Imagery/Visualization/Self-Hypnosis

Imagery has been considered a healing tool in virtually all of the world's cultures and is an integral part of many religions. Navajo Indians, for example, practiced an elaborate form of imagery that encouraged the subject to "see" himself as healthy. Ancient Egyptians and Greeks, including Aristotle and Hippocrates, believed that images release spirits in the brain that arouse the heart and other parts of the body. They also found that strong images of a particular disease were enough to cause its symptoms.

### The Basics of Imagery

Imagery is a technique that anyone can learn. The main factor in determining success is practice: the more you put in the time and discipline, the more you will reap the benefits of mind control through imagery. Most proponents suggest that you practice imagery for fifteen to twenty minutes every day. As you become more skilled, you will be able to spend less time and still get the same results. Think of it as learning a new foreign language; you need to put in the time up front, and then it gets easier.

Imagery is more effective if you choose images that are meaningful to you. The more powerful, "real," and personal your images, the more they will be able to rewire your anxiety centers and unlearn anxious memories. Major cancer centers use imagery techniques with consistent success as an adjuvant therapy in combating malignant cells. One exercise is to ask cancer patients to imagine their healthy cells as being strong, plump, and undamaged—like a bunch of juicy grapes. Then imagine the cancer cells as dried up, sick, weak raisins. Now imagine your immune system as a cleansing wind that sweeps away the lighter raisins and leaves the grapes unharmed.

Kids who are more into video-game technology are told to imagine their immune systems as silver laser bullets shot from space ships that annihilate the helpless low-tech tumor cells.

Other experts recommend personifying your condition so that you can reason with it. This technique also gives you a chance to gain some insights from your condition. If you are suffering from headaches, for example, imagine that there is a gremlin standing on your shoulders digging his thumbs into your temples. Talk to your gremlin and ask him why he is there and what you need to do to get him to release the pressure. He might "talk" to you about your poor sleep patterns, junk food diet, uncontrolled work stress, and low exercise level. If you listen, there's a good chance he will reward you by letting up on the pain level.

### Step-By-Step Imagery

Imagery works best when it is used in conjunction with a relaxation technique. When your physical body is relaxed, you can give your mind the freedom to daydream. Meditation, progressive relaxation, and yoga are the most common relaxation techniques used with imagery.

Loosen your clothing, take off your shoes, and sit in a comfortable position on a chair or pillow. Dim the lights or close your eyes. Take in a few deep breaths. Picture yourself descending an imaginary staircase. With each step, notice that you feel more and more relaxed.

When you feel relaxed, imagine a place you would like to spend some peaceful quiet time. It could be a beach, a mountain, a monastery, or the shore of a serene lake or waterfall you enjoyed in childhood.

Try to go into this scene each time you practice your imagery. Make sure your scene has special meaning to you and that you feel safe and secure here. No one can find you or hurt you. If you feel this way, it will make you more receptive to other images.

Once you feel comfortable in your special place, gradually direct your mind toward the problem or fear that you're concerned about. Let your mind create images as you think about this concern. Try to let the images become more vivid and in focus, but don't worry if they fade in and out at times. If several images come to mind, choose one and stick with it for that session.

Your images may take different forms, sensations, sounds, smells, or colors. Let your mind find the images that reflect your emotions. Don't expect great revelations or insights to strike you; just allow your mind to rest and do its daydreaming. Let yourself loiter in your thoughts.

At the end of each session, spend some time imagining that your problem is completely resolved. Take a few deep breaths and picture yourself reclimbing the imaginary staircase and gradually becoming aware of your surroundings. Open your eyes, stretch, smile, and go on with your day.

*TOOL: See if guided imagery is a skill you would like to learn. Find out more at www.academyforguidedimagery.com

## Autogenic Exercises

Autogenic training helps to shift your anxiety centers from the fight-or-flight stress response to a calming of mind and body. The following exercise uses autogenic training to help you relax and manage stress. This exercise is very easy to do, and it works.

1. Concentrate on the extremities of your body: your arms, legs, feet, and hands. Feel them getting heavy. Repeat to yourself, over and over again, "My left arm is heavy, my right arm is heavy, my left leg is heavy, my right leg is heavy." Then, "My arms and legs are heavy."
2. Concentrate on the extremities of your body and feel them getting warmer. Repeat to yourself, over and over again, "My arms and legs are warm." Say it until you feel the warmth flowing into your extremities.
3. Now concentrate on your pulse rate. Feel it beating calmly. Repeat to yourself, over and over again, "My pulse is calm and regular." Say it until you feel your heart rate slowing and beating softer.
4. Concentrate on your breathing. Listen to your breaths coming slowly and regularly. Repeat to yourself, over and over, "My breathing is calm and regular."
5. Concentrate on your solar plexus (the area of your upper abdomen and breastbone). Feel it getting warmer. Repeat to yourself, over and over again, "My solar plexus is warm."
6. Lastly concentrate on your forehead. Feel it getting cooler and cooler. Repeat to yourself, over and over, "My forehead is cool."

After experiencing the above sensations of heaviness, warmth, calm heartbeat and respirations, more warmth, and then coolness, take a few moments to enjoy your state of calm and take some slow, deep breaths. When you have done this exercise many times, you will be able to do it fully in just a few minutes.

*TOOL: If you are a person who is "body aware" and who focuses on bodily functions and sensations like the rhythm of your heartbeat and breathing or the tension in your muscles, then autogenic exercises may be natural for you!

## Self-Hypnosis

Hypnotherapy has been used to overcome phobias, such as the fear of flying, injections, and spiders, and has also proven helpful with performance fear, such as fear of examinations, making public speeches, and sporting contests. It can also help as a daily program for those with general anxiety.

Imagery and self-hypnosis are beneficial for the treatment of stress. They have been shown to effectively increase brain chemicals that have a tranquilizing effect, lowering blood pressure, heart rate, and anxiety levels. Emotive imagery and visualization are especially helpful to the treatment of phobic disorders and are used by a variety of practitioners, including biofeedback therapists, hypnotherapists, psychotherapists, and holistic practitioners. The basic technique is that the patient is guided by the therapist to imagine the anxiety-provoking phobia while at the same time learning how to relax. Biofeedback may be used to measure the degree of relaxation and progress of the patient.

Visualization techniques involve teaching people how to quiet their minds, focus, and use imagery to imagine a successful result. This has been used very effectively in professional athletes to enhance performance and consistency. A golfer may imagine the perfect swing and practice it repeatedly in her mind while breathing calmly and learning to relax and focus. When it comes time to hit the ball, her mind is in a focused, familiar, and calm space. An example of a self-hypnosis technique that uses visualization and imagery is as follows:

- Sit comfortably with your arms and legs uncrossed.
- Take deep breaths and relax slowly from head to toe, feeling waves of relaxation washing over you. Let your eyes close gently.
- Take yourself to a place that contains a feared situation. Visualize your fear in an objective way. Be an observer, disassociated from the event that is taking place.
- Imagine yourself performing a particular task with great ease and comfort. If you have a fear of social gatherings, imagine being the life of the party, able to converse with a variety of people from varying backgrounds. If you fear distraction while swinging a golf club, imagine yourself maintaining perfect focus on the ball throughout your perfect swing. If you fear birds, imagine yourself walking among a flock of pigeons unruffled.
- Complete the activity in your mind, being thoroughly satisfied with your performance and interpersonal skills.
- Give yourself positive affirmations that you are capable and worthy, and slowly open your eyes.

*TOOL: For better performance in sports or to help overcome a phobia, learn more at the following websites:
www.hypnos.info
www.bcx.net/hypnosis
http://biocentrix.com

## Positive Affirmations and Relaxation Exercises

The power of positive thinking is well established. Affirmations are an attempt to reprogram the mind. They are not lies that we tell ourselves to cover the truth but are corrections to an overly critical and judgmental attitude. Negative thinking always stems from a deep wound in our psyche. The only way to truly heal this wound is to look at it unflinchingly and accept it—no, embrace it. When we treat our wounds and shortcomings with love and acceptance and see the wisdom of our pain and suffering as part of a grand design beyond our comprehension, then the healing process has begun.

Rather than repeating meaningless affirmations that you don't truly feel on an emotional level, I recommend you seek a life-affirming mind-set in combination with any number of relaxation techniques. Below is a simple, five-step exercise for developing a positive mind-set:

1. Relax. First off, invoke the relaxation response by any number of methods: deep breathing, yoga, rhythmic exercise, meditation, self-hypnosis, etc. Be silent and completely relaxed. Be your natural self and let your mind float freely.
2. Be grateful. Say a simple expression of gratitude. Give thanks for all of life, including your disappointments and failures, for they may be your greatest gifts in the larger scheme of things. Have faith that there is meaning in your suffering, illness, and pain, and be thankful for it. Read more about the power of gratitude in the last chapter of this book.
3. Affirm the truth. Admit the truth to yourself. See yourself as you truly are. Acknowledge your weaknesses, mistakes, flaws, and your dark and ugly sides. Then throw away any judgment or feelings of guilt or regret. Look at your strengths and think of what you can do to build on them. Accept all aspects of yourself as a necessary part of the growing processes. Affirm that you have a desire to find purpose, meaning, and happiness in your life, and that you seek a positive road to this end. Acknowledge that you can achieve this without harming the rights or happiness of others.
4. Set your goals. Focus on your intention. See clearly what you would like your life to be. See the financial success you would like to have. See the healthy and fit body in the mirror. See yourself having the right person in your life and being happy with your career. If you cannot visualize your goals and intentions, they cannot happen. No one will walk up and give you your dream; you have to see it first and then move in that direction.
5. Take action. "Moving in that direction" means to take action. Nothing happens if we stay in a relaxed, dreamlike state. Put in the effort and energy and be persistent. Face your problems and find solutions to the obstacles that stand in your way. Don't let negative thinking or doubts deter or discourage you.

*TOOL: Consider one or more of the following tools: meditation, visualization and imagery, self-hypnosis, autogenic exercises, or affirmations. Deep breathing, progressive relaxation exercises, yoga, and prayer may have similar results in eliciting the relaxation response. The trick is to choose a technique that appeals to you and practice it daily.

## Biofeedback

Biofeedback operates on the principle that we all possess the innate ability to exert control over the automatic functions of our body through training of the mind. A variety of instruments that monitor various body systems are used to train us to use and develop our mind-body connections to control anxiety and panic symptoms. The electromyogram (EMG) measures muscle tension. Two electronic sensors are placed over the muscle to be monitored. Biofeedback practitioners will most commonly use the glabellar and frontalis muscles in the forehead, the massater muscle of the jaw, and the trapezius muscle in the neck and upper back. In anxiety and stress management, the EMG is used to promote relaxation in muscles that have become tense in response to stress. In what is known as the *body-mind connection*, the relaxation of the body leads to a more relaxed and positive state of mind. The EMG works by transforming the tension signals in the muscles into a light or sound signal so you can hear or see your muscle activity. Once you are made aware of the degree of tension, your mind can learn how to allow relaxation to occur.

**Temperature biofeedback** uses a device that monitors skin temperature. Usually the sensor is placed on your hand or foot. During anxiety and stress, skin temperature drops as blood is redirected to the muscles and internal organs. Learning to redirect blood back to the skin will help abort the anxiety episode and allow the relaxation response to take over.

**Galvanic skin response (GSR) or electrodermal response** measure electrical conduction in the skin. A very slight electrical current (unnoticeable to you) is run through your skin. The machine measures changes in the salt and water of your sweat gland ducts. The more emotionally aroused you are, the more active your sweat glands are and the greater the electrical conductivity of your skin. The GSR is effective in treating phobias, anxiety, and excessive sweating. It is also used in the lie-detection test. Athletes can use this technique to prepare for competition—making sure they are not too anxious and to calm the pregame jitters.

The **EEG** monitors brain-wave activity. The brain emits many electrical signals of various frequencies. A few of the frequencies that have been classified are beta (awake), alpha (calm relaxation/daydreaming), theta (light sleep), and delta (deep sleep).

Learning to enhance and amplify alpha waves through biofeedback helps achieve a more relaxed state without having to take a medication.

William Barton, PhD, a long-time practitioner of biofeedback technology in the Bay Area, has helped many resolve their phobias through a variety of simple-yet-effective strategies. For instance, to help a patient get over a fear of traveling through tunnels, he teaches him or her how to use the GSR apparatus. The basic GSR device attaches to the person's fingertips and is able to detect minute amounts of perspiration on the skin. The tenser you are, the more perspiration is measured, and the machine emits a buzzing noise. As you become calm, the perspiration, and also the buzzing noise, diminishes. Dr. Barton accompanies the patient on a number of sessions involving driving through tunnels. The patient is instructed to practice relaxation techniques that reduce the buzzing noise while traversing the tunnel. Once the patient figures out how to do it with the help of the machine, he or she can then often accomplish relaxation and abort an anxiety attack without the help of the machine.

Once a reasonable level of success and confidence has been achieved, Dr. Barton allows the patient to "solo" (that is, drive through the tunnel alone). As discussed earlier, emotional learning can occur only when we realize we can do it all by ourselves without the help of a drug, a machine, or another person by our side. Only this deep realization both consciously and subconsciously allows true healing and long-lasting recovery from phobias. For most phobias, ten to fifteen sessions of biofeedback are all that is necessary to achieve significant results. You can visit Dr. Barton's website at www.biobill.org.

*TOOL: Consider getting a personal biofeedback device to teach yourself the relaxation response or for use in graded desensitization exercises. Follow the URLs below to learn more about affordable personal biofeedback instruments for sports performance and desensitization from phobic fears.
   www.wilddivine.com
   www.stens-biofeedback.com
   www.lifematters.com

## Aromatherapy

Aromatherapy means "treatment using scents." It is a holistic treatment using pleasant-smelling botanical oils to care for the body and improve the state of mind. Rose, lemon, lavender, and peppermint are common essential oils that may be added to a bath, massaged into the skin, inhaled directly, or diffused to scent an entire room. Aromatherapy may be used to energize, stimulate, and invigorate—or to relax, calm, and prepare for sleep. They are most commonly used to reduce anxiety and promote relaxation. When inhaled, they work on the brain and nervous system through direct stimulation of the olfactory nerve, which is evolutionarily the oldest and most primitive of our cranial nerves. The olfactory nerve has direct connections with the hypothalamus and limbic areas, including the amygdala, which are the seat of our emotional response.

The essential oils are aromatic essences extracted from plants, including flowers, leaves, bark, fruits, grasses, and seeds, with distinctive therapeutic, psychological, and physiological properties. There are about 150 essential oils. To get the maximum benefit, the oils should be made from raw, pure, natural products. Aromatherapy is one of the fastest-growing fields in alternative medicine. It is widely used in private homes, clinics, and hospitals for a variety of applications such as pain relief for women in labor, relieving the side effects of chemotherapy in cancer patients, and improving the energy and vigor in patients who have suffered heart attacks. Aromatherapy is also slowly making its way into mainstream society. In Japan, engineers and architects are incorporating aroma systems into new buildings. In one such application, the scent of lavender and rosemary is pumped into the customer area to calm those waiting in line, while the perfumes from lemon and eucalyptus are used behind the counters to keep the clerks alert and responsive.

*TOOL: Find a local scent shop or aromatherapy practitioner to experiment with how your emotions are influenced by this modality. We have also provided some URLs below where you can do your exploring online.
   www.aromaweb.com
   www.naha.org
   www.aworldofaromatherapy.com

## Light Therapy
### Overview
One of the most useful applications of light therapy is in the treatment of seasonal affective disorder. Although how light therapy works is not fully understood, there is a large body of scientific evidence vouching for its effectiveness.

Our daily rhythms are affected by the availability of the natural sunlight. Many of us work in artificially lit buildings and do not get enough natural light. Most artificial lighting cannot replace the natural light. The reason for this is that indoor lighting is not of sufficient intensity to affect the hormonal mechanisms that control our bodily rhythms. Intensity of light is measured in a unit called *lux*, an abbreviation for *lumens per square meter*. Lumens are a measure of brightness and light output, not energy use (like watts). The intensity of light at any point is determined not only by the strength of the illumination source but also by how far it is from the source. The electric light used in most homes and workplaces rarely exceeds five hundred lux. A sunny afternoon could be as much as one hundred thousand lux, and even the cloudiest day is rarely below ten thousand lux. Researchers have discovered that light of at least 2,500 lux is necessary to suppress melatonin production in humans. Most of the bright-light therapy uses five thousand lux light (ten thousand lux preferred.)

The artificial light we use indoors is not of sufficient intensity to suppress melatonin and to correct the circadian rhythm. Night-shift workers and people who live in Arctic climates are usually exposed to light levels of only fifty lux. Light specialists believe this "malillumination" may be at the heart of many common disorders, including fatigue, depression, skin problems, suppressed immune function, and, of course, sleep disorders.

Light therapy for seasonal affective disorder and circadian-rhythm disorders involves sending visible light through the eyes so that it reaches, and triggers, the pineal gland. There are several different forms of light therapy in use today; the oldest is sunlight itself. The sun is the ultimate source of full-spectrum light, which means it contains all possible wavelengths of light, from infrared to ultraviolet (UV). Generally speaking, light therapy involves the use of equipment that sheds either full or bright-white light.

In most cases, the purpose of light therapy is to increase the amount of light to which we would otherwise not be exposed. Bright-light therapy consists of looking at special broad-spectrum bright lights from one-half to three hours a day, generally in the early-morning hours. One should not stare directly into the lights because of possible eye damage.

In the mid-1980s, bright-light therapy (phototherapy) was the treatment of choice for seasonal affective disorder. But many people found it difficult to allocate the four hours recommended daily. Researchers conducted additional studies to determine how to optimize light therapy. They found that similar benefits can be obtained from a morning-only therapy, effectively slashing the time by half. Later, by increasing the brightness or the intensity of the lights used, the therapy time was further reduced. For example, ten-thousand-lux light required only thirty minutes of exposure per day to improve the symptoms of seasonal affective disorder. Seasonal affective disorder symptoms typically begin to lift about a week after the start of phototherapy. But they return shortly after discontinuing the treatment. As a result, people with seasonal affective disorder in the northern hemisphere should be exposed to bright light daily from October through April.

### Light Therapy for Bulimia
This binge/purge eating disorder typically develops in women during their teenage or early-adult years. Bulimia is an anxiety disorder that is often successfully treated with the use of SSRI drugs. If bulimia remains untreated, it can cause serious physical and emotional problems. Some researchers have noted that bulimic episodes seem to occur most frequently in winter, leading to speculation that the illness might have a seasonal component. People who undergo high-intensity light therapy show a remarkable improvement in this condition.

### Full-Spectrum versus Broad-Spectrum Light
**Full lightbulbs** are made to try to imitate natural sunlight, and like sunlight, they also produce UV rays. Typically, full bulbs have a color-rendering index (CRI) of ninety or above (outdoor light has a CRI of one hundred) and a Kelvin temperature of five thousand or above. Full light is described as having a purplish or a bluish cast. Most light-box companies using full lightbulbs now block these UV rays through their diffuser screens. Make sure they do before purchasing their products.

**Broad-spectrum light boxes** are often described as being as close to full as you can get without the UV rays. Typically, they have a CRI of around eighty-two and a Kelvin temperature of around 4200. Broad-spectrum lightbulbs are described as being a pure white light. Most light-box companies use a broad-spectrum lightbulb so that there is no danger of UV rays.

***TOOL:** If you believe you suffer from a condition caused by light deprivation, try light therapy. Some URLs to get you started are below.
www.fullspectrumsolutions.com
www.alaskanorthernlights.com

## Music/Sound Therapy
### Overview
We have all used music as a mood changer and stress reliever. We have playlists on our smartphones and iPods to facilitate relaxation for a massage, to jack us up before a sports competition, to get us in the mood for sex, to console us when we're going through a breakup, and to calm us as we fall asleep. Many experts suggest that it is the rhythm of the music or the beat that has the calming effect on us, although we may not be consciously aware of this. They point out that when we were still developing in the womb, we were probably influenced by the rhythm of our mother's heartbeat. We respond to soothing music later in life, perhaps because we associate it with the safe, relaxing, and protective environment of a simpler time.

Music and rhythm influences have been shown to help us control our brain-wave patterns to enhance productivity and creativity in wakeful states, to help induce relaxation and deep meditative states, and to potentially even guide us toward deeper sleep cycles.

- **Gamma brain waves (thirty-eight to forty-two cycles per second, or hertz):** These are the highest frequency (fastest) brain waves that have the lowest amplitude (smallest variation up and down). They are associated with the formation of ideas, linguistic processing, memory processing, and attention. Gamma waves have been shown to disappear during deep sleep. A 2005 *Scientific American* article discussed gamma waves in conjunction with long-term Buddhist meditation practitioners. It was found that experienced meditators demonstrated self-induced, high-amplitude gamma oscillations during meditation. Researchers also noted that their gamma activity differed significantly from those in a control group, both during the meditation and before they even began. Interestingly enough, a similarly strong presence of gamma waves throughout the cortex has been observed in musicians listening to music, compared with a control group of nonmusicians.

- **Beta brain waves (twelve to thirty-eight hertz):** Beta brain waves dominate our normal waking state of consciousness when attention is directed toward cognitive tasks and the outside world. Beta is a "fast" activity, present when we are alert, attentive, engaged in problem solving, using judgment, making decisions, and in focused mental activity.
- **Alpha brain waves (eight to twelve hertz):** These are the slower waves that are the gateway to deeper states of consciousness. Creativity, problem solving, meditation, and relaxation all are commonly supported in the alpha brain-wave state. Also, the brain produces higher levels of natural melatonin in alpha rhythm, so those who experience more of this pattern often sleep better.
- **Theta brain waves (three to eight hertz):** Theta brain waves occur most often in sleep but are also dominant in deep meditation. They act as a gateway to learning and memory. In theta rhythm, our senses are withdrawn from the external world and focused on signals originating from within. It is that twilight state that we normally experience only fleetingly as we wake up or drift off to sleep. In theta, we are in a dream—vivid imagery, intuition, and information beyond our normal conscious awareness. It's where we hold our "stuff," such as our fears, troubled histories, and nightmares.
- **Delta brain waves (half to three hertz):** Delta brain waves are slow, low frequency, and deeply penetrating, like a drumbeat. They are generated in deepest meditation and dreamless sleep. Delta waves suspend awareness. Healing and regeneration are thought to be stimulated in this state, and that is why deep, restorative sleep is so essential to the healing process.

Science has shown that various tonal structures and instrumental arrangements are powerful influences on brain waves and activation in the emotional brain. Different instrumental tones affect us in different and predictable ways. In extensive studies on how any given piece of music affects the physiological response system, some unexpected things were discovered. Many of the so-called meditation and relaxation recordings actually produced adverse brain waves on the EEG, as harsh as hard rock and heavy metal. Surprisingly, many selections of Celtic, Native American, and other music containing loud drums or freely improvisational flute were extremely soothing. The most profound finding was that any music performed live, even if discordant or played at moderately loud volumes, had a very beneficial response. Whenever the proper sounds for an individual were experienced, remarkable right-left brain hemisphere synchronization occurred. The normal voltage-spiking pattern coming from the brain changed to a smooth sinusoidal wave form, and the usual voltage differential equalized. There were also clear benefits when the music was being created and played by the individual being studied.

## Conti Music

Tom and Chris Conti are a husband-wife team who have composed and published extensively in the field of music therapy. They are the founders of Emotion Transitional Music Therapy (ETMT), which helps people reduce stress and anxiety in a natural way. As they explain it, "All of our albums contain music-therapy techniques, such as bilateral stimulation, brain-wave entrainment, and isochronic tones. These techniques by themselves are not always good sounding, to say the least! But, nonetheless, they are very effective, so we made it our challenge to incorporate them into our music without compromising the music or the effectiveness of the therapeutic benefits while finding a good balance. ETMT does exactly that but also uses the different techniques within every track where most appropriate, considering chord progressions and their effect on emotions."

I have reviewed two of Tom and Chris Conti's most popular albums, *Modern Classics* and *Sound Therapy for the Senses*. *Modern Classics* represents their classical music-therapy album, whereas *Sound Therapy for the Senses* is ambient based and, at the same time, it is the album that incorporates the most advanced music-therapy techniques. Both are well conceived and very helpful. From their website, Chris and Tom explain their journey:

> Together, we have been composing and publishing Relaxing Music, Therapeutic Music, EMDR Music, Guided Meditation and Sound Therapy albums for professional and private use. We have long been aware that listening to music can alleviate stress from life in general, as well as stress from PTSD (Post Traumatic Stress Disorder), anxiety, panic disorders, phobias, and many other mental health problems.
>
> We know that life is not always easy. There are many different problems that arise from living in our world today. Besides traumatic events and mental disorders, much of the difficulties stem from the amount of stress we all have throughout the day that is never fully expunged from the body.
>
> Music has long been a tool to relax and destress. All of our projects incorporate different healing and sound therapy techniques within the music. We have received many reviews over the past few years and have gradually made changes with every new album.

You can learn more and order their music-therapy products at https://www.contimusic.com.

## Music for Stress Reduction

Among the many stress-reducing effects of music is the increase in deep breathing that occurs when we are focused on a particular piece. Brain serotonin levels also begin to increase. Music has been found to reduce the heart rate and increase core body temperature, an indication of the relaxation response. Stress is reduced by background music, even if we are unaware it is playing. This is why music is often piped into elevators or telephones when you are on hold. Music also reduces fear and increases the pain threshold during medical procedures, and headphones and earbuds are now a common fixture in the modern dental office. Airlines offer a varied selection of music to keep passengers relaxed and distracted from their fear of flying.

Here are a few recommendations for helping you create your own music-therapy program. Remember, the same type of music does not work for everybody, because people have different tastes. The important thing is that you choose music you like.

- To wash away stress, try a twenty-minute "sound bath." Put some enjoyable, relaxing music on the stereo and lie near the speakers in a comfortable position on the floor or a couch. To help you focus and avoid distractions, it may be best to wear headphones.
- Choose music with a slow rhythm—slower than your natural heartbeat. Music with a cyclical or repeating pattern is effective for most people.
- As the music plays, imagine it flowing over you, washing away all the frustration and stress of the day. Focus on your breathing and let it slow and deepen. Focus on the silence between phrases; this keeps you from analyzing the music and makes relaxation more complete.
- If you need to be energized and stimulated due to a sense of exhaustion and fatigue, choose a more rapid, upbeat tempo you can dance or tap your foot to.
- Familiarity often helps the calming response. Choose an old favorite that you know by heart.
- Try combining exercise and imagery to your experience of music. Take a brisk walk with your favorite tunes playing on your music device. Inhale and exhale in rhythm with the music. Sing or hum if you like. Imagine yourself being taken to whatever fun and relaxing place the music is leading you.
- Listen to the sounds of nature, such as the pound of the ocean surf, the calm and quiet of a deep forest, the drone of bees, the sound of wind rushing through the grass or rustling the tree leaves, the singing of birds, the sound of a peaceful stream, or the falling of tropical rain on a canopy of jungle vegetation. If you don't have time to experience these sounds in nature, you can find recordings of them.

***TOOL:** Follow one or more of the above recommendations to treat yourself to music and sound therapy. The websites below specialize in sound therapy and relaxation sounds, beats, and music. Learn how to guide your brain-wave patterns through sound and music.
   https://transparentcorp.com
   www.brainsync.com
   www.global-journey.com

And, again, try an album by Tom and Chris Conti. They have put a lot of thought and expertise into their therapeutic products: https://www.contimusic.com.

## Humor Therapy

Laughing has been found to lower blood pressure, reduce the secretion of stress hormones from the adrenal glands, increase oxygen delivery to the brain and muscles, and boost immune-system elements such as the infection-fighting T cells, disease-fighting gamma-interferon proteins, and antibody-producing

B cells. Laughing also triggers endorphin release from the brain, which reduces pain and produces a general sense of well being. Unfortunately, we often lose our sense of humor when we are anxious or depressed—just the time it is most needed. Laughter is a powerful tool to quiet the mind's overactive thought processes, thereby clearing the head of obsessive patterns of worry and fear.

***TOOL:** Practice humor! Rent a funny movie or stand-up comedy act. Hang out with your funniest, most upbeat friends. Think back on funny memories from your past. Start creating a scrapbook of things you find particularly hilarious. Try making others laugh by creating or learning jokes or funny stories (just don't laugh at your own jokes). Buy *The New Yorker* magazine just for its cartoons! Start by reading a few jokes at these sites:

    www.ahajokes.com
    www.the-jokes.com
    I'll bet you will find other sites that are funny—let me know!

# CHAPTER 10

## Toolbox Compartment Number Seven: Body-Mind Tools

These tools work through the peripheral nervous system to feed back and inhibit the anxiety centers of the central nervous system, which, in turn, elicits the relaxation response. These tools include EMDR, sensory-deprivation flotation tanks, deep-breathing exercises, reflexology, yoga, massage therapy, acupuncture, and hydrotherapy.

### Eye Movement Desensitization and Reprocessing

EMDR really works quickly to calm anxiety and improve a depressed state. In fact, I am somewhat surprised at the high rate of positive response from my patients who have tried it. Therapist Francine Shapiro developed and studied this form of psychotherapy for individuals with PTSD.

According to Shapiro, a traumatic or distressing experience overwhelms normal cognitive and neurobiological coping mechanisms. The memory and associated stimuli are inadequately processed and stored in an isolated memory network. The goal of EMDR therapy is to process these distressing memories, reducing their lingering effects and allowing patients to develop more adaptive coping mechanisms. Patients are asked to recall traumas while following the therapist's hand movements.

Shapiro noted that when a patient was experiencing a disturbing thought, his or her eyes would be rapidly moving involuntarily. She noted that if this eye movement was brought under voluntary control while remembering the traumatic thought, that anxiety caused by the trauma was reduced. The use of EMDR was originally developed to treat adults with PTSD but was soon found to be effective in children who had experienced trauma.

Although EMDR has been rated as an effective treatment for PTSD based on a review of thirty-three randomized controlled studies, it has not been shown to be superior to trauma-focused, cognitive-behavioral therapy; stress-management treatments; or exposure-desensitization therapy. A comparative study showed EMDR to be of similar efficacy to other exposure therapies and more effective than SSRI medications for PTSD. Shapiro proposed that a number of different processes underlie the benefits of EMDR and that the eye movement component contributed to the therapy's effectiveness by evoking neurological and physiological changes that aid in the processing of the traumatic memories being treated. Another perspective is that the eye movements are an unnecessary epiphenomenon, and EMDR is simply another form of desensitization therapy. In any case, I have had patients vouch for its effectiveness in recovering from the trauma of rape, life-threatening car accidents, and traumatic cancer-related diagnoses and treatments.

**\*TOOL:** If you suffer from PTSD, consider an EMDR therapist. Visit the websites below to learn more about the EMDR process, which involves eight separate stages.
https://www.emdr.com/what-is-emdr/
www.emdr.com

## Sensory-Deprivation Flotation Tank

Sensory-deprivation flotation tanks are filled with warm Epsom salt water and magnesium to achieve a density that allows the body to float in a neutral state of complete musculoskeletal relaxation. With stimulation from the sensations in our body and external factors of sound and sight removed, amazing changes happen in the mind that have been shown to be helpful for both physical tension and emotional turmoil.

There are seven theories as to why flotation in a sensory-deprivation flotation tank has a healing, calming, and regenerative effect on the mind, body, and spirit.

1. Escaping gravity. During our waking hours, it is estimated that up to 90 percent of our nervous system activity is expended on adjusting to gravitational forces. Gravity also is at the root of many degenerative conditions involving our joints and intervertebral discs. Being released from the effects of gravity on our feet, knees, backs, neck, and muscles, as well as freeing the nervous system of its busy work fighting gravity, allows the brain to use vast amounts of freed space to deal with matters of mind and spirit and to develop enhanced awareness of internal states.
2. Brain waves. We often talk about the relaxation response and activating alpha and theta brain-wave patterns in accomplishing this. In fact, many of the tools in the ATP are designed to help the brain make this transition. Beyond the relaxation of alpha waves are the slower, theta brain waves, which are accompanied by vivid memories, free association, sudden insights, creative inspiration, and feeling of serenity and oneness with the universe. Most of the time we are asleep during theta-wave activity. But occasionally, you will have a theta experience while conscious. You may have experienced this in a warm shower in a quiet, candlelit bathroom. You let your mind wander during some downtime. Suddenly, a fantastic idea or solution to a problem you have been struggling with comes into your conscious mind, and you wonder how it got there. Theta wave is a mysterious, elusive state, potentially highly productive and enlightening, but experimenters have had a difficult time studying it, and it is hard to maintain, since people tend to fall asleep once they begin to generate theta waves. Zen monks who have practiced meditation for more than twenty years are able to move in and out of theta states during their meditations. But studies at Texas A&M and the University of Colorado have shown flotation in sensory deprivation to enhance theta-wave experiences. Floaters quickly enter the theta state while remaining awake, consciously aware of all the vivid imagery and creative thoughts that

pass through their minds, and after getting out of the flotation environment, floaters continue to generate larger amounts of creativity-promoting theta waves for up to three weeks.

3. The right hemisphere takes over. The two hemispheres of the brain have different functions. The left hemisphere excels at detail. It processes information that requires fine resolution and operates analytically by splitting or dissection. The right hemisphere, on the other hand, is good at putting all the pieces together. It operates by pattern recognition—visually, intuitively, rapidly absorbing large-scale information. Just as in the sunshine of a bright day it is impossible to see the stars, so are the subtle contents of the right hemisphere usually drowned out by the noisy chattering of the dominant verbal/analytical left brain, whose qualities are the more cultivated and valued in our culture. But recent research indicates that floating increases right-brain (or minor-hemisphere) function. Floating turns off the external stimuli, plunges us into literal and figurative darkness—then suddenly the entire universe of stars and galaxies is spread out before our eyes. The right hemisphere has been released to come out and play.

4. Coordination of our three brains. The brain is sometimes looked at from an evolutionary perspective from primitive to advanced. The primitive brain, also called the *reptile brain*, resides in the brain stem and is involved in self-preservation and reproduction. Above this, in our midbrain, the amygdala, hippocampus, and basal ganglia are where emotions are processed and then filtered through the higher brain cortex, which is responsible for cognitive functions of abstract thinking, memory, intellect, language, and consciousness. While many of these three separate brains have overlapping functions, they are all quite different in chemistry, structure, action, and design. Three brains should be better than one, but unfortunately, there is often insufficient communication and coordination between the three levels. This lack of communication results in a chronic dissociation between the higher and lower brains, which can cause conflicting drives—unconscious and conscious, savage and civilized, lusty and loving, ritualistic and symbolic, and rational and verbal. There are times when the levels do act in harmony, when body and mind unite in exhilarating moments of vitality, and our actions become effortless and spontaneous. (I think this must be happening when Stephen Curry and his Golden State Warriors basketball teammates get in a rhythm.) But it's hard to predict when these perfect moments will occur. Now there is evidence that suggests that, due to heightened internal awareness and decreased physical arousal, floating increases the vertical organization of the brain, enhancing communication and harmony between the separate levels. Floating, it has been hypothesized, can provide us with peak experiences almost at will.

5. The neurotransmitter explanation. As discussed earlier, our brain runs on chemical hormones that stimulate various pathways and connectivity in the brain. These hormones influence whether we are feeling happy, anxious, depressed, shy, sleepy, or sexy. Each of us creates different amounts of these various neurotransmitters, and those who create, for example, more endorphins—natural opiates—experience more pleasure as a result of a given experience than those who create fewer endorphins. Tests indicate that floating increases the secretion of endorphins at the same time it reduces the levels of a number of stress-related neurochemicals, such as adrenaline, norepinephrine, ACTH, and cortisol—substances that can cause tension,

anxiety, and irritability. Since pregnant women produce up to eight times the normal endorphin levels, the fetus is always in a good mood. When a floater is suspended in the dense, warm solution, enclosed in darkness, body pulsing rhythmically and brain pumping out endorphins, it's possible that subconscious memories are stirred and profoundly deep associations called up. It is no coincidence that at least one commercial float center is named "The Womb Room."

6. The biofeedback explanation. Biofeedback research has shown that humans can learn to exercise conscious control over virtually every function of their minds and bodies. Processes long thought to be involuntary, such as the rhythm and amplitude of our brain waves, healing, blood pressure, the rate or force of heart contractions, respiratory rate, smooth-muscle tension, and the secretion of hormones and neurotransmitters, are now thought to be controllable. The way biofeedback machines work is by enhancing or having the ability to concentrate on a single, subtle change in the body. This change is amplified by the machine so that we are able to hold concentration on that internal signal and shut off our awareness of the external environment. This shutting off of external stimuli is exactly what the flotation environment does best—almost as if in an "organic" biofeedback machine. In the tank every physical sensation is magnified, and because there is no possibility of outside distraction, we are able to relax deeply and focus at will upon any part or system of the body. Progressive relaxation discussed above involves focusing on one body part at a time and consciously sending relaxation signals to that area. This would be much easier to accomplish in a flotation tank.

7. The homeostasis explanation. The human body has an exquisitely sensitive self-monitoring and self-regulating system that is constantly working to maintain the body in homeostasis—an optimal state of balance, harmony, equilibrium, and stability. Considered in these terms, we can define stress as a disruption of our internal equilibrium, a disturbance of our natural homeostasis. Research now indicates that many of floating's most powerful effects come from its tendency to return the body to a state of homeostasis. When we view the mind and body as a single system, it becomes clear that external stimuli are constantly militating against the system's equilibrium—every noise, every degree of temperature above or below the body's optimal level, every encounter with other people, and everything we see and feel can disrupt our homeostasis. But when we enter the tank, we abruptly stop making constant adjustments to outer stimuli. Since there are no external threats, no pressures to adapt to outside events, the system can devote all its energies to restoring itself. The normal state, of course, is health, vigor, enthusiasm, and a sense of pleasure in being alive.

*TOOL:* Seek out a well-established flotation tank facility near where you live or work. Try a few sessions and see how you feel. Is there a stabilizing effect? Are you sleeping better? Are your headaches or body pains reduced? Write down any benefits you feel and decide if this should be part of an ongoing program. I have a patient who was so sure that this was helpful for her stress and anxiety that she bought a flotation tank and installed it in her home! I live near Fairfax, California, and recommend you visit Conscious Drift to try this out if you're in the Bay Area:

http://consciousdrift.com

If you live in another location, search the Internet for a flotation tank facility near you.

## Deep Breathing
### Overview

Most people think your body knows how to breathe instinctively. After all, who thinks about how they are breathing in the normal course of the day? But breathing is more than what it appears on the surface: a way to get oxygen into the lungs and expel carbon dioxide waste product. Breathing is also a powerful tool in the relaxation response. When we are under stress or feel anxiety, we tend to hold our breaths or breathe shallowly. This is the opposite of what our body and mind needs and leads to an improper balance of gases in the bloodstream, increasing anxiety, sense of panic, muscle tension, moodiness, headaches, and fatigue. Luckily, we can learn good breathing habits and use them alone or with other relaxation-response techniques whenever anxiety strikes.

It is helpful to understand the anatomy and physiology of breathing and have an image in your mind of what is going on each time you take a breath. As you inhale, the nose and upper throat warms and humidifies the air. To help create a vacuum in the chest so that air will flow deep into the lungs, your diaphragm muscle, the large, flat muscle that separates the chest from the abdomen, expands and lowers. Because the lungs are attached to this muscle as well as to the inside of the rib cage and chest wall, they have no option but to expand, creating a negative pressure void that the air then rushes in to fill ("nature abhors a vacuum").

Inside the lungs are the big pipes, the trachea and bronchi, which lead to smaller and smaller branches (bronchial tubes) and finally to tiny sacs called *alveoli* where the actual exchange of gases takes place. These elastic sacs expand and contract as you breathe in and out. They are rich in small blood vessels called *capillaries* that have very thin membranes across which oxygen can enter and carbon dioxide can leave the bloodstream. The oxygenated blood is then transported to the heart through the pulmonary veins (this is the only place in the body where veins carry oxygenated blood). The heart then pumps the oxygen-rich blood to the brain and body. In the small capillaries of the body tissues, oxygen is delivered to each cell, and carbon dioxide is collected and transported back to the lungs. This continuous method of gas exchange and transportation is fundamental to the sustenance of life.

There are two basic ways to breathe: from your chest or from your diaphragm. Let's review each of these.

Chest breathing is common when you feel stress or anxiety. In this pattern, you expand your chest wall and raise your shoulders to create the negative pressure vacuum in the lungs. You are more likely to breathe this way if you are overweight, as your belly fat restricts the ability of your diaphragm to expand. Chest breathers do not have deep, relaxed, effective breathing. At times, they will breathe too fast and shallow, and at other times they will hold their breath. Chest breathing requires some level of conscious input, so it is tied to your emotions. Because this pattern of breathing results in an erratic and overall decrease in oxygen delivery to your organs, muscles, and brain, the result is increased heart rate, muscle tension, and fatigue and a sense of stress and anxiety.

Diaphragmatic or abdominal breathing is the breathing pattern of the newborn and the sleeping adult. When we turn off our conscious minds, our respiratory centers deep in the brainstem restore our natural breathing pattern. Inhaled air is drawn deep into the lungs and then released effortlessly as our diaphragm muscle contracts and expands. This pattern is even and unrestricted. The result is an efficient delivery of oxygen so each cell can do its job.

Because diaphragmatic breathing is the breathing of a relaxed, nonanxious person, using this pattern tells the brain that we are in a relaxed state. This is how the body-mind feedback loop works: if the body tells the mind we are relaxed, the mind will feel a calming influence on the emotions.

Try the following simple experiment. First pull in your stomach as if you are wearing a very tight pair of pants or a girdle. Actually grab your belly with both hands and hold in your gut. Now take in a deep breath. Notice that you are forced to expand your upper chest and raise your shoulders to get the breath in. Even then, you will feel that the bottom of your lungs does not fully inflate. Now whistle or sing a single tone as you exhale, seeing how long you can sustain this tone. Time yourself with the second hand of a clock or watch. Then let your belly relax. Actually push it out like you are eight months pregnant. Take in another full, deep breath. This time you should feel the air go deep into the lower lungs. You should also notice that you can hold the tone significantly longer.

As a wind instrument player (bassoon), I remember my teacher focusing on my breathing to make sure I was using my diaphragm, because this would allow me more air to sustain a longer phrase in the music.

## Practicing Deep Breathing

To make deep abdominal (diaphragmatic) breathing come naturally, you may need to spend time practicing with proper technique. After a while, you will be able to use this technique to invoke the relaxation response spontaneously and effortlessly. Follow the steps below until you feel you fully understand deep breathing:

- Lie down on the floor on a mat or blanket. Place your back flat against the floor with your legs slightly apart and your arms away from your body with the palms facing up. Your toes should fall outward comfortably.
- Close your eyes and scan your body for any tension. Allow any areas of tension in your face, shoulders, arms, or legs to release.
- Take slow, deep breaths in through your nose. Let the air escape through your mouth as you exhale. Pay attention to which part of your body rises and falls as you breathe. Is it your chest, abdomen, or a combination of the two?
- Place your left hand on your abdomen and your right hand on your chest. As you breathe in, feel your left hand being actively pushed up by your abdomen. Feel your chest moving less actively and only to follow your abdominal movements.
- Take slow, deep breaths in through your nose, filling your entire lungs, and then let the air out through relaxed, slightly open lips. Make a quiet, relaxing sound like an afternoon breeze as you gently exhale. Make sure your jaw, tongue, and mouth are relaxed.
- Continue this method of breathing for five to ten minutes, making sure your abdomen is expanding more actively than your chest and that your chest is just going along for the ride. Continue to scan your body for tension.

**\*TOOL:** Once you feel comfortable with deep breathing while lying down, try a session while sitting in a comfortable chair or in a car, bus, or train. Notice you can choose to breathe deeply anytime, even in a stressful board meeting. Whenever you feel tension or anxiety, shift your attention to your breathing.

Slow it down with deep abdominal inhalations through your nose and relaxed exhalations through your mouth. Scan your body and release areas of tension. This is the simplest and fastest way to trigger the relaxation response.

## Controlled Breathing

Learning this technique is essential for those who experience panic attacks, particularly those with agoraphobia and panic disorder. When we feel panic, we tend to forget to exhale fully. Instead, we gasp, trying to take in more air and holding the air already in our lungs. The result is a quick and shallow breathing pattern that is the hallmark of hyperventilation. In the state of hyperventilation, we are actually getting less oxygen in as we breathe more of the carbon dioxide out. This leads to an imbalance of blood gases that triggers more panic and a sense of suffocation, dizziness, nausea, and sweats and may even lead to a fainting spell.

Controlled breathing first emphasizes the need to exhale fully to be able to breathe properly. It then relies on a conscious switch from our anxiety-driven abnormal breathing to a counting technique that forces you to pace yourself and takes the focus away from the catastrophic thinking of a panic attack. When you feel a panic attack coming on, follow these steps:

- Exhale first. At the first sign of catastrophic thinking ("What if I have a panic attack right here in public?"), open your mouth and let you lungs empty completely.
- Inhale and exhale through your nose, as this will tend to slow down your breathing. An alternative method is to breathe in through your mouth and then exhale with pursed lips as if you are blowing out through a straw.
- As you inhale, make sure your abdomen expands before your chest, counting "one…two…three." Pause for a second, then breathe out counting "one…two…three…four." Make sure that the exhalation phase is longer than the inhalation.
- After you feel comfortable with the last step, try to slow your breathing even more by counting "one…two…three…four" while breathing in and "one…two…three…four…five" during exhalation.

*TOOL: Practice controlled breathing for five minutes a day. If you invest a little time in it on a regular basis, it will be there for you when you need it. You can even make a recording that forces you to breathe in the proper rhythm and timing. First, figure out what your resting breathing rate is by sitting quietly and counting how many times you breathe in and out in a three-minute period. Divide this number by three for the rate per minute. If your rate is more than ten breaths per minute, make a twelve-breaths-per-minute recording. If it is less than ten breaths per minute, make an eight-breaths-per-minute recording:

- Twelve breaths per minute: Using a watch with a second hand, make a recording by saying one word every second for five minutes in the following manner: "in—in—out—out—pause, in—in—out—out—pause." This gives two seconds of inhalation and two seconds of exhalation, followed by a one-second pause. With one breathing cycle taking five seconds, you will be on pace for twelve breaths per minute.

- Eight breaths per minute: Using a watch with a second hand, make a recording by saying one word every second for five minutes in the following manner: "in—in—in—out—out—out—pause." This seven-second breathing cycle will put you close to eight breaths per minute.

## Progressive Relaxation Exercises

In this section, you will learn to:

- Differentiate between when your muscles are tensed and when they are relaxed
- Progressively release tension in all the muscles of your body
- Use this relaxation technique quickly during times of stress or anxiety

## A Little History

Edmund Jacobson, a Chicago physician, described the technique of deep-muscle relaxation in his 1929 book, *Progressive Relaxation*. He claimed that this technique required no imagination, willpower, or suggestion to work. Dr. Jacobson believed that we hold tension in our bodies in response to anxiety-provoking thoughts and stressful situations, and this in turn increases our psychological experience of anxiety and stress. He felt that one cannot be physically relaxed and psychologically anxious at the same moment, and anxious emotions could be stopped purely by successful relaxation of all the muscles in the body. Today, our understanding of the body-mind response validates Dr. Jacobson's premise, but at the time, his beliefs on progressive relaxation were met with skepticism and even ridicule.

## Basic Instructions

Progressive relaxation can generally be mastered in one to two weeks by committing to only two fifteen-minute sessions per day. Think about how many hours of your life you have spent in a state of anxiety. What if you could learn a new technique in four to six hours that would successfully negate and block those anxious emotions? Progressive relaxation may be the ticket. It has been found effective for treating related conditions as well, such as insomnia, depression, fatigue, irritable bowel syndrome, muscle pain and spasms, high blood pressure, mild phobias, and stuttering.

Progressive relaxation may be practiced lying down or sitting in a comfortable chair. Each muscle group will be tensed from five to seven seconds and then allowed to relax for twenty to thirty seconds. Each muscle group is tensed and relaxed two to five times, with difficult, tight muscles requiring more repetitions. As the muscle group is allowed to relax, it may be helpful to say to yourself a guiding phrase, such as:

"Let it all go…"
"Relaxing deeper and deeper…"
"Tension is melting away…"
"Calm and rested…"
"Let go more and more…"

Spend time memorizing the progressive relaxation script before each session so that you can relax and close your eyes as you focus on each muscle group individually. Each muscle should be allowed to relax fully and immediately, causing sudden limpness like a rag doll. Don't try to slowly and gradually relax the muscle, as this method causes sustained tension. When tensing, do not tighten to the point of pain or discomfort. This is especially true in the neck, back, and feet, where excessive tensing can cause a spasm or cramp. While it is best to learn progressive relaxation in a quiet place with comfortable attire, over time you will be able to employ this technique anytime and anywhere you feel anxiety or stress.

## Progressive Relaxation

Find a comfortable position in a quiet room free from distractions or interruptions. Wear comfortable, loose clothing and take off your shoes. Now follow the following script:

- Begin relaxing by taking in several slow, deep abdominal breaths. Imagine all your worries and concerns leaving your body as you exhale.
- Let your entire body go completely limp and relaxed as you continue your deep, slow breathing pattern.
- With everything relaxed, tighten only your fists, bending them back at the wrists. Feel the tension in your hands and forearms for five to seven seconds. Now relax and feel the looseness in your hands and forearms for twenty to thirty seconds. Notice the contrast between the tensed and relaxed states. Repeat the same exercise at least one more time.
- Now bend your elbows and make your biceps tense up. Make the biceps muscle form a tight ball for five to seven seconds, followed by complete relaxation for twenty to thirty seconds. Feel the blood flowing into the resting muscle group.
- Next, wrinkle your forehead by raising your eyebrows as high as possible. Feel the tension to your scalp and ears. Then let your entire forehead and scalp relax and go smooth.
- Now frown down with your forehead, creating full tension between your eyes and creating deep frown lines (skip this part if you just got Botox!). Then allow your brow to become smooth and relaxed again.
- Squeeze your eyes closed tight and then allow them to relax. Let them remain closed gently and comfortably.
- Alternatively smile and frown using all the muscles of your cheeks, then let go of all the tension. Give it a full twenty seconds.
- Push your tongue into the inside of each cheek and the roof of your mouth, then relax.
- Bring your chin down toward your chest and hold a few seconds. Then lay your head back and gently roll in all the way to each side. Then bring it back to a central position and feel complete relaxation.
- Shrug your shoulders up toward your ears and then pull them downward as if someone is pulling on your hands. Bring them back to a comfortable position and feel all the tension melt away.
- Scan your entire head, neck, and shoulders and upper body. Let go of every last bit of tension in your face, jaw, throat, scalp, forehead, neck, shoulders, and arms.

- Now feel your stomach as you check your abdominal breathing. Your hand should be pushed up by each breath. Breathe in deeply and slowly, feeling the air expanding your lungs, then let the air out by relaxing the entire chest and abdomen.
- Arch your back by putting your feet flat on the ground with knees bent and lifting your hips off the floor. Don't strain. Hold the position for several seconds, feeling the tension in your low back. Bring your hips back down and relax. Do this one or two more times, relaxing more and more. Then let your legs go straight and relaxed with the feet pointing slightly outward.
- Tighten your buttocks and thighs, then relax and feel the difference. Repeat a few more times.
- Straighten and tense your legs with your toes curled downward. Hold and then relax. Now straighten and tense your legs with your toes bent upward. Hold and relax.
- Scan your chest, abdomen, back, hips, thighs, calves, ankles, and feet. Let go of every last bit of tension.
- Feel deeper and deeper relaxation throughout your entire body. As you breathe slowly and deeply, experience the warmth and heaviness of complete relaxation. Everything is loose, heavy, and comfortable. Focus on slow, deep abdominal breathing and notice that your entire body is loose and relaxed, calm and rested.

## The Shortened Version

Once you have mastered the basic technique above, it will be easy to employ an abbreviated version when you need to quickly reduce your anxiety and stress. This is accomplished by tensing whole groups of muscles simultaneously for five seconds and relaxing for ten seconds. The shortened version can be done in any position but should be practiced sitting, as this is more convenient. Below is a sample script to follow; you may write a script that works best for your body:

- Curl both fists and tighten your biceps and forearms by bending your arms like a body builder in competition. Now relax.
- Gently roll your head clockwise three times and counterclockwise three times, pulling the muscles in your neck up and tight. To ensure proper technique, think of your chin tracing a large circle in the air. The bottom of the circle is when your chin meets your chest, and the top of the circle is when your neck is fully extended and your nose is straight in the air. Now relax the neck for ten seconds.
- Wrinkle your face while hunching your shoulders. Get all the muscles in the face involved as you squint, smile, frown, scrunch your nose, and raise your eyebrows. Raise the shoulders all the way up and then pull them all the way down. Then take ten seconds to completely let go of all the upper-body tension.
- Arch your back and shoulders as you take a deep breath in while holding your abdomen. Feel the abdomen and chest expand fully three times and then relax.
- Straighten your legs while tightening your thighs, buttocks, and calves, curling your toes first downward and then pointing them upward. Now relax.
- Scan your entire body as you allow your breathing to slow into a deep diaphragmatic pattern. Let go of all tension as your body goes limp and relaxes deeply into the chair.

**\*TOOL:** Spend fifteen minutes twice a day for one to two weeks doing the longer version of progressive relaxation. After that, use the shorter version from time to time during the day. If you have a private cubicle or office space, take a five-minute break every hour during a stressful day to perform the shorter version.

## Yoga

"Yoga is best known as a set of physical practices that include gentle stretches, breathing practices, and progressive relaxation. These physical practices are intended to ready the body and mind for meditation as well as for a meditative perspective on life. These meditative practices also follow a sequence. First developed is the capacity to withdraw the senses from focus on the outer world, then, the capacity to concentrate on a meditative subject—a candle flame, a sacred or uplifting word or image, or the movement of the breath. Finally, and for most of us only occasionally, the concentration leads into a wordless and timeless experience of inner peace. The yoga masters describe various subtleties among these states of inner peace, but most of us, at best, achieve moments of this experience only from time to time."

—Michael Lerner, *Choices in Healing*

Before participating in the mind-body therapy known as *yoga*, one should appreciate the underlying philosophy of this practice. Practitioners of the belief system teach that we are naturally programmed to search for happiness but that most of us settle for the watered-down version of brief and transient pleasures. The *yogis*, as the teachers are called, believe that in some stage of our spiritual evolution over many lifetimes we will become dissatisfied with these temporary pleasures and begin a quest for eternal bliss. Methods to achieve this were developed and perfected by the yogis thousands of years ago. They consider that the laws of nature are so designed that we have no choice but to evolve. In the early stages, nature uses pain as the main mechanism for this spiritual evolution (both physical and emotional). Eventually, we find that the things of the world—like money, sex, relationships, drugs and alcohol, or fame, for example—do not produce happiness or a sense of purpose, and we start looking more deeply into life for answers. In the later stages of spiritual evolution, we no longer need suffering to spur us on. Each stage of progress produces such an enhanced sense of peace and happiness that we look forward to the next level. Instead of anxiety and pain, reward becomes the prime motivator. Yoga philosophy is so comprehensive that it deals with every aspect of life and delves into the nature of reality itself.

In practice, yoga is an applied science of the mind and body. It is derived from the Hindu Vedas (scriptures). Practice and study of it helps to bring about a natural balance of body and mind so that a healthy state can manifest itself. Yoga itself does not create health; rather, it creates an internal environment that allows the individual to come to his or her own state of dynamic balance, or health. Basically, yoga teaches that a healthy person is a harmoniously integrated unit of body, mind, and spirit. Therefore, good health requires a simple, natural diet; exercise in fresh air; a serene and untroubled mind; and an awareness that man's deepest and highest self is an image of the spirit of God. For some, yoga becomes a philosophy that offers instruction and insight, but for others, yoga is equally satisfying as a physical exercise alone.

For our purposes, one of the most beneficial applications of yoga is in relieving stress, anxiety, and fatigue and its use in relaxation therapy. Indra Devi, author of many books on yoga, suggests that with yoga: "You will be able to enjoy better sleep, a happier disposition, a clearer and calmer mind. You will learn how to build up your health and protect yourself against colds, fevers, constipation, headaches, fatigue, and other troubles. You will know what to do in order to remain youthful, vital and alert, regardless of your calendar age." The clinical benefits have been well documented in myriad respected studies on such divergent conditions as asthma, premenstrual tension, heart disease, obesity, diabetes, alcoholism, tobacco addiction, stomach ulcers, high blood pressure, back pain, arthritis, and the development of cancer. In addition, yoga has been found to improve cognitive mental performance and reduce subjective complaints of fatigue, depression, anxiety, and stress. Yoga can be a ready and enjoyable tool to combat any number of physical or emotional ailments. Whether to help you keep on track with a diet plan, quit a cigarette habit, improve concentration while studying or taking an exam, or melt away stressful emotions, yoga is an ancient, tried-and-true remedy.

Yoga's benefits for anxiety conditions are many. It combats the physical and mental exhaustion caused by stress that makes us more vulnerable to anxious emotions. The goal of yoga is fearless, confident living. Its aim is to replace worry and pessimism with a "yea-saying" appreciation of life and acceptance of the universe. Fear is replaced by the positive mental values of poise, contentedness, patience, assurance, and faith in life. By recurrent, regular efforts to reduce tension through yoga exercises, we reduce our tendency toward emotional stress derived from fear. The long-range benefit of yoga is the ability to live a relaxed-yet-agile life and to gain a peaceful perspective.

Spiritual perspective has long been recognized as a useful tool in reducing vulnerability to stress, anxiety, and depression. We will discuss this more extensively in the last compartment of the toolbox. Yoga may help develop a stronger spiritual framework to fall back on at times of stress and disappointment, no matter what your individual religious beliefs might be.

***TOOL:** Practice yoga. There are many different forms and schools of yoga, including sivananda, Ashtanga, hatha, bikram, iyengar, pranayama, and many others. There is also a plethora of yoga studios and yoga retreats to choose from. You may be surprised to find a regular yoga class that meets very near your home or work. A wide variety of yoga books and videos is available through Amazon. Here are some websites to get you started:

www.yogasite.com
www.yoga.com
www.yogadirectory.com

## Tai Chi

Tai chi is sometimes described as a combination of moving yoga and meditation. It involves practicing breathing exercises and performing a series of slow, graceful, flowing postures (also called *poses*) simultaneously. The postures consist of movements that are said to improve body awareness and enhance strength and coordination. Many people who practice tai chi say that they feel more peaceful and relaxed after a session.

Like with many other Eastern techniques, tai chi is thought to redirect and augment the flow of vital energy, or chi. Practitioners believe that a person can help improve the flow of chi throughout the body and improve health by practicing tai chi exercises.

There are many different styles of tai chi, including chen, hao (or wu shi), hu lei, sun, yang, and zhao bao. The different types vary in intensity and focus. For example, sun style is known for its fast footwork. The low-impact movements of hao style can be practiced by people who are elderly or have special needs. In general, though, practicing tai chi improves strength, flexibility, and respiratory function.

You have many choices when it comes to choosing a tai chi workout. Many fitness centers and YMCAs offer tai chi classes, and many tai chi instructors also offer private classes. You may also want to try a tai chi video—there are several excellent videos just for beginners. Instructional websites, CDs, and books are also available to help you learn more about tai chi.

Before you start your first tai chi workout, you should dress comfortably so you can move and stretch easily. Shorts or tights and a T-shirt or tank top are great choices. Because tai chi is a martial art, some people who practice it wear a martial arts training uniform. Tai chi is considered completely nonviolent and is usually practiced barefoot or in comfortable socks and sneakers.

During a tai chi class, you'll participate in forms. Each form is a series of movements performed in a specific order. The poses that make up the forms sometimes have visually descriptive names, such as "white crane spreads its wings" and "grasp sparrow's tail."

Here are a few poses that you might encounter if you take a tai chi class or watch a tai chi video:

- Hands strum the lute: Slightly bend your left knee and place your weight on your left foot. Move your right foot and place it behind your left foot. Shift your weight back to your right foot and extend the left foot forward with the toes up. At the same time, slightly turn your body to the right, raise your left hand until it is level with your nose, and move your right hand horizontally to the inside of your left elbow. Direct your eyes toward the left hand.
- Needle at the bottom of the sea: Shift your weight to your left foot and move your right foot, placing your toes behind your left foot and shifting your full weight to the right foot. Extend your left foot forward. Turn your body to the right, and circle your right arm to the right while moving your left hand to the front of your face. Look at the floor in front of your feet.
- Closing form: With your feet at hips' distance apart, extend both arms forward while turning your palms down. Lower both of your arms slowly to the sides of your hips and look straight forward. Shift your weight to the right foot and move your left foot toward the right foot.

Before you begin any type of exercise program, it's always a good idea to talk to your doctor, especially if you have a health problem. But unlike many other sports, tai chi is based on continuous, flowing, low-impact movements, so it's a good workout choice for just about anyone. Is your schedule jam packed with school, work, and social activities? Here are a few tips for fitting in fitness and staying motivated:

- Try a little at a time. If you don't have time to go through an entire form in your regular tai chi routine, try breaking up your workout into ten- or fifteen-minute chunks. During a long study session, reward yourself every hour with a few minutes of tai chi.
- Go slow. Keep your expectations reasonable. Don't expect to be able to do all the moves perfectly right away. Masters of tai chi work on the forms continuously for years to perfect them.

As you become more proficient, remember: the postures of tai chi are meant to be done slowly for best results.
- Do what works for you. Some people have more success working out in the morning before the day's activities sidetrack them; others find that a nighttime workout helps them unwind before hitting the sack. Experiment with working out at different times of the day, and find the time that fits your schedule and energy level best.
- Get in a group. If you find that you aren't motivated to work out by yourself, attend a few tai chi classes and get social. An added benefit of taking a class is that the teacher can help you with your form and give you tips to make your workout more effective and enjoyable.
- Keep boredom at bay. Many people who work out regularly say that preventing boredom is the key to consistent workouts. If you've been doing tai chi every day and are feeling a little blah, mix it up with walking, a yoga video, or a new outdoor location.

There's one caution about starting a tai chi routine, though: once you start, you might not be able to stop!

*TOOL: Learn more about tai chi by finding a class in your area. You can read more about tai chi and search for a teacher in your area by visiting these websites:
www.tai-chi.com
www.patiencetaichi.com
www.taichichih.org

## Reflexology

Reflexology works on the principle that pressure points in the hands and feet trigger improved energy flow and thereby improve functioning of the body, organs, and mind. These pressure points are mapped out on the hands and feet and are based on the same meridian system as acupuncture and emotional freedom therapy (EFT). Typically, a practitioner will ask you questions about your symptomatology and may perform an exam of your pulse, oral cavity, or other aspects of your physical health. They may then perform acupressure point massage manually or with various instruments to influence the energy field responsible for your particular complaint or ailment.

*TOOL: Try a session of reflexology. If you are ticklish or a tenderfoot, this may not be the tool for you. If not, it can't hurt. Reflexology is usually not covered under insurance, although it doesn't hurt to ask, especially if the practitioner is practicing in a licensed physical therapy clinic. You can learn more by visiting the Reflexology Association of America at www.reflexology-usa.org.

## Massage Therapy

Massage therapy is the systematized manipulation of soft tissues for the purpose of normalizing them. Practitioners use a variety of physical methods, including applying fixed or movable pressure, holding, or causing stretching or movement to the body. Therapists primarily use their hands but may also use their forearms, elbows, or feet. Touch is the core ingredient of massage and combines science and art. Practitioners learn a variety of massage techniques and use their sense of touch to determine the right amount of pressure to be applied to each person, while also locating areas of tension and other soft-tissue problems. Touch also conveys a sense of caring, an important component in the healing relationship. When muscles are overworked or when emotional stress causes tension to build up in the muscles, waste products such as lactic acid can accumulate, causing soreness, stiffness, and even spasm. Massage improves circulation, increases blood flow, brings fresh oxygen to the tissues, and helps speed the elimination of waste products. This speeds healing after injury and can enhance recovery from disease. Therapeutic massage can be used to promote well being and increase self-esteem while boosting the circulation and immune systems. It has been incorporated into many health systems, and different massage techniques have been developed and integrated into various complementary therapies.

***TOOL:** Find a local massage therapist or spa that specializes in a variety of massage styles. Tell them you are looking for a relaxing (not necessarily painful) experience. Over time, your therapist will figure out the right amount of pressure to apply to reduce the tension in your muscles while letting your mind drift into a state of relaxation and even sleep. Starting with the Swedish-style or hot-stone relaxation massage is recommended. Massage therapy of this type (as opposed to deep tissue or Rolfing) can be enjoyed as often as you like (or can afford!). Some insurances pay for massage therapy; you might want to ask your doctor to give you a referral. Get more information at https://www.massagebook.com.

## Acupuncture/Chi Kung

Acupuncture and chi kung are alternative practices rooted in Eastern mysticism that are often met with skepticism by Western practitioners. This may be because of the many claims about healing, longevity, and disease prevention that have failed scientific scrutiny. In this discussion, we encourage you to explore these modalities purely as methods to help relieve stress. They are often used in conjunction with herbal remedies to help calm the nervous system.

Eastern medicine operates on the principle of vital energy, spelled "chi" or "qi" (pronounced "chee"), that flows along defined pathways in the body known as *meridians*. If the natural flow of energy is disrupted, then pain, illness, or anxiety can be the result. By placing fine needles into the blocked meridians, the acupuncturist restores the flow of chi so that the dysfunction is corrected. The practice of chi kung in Chinese medicine is built on the same principle of manipulating and directing vital energy for the purpose of promoting and maintaining physical and emotional health.

In the view of Chinese medicine, many illnesses are caused by blockages in these channels. Practitioners of these arts claim that by learning to recognize, use, circulate, and direct the internal energy of the human body, an individual can also connect with the energy of the universe and of the earth and learn to interact with all of nature as a whole. Through use of certain energies and techniques, they assert, chi kung can relieve pain, strengthen the body's constitution, improve intelligence, and prolong life.

Although once dismissed by Western medicine as a placebo remedy (works only as good as a sugar pill), acupuncture and chi kung have attained wider acceptance over the last fifteen years, especially after a National Institutes of Health conference concluded that "acupuncture may be useful as an adjunct treatment or an acceptable alternative" for a wide variety of conditions.

One mechanism by which acupuncture is thought to work is by releasing negative ions that accumulate in damaged muscles and can cause spasm. This reduces muscular tension and allows a body-mind relaxation to occur. In addition, acupuncture directly triggers the release of happy, pain-relieving chemicals from the brain known as *endorphins*. These proteins enable a mind-body relaxation reaction to occur simultaneously. While the meridian theory of energy flow is still not widely accepted by Western physicians, the negative ion release, blocking of neuronal "gates," and endorphin mechanisms are well-studied phenomena.

*TOOL: Try a session of acupuncture or chi kung with a reputable practitioner in your area. Let the practitioner know you are primarily interested in reducing tension, stress, and anxiety symptoms in advance, so he or she can tailor the session to your needs. If it seems to have benefit and is not uncomfortable, you may be inspired to try more sessions, maybe once or twice a week for a few weeks, just to get a better idea of its effectiveness. Here are some applicable websites:
www.nccam.nih.gov/health/acupuncture
www.chigong.com

## Emotional Freedom Techniques

Although this technique will seem awkward and downright goofy to many, it seems to have merit and a grateful following. But first, I noticed that the websites and some practitioners are overenthusiastic about the value of their technique, which may belie some insecurity about their place among other therapeutic techniques. They may make claims of success above other modalities of therapy that are unfounded. Second, I think their choice of a name is unfortunate. After all, we are not seeking to be free or emancipated from our emotions but are striving to be free from uncontrolled and unhealthy emotional imbalances and to understand how our feelings are influenced by our reactions and perceptions. Perhaps "emotional modulation therapy" or "emotional adjustment therapy" would be better (except the acronyms would be either *EMT*, which is a stressful job, or *EAT*, which isn't always a good strategy for improving emotional health). This being said, I think EFT is a useful technique for specific individual conditions. We often find by serendipity that a medication invented for one thing helps a completely different condition. It could be that EFT releases past emotional trauma though mechanisms similar to other standard experiential/desensitization therapies, rather than facilitating energy flow through meridian pathways. So with EFT, they may have stumbled upon a helpful therapy without fully understanding how it works, and who really cares, as long as it provides relief and fits your belief system?

Here are the basic premises of EFT:

- Every negative emotion we experience (anger, anxiety, frustration, grief, jealousy, fear, etc.) is the result of an energy blockage somewhere along our meridian pathways.

- As with acupuncture, energy fields in the body align themselves along meridian pathways, and these energy fields can be facilitated and "unblocked" by applying pressure to specific points along these pathways.
- By saying positive affirmations, focusing on a traumatic event or a physical symptom, or stating a specific fear or phobia while tapping on acupressure points, the energy block is relieved, allowing the negative emotions to dissipate.

Traditional psychotherapy would remind us that all negative emotions are due to our thoughts and perceptions about events, not the events themselves. EFT would say it is not even our thoughts or perceptions, but an actual physical block of energy that causes the unwanted emotions. Of course, one could argue that the negative thoughts led to a blockage of energy, and EFT is really a body-mind technique that feeds stimuli directly to the emotional centers of the brain that are remembering a specific fear or trauma. These energy signals in the brain may serve to cancel or desensitize the area of the brain where emotional memories are stored. This may then cause a rewiring of a response that had previously been wired to react in a negative way to certain thoughts, experiences, and phobic stimuli. If it works for you, that's all that matters, and I certainly see no harm in trying.

*TOOL: You can look into whether EFT sounds good to you by reading more at www.emofree.com.

## Psychodrama and Experiential Therapy

I recently saw a woman who had completed a forty-five-day inpatient program for alcohol dependence after a hospitalization for acute alcohol withdrawal. I'm always curious about the latest therapeutic techniques. She had been in many twelve-step programs and attended regular meetings. But she felt she had experienced a breakthrough with psychodrama and experiential therapy and felt more positive and confident about her sobriety than ever before. In psychodrama, patients act out traumatic events from their pasts to gain new insights and to diffuse some of the pain and discomfort of those memories. In the case of my patient, she would give others in her support group the background they needed to reenact a particularly difficult and challenging scene from her life. It was spontaneous, organic improvisation and allowed her a degree of healing.

Like psychodrama, experiential therapy encourages patients to identify and bring to the surface their hidden or subconscious emotional trauma through activities like role playing, guided imagery, the use of props, and the active participation of others in the reenactment of the unpleasant experience. As in group therapy, there is a powerful force when two or more people set about to identify and solve a problem, a healing force that is uniquely human. Like desensitization therapy, there is a benefit to being exposed to the trauma and diffusing it, even if it is done using a virtual-reality program to reenact the event. We see this in speaker's nerves, where a virtual audience is almost as effective as a real, live audience to desensitize the anxious speaker and make him or her feel confident in front of a crowd. EMDR also helped this patient above.

*TOOL: Consider these dynamic methods of therapy in a group setting.

## Hydrotherapy

Hydrotherapy is the use of water in the treatment of disease. Hydrothermal therapy additionally uses the temperature effect, as in hot baths, saunas, wraps, etc. These therapies have been used in many cultures, including those of ancient Rome, China, and Japan. The ancient Greeks made therapeutic baths a way of life. Water is also an important ingredient in the traditional Chinese and Native American healing systems. A Bavarian monk, Father Sebastian Kneipp, helped repopularize the therapeutic use of water in the nineteenth century. There are now dozens of methods that apply hydrotherapy, including mineral baths, hot and cold showers, steam therapy, wet saunas, douches, body wraps and packs, hot and cold moist compresses, sitz baths, and foot baths.

The recuperative and healing properties of hydrotherapy are based on its mechanical and thermal effects. It exploits the body's response to hot and cold stimuli, to the protracted application of heat, to pressure exerted by the water, and to the sensation it gives. The many different specialized superficial nerves then carry impulses felt in the skin deeper into the body to the spinal reflexes and to the brain, where they are instrumental in stimulating the immune system, influencing the production of stress hormones from the adrenal glands, invigorating the circulation and digestion, encouraging blood flow, and reducing pain sensitivity.

Generally, heat quiets, relaxes, and soothes the body, slowing the activity of the internal organs. Cold, in contrast, stimulates and invigorates, increasing internal activity. If you are experiencing tense muscles and anxiety, a hot shower or bath is in order. If you are feeling tired, lethargic, and stressed out, you might want to try taking a warm shower or bath followed by a short, invigorating, cold shower to help stimulate your body and mind.

***TOOL:** Try to get some more ideas on how to add hydrotherapy to your armamentarium against stress: http://www.holisticonline.com/hydrotherapy.htm.

# CHAPTER 11
## Toolbox Compartment Number Eight: Cognitive-Behavioral Therapy Tools

Cognitive therapy begins with making corrections in our thought processes. Any misperceptions or misconceptions about ourselves, others, or the world around us are challenged. We also emphasize and teach both stress and anger management, focus on assertiveness training to resolve inhibitions, as well as teaching social skills, which may be deficient in those with social phobia. For those with phobias, graded desensitization and extinction through real or virtual-reality exposure to social situations and to uncomfortable sensations is a tool that reprograms the brain to respond to stressful stimuli without triggering the anxiety response. Medical treatment to speed up desensitization is also available. This chapter is to help you get used to the ideas behind cognitive therapy, not to serve as a substitute for therapy.

## Cognitive Distortions
### Overview

Your perceptions and beliefs may be toxic and should be challenged, at first with the help of a therapist. The myths you grew up with, as well as your own misinterpretations about the scrutiny of others and your own misperceptions about internal sensations, must be countered regularly by reality and truth.

One of the core assumptions of wrong thinking, false beliefs, and irrational ideas is that things are being done to you: "That really got me upset." "He makes me nervous." "Dogs scare me." "Being lied to like that really makes me angry." In reality, nothing is done to you. Events happen in the world that are not under our control. How we react to these events, however, is under our control. If we react with unrealistic, irrational self-talk, we will get our emotions all worked up for no purpose.

Two forms of irrational self-talk are catastrophic thinking and absolute thinking. During catastrophic self-talk, we think of all the awful possibilities and come up with nightmarish interpretations of our experiences. We imagine the worst-case scenario, no matter how improbable, and let our emotions get carried away. A momentary chest pain is a life-threatening heart attack; a criticism from your supervisor means you will be fired; your spouse has to take a business trip for a week and the thought of being alone is unbearably terrible. The emotions that follow have nothing to do with your brief chest pain, supervisor's comment, or spouse's decision. They have everything to do with your own self-talk about the events. Again, the events do not cause the emotions; your self-talk determines your emotional response.

In absolute thinking, words such as "should," "must," "always," and "never" are common. This is because we believe things must be a certain way or that we must react in a certain way. If you don't live up to a certain value or standard, you feel you are bad or have failed in some way. In reality, your irrational standard is what's bad because it sets you up for unrealistic expectations of yourself and the world that can never be satisfied. Absolute thinking is sure to bring you frustration, disappointment, unhappiness, and anxiety—all for nothing.

Replacing the false beliefs and irrational thoughts with the truthful reality is the focus of cognitive therapy. While reading through this chapter, make a check mark on any thought or belief that coincides with your own thought or belief system. Be honest now, and remember that this is just for you; no one else can see.

*Cognitive distortion: I have no control.*
**Correction:** Sooner or later we must accept the reality that many things are not under our control, nor should they be. Control freaks think they can lessen their anxiety by insisting on controlling every situation. This gives them difficulty in working and living with others. On the other hand, it is useful to recognize what we can and should control. While agoraphobics wish for a life that is spontaneous and free from fear, they focus on the opposite. They focus on the limitations imposed by the fear and their failure to control the fear, resulting in a life of self-confinement. The paradox is that the more energy you expend trying to control anxiety, the more fearful you will become.

*Cognitive distortion: I'm trapped.*
**Correction:** We must practice looking at how we are free instead of how we are trapped. Dismantling a false sense of entrapment begins with your perceptions. We are only trapped if we perceive that we have no options or choices. This is rarely the case, in reality. For example, of his many imprisonments, the Indian spiritual leader Mahatma Gandhi later stated that it was during these times that his mind and heart was most free to focus on the truth. Here, perception was the difference between four cold, stone walls and the limitless universe of the mind. Similarly, if you are temporarily confined in an airplane, train, or dentist's chair, it is probably wise to stay put and let your mind wander via a good book or visions of someplace you've always wanted to go. If you're in a movie theater, reassure yourself that if you had to leave, it would be no big deal. Others will not sense your anxiety or turn their focus to you. In any case, people get up and leave a movie for a number of reasons, like to get a snack, go to the bathroom, call a friend, or just to stretch their legs. No one is inconvenienced or upset by this. Most people are subjected to the same constraints in a number of situations, but they don't feel anxious because they correctly perceive that there is no realistic danger and therefore no need to escape.

*Cognitive distortion: I am frail and vulnerable.*
**Correction:** You are what you think. In reality, it is just as easy to say, "I'm strong and a good survivor." Changing a negative into a positive thought is simply a matter of choice and repetition. All those times you told yourself you couldn't do it must now be replaced with the affirmative mind-set over and over again. In truth, we all have inner strengths and abilities equal to the tasks we are asked to complete. We are all vulnerable to things that are beyond our control. There is no guarantee of security in this world, as the survivors of 9/11 will tell you. But they will also remind you that such risks are part of life and should not be used as an excuse for living a fearful, unfulfilled life. Tapping into our inner source of resourcefulness, strength, and power is the goal of therapy.

*Cognitive distortion: Anxiety and fear are weaknesses.*
**Correction:** Many carry the misperception that if they admit their phobias and fears, others will see them as emotionally weak. But it requires bravery to rise above and overcome anxiety and fear. There is nothing more courageous than admitting and facing your fears.

*Cognitive distortion: I'm strange because I feel anxiety.*
**Correction:** Anxiety is an integral and natural part of the human experience. Anxiety is a necessary and useful emotional experience that allows adaptive, experiential learning and teaches us about ourselves. Absence of anxiety and fear is not our goal in life. However, understanding and respecting anxiety and learning the lessons it has to teach without misinterpretation is within our capability.

*Cognitive distortion: Anxiety is harmful.*
**Correction:** Anxiety is not out to kill you. Anxiety is a gift designed to protect and motivate us, not to destroy or damage us. It can only damage us if we give it more attention than it deserves. I will not go on record as saying that no one dies of an anxiety attack. Anxiety, like anger, is a strong emotion that causes strong physical responses. A person with a weak heart or untreated blood pressure could experience a fatal event during overwhelming stress or anxiety. On the other hand, only one patient death in our clinic over the past thirty years was directly linked to an anxiety attack. That means that thousands and thousands of documented anxiety attacks have caused no physical damage whatsoever. A healthy person has nothing to fear from anxiety.

*Cognitive distortion: If the anxiety lasts too long, I will die or go crazy.*
**Correction:** Anxiety and panic attacks have natural limits. Even if you do nothing, your parasympathetic nervous system will eventually counteract the anxiety attack, as it is designed to. You won't go crazy. Even if you actually faint or vomit, this will usually abort the attack very quickly. This book will recommend that you consider learning biofeedback and techniques of proper breathing to shorten your attack and regain control.

***Cognitive distortion: I'd be fine if I could just avoid the object or situation that I fear.***
**Correction:** The object of your fear is not the problem. Don't blame the phobic stimulus for your anxiety condition. If you have a phobia, it is not the object of your phobia (birds, heights, spiders, water, tunnels, bridges, social situations) that is the problem. It is how you interpret and perceive the situation or object of your anxiety that is dysfunctional and needs to be corrected.

***Cognitive distortion: I should have the strength to control my anxiety problem.***
**Correction:** The more you try to control anxiety, the more it will control you. The paradox of anxiety is that you must resign yourself and accept your anxiety to neutralize and render it powerless. Ignore it and it will go away—focus on it and it will become more acute. Have you ever noticed how hard it is to swallow a mouthful of vitamins if you concentrate on the act of swallowing rather than diverting your attention and letting them slide right down?

***Cognitive distortion: Anxiety is taking over my life.***
**Correction:** Anxiety takes what you give it. The more of your life that you give over to anxiety, the more it will take. The more you let anxiety determine your choices and make your decisions, the more limited your choices and decisions will become.

***Cognitive distortion: I can't stop an anxiety attack.***
**Correction:** Anxiety attacks will last as long as you allow them to. Fear is fuel to the fire of anxiety. The more you fear an attack and let yourself get worked up over it, or stress about when it will stop, the more it will spread and magnify. Self-hypnosis, biofeedback, and breathing exercises work by turning the mind's hypervigilant state of attention to a state of nonfocus and nonrecognition.

***Cognitive distortion: I'll get over this anxiety by avoiding the things I fear.***
**Correction:** Avoidance ensures that your anxiety problem will get worse. You can't overcome a fear by avoiding it. The less you know about your fear, the further away you are from conquering it. Avoiding exposure increases apprehension and decreases confidence. Although medication can help stabilize the nervous system, you will still need to build your self-confidence through the experience of exposure.

***Cognitive distortion: It is absolutely necessary for me to have love and approval from my peers, family, and friends.***
**Correction:** It is impossible to please all the people in your life all the time. Even close family and friends will tend to take whatever you give to them. This means you will give up more and more of what you need and want to satisfy others. Eventually you will feel that others are taking advantage of you, causing resentment and anger. But you have no one to blame but yourself. Only you can stand up for your rights

by saying no and directly asking for what you want. Get used to the fact that, even with your strongest effort and best behavior, others may choose to reject you at times. Don't let your happiness depend on the whims and fickleness of others.

*Cognitive distortion: Some people are wicked and evil and should be punished.*
**Correction:** All people have faults and unpleasant behaviors at times. They may have dysfunctional personality disorders or be devious, arrogant, or just plain selfish. They may be ignorant, racist, antisocial, or neurotic, causing them to display a wide range of inappropriate behaviors. Rather than getting upset or angry or vilifying others, recognize their faults and your own shortcomings, as well. Use their behaviors as examples of how you do not want to behave. Stand up to those who offend or abuse you, letting them know they will not have the benefit of your company unless they change their behavior.

*Cognitive distortion: It is terrible when things are not the way I expect them to be.*
**Correction:** This is known as the *spoiled child syndrome*. As soon as things don't go the way you planned, you immediately start complaining: "I should have seen this coming." "How could this be happening to me?" "This is just miserable." "You forgot the umbrella? Now I'll get all wet and catch pneumonia!" Every small situation gets turned into a big blame-a-thon, and you seem to enjoy moaning about it until everyone's day is ruined. Even *you* feel aggravated and emotionally spent. A healthy response to unexpected problems is to immediately look for positive solutions and alternative options. Give others a break and laugh it off. People will admire and respect your good nature and positive resourcefulness. Otherwise, they'll be looking for ways to avoid spending time with you.

*Cognitive distortion: External events cause our emotional problems. If everything out there in the world went well, I would not be anxious.*
**Correction:** The logical extension of this thinking is that controlling events in the world will lead to less anxiety, less sorrow, and greater happiness. But because our control over life events has limitations, especially when it comes to controlling the will and desires of others, a sense of helplessness, frustration, and chronic anxiety results. You can never truly relax because, even during good times, your thoughts of "what should I be doing to make sure everything is under control?" will be intrusive. It is much easier and possible to control your own emotional response to external events than to control the events themselves.

*Cognitive distortion: I should feel anxious about anything that is new, unknown, uncertain, unfamiliar, or potentially dangerous.*
**Correction:** I can learn to become comfortable with unfamiliar situations and places. New experiences are good for me, and I look forward to new opportunities for learning and growth that the outside world has to offer.

*Cognitive distortion: It is easier to avoid than to face most of life's problems and responsibilities.*
**Correction:** Avoiding problems and responsibilities leads to more difficulties, just as lies lead to more lies. You may know a relationship is over but delay telling the other person, hate your job but not proactively look for another, put off completing a chore that should have been done weeks ago, or tell others you'll be there when you have no intention of making good on your commitment. All these examples of avoiding responsibility will lead to aggravation and hardship, as well as hurt feelings, frustration, and anger from others.

*Cognitive distortion: I am not competent to succeed. I need something stronger or greater than myself to rely on.*
**True correction:** Constantly relying on a higher authority for answers will often undermine your true beliefs, judgment, and awareness of your individual worth. Learning to trust your feelings and instincts is more likely to empower you to make decisions that are in your best interest.

*Cognitive distortion: The past has a lot to do with determining the present.*
**Correction:** This belief causes a psychological trap in which we feel overly attached to past experiences. We then repeat past patterns of behaviors and coping strategies, which may not be appropriate for the new situation we face in the present moment. The belief that "today is the first day of the rest of your life" would apply here. Every day we start out with a clean slate. Every day we have the ability to change our behaviors and responses to life in a way that is more healthy and positive. This perspective is necessary for personal growth and gives us a sense that our lives are moving forward in a healthy direction.

*Cognitive distortion: Happiness can be achieved by doing nothing and by seeking inactivity and leisure.*
**Correction:** Many people feel retirement will finally lead to happiness by providing an endless "Club Med" where they can "exercise their right to do nothing at all." Disappointment is common when boredom and loss of direction result. Happiness is a state of mind that we must create for ourselves; it is not a place or external situation we can build and then expect happiness to be there when we arrive.

*Cognitive distortion: I am helpless and have little control over how I feel.*
**Correction:** This belief is often responsible for perpetuating anxiety and depression. It places responsibility for how we feel on external events and situations rather than on our own thought processes and interpretations of those events and situations. The truth is that we exert considerable control over our environments. We control the direction of interpersonal interactions by our behaviors and actions. This determines whether we develop a positive and supportive network of family and friends around us. We control our financial situations by decisions to be consistent and productive while saying no to negative, self-destructive thoughts and behaviors. But, most importantly, we control how we react and interpret

each life event. We *decide* whether to be angry, bitter, vengeful, irritated, or upset. We could just as easily decide to forgive, let go of hostility, and let our emotions turn toward a positive direction.

*Cognitive distortion: People are fragile and should never be hurt.*
**Correction:** Life is all about give-and-take and negotiating a balance with those around us. The belief that others are fragile leads to too much "give" and an unhealthy balance in which your needs are ignored. Lack of communication then leads to frustration and a sense of deprivation, depression, and anxiety. People are actually remarkably resilient and are able to adapt to accommodate your needs and desires as well as their own. Proper assertive communication strategies are needed to get your message across without offending others or putting them on the defensive.

*Cognitive distortion: A good relationship is built on self-sacrifice and giving.*
**Correction:** Some believe that, if they are good, considerate, and giving, their hidden needs will be divined and provided for. Many times, however, frequent self-denial and failure of others to reciprocate leads to bitterness and withdrawal. Good relationships are based on good communication and frequent negotiation that allows the needs of both parties to be met in a mutually satisfactory way.

*Cognitive distortion: If I don't work hard to please others, they will abandon or reject me.*
**Correction:** This is the thought process of those with low self-esteem. They believe that they are not worthy to be loved and accepted. They feel they have to work extra hard to put forth a pleasing image, even to the point of embellishing on their abilities and achievements. Actually, you run less risk of rejection by being yourself and letting go of what others think. Let them take it or leave it, but be honest and uncompromising when it comes to who you are. Then you will be able to relax and stop the charade of being someone you're not. Others will eventually see through your act and think of you as insincere. Why set yourself up for rejection later?

*Cognitive distortion: If people disapprove of me, they must be right.*
**Correction:** This belief also comes from low self-esteem and derives from the thought that others are more capable to render a decision or commentary about us than we are. It leads people to think that one particular fault or mistake is a total indictment of the self. Those who are perfectionists are particularly vulnerable to this belief, thinking that a small failure would be a complete catastrophe as it would draw the disapproval of others.

*Cognitive distortion: Being alone is horrible and leads to loneliness, boredom, and emptiness.*
**Correction:** All of the elements of a happy life can be experienced alone, including pleasure, self-worth, and fulfillment. In fact, being alone is sometimes preferable for positive self-growth and perspective.

***Cognitive distortion: There is a perfect love and relationship for each person.***
**Correction:** This belief puts unrealistic pressure on the other person to conform to your ideal of a "perfect fit." Rather than accepting relationships as evolving and uncertain, requiring that each individual adapt and change for the benefit of both, you feel there should be a "magic chemistry" that takes away all the effort and stress. A lifelong love takes years of hard work, and the road to love has many bumps, turns, and disappointments.

***Cognitive distortion: If I do everything right, I deserve to have no disappointments or pain in life.***
**Correction:** This belief falsely assumes that life is fair or that there is some guarantee that you will be rewarded for hard work and fair play. In truth, life holds no guarantees, and you should strive to do the best you can without being attached to a particular reward or outcome. Doing the job right should itself be the reward, just as the journey of life is more important than the destination or outcome.

***Cognitive distortion: My worth as a person depends on how much money I make, what I produce, and what I accomplish.***
**Correction:** Pinning your self-worth on these items alone will often lead to a diminished sense of self-worth when business takes a bad turn, you get fired from a job, or an injury or illness prevents you from working. Self-worth should also be defined by your ability to make others laugh and feel good about themselves. It should include your capacity to appreciate music and art, to show compassion, to forgive a transgression, and to learn from mistakes and failures. There are many factors, gifts, talents, and abilities unique to you that more clearly define who you are than your net worth on paper or ability to generate income.

***Cognitive distortion: Anger is always destructive and unhelpful.***
**Correction:** Anger is often an honest emotion that clearly states your feeling and position. Used in a healthy way, it does not need to attack or threaten others but simply and directly convey your displeasure. If used too frequently, like a cliché, it loses its power and meaning.

***Cognitive distortion: It is wrong to think of yourself first.***
**Correction:** Your happiness is your responsibility. Considering your needs and pursuing what you want means that you accept this responsibility. It is worse to blame others for your unhappiness. How are others supposed to know what you need if you don't tell them? Of course, life is a two-way street, and if we want to express our needs, we must be willing to listen to and consider the needs of others.

***Cognitive distortion: If I worry enough, my problem(s) should get better and go away.***
**Correction:** Worrying does not help to solve anything; only positive action does.

*Cognitive distortion: I can't cope with difficult or scary situations.*
**Correction:** I can learn to handle any difficult situation if I approach it slowly and think it through, taking one step at a time.


*Cognitive distortion: I should always look good and act nice no matter how I feel.*
**Correction:** It's OK to be honest about how I feel. I have the right to be accepted for who I am.


## Cognitive Distortions in Specific Phobia
Typical distorted thinking in the case of specific phobias includes the following:

- That plane/car/train/boat is unsafe. It could crash/sink/explode, and that would be the end of me.
- The injection will injure me or cause pain, and I might have an anxiety attack and faint.
- The mice/spiders/cockroaches/birds may attack/bite/contaminate/kill me.

**Correction:** These thoughts are examples of irrational fears experienced by those with specific phobias. Even though they know the degree of fear and reaction is unreasonable given the level of the actual threat, they cannot stop the response from happening. Although most of these fears must be unlearned by exposure therapy and desensitization, an attempt should be made to correct cognitive misperceptions about the real and true risk that the activity or object presents.


## Cognitive Distortions in Social Phobia
Distorted thinking in cases of social phobia includes these assertions:


*I have no control in social situations.*
**Correction:** Social phobia patients often avoid social events because of a perceived inability to perform well in that environment. They realize that parties and social gatherings are not their strong suit because they feel they don't have the social skills to control the situation. They only see all the things that could go wrong, resulting in humiliation or embarrassment. Therapy tries to show those with social anxiety the ways that they *do* have control. For instance, it would be natural to be fearful in a party with lots of new faces. Instead of saying, "There are too many people here that I don't know and I can't control all the judgment and scrutiny coming my way," say the real truth; "There are lots of people I don't know here, but I can go outside and distance myself if I need to. Actually, I can move around just fine, and it seems most people are not focused on me, but are just enjoying their conversations and having a good time. These people really aren't trying to bother me; they even seem friendly and polite." Remember that you can never control how others behave, only how you respond to their behaviors. Assessing what you can and should control as opposed to what should be released and let go of is a focus of therapy.

*I have to be perfect.*
**Correction:** Let's decide here and now that nobody is perfect, nor would they want to be. Not making mistakes means we are not challenging our potential. Being perfect is no fun, either, and most people find perfection to be annoying and uncomfortable to be around. Accepting your faults allows you to laugh at yourself, which is a great way to endear yourself to others. Start having fun today by shedding your futile attempts at perfection.

*Everyone is judging me.*
**Correction:** Get over it. People have better things to do with their time than to think about you. Most people are too busy scrutinizing themselves and dealing with their own problems to leave time for you and your problems. Remember the old eighteen/forty/sixty rule: When you're eighteen, you hope nobody thinks negatively of you. When you're forty, you don't give a damn about what anyone thinks about you. When you're sixty, you realize no one was ever thinking about you!

## Cognitive Distortions in Agoraphobia
*My phobic anxiety will lead to a catastrophe.*
**Correction:** Fear of a catastrophe is a large component of agoraphobia. Whether it is death, complete humiliation, or insanity that will happen as a result of your anxiety symptoms, the fear of a catastrophe is your greatest fear and the strongest factor in the development of avoidance behaviors. In truth, most agoraphobics have experienced their anxiety symptoms many times but have never experienced a catastrophe. Few can claim to have experienced death, insanity, or such humiliation that no one ever talked to them again. When it is said like this, the rational mind laughs and says, "Of course, it is unlikely a catastrophe will ever happen." But the emotional mind feels differently. It perceives itself as being unable to cope with what most of us would consider very "small catastrophes," like being ridiculed for trembling or blushing during a wave of anxiety. Cognitive-behavioral therapy allows us to put our feared catastrophes back into perspective.

## Refuting False Beliefs
The following are six rational statements will help remind you to challenge and correct false beliefs and replace them with rational thinking before they affect your emotions. In this section, I was helped by the thoughts of David Goodman in his book *Emotional Well-Being Through Rational Behavior Training*, 1978.

*Events and situations are not the cause of my anxiety or unhappiness.*
Events and situations do not bring unhappiness or anxiety; only how I think about those events and situations affects my emotions.

*Everything is the way it is meant to be.*
The way your life has turned out to this point is exactly as it should have turned out, and the conditions for things to be otherwise do not exist. To say that things should have turned out differently is to believe in a fantasy. Things are the way they are because of a long series of causal events in life, including those things we have no control over and those things directly affected by our own interpretations, reactions, irrational self-talk, and so on. To say things ought to be different is to throw out causality.

*All humans are fallible creatures.*
You must set reasonable expectations for yourself and others, allowing for reasonable quotas of failure. Otherwise, small mistakes will open up the possibility of excessive self-blame and self-loathing or negative personal assessments of others.

*It takes two to make a conflict.*
It always takes two to keep a conflict going. The "30 percent rule" states that any party to a conflict is contributing at least 30 percent of the fuel to keep it going. Being inflexible and rigid in your stance just because you are right is not always healthy. There may be times when you are wrong and would appreciate it if others were to allow you to save face by backing down a bit. Giving others the benefit of the doubt and the chance to recover from a conflict without feeling defensive will give you a reputation for strength and fairness.

*The original cause is clouded by time.*
Trying to make sense of what happened or searching for the original cause of a painful emotion is a waste of time. Trying to find out who did what first is impossible and never leads to healing or understanding. It is a better use of your time and energy to work on changing your thinking and behavior from now on to help improve future outcomes of interpersonal interactions.

*We feel the way we think.*
This is a more direct way of stating the first guideline above: events don't cause negative emotions; our interpretation of events triggers our emotions.

## Changing Anxious Self-Talk

Our own internal dialogue determines our emotional response to any given situation. This dialogue with ourselves is called *self-talk*, and we all do it throughout the day. When self-talk becomes negative and distorted, we can't help but feel anxious and insecure. A sure way to stay afraid is to allow ourselves to get worked up into a cycle of negative thoughts about the fear. Your thoughts may lead to *images* of worst-case scenarios coming true. This leads to *anticipatory worry* that keeps our emotions on high alert and sets us up for a full-blown panic attack. Worry also undermines your confidence that you have the ability to overcome your fears.

Anxious self-talk and negative images lead to avoidance and a refusal to face your fears. In truth, they are distortions of our own creation, and only we can destroy them by confronting and challenging the rationality of those thoughts. Whether you are afraid of speaking in front of a group, throwing up in public, crossing a bridge, or being attacked by a flock of birds, the types of anxious thoughts that perpetuate your fears are the same and involve three basic distortions:

- *Overestimating the possibility of a negative outcome.*
- This is known as *"what if" thinking*: "What if I fail the exam?" "What if I am rejected?" "What if I panic and can't catch my breath?" "What if others see me panic and think I'm crazy?" People with anxiety tend to greatly overestimate the possibility of something bad happening. In fact, if you ask them, most will say they have never experienced the negative outcome that they worry about.
- *Catastrophic thinking.*
  This is the belief that if a negative outcome did happen, it would be terrible, overwhelming, and unmanageable. Those with catastrophic thinking might make statements like, "I'd rather die than have that happen," "I'd never be able to live it down," "It would ruin me forever," "I couldn't handle it," or "They'll never forgive me."
- *Underestimating your ability to cope.*
  If you thought about it, you've been in many uncomfortable situations before and you came through each of them intact. Did you ever really completely fall apart, have to change your name and move to a new town, or find you couldn't carry on due to overwhelming circumstances? We all have amazing capabilities of resilience and recovery. Think of the people who actually benefited from their worst nightmares, like Donald Trump's bankruptcies or Martha Stewart's jail sentence. People admire and forgive those who have a setback and move on without loss of enthusiasm. And remember that even the biggest problems are eventually seen in the rearview mirror and are no longer an issue.

Those with persistent fears and phobias will find elements of these distortions in their thinking, both the tendency to overestimate the threats they face and the tendency to underestimate their abilities to deal with it. Recognizing and challenging these thoughts is fundamental to controlling fear reactions that are conditioned responses.

## Stopping Automatic Negative Thoughts

Again, most of the stress we feel in life is self-manufactured by our own thoughts and perceptions. We feel the way we think. Stopping negative patterns of thinking takes mindful attention to your thoughts and persistent challenges to those thoughts. To stop negative self-talk that magnifies and perpetuates your anxiety, follow these steps:

*Be aware of your thoughts*
To be able to stop negative thoughts, you must first "catch yourself in the act." Be on the alert for negative thoughts in the following situations:

- Anytime you feel anxious, ask yourself if you are overestimating the threat or worrying about catastrophic outcomes.
- Whenever the feeling of panic starts to come over you, look for overestimation of the threat, distortion of the real danger, thoughts of catastrophic outcomes, and underestimation of your own ability to deal with it.
- In anticipation of facing a difficult task or phobic situation, look for catastrophic thinking and overestimating the difficulty and frightfulness of the exposure or task.
- In situations that have led to bad outcomes or in which you made mistakes in the past, look for critical thoughts about your ability and competence or automatic expectations of a repeat negative result.
- At times when you feel discouraged or depressed, look for thoughts of being a victim, overestimating the difficulty you face, underestimating your resources to overcome your problems, overgeneralizing that bad experiences from the past are destined to be repeated, and the tendency to paint everything with the same dismal negative tone.
- At times when you're angry at yourself or others, look for critical thoughts about yourself, thoughts that things should be different, and unrealistic perfectionist expectations of yourself or others.
- In situations in which you feel guilty, ashamed, or embarrassed, watch for thoughts of unrealistic expectations, how things "should" be different, overestimating your responsibility for a situation, or the unforgiving attitude of others.

*Stop and Consider*
Stop and ask yourself the following questions:

- What thoughts are making me feel this emotion?
- Is it necessary to do this to myself?
- Is there any benefit in making myself upset/anxious/depressed?

If you have decided that the emotion you are feeling is unwanted, proceed to the following steps:

*Relax*
During times of emotionality, we tend to tense up as our mind shifts into high gear and we dwell on danger and potential problems. To really evaluate our patterns of negative self-talk, we will first need to relax and slow down our racing minds.

Disrupt the pattern of negative thinking by distracting yourself. One easy way to do this is to momentarily focus on deep abdominal breathing patterns. Use the progressive relaxation or meditation techniques we discussed earlier. Hopefully, you have already spent time practicing them so that they can be quickly and easily employed to stop the cycle of negative thoughts.

### Document

Now write down in your personal anxiety assessment plan the negative self-talk that caused you to become anxious, upset, or depressed. The important task here is to separate your thoughts from your feelings. You want to identify the thought that led to the feeling. You may want to start with the feeling, such as "I felt upset and hurt." Then ask yourself why: "Because he made me feel angry, stupid, and incompetent by yelling at me." Notice that, in this last statement, thoughts and feelings are still mixed up. A statement about your thoughts should not include emotions like hurt, sad, or angry, or comments about how you felt. The real thoughts here are "I am stupid" and "I am incompetent." If you tell yourself these things, you will become angry and upset. On the other hand, if you did not believe them, you would not have felt the emotion. It is annoying when someone yells at you, but if you believe you are being wrongfully attacked, you would see that the other person has the problem, not you, and that this really has nothing to do with you and should not affect your emotions at all.

In another example, you may write down, "I feel too afraid to give this speech." Here, you are talking about feelings. If you think about it for a while, you may find the thoughts behind the feeling of being afraid are, "I am not prepared as well as I should be." "People will think I'm stupid." "I'm stupid." "They'll never forget or forgive." "I'll never work in this town again." Notice the first thought may be true; maybe you should have prepared better, and this will stimulate you to work harder next time to avoid feeling unprepared. The other thoughts are overly self-critical and excessive worries about catastrophic possibilities that are overblown and untrue.

### Identify

Now write down the type of negative self-talk you are engaging in. There are four types:

1. The perfectionist: You constantly push yourself to do better, but your efforts are never quite good enough. The perfectionist uses expressions like "I should," "I must," and "I have to." Examples include the following:
   o "I should work harder and try harder."
   o "I should be well liked and popular."
   o "I should always look good."
   o "I should always be nice and pleasing to others."
   o "I should always have my life under control."
   o "I have to stay ahead of the pack."
   o "I must be the best."
   o "I have to get this job, make this amount of money, and be respected and admired by my peers."
   
   The problem with these kinds of beliefs is that they convince you that your self-worth depends on external factors like looks, money, popularity, respect, or your ability to be nice and pleasing, rather than on your own intrinsic and inherent talents and attributes.

2. The worrier: The worrier fuels and promotes a state of anxiety by imagining all that can go wrong and dwelling on worst-case scenarios. The worrier anticipates the worst, overestimates the possibility of something bad or humiliating happening, and creates catastrophic visions of potential failure. People who are worriers rarely let their guards down; they are constantly on the watch for the smallest sign or sensation that trouble is near. With uneasy apprehension, they frequently ask "what if…" questions, such as the following:
   - "What if I have a panic attack right now and my neighbor sees me?"
   - "What if that slight dizziness I just felt is really the start of a panic attack?"
   - "What if my heart beats too fast and I have a heart attack or stroke?"
   - "What if people notice my voice is shaky during my speech?"
   - "What if I'm alone and no one calls me back?"
   - "What if I don't find a husband/wife and I end up old and alone?"
   
   The problem with worrisome thoughts is that they get us worked up about things that haven't happened and probably won't happen, unless we keep worrying about them. Worrying keeps our minds and bodies in a constant state of apprehension and tenseness, leading to the release of stress hormones that really might hurt our health and give us something real to worry about. Worrying also accelerates the panic attack by focusing on the first symptom and setting off the fight-or-flight response.

3. The critic: Critics promote low self-esteem by telling themselves that they are not capable or competent. Critics constantly judge and evaluate themselves, looking for flaws and mistakes to pick at. The problem with being a critic is that you only see your weaknesses and inadequacies without taking into account your positive strengths and attributes. This leads to an overall negative view of yourself, putting unnecessary stress and blame on your shoulders. The critic will have thoughts like "You're stupid," "Any idiot could have done a better job," or "Why can't you ever get it right the first time?"

4. The victim: The victim is the defeatist part of you that tells you the situation is hopeless and helpless. It is the pessimist that says you'll "never make it." Victims believe they are fundamentally flawed and unworthy. Because of this, a positive outcome is just not possible, nothing will change for the better, and it's no use to try. Victims complain about the way things are and regret past failures. Their thoughts might run something like: "I can't do that," "I'll never be able to accomplish that goal," "It's too late for me now," "It'll never work," "I'll fail again," or "What's the point in trying?"

### *Correct or dispute*

The final step is to write in your personal anxiety assessment plan journal note a positive counterstatement that is more rational and true. In forming a self-supporting, positive correction, ask yourself these questions about your negative self-talk:

1. What is the real evidence for this thought?
2. Is it always true?
3. Has it proven to be true in the past, and how often?

4. What are the odds of it really happening?
5. What if the worst did happen? Would I be able to cope? Would my life really be ruined?
6. Am I being objective and looking at the whole picture?

Now write your counterstatement based on your answers. It should be believable and feel correct to you. After a few weeks of doing this, you will recognize negative self-talk, identify the type of thought you are having, and counter it with a positive affirmation automatically and without effort. The more you do it, the more you will balance your negativity with a true and accurate perspective.

*TOOL: Stop your automatic negative thoughts using the above method for two to four weeks until it becomes second nature.

## Stress-Resistant Thinking Tips

Using the following tips when confronting a stressful situation will often decrease or eliminate the stress altogether. If you can control your stressful thoughts, then you can control the amount of stress you feel.

### *Stop "catastrophizing."*

Here are some examples of phrases that often belie our catastrophic thinking:

- "This is just terrible."
- "This is the worst possible thing that could happen."
- "I can't believe how miserable and awful this situation is becoming."

A catastrophist is an expert in creating problems and making mountains out of molehills. They seem to thrive on misery and go looking for it if it doesn't exist. Whenever you find yourself using the above type of catastrophic expressions, stop and ask yourself these things:

1. Is it really important to get worked up over this? Is my aggravation helpful to the situation, or does it just make things worse?
2. Is this really a catastrophe that I will remember the rest of my life, or is it something that I will likely forget by dinnertime?
3. Am I being unrealistic to expect that everything should work out according to my plans and wishes?

### *Stop exaggerating and overgeneralizing.*

See if you recognize yourself in any of these expressions that exaggerate or overgeneralize:

- "I always end up with the lousy assignments."
- "I never get any respect."
- "Nobody cares."
- "People always lie and take advantage."
- "You never listen."
- "I can't stand it any longer."

Such expressions cause you to distort reality and then react with inappropriate anger and emotional upset. By thinking in black-and-white terms—all or none, good or bad, right or wrong—you invite your stress level to increase. When you find yourself in this pattern of thinking, ask these questions:

- Am I being fair and balanced in my assessment?
- Am I making assumptions and jumping to conclusions?
- Is it true that it is "always" or "never" this way?
- Are there ways in which this person or situation *does not* fit my overgeneralization?

**Stop the what-ifs.**
People hoping for more stress in their lives look for potential or theoretical situations to worry themselves and others about:

- "What if there is a terrorist attack?"
- "What if I get laid off?"
- "What if I have a brain tumor?"
- "What if they laugh at me?"
- "What if I fail the test?"

The problem with what-if statements are that they take a condition that *could* happen and turn it into something that *probably will* happen in your mind. Most of these things you worry about never happen. Some of them do happen, but being in a state of worry did not prevent them. This is unnecessary and unproductive worry that makes you less able to deal with the real problems in your life. In fact, you're creating a real problem by being difficult to live with or be around. People who worry about what-ifs expect others close to them to share their same concerns. But those not inclined to worry will only feel uneasy and uptight in your presence.

**Stop jumping to conclusions.**
Jumping to conclusions makes you vulnerable to being wrong and losing credibility in the eyes of others. This pattern of thinking makes it difficult for you to be objective and balanced in your assessment of a person or situation. Here are some examples:

- Your wife does not answer her cell phone, so you conclude she is cheating on you.
- You don't get a call back the day after a first date and conclude the person hates you.
- You meet someone at a party underdressed for the occasion and conclude they are unsuccessful and lazy.
- A neighbor has a same-sex visitor for a few days, and you conclude she is a lesbian.

If you make a conclusion about a person or situation, ask yourself the following:

1. Have I really gathered enough evidence and weighed it carefully before coming to this conclusion?
2. Would others respect and agree with my conclusion?
3. Does it matter, or is it any of my business to be dwelling on this issue?

***Stop your unrealistic expectations.***
If your expectations are unrealistic, chances are you will be disappointed or overreact. Unrealistic expectations often arise if you have an inflated sense of self-importance or a rigid, fixed idea about the way things should be. When things don't live up to our expectations, frustration and anger are the result. You likely have unrealistic expectations if you use terms like "must' or "should" in your self-talk:

- "I should never have to wait in line!"
- "People shouldn't be rude!"
- "I must win!"
- "Life should be fair!"

Another sign of unrealistic expectations is if your self-talk ends in an emotional exclamation point:

- "This is ridiculous!"
- "How could you be so thoughtless?!"
- "I don't believe this!"
- "What were you thinking?!"
- "I'm so pissed off!"

Implied in these unrealistic shoulds, musts, and exclamation points is the expectation that others conform to your standards and behave the way you expect them to. Those with inflexible ideals about the way things should be have very little chance of having life dished up the way they want it, leading to self-created stress, frustration, and higher risk for abandonment and isolation.

***Stop the self-rating.***
A person's self-worth should not be determined by their net worth, accomplishments, or acceptance from others. It should be derived from more personal criteria, like core values, talents, capacity for kindness and mercy, unique individual qualities, and strength of character.

When we look at ourselves in terms of money, looks, intelligence, performance, or accomplishments, we are comparing and rating ourselves as better or worse than others. This makes us vulnerable to unnecessary stress and loss of self-esteem when life takes a difficult turn. Ask yourself the following:

1. Do I need the approval of others to feel good about myself?
2. Do I really have to be better off than others to feel good about myself?
3. Do I need to be the center of attention and be the best looking to have good self-esteem?
4. Do I have to show off money and possessions to feel worthy?

*TOOL:* Change to a stress-resistant thinking pattern. Whenever you feel stressed, frustrated, or angry, try to determine how much of a role your thinking is playing in contributing to your stress level. Go through the list:

1. Am I catastrophizing?
2. Am I exaggerating or overgeneralizing?
3. Am I using what-ifs?
4. Am I jumping to conclusions?
5. Are my expectations unreasonable?
6. Am I self-rating and comparing myself to others?

Once you recognize a stress-creating thought pattern, stop and correct it. Take a deep breath. Give yourself and others a break! Remember to identify and correct your stressful thinking patterns in the section provided in the personal anxiety assessment plan.

## Identifying, Expressing, and Communicating Feelings

People with anxiety tend to have overly reactive, strong emotions that they hold inside. This leads to restricted breathing patterns, psychological and physical tenseness, and the release of stress hormones that damage our health and make us feel ill. Here is a three-step process to successfully deal with your feelings.

### Identify Your Feelings

1. **First of all, learn to recognize when you are experiencing suppressed emotions.** You may feel several symptoms when you hold in unidentified emotions:
   o Anxiety. Do you feel a general sense of uneasiness, apprehension, or worry about uncertainty? Each emotion carries energy. If not handled properly, this pent-up energy may lead to a vague sense of anxiety. I find that a cup of strong coffee will give me a sense that something is not right or about to go wrong, and I just can't put my finger on it. It could be that caffeine, as a stimulant, adds to the energy of our unexpressed emotions and magnifies our

fears. Notice that unexpressed excitement and enthusiastic anticipation can also lead to feelings of free-floating anxiety.
- Depression. Depression has been described as grief or sadness over a past loss. But often we feel depressed due to chemical imbalances that may be genetic, hormonal, or situational. When we hold in depressed feelings, we tend to feel "stuck" and unable to move on or enjoy the positive aspects of our lives. Perhaps there has been no recent loss and we can't understand why we feel depressed. Of course, human beings want answers and explanations and will often come up with a reason (job, spousal problems, health issues). But if you thought about it, you'd find that these things are no different than last month when you were not depressed. Gestalt psychologists point out that depression without an obvious source may be the manifestation of self-anger. Check to see if your internal "self-talk" is overly critical. Depression and anxiety become black holes that suck any positive energy away from us and leave us feeling empty and lost. Letting go of depressed emotions by expressing and communicating them is the first step in reducing their influence over us.
- Physical symptoms. Unexpressed emotions often present themselves as psychosomatic complaints, such as headaches, irritable bowels (diarrhea or constipation), stomach ulcers, high blood pressure, physical pain, and asthma attacks. Learning to express and let go of toxic emotions can lead to much better control of these conditions, even reducing or eliminating the need for medical treatment.
- Muscle tension. In our section on progressive relaxation exercises, we talked about scanning your body to identify areas of muscle tension. Because of the mind-body response, tensing up emotionally also causes our physical body to tense up. Conversely, relaxing physically facilitates the release of stored emotional tension. The relationship between suppressed feelings and muscular tension is explored in depth in the books of Dr. Alexander Lowen, and this school of thought is known as *bioenergetics*. For instance, those who subscribe to bioenergetics would point out that grief and sadness cause a tensing up of the muscles of the face and chest, while fear causes more of a tensing in the stomach region. They believe that gaining control of these emotions can be accomplished through relaxation of the affected areas. This body-mind response is demonstrated in my patients who say that cosmetic Botox in the forehead reduces stress.

2. **Secondly, pay attention to how your body is feeling**, rather than what your head is thinking. Feelings cause a physical response that we can tune into to discover when our emotions are not in check. Common expressions, such as "pain in the neck," "heartbreak," and "gut feeling" attest to this connection. Scan your body for how you feel and focus on relaxing areas of tension and discomfort.

3. **Next, write down your feeling as succinctly as possible**. What exactly is the emotion you are feeling? If it is a positive emotion, like "alive," "loved," "calm," "confident," or "proud," you probably won't be feeling negative tension. It will probably be a negative feeling you are trying to identify, like "ashamed," outraged," disappointed," "unappreciated," hostile," inferior," "insecure," "uneasy," and so on.

## Express Your Feelings

Expressing feelings must be done in a healthy and constructive way. You should not dump on or blame others whom you perceive as being responsible for your feelings. Letting out emotions in a healthy way includes the following:

- Sharing them with someone else not directly involved in the source of your feelings
- Writing them down in your journal
- Physically discharging them by punching a punching bag (with proper protective gloves), crying, screaming out the window (maybe better to keep the window closed), or going for a brisk run or gym workout

## Communicate Your Feelings

Probably the best way to express feelings is to communicate them to supportive friends, your spiritual counselor, or a trusted therapist. Talking it out in a supportive atmosphere is the foundation of group therapy and many forms of individual therapy. It is best to talk to a good listener, rather than someone who continually interrupts with his or her own opinion or advice.

Writing out your feelings is also effective for discharging emotions and can be accomplished anytime, anywhere, and without needing to involve others. You can keep a journal handy for this purpose and use it to identify emotions and patterns of thinking and feeling.

Feelings can also be communicated by your physical response, which may be crying, laughing, jumping up and down, or waving your arms in the air during a lively conversation. In some cultures, it is natural and expected to emote freely, while others are uncomfortable with this.

## Stress/Anger Management

Stress and anger seem epidemic in today's society. You only have to go out into your neighborhood to sense it. You can feel the tension on the roadways and the lack of consideration in the store as people push and shove their way around as if their problems and burdens outweigh everyone else's. Stress often comes in the form of work pressures, financial worries, or family demands. As we have less time for ourselves, we feel cheated, irritable, and angry. Poor sleep pattern and hormone imbalances only make it worse. As with anxiety, the management of stress and anger requires a toolbox of strategies, tactics, and techniques to be managed successfully.

Does it pay to manage stress? Let's look at the cost of stress to American society. The American Medical Association has stated that stress is the number-one killer in the country, causing or contributing to 80–85 percent of all human illness and disease. Every week, 95 million Americans take some kind of medication to relieve symptoms caused by stress. American businesses lose $200–300 billion dollars per year to stress-related injuries, illness, and loss of productivity. This cost is probably greatly underestimated. What is the cost to you and your family?

## Counseling for Stress Management

As we have learned, the inability to cope successfully with stress and anger damages our emotional nervous system as well as cardiovascular system and makes life difficult for everyone around us. So where's the payoff? Why do we allow ourselves to get worked up, stressed out, and upset over things that really don't matter and won't be helped by our reactivity?

Regarding stress, much of the pressures and frustrations that we perceive are completely self-imposed—especially if we take responsibility for everything and everybody. Anything that goes wrong is our fault. We insist on an unrealistic level of performance and perfection. Our priorities are all wrong, as we often lose track of what really has meaning and chase after material measures of success.

The anxiety that follows may be the Creator's way of telling you to look inside at your belief system and reassess your choices and direction in life. A therapist may ask you, "What will really be remembered and matter twenty years from now?" A good therapist will help you get back to your core values and beliefs. From here, you can begin putting life back into a healthy balance.

Another cause of undue stress is our failure to seek help and advice. We wait until we are overwhelmed and at our wits' end or have lost our job or marriage before getting the support we need. Stress management teaches us to recognize the signs of overload before we become dysfunctional and experience irrevocable loss. Recognizing our limitations, setting boundaries, setting reasonable goals and expectations, learning organizational skills, and identifying our resources and support structure are all helpful elements of stress-management counseling.

Learning to facilitate the relaxation response through hypnotherapy, biofeedback, music, meditation, or deep breathing exercises will enhance the benefits of stress-management therapy.

## Counseling for Anger Management

Anger is often a dysfunctional means of attempting to control our environment. Unfortunately, it usually backfires on us, leading to social isolation, rejection, personal failures, and less control over our lives. The notion of "karma" holds valuable truths.

The match that touches off explosions of anger can be one of the following: (1) an unrealistic expectation of the way things should be, and (2) an inflated sense of self-importance. For instance, people with road rage have the unrealistic expectation that everyone should respect their time schedule and get out of the way and the firm conviction that where they are going and what they are doing is more important than anyone else's plans. This way of thinking causes us to trigger our anger centers whenever the world does not conform to our expectations or we feel others don't recognize our importance.

The "three Rs" for managing anger include the following:

- **Reframing** expectations and deciding what is really important to get angry about and what is not (choose your battles wisely)
- **Relaxing** physically, taking a deep breath, and pausing before reacting emotionally with anger
- **Responding rationally** using the higher brain (cortex) to inform the emotions what the appropriate reaction to the situation should be. The higher frontal cortex area takes more than thirty

years to complete development, which makes responding rationally difficult for children, adolescents, and young adults.

Anger is really a full range of emotions that includes irritation, impatience, frustration, and full-blown rage. As you will learn in the next section, feelings of anger should be communicated with an assertive style, not an aggressive style. It is counterproductive to get in the habit of overly expressing anger, as this tends to only produce more anger. People who seem to enjoy the stimulation of angry encounters are sometimes called *rageaholics*. Some people with ADD create angry drama wherever they go because stimulating emotions improves focus and concentration. Most are unaware of what they are doing and why. One goal of this program is to help readers to focus their efforts on recognizing when they are angry, identifying the negative self-talk that is behind it, and finding healthier ways of viewing themselves and others.

## Assertiveness Training
### Overview
When I first heard about it, I thought assertiveness training involved making passive people more assertive in their social interactions. In reality, it is about teaching people with both passive and aggressive communication styles that there is a better, more-effective and less-stressful way to communicate by using the assertive style. The assertive method respects the rights and feelings of others while clearly expressing the views, concerns, and needs of the individual. An assertive person is able to do the following:

- Express how they feel
- Ask for what they want
- Ask for help
- Say "no" to things they don't want

In short, assertiveness training is really training in social communication skills. It is designed to help reduce misunderstandings and avoid manipulation, both of which are often the source of relationship and work-related stress and anxiety. Everyone could learn something from assertiveness training to help become a better communicator. One study showed that successful social skills are a better predictor of success than IQ. Good communication skills are the primary tool of a good negotiator, especially for those who work with the public, manage others, or are thinking of going into politics.

In 1949, Andrew Salter described assertiveness as a personality trait. He thought that you were either born with or without an assertive nature. But it was subsequently found that anyone can learn assertiveness, which is defined as "the ability to express personal rights and feelings." Being assertive means that you stand up for your rights without violating the rights of others. An assertive person is able to discuss their likes and dislikes freely, talk about themselves without feeling self-conscious, accept compliments without discomfort, disagree with someone openly, ask for clarification of the other person's point of view, and say "no." Because of these skills, an assertive person is more relaxed in interpersonal situations and is able to enjoy interaction with others more fully.

To become an assertive person, you must first be aware of your present behavior style and see how that leads to problems. Look at the following descriptions of various behavior styles to see which sounds most like you:

**Submissive behavior:** The submissive person tends to yield to the wishes and desires of others, feeling that their own rights and needs are not as important. Because of this, they will not volunteer to tell others what they want or how they feel. Others are left in the uncomfortable position of trying to guess what they want and may be unfairly blamed when they don't respond to the feelings and needs of the submissive friend or spouse. When they do ask for what they want, submissive people often sends the message that they feel guilty for imposing. Showing insecurity about their right to express their needs causes others to discount them as well. Often, those with anxiety are afraid of losing friends or the support of others. They will strive to "not make waves" and work hard on being nice and pleasant so as not to offend others.

**Aggressive behavior:** Those who have adopted an aggressive style of behavior will typically demand, intimidate, or use hostility and anger to power their way to getting what they want. They have learned that most people can be cowed into submission if they are sufficiently abrasive. The nature of their methods shows that they have no regard or respect for the desires, needs, or rights of others. This behavior often results in conflict, hurt feelings, and other negative consequences.

**Passive-aggressive behavior:** Passive-aggressive people will not openly confront someone but rather show their anger and hostile feelings in a covert fashion through passive resistance. Instead of asking directly for something they want, they will continually complain about what they don't have. If they disagree with a family decision to spend Saturday dinner together, they will show up as everyone else is finishing their plates. If they don't like the fact that their spouse has asked them to perform a chore, they will conveniently forget to do it, do it poorly, or create a new problem while doing it. If they don't like that the boss has asked them to help train a new staff member, they will ignore the trainee's questions and call a friend on their cell phones instead. Because they never make clear what is bothering them or what they really want, passive-aggressive people rarely get what the want, making them even more irritable and unhappy. Their behavior leaves others feeling confused, annoyed, and resentful, as well.

**Manipulative behavior:** Manipulative people use guilt or pity to get what they want from others. By taking on the role of victim or long-suffering parent/friend/spouse, they are able to get others to take care of their needs. Rather than taking responsibility for themselves and "getting a life," they will play helpless and weak so that others will feel sorry for them. They may hint that they will hurt themselves, get sick, have a heart attack, or starve to death unless you give them what they want. Examples of manipulative behavior include, "You're breaking your mother's heart," "You want me to have another heart attack?" "I haven't eaten a decent meal in weeks," and "Don't worry about me; I'll probably survive until you get back." Of course, manipulation works only as long as the people being manipulated allow themselves to get sucked into it. When the manipulators fail to get what they want, they may become angry or act like they don't care. If the people being manipulated fail to recognize the game that's being played, they will feel confused and stressed out. Later, they may feel resentment and anger once they figure out the con.

**Being assertive:** Assertive people understand and believe that they have legitimate rights. They feel they are the best judge of their own wants, needs, thoughts, feelings, and behavior. They can ask for what they want or simply say "no" in a direct, kind, and clear fashion. In this way, they are careful not to negate, attack, or manipulate others. Feelings and needs are communicated honestly in a straightforward way while maintaining respect and consideration for others.

**What Is Your Behavior Style?**
Take a look at the following situations and then read the different behavioral responses. Think which style most closely resembles how you see yourself responding.

**1. Your doctor keeps you waiting more than thirty minutes for your appointment.**
*Submissive:* You keep waiting, even though others who came in after you are taken in to see the doctor. After all, it's not your place to question the doctor's schedule, and your problems are probably not as important as those of the other people.

*Aggressive:* After five minutes of waiting, you yell at the front-desk person: "Does the doctor think his time is more important than mine? I was here on time and I want to be seen now. This is ridiculous!" You stand over the front desk glaring and tapping your fingers on the counter.

*Passive-aggressive:* You keep looking at your watch and sighing, making sure the front-desk person can see your discomfort and impatience. You stand up as if you might be deciding to walk out. Or you call a friend on your cell phone to tell them how annoyed you are that the doctor is running late, making sure the staff and waiting-room patients can hear every word. You then show up late to future appointments, pointing out that the doctor kept you waiting the last time.

*Manipulative:* Of course you want to make the doctor and staff feel guilty or pity you, so you groan in pain and hold your leg/back/stomach/head. Or you ask to go use the bathroom, telling the staff you need someone to help you because you feel faint and are about to throw up. You might even gag yourself in the bathroom so everyone can hear you retching.

*Assertive:* You announce yourself when you first walk in to the receptionist: "I'm Joe, and I have a 3:30 appointment to see Dr. Smith." After a ten-minute wait, you ask the front desk how much longer the doctor will be and confirm that you were scheduled ten minutes before. You tell them how much longer you are willing to wait and ask if the doctor's schedule will be able to accommodate this. You reschedule for another time if you feel you cannot wait. If there has been a pattern of lateness and disregard for your schedule, you find another doctor and write a letter to your physician explaining the reason for your decision.

**2. You are seated before the movie starts and a lady sits right in front of you wearing a big feather hat that is distracting or obstructs your view of the screen.**
*Submissive:* You quietly move to a different location that is less desirable than the place you had originally chosen. Or you stay put and endure the distraction, not really enjoying the movie that much. Inside you are angry that this person is so rude.

*Aggressive:* You say, "Hey bird brain! Either take off that hat or you'll be eating it!"

*Passive-aggressive*: You start talking loudly in an attempt to annoy the person, without saying anything about the hat. You "accidentally" keep kicking the back of her chair so she can't enjoy the movie, either.

*Manipulative*: You pretend you are having a sneezing attack because you are allergic to bird feathers, when you're really not. You sigh and exclaim to your friend next to you, "I've been looking forward to this movie for weeks and weeks, but I guess I'm not going to see much of it now."

*Assertive*: You lean forward and say, "I'm sorry, but you may not be aware that your hat is distracting and obstructing my view. Would you be willing to remove it during the show?

## 3. An aggressive salesperson calls you on Saturday morning wanting you to buy something you don't need. You don't want her to call your house again.

*Submissive*: You listen to her whole sales pitch, feel guilty you've taken so much of her time, and buy whatever it is you don't need. Telemarketers make their living preying on submissive types.

*Aggressive*: You slam the phone down in her ear. That should get the message across!

*Passive-aggressive*: You say, "Just a minute, I've got another call coming in," and put her on hold until she hangs up. Hopefully, she will get sick of calling and being put on hold.

*Manipulative*: You say that she woke you up from a deep sleep or that you have sick family members who may be resting at any time and should not be disturbed by the phone ringing. You hope she feels badly enough that she doesn't call again.

*Assertive*: You ask how she got your phone number and request that your name be taken off any calling list for solicitations. You explain that this is your home phone and is for personal use only.

## 4. A friend asks you for money that you can't really afford to give him, especially since he has a pattern of not paying you back.

*Submissive*: You avoid him until he goes away, not answering calls, pretending you're on vacation and never got his message, and parking in a different spot so he can't wait for you after work. Or you give him the money and feel anxious about your own financial situation.

*Aggressive*: You yell back, "What?! Do you think I'm made out of money? What kind of idiot do you think I am that I would fall for your bull again? Go get a job and leave me alone."

*Passive-aggressive*: You are angry that he has asked you for help again. You resist making a decision or getting involved by changing the subject, acting as if you didn't understand his request. You don't talk to him for a few weeks as a punishment for asking. You ask him for something that you know he can't afford to give you as a condition of the loan.

*Manipulative*: You say "yes" or "maybe" and then tell him that you are having problems yourself and that it really puts you in a bind. You let him know all about your bills, expenses, and financial misfortunes. You keep him hanging as long as possible because he is very attentive to your needs when he wants something. You let him do errands for you and talk to him when he calls daily to ask how you're doing. Finally, you tell him that you are broke, the paycheck didn't come through, or you got an unexpected bill and can't give him the money.

*Assertive:* You explain that you are not able to help him because you can't afford to or don't think it is healthy for your friendship. You remind him that he promised to repay in the past but has been unable to do so. You may offer to help him find a job, but you make it clear that you are not interested in loaning money now or in the future and request that he not ask again.

One important thing you'll notice about the assertive style: assertive people protect their rights by making direct and clear requests, not by making demands or trying to get their points across indirectly. To become assertive, you must work on the following areas:

- Recognizing and exercising your basic rights
- Knowing your own needs and desires
- Practicing assertive responses
- Saying "no" firmly and kindly
- Avoiding manipulation

## Recognizing and Exercising Your Basic Rights

To be assertive, you must first believe that you have the right to be assertive. Many people have forgotten this or were taught as children that they do not share some basic rights as the opposite sex or those of a higher socioeconomic status or different race. In adulthood, this may lead to the false assumption that they don't deserve these rights and should not expect or ask for them. Read the items below and ask yourself if you believe that you have this right as much as anybody else. If the answer is no, then take some time to give yourself that right here and now. Just say, "I do have the right to _____." Say it until you believe it.

1. I have the right to ask for what I want.
2. I have the right to express all my feelings, positive or negative.
3. I have the right to change my mind.
4. I have the right to put myself and my program first.
5. I have the right to have my own convictions and opinions.
6. I have the right to object to unfair treatment or criticism.
7. I have the right to be the final judge of my feelings and accept them as legitimate.
8. I have the right to ask for help or emotional support.
9. I have the right to interrupt to ask for clarification, if the situation is appropriate.
10. I have the right to ignore the advice of others.
11. I have the right to choose not to respond to a situation.
12. I have the right to not be concerned about the opinions or welfare of others who are not my responsibility.
13. I have the right to be alone.
14. I have the right to say "no" to things I don't want to do.
15. I have the right to make mistakes.
16. I have the right to not be perfect at everything all the time.
17. I have the right to my own personal beliefs and values.

18. I have the right to say "no" to things I feel are unsafe, I don't agree with, I am not ready for, or that violate my values.
19. I have the right to make my own goals and priorities.
20. I have the right not to accept responsibilities for the problems, behaviors, actions, or feelings of others.
21. I have the right to expect honesty from others.
22. I have the right to be angry at a friend or spouse.
23. I have the right to be myself.
24. I have the right to ask questions when confused and say, "I don't know."
25. I have the right to say, "I'm afraid.
26. I have the right to make a decision based on how I feel.
27. I have the right to laugh at what I think is funny and cry when I am sad.
28. I have a right to my need for personal space and downtime.
29. I have the right to be goofy, playful, and frivolous, as long as I'm paying my way.
30. I have a right to my sense of humor.
31. I have the right to be wealthier, healthier, and wiser than others around me.
32. I have the right to be free from abusive environments.
33. I have the right to make new friends and expand my horizons.
34. I have the right to change and grow.
35. I have the right not to have to anticipate the needs and wishes of others.
36. I have the right to be treated with dignity and respect.
37. I have the right to be comfortable around others at work and in my social life.
38. I have the right to have my needs taken seriously by others.
39. I have the right to feel and express pain.
40. I gave the right to a workplace free of emotional abuse and sexual harassment.
41. I have the right to be happy.

Of course, having the above rights is a two-way street. To claim any of these rights, you must be willing to afford that right to everyone else. You can't say, "I have the right to make new friends and expand my horizons, but my wife does not." Also, exercising your rights must not be at the expense of the rights of others. You may have the right to "be yourself," but not if that means running naked through the grocery store. When two justifiable rights are in conflict, then there must be negotiation. For instance, your right to be goofy and playful might conflict with your wife's right to enjoy an evening at the opera with a sophisticated adult. Wearing your bowtie on your nose in this case might be something you want to discuss.

Next, you must believe in your rights strongly enough that you are willing to take responsibility to exercise them in situations in which they are threatened or infringed upon. Learning and practicing the material in the next four sections will help you exercise your assertive skills effectively.

## Knowing Your Own Needs and Desires

Although it sounds trite, being assertive requires that you "be in touch with your feelings." You must frequently ask yourself, "What am I feeling?" and "What do I or don't I want?" Unless you can answer these questions, you have very little chance of getting what you want. Other people are not mind readers, and you cannot expect them to guess correctly. Here are some examples:

1. **You've just been fired and want to share your disappointment with a friend, but she keeps changing the subject to talk about her child's problems in school.**
   Q. How do I feel?
   A. I feel disappointed with my termination and upset that my friend does not seem to give much weight to my loss and concerns.
   Q. What do I want?
   A. I want my friend to listen to me.
2. **You're sick with a headache and would like to rest, and your roommate is entertaining in the next room with the stereo up full blast.**
   Q. How do I feel?
   A. I feel annoyed that my roommate knows I'm not feeling well and is showing no consideration.
   Q. What do I want?
   A. I want my roommate to take the party somewhere else or turn off the stereo and talk quietly.
3. **A date you've been looking forward to all week stands you up for Sunday brunch after you confirmed with him on Thursday.**
   Q. How do I feel?
   A. I feel disappointed and angry at the same time.
   Q. What do I want?
   A. I want to be treated with more consideration by this individual.
4. **You receive food at a restaurant that is over- or undercooked.**
   Q. How do I feel?
   A. I feel that the cook did not pay attention to my order and got it wrong.
   Q. What do I want?
   A. I want the dish cooked to my preference.
5. **You've been standing in line for some time and someone cuts in front of you.**
   Q. How do I feel?
   A. I feel angry and annoyed.
   Q. What do I want?
   A. I want the person to go to the back of the line where he belongs.
6. **A woman in the supermarket has thoughtlessly blocked the aisle with her cart while she reads a label.**
   Q. How do I feel?
   A. I feel irritated and inconvenienced by her behavior.
   Q. What do I want?
   A. I want her to move her cart so I can get by.

Whenever you are feeling a negative emotion as a response to another person's behavior, stop and define that emotion more clearly (angry, hurt, worried, insecure, disrespected, etc.). Next, ask yourself what you want to feel better about the situation. Only then can you respond in an assertive way.

## Practicing Assertive Responses

To make sure you are making an appropriate assertive response, go through the following checklist:

- Determine your rights.
- Designate an appropriate time to discuss the situation.
- Express your feelings.
- State how the problem affects you directly.
- Request what you want.
- State the consequences of gaining (or not gaining) cooperation.

1. To determine the legitimacy of your rights, review in your mind the list of personal rights above, or just ask yourself if you would afford these rights to others.
2. If it is more appropriate to address the problem at another time, choose a time that is mutually convenient to discuss your concerns with the other person(s) involved. It is often necessary to be assertive on the spot, of course.
3. Remember that you have a right to your own feelings and that your feelings hold equal merit with those of anyone else. By letting others know how you feel, you give them the opportunity to understand how their behavior affects you. Remember to start the statement of your feelings with *I* rather than *you*. When you use "I statements," you are taking responsibility for how you feel. When you use "you statements," you are accusing or judging others, which leads them to throw up a defensive wall and think more of how they will return the attack rather than listen to your point of view. Consider these examples:
   a. "You never listen to what I have to say!" versus "I feel better when you listen to me."
   b. "You're lazy and selfish because you won't help out around the house," versus "I feel angry and devalued when you don't help with the housework."
   c. "You don't care about how I feel," versus "I feel unloved and lonely when you don't show an interest in my concerns and feelings."
4. State how the problem affects you directly. For example:
   a. "When you don't listen to me, I feel frustrated and upset."
   b. "When you don't help me, I feel used and taken advantage of."
   c. "When you show indifference toward my feelings, I feel insecure and unhappy."
5. When requesting what you want, there are some basic rules:
   - Be assertive with your nonverbal behaviors. Remember to maintain eye contact, stand or sit with confident posture, and keep your voice calm and your demeanor self-contained. Do not yell or use aggressive gestures. Do not shake your head in disbelief or roll your eyes with sarcasm.
   - Keep your request simple, singular, and to the point. Don't make more than one request at a time, and be clear. Think of a one- or two-sentence statement of your request, such as, "I want us to go to marriage counseling," "I want you to stop smoking marijuana around me," and "I would like to drive home" (when your spouse has been drinking).

- Use I statements such as, "I would like," "I want," "I could use," and "I would appreciate." You statements at the beginning of a request can be seen as threatening or coercive.
- Object to the behavior, not the person. Let the person know that you have a problem with what he or she is doing, not with who he or she is as a person. This will preserve respect for the other person, and mutual respect is the first rule of any debate or negotiation. For instance, "I would like you to keep your agreements with me" is better than "You're an untrustworthy person." Or, "I would like you to call me if you can't keep our lunch date," rather than, "You're an inconsiderate jerk."
- Don't apologize for your request. For instance, say, "I would like you to stop smoking near my children," rather than "I know this is a little bit of an imposition, but I was hoping you might consider…" Another example of a polite-yet-firm and unapologetic request is, "No, thank you, I'm not interested," rather than, "I know I'm probably making a mistake, and I hope you're not angry with me, but I'm not quite ready to make a commitment." Apologizing shows a weakness and lack of resolve that invites further discussion and stressful pressure.
- Make requests, not demands or commands. I have had to discharge patients from my medical practice for this failure alone. Patients who are in the habit of demanding everything they want soon wear out their welcome by putting unnecessary stress on the office staff. For example, an aggressive patient will call at the last minute and say, "I'm here at the pharmacy and I want to pick up a refill of my medication right now!" rather than, "I'll be going to the pharmacy tomorrow, and I wondered if the doctor would authorize a refill of my medication." Here's another example: "I'm very sick and the doctor needs to see me today, even if he has to stay late or cancel other patients!" (This is an actual verbatim quote.) An assertive patient would have said, "I feel sick today and would like to see the doctor. Would it be possible to be worked into her busy schedule?" Demands and commands do not respect the humanity and rights of others. Demanding and commanding are aggressive styles of behavior and are based on the false assumption that you are more important than others, that you are always right, or that you deserve to have everything your way. Needless to say, such behavior is poisonous to healthy relationships, be them between coworkers, marriage partners, or the doctor and patient.
- Before stating the consequences, you should consider carefully what is most appropriate for the given situation. With close friends or spouses, it's best to present a positive consequence as an honest offer of give-and-take rather than threatening a negative consequence. For example, "Honey, if you come to lunch with me and your mother-in-law, you'll probably get lucky tonight." Or, "If you come with me to the museum, I'll go to the baseball game with you next week." If you are dealing with someone who has been difficult and uncooperative in the past, you might want to describe the *natural consequences* of his or her resistance, rather than a negative consequence that is *arbitrarily imposed* by you. For instance, "If you're not ready to go when the carpool arrives, them we will have to leave without you to stay on time." Here's another example: "Your yelling is not conducive to a constructive exchange. If it continues, I will have to excuse myself and come back once you

have calmed down." You can see how it is important to think of how you will phrase your statement of consequences beforehand if you anticipate a particular situation (like your boss yelling at you). Otherwise, you may do something you regret or later realize was childish, like crying and kicking the wastebasket or slamming the door as you leave the office.

## Sample Scenarios

Let's use the six cases from the section on "Knowing Your Own Needs and Desires" above. In each case, I will give the correct assertive response. Imagine yourself thinking and behaving this way.

1. **You've just been fired and want to share your disappointment with a friend, but she keeps changing the subject to talk about her child's problems in school.**
    a. **What is my right?** I have the right to have my concerns count as much as those of my friend.
    b. **What is the best time to discuss this?** Now, when she can clearly see how one-sided this conversation has been.
    c. **How should I express my feelings?** By saying, "I feel ignored when you redirect the conversation to issues going on with your son. We can talk about that in a moment, but first I would like to get your feedback on some of the concerns I brought up earlier."
    d. **How does the problem affect me directly?** It makes me even more emotionally upset because I'm not getting the support of my friend (state this to her directly).
    e. **What do I want?** "I would like to have equal time for issues important to me."
    f. **What are the consequences if I do or don't get cooperation?** "I will be there for you if you treat my problems equal to your own."
2. **You're sick with a headache and would like to rest, and your roommate is entertaining in the next room with the stereo up full blast.**
    a. **What is my right?** I have the right to a peaceful home environment when needed.
    b. **What is the best time to discuss this?** Now, since I need the rest now.
    c. **How should I express my feelings?** By saying, "I feel cranky because you are not honoring my right to have some peace and quiet when I'm not feeling well."
    d. **How does the problem affect me directly?** If I don't get some rest, the headache will last longer and get worse.
    e. **What do I want?** "I want you to turn off the stereo and take the party elsewhere."
    f. **What are the consequences if I don't get cooperation?** "It will harm our relationship."
3. **A date you've been looking forward to all week stands you up for Sunday brunch after you confirmed with him on Thursday.**
    a. **What is my right?** I have the right to have people respect the agreements they make with me or have a very good excuse and express regret.
    b. **What is the best time to discuss this?** I will call them when I know they are home from work and I can talk to them directly without interrupting their workday.

c. **How should I express my feelings?** By saying, "I'm disappointed and a bit hurt that you didn't show. I was looking forward to spending time with you. It made me feel embarrassed to be sitting alone as if I was waiting for someone who had forgotten about me. I could have used that time more productively. It's OK if you're not interested; just say so."

d. **How does the problem affect me directly?** I feel upset and angry for the rest of the day, which I don't deserve.

e. **What do I want?** "I would like you to call and cancel within a reasonable amount of time so I can make other plans for my afternoon."

f. **What are the consequences if I don't get cooperation?** "I will not be available to see you." Again, you don't have to state a consequence if you accept the apology or initial response.

4. **You receive food at a restaurant that is over- or undercooked.**
   a. **What is my right?** I have a right to have it cooked the way I ordered it.
   b. **What is the best time to discuss this?** Now, because I'm hungry.
   c. **How should I express my feelings?** By saying, "This food is undercooked; I ordered it medium-well."
   d. **How does the problem affect me directly?** "I can't enjoy the meal this way."
   e. **What do I want?** "I would like you to put it back on the grill until it is done."
   f. **What are the consequences if I don't get cooperation?** If there is not an appropriate response to your request, you might say, "I will not eat or pay for this meal if it is not prepared as I have requested," or "This won't be a good Yelp review."

5. **You've been standing in line for some time and someone cuts in front of you.**
   a. **What is my right?** I have the right to have my place in line respected.
   b. **What is the best time to discuss this?** Now.
   c. **How should I express my feelings?** "I do not appreciate your disregard for the integrity of the line."
   d. **How does the problem affect me directly?** It makes me angry, and I will have to wait even longer.
   e. **What do I want?** "I would like you to get back to your place in the line, please."
   f. **What are the consequences if I don't get cooperation?** "I will complain to the bank/theater/club/store manager."

6. **A woman in the supermarket has thoughtlessly blocked the aisle with her cart while she reads a label.**
   a. **What is my right?** I have the right to get through without undue delay.
   b. **What is the best time to discuss this?** Now.
   c. **How should I express my feelings?** "Excuse me, I feel trapped!"
   d. **How does the problem affect me directly?** I can't get to the item I'm shopping for.
   e. **What do I want?** "I would appreciate being able to maneuver around your cart."
   f. **What are the consequences if I don't get cooperation?** "I will ask for help from the manager."

By practicing assertiveness, you will soon sense your rights without having to think about them. You will likely adopt a shortened form of this exercise by stating simply how you feel and requesting directly what you want, hopefully with a kind and sincere smile. You will learn a style that is polite yet firm and that respects the feelings and rights of others.

## Saying "No"

An important part of being assertive is the ability to exercise your right to say "no." This enables you to put your own needs and desires ahead of the demands that other people make on your time and energy. After all, it is *your* time and *your* energy, and you should not feel guilty or make apologies about how you decide to spend it.

If you are not interested in the advances of a stranger or casual acquaintance, a polite-yet-firm, "No, thank you, I'm not interested," should be clear enough. Sometimes the phrase needs to be repeated with direct eye contact and an unwavering voice for those aggressive types who don't like to take "no" for an answer.

For friends, family, coworkers, or closer acquaintances, it may be helpful to say "no" using this formula (the REST formula, as in "give it a rest"):

1. **R**epeat the request so the individual knows you heard and understand what he or she is asking.
2. **E**xplain why you are declining the request.
3. **S**ay "no" clearly.
4. **T**ake a rain check. If appropriate, offer an alternative proposal that is acceptable to you and the other person.

Check out this example: "I understand you want me to join you and several other classmates at the jazz club tonight (repeat of the request). Unfortunately, I have an early chemistry lab class, and I need to prepare for my experiment (explanation). I won't be able to make it (saying "no"). If you go out on a Saturday sometime, try me again." (Take a rain check, but only if you really want to spend time with this person. Otherwise, you will be inviting more invitations.)

## Avoiding Manipulation

Avoiding manipulation means you understand how a manipulative person behaves. As we said earlier, those with a manipulative style of behavior try to make others feel guilty or pity them to get what they want. Usually, such people are lonely and insecure, but occasionally, they can be downright selfish and inconsiderate.

If you think about it, manipulative people believe that their needs and wants are more important than yours. They would rather have you stay home and take care of them than see you out having a good time. Where do they get the right to treat you this way? The answer is from you. Only you can give manipulative people the right to control your life and exert their wills over yours.

Of course, some people want to be led around like sheep and told what to do and when to do it. But more often, those being manipulated allow themselves to believe they have an obligation, and they feel guilty if they don't live up to it. But ask yourself this: "When did I accept this obligation? How did it become my responsibility to make this person happy at the expense of my needs and wishes?"

Often, the person who benefits from your feelings of guilt or pity—the person who is manipulating you—is a parent, spouse, family member, or close friend. Because of this, the situation may be quite complicated, with a long history of intertwined manipulation and game playing on both sides. You may have already had some blow-up moments and fights when your anger and frustration boiled over. You may have even said, "You're trying to manipulate me again!" But a few days later, you're back to the same pattern of devaluing your rights in favor of the other person's needs, seeing to it that the person gets what he or she wants first.

Very commonly I see the manipulative parent(s) who want their children to put their needs ahead of the other responsibilities in their lives. Here are some things parents say to manipulate their kids:

- "You never call me anymore."
- "I won't be around much longer."
- "I had a beautiful figure before you were born."
- "I won't be seeing too many more holidays; I sure hope you can visit."
- "You're all busy with your families; no one has time for old dad anymore."
- "I was always there for you."
- "You shouldn't turn your back on your family."
- "Don't you walk away from me; I gave the best years of my life to you."
- "I raised you right, that's why I know I can always count on you to do the right thing by me."

The old saying, "You can choose your friends, but you can't choose your family," may make some feel trapped by the demands and expectations of their parents or siblings. Remember that your first responsibility is to yourself. If you are not happy and healthy, you can't contribute to the welfare of anyone else. Your second responsibility is to your wife, partner, and children. They have more of a right to your time and attention than your parents do. Make sure to keep these priorities straight.

Set limits on manipulative parents: "This is what I can and can't do for you." Do not be available anytime they want to reach you. Give them a specific time each week you will be able to talk to them: "I'll call you Saturday morning for thirty minutes before my run. Please don't call me other times as I won't be able to give you quality time."

How about some things a manipulative significant other or spouse might say:

- "But honey, I don't feel safe staying home alone, and I don't know your friends that well, so let's both stay home and watch a movie on TV."
- "I'm just not as smart and strong as you are; I'll let you make the decision."
- "Your mother hates me. If you loved me, you wouldn't accept her invitation to Thanksgiving dinner."
- "My mother is old and sick, and I would never be able to put her in a nursing home. If you cared about me, you'd let her live with us."

A manipulative friend might start the manipulation with something like, "If you were my friend…"

- "…you'd let me use your car this weekend."
- "…you would go with me to the party."
- "…you'd loan me the money."

I think you're getting a good idea of manipulative statements. Go ahead and jot down a few of your own to add to the list. Identify people who are manipulating you and write down some of the expressions they use to make you feel guilty or feel sorry for them. Then write down the ways you give up what you want to meet their needs. Lastly, think not only how this affects your life but the lives of your spouse, partner, or children who have a right to receive their share of your time and attention.

Only you can stop manipulation, because manipulation only works if you fail to recognize it or because you allow it to happen. Remember, you don't owe your parents anything. They had you for selfish reasons (this is always the case), and it is their responsibility to raise you and give you a good start in life. They have no right to expect anything in return. Maybe your culture and upbringing tell you differently; after all, the earlier the manipulation starts, the more effective it is for the manipulator.

A manipulative spouse may have real insecurities. In this case, seeing a marriage counselor is the best way to learn healthier methods of communication. Simply say, "Honey, I want to give you what you need, but I don't know how to do this in a way that we both can be happy with. Let's get some professional advice." Never attack or dismiss the insecurities of your intimate partner; it's unkind and hurtful. On the other hand, be firm in insisting that you go to counseling together, as you owe that to each other.

Your spouse or partner also has a right to decide how you as a couple will deal with your aging parents. This must often be negotiated with the help of a counselor.

Who needs manipulative friends? You deserve better than that. Simply say, "If you were my friend, you would not try to manipulate me. I'm not interested in a relationship based on manipulation." If the friend admits fault and wants a second chance, that is up to you. My experience is that people rarely change unless they truly value what they have lost. Maybe it's time to see how much they truly value you by not making yourself available for a while. Chances are they won't be interested in having a "friend" they can't manipulate.

***TOOL:** So now that you've read a bit on the subject of assertiveness, why not make it a daily tool or exercise? In your personal anxiety assessment plan under "My Assertiveness Issues," fill in the questions about your behavior style, your rights, things that deserve a "no" answer, and ways you are typically manipulated. Now think of ways you could show a more assertive style and do better at being an assertive communicator. To change, you need to first think about everything you say and do. Don't go through life letting others get what they want at your expense. Practice assertive behaviors as outlined in this chapter. Say no without apology or guilt whenever you want. And don't let others manipulate you.

## Social Phobia and Social Skills Training
### Overview
People with social anxiety have a tendency to feel nervous or uncomfortable in social situations, usually because they fear doing something embarrassing or foolish, making a bad impression, or being judged

negatively by others. A detailed discussion of social phobia can be found in my book, coauthored by Art Bell, PhD, *Phobias and How to Overcome Them: Understanding and Beating Your Fears* (2005).

There are many types of social anxiety. Some people fear only specific situations, such as using a public restroom or speaking in front of a group of people, while others feel uncomfortable in almost every social situation. Some famous actors and actresses have admitted to feeling comfortable in front of a large, anonymous audience, but shy and nervous in dealing with one-on-one or small-group situations. Some people with social anxiety will experience symptoms only in formal locations, like the workplace, while others find that only casual, unstructured social interaction makes them uncomfortable.

No matter what type of social phobia you may have, the information in the following pages should be useful. The cognitive behavioral approach to treating social anxiety involves identifying your specific pattern of response to social anxiety and applying specific strategies to gain control over these response patterns. There are three types of anxiety reactivity:

## 1. Physical feelings and sensations of anxiety

These physical aspects include racing heart, difficulty breathing, dizziness, blushing, nausea, diarrhea, sweating, trembling, shaky voice, crying, nervous laugh, numbness and tingling sensations, chest pain, dry mouth, weak legs, and feelings of unreality or being detached.

Those with these physical symptoms are especially concerned that others will notice their blushing, shaky voice, or tremors and will judge them harshly. They are also concerned that their symptoms (nausea) will lead to a perceived catastrophe (throwing up in front of the class). These people tend to overestimate the degree to which their discomfort is noticeable to others. If they had no concern about experiencing these symptoms in front of other people, they would probably feel much less anxiety in social and performance situations.

## 2. Anxious cognitions (thoughts)

The cognitive aspects of social anxiety are the thoughts, expectations, and predictions that one has about social situations. Remember, you don't react emotionally to the actual situation or event but rather to your *beliefs and interpretations* of those situations and events. People who have faulty anxious beliefs are likely to have an anxious emotional response. Here are some examples of beliefs that might get you into trouble, many of which we have discussed in previous sections:

- It is important that people like me.
- If I speak in public, I will look like a fool.
- If I make a mistake, people will be angry with me or think I'm stupid.
- It is terrible to blush, shake, or sweat in front of other people.
- If someone rejects me, I am unlikable.
- Anxiety is a sign of weakness.
- I should find ways to hide my anxiety symptoms.
- If people do not show interest in what I say, they don't like me.

For instance, in this last statement, the reality could be that other people are not showing interest in what you are saying for a completely different reason that has nothing to do with you. Maybe they are distracted by their own problems, are hungry, are late for an appointment, are sick or tired, are shy, or don't like conversations. To assume that their disinterest is related to what you are saying or your likability is a common cognitive distortion in social anxiety.

### 3. Anxious behaviors (avoidance)

Avoidance of social situations as well as "safety behaviors" are behavioral aspects of social anxiety. This means the person will attempt to avoid anxiety-provoking situations whenever possible or will develop elaborate strategies to reduce the anxiety. Unfortunately, while these strategies may help in the short term, they block long-term recovery from social anxiety by preventing you from learning that your anxious predictions are unlikely to come true. It takes exposure to the feared situation without any behavioral crutches to really believe that you are capable to perform well in that situation without anything terrible happening. Even taking a medication that allows you to feel more relaxed in the feared situation may prevent recovery if you think that you could never have been able to do it without the medication. Here are some examples of anxious avoidance/safety behaviors:

- Never raising your hand in class to answer a question
- Making an excuse not to go to a party
- Making your pager alarm sound as if you have a call that you must attend to to get out of an uncomfortable conversation
- Helping with the dishes at a party to avoid talking to the guests
- Avoiding eye contact and speaking softly in conversations
- Turning down the lights while giving a presentation so that the audience won't notice your shaking/blushing/sweating
- Needing to have a close friend or spouse accompany you to events because you feel uncomfortable going alone
- Wearing makeup and a turtleneck sweater to hide blushing
- Having a couple glasses of wine before entering a party situation

## Factors Contributing to Social Phobia

Social anxiety or phobia may be exacerbated or made more intense by a number of factors, including panic attacks, the trait of perfectionism, depression, substance abuse, negative body image, and difficulty trusting others, as discussed below.

### *Panic attacks*

Panic attacks are intense physical symptoms of anxiety without any realistic danger or threat. The attack peaks within a few seconds to ten minutes and involves at least four of thirteen symptoms, including racing heart; chest discomfort; dizziness; breathlessness; shaking; stomach discomfort; sweating; choking feelings; hot flashes or chills; feelings of unreality or detachment; numbness and tingling; and fears of doom, dying, losing control, or going crazy. These attacks can be triggered by an actual social situation or even just thinking about being in a feared situation. Once people have had panic attacks, they tend to avoid the situations that triggered them in the first place. They worry in advance about whether they might have a panic attack in a particular situation, and this apprehension makes another panic attack more likely. Eventually, they may avoid many different places and situations because they fear they will have to endure a panic attack that others might witness.

*Perfectionism*
Social anxiety has been associated with elevated levels of perfectionism. Perfectionism is the tendency to hold standards that are unrealistically high and overly rigid. Perfectionists are overly worried about making mistakes and what other will think of them if they make mistakes. Because of these worries, it is often easier to avoid situations in which others might see them make a mistake. Perfectionists fear they may not make a perfect impression on others and worry that they will be rejected or not liked. To reduce the risk of feeling uncomfortable, perfectionists tend to overprepare and rehearse for tasks that others will evaluate. They also tend to procrastinate (such as putting off a presentation with a variety of excuses) and to be overly critical of their performances.

*Depression*
It may be argued that social anxiety leads to poor social functioning, isolation, and eventually depression; or that depression leads to isolation, low success in social situations (no one likes being around someone who's depressed), and eventually to social anxiety. Both scenarios are possible. It is interesting that many of the medical treatments for depression have also been approved for treating social anxiety. This has led some to postulate that both depression and social anxiety share similar brain chemistry imbalances.

*Body Image Problems*
Body dysmorphism is a condition that causes sufferers to be unhappy with all or some specific aspect of their physical appearances. Often, they perceive that they have a flaw that is obvious and offensive to others. They may feel that they are too fat, even though they weigh only eighty pounds, or that their nose is too big, even though they have had four nose surgeries that have whittled their nose down to just about nothing. With this kind of frame of mind, it is easy to understand why these people develop severe social anxiety and find it difficult to feel comfortable in the presence of others.

*Substance Abuse Problems*
Many with social anxiety turn to drugs or alcohol as a form of self-medication. In fact, it has been estimated that 85 percent of those with social phobia self-medicate in some way. This must be recognized

as a type of avoidance or safety behavior that must be addressed and overcome if you are going to successfully get over a social-anxiety condition.

*Anger and Mistrust*
Some people with social phobia fear others are not trustworthy and should not be confided in. They may have increased levels of anger or hostility, especially if they feel others are "looking at them wrong" or rejecting them. Because of these feelings, their previous social interactions have likely resulted in failure and rejection, which makes them even more resentful, paranoid, and withdrawn from further social situations.

## Overcoming Social Phobia
The key to overcoming social phobia lies in both medical and psychological strategies. I believe that a combination of the two is most helpful, although many psychotherapists would not agree with me.

*Medical Strategies*
As discussed earlier in the chapter on medical treatment, many types of medications have proven helpful in getting phobias and panic attacks under control in a relatively short period of time—sometimes overnight. Serotonin reuptake inhibitors, such as Paxil and Zoloft, are often helpful but may take a few weeks to really kick in. Anxiolytics, both long acting—such as Clonazepam, Valium, and Xanax XR—as well as short acting—such as Xanax and Ativan, are often used in the emergency room to stop anxiety attacks immediately. They may be used for limited periods of time until anxiety has decreased to reasonable levels and other longer-term medications have started to work. Two more recent types of medications, known as *mood stabilizers* (Lamictal, Trileptal, Depakote) and *atypical antipsychotics* (Zyprexa, Seroquel, Risperdal, Abilify) have shown great benefit in those who are overly agitated or can't turn off their minds from overactive thoughts and ruminations. Taken at bedtime, these medications often will stop the common complaint of morning anxiety the first day they are taken! Beta-blockers, like Inderal, have been used for several decades to treat autonomous nervous system dysfunction caused by anxiety reactions. This helps the sweating, shaking, heart palpitation, and tremor symptoms often experienced by those with social anxiety. For instance, it can be taken a half hour before a presentation. The confidence it gives to those who worry that others will see them sweat or shake is often all it takes for them to get through the presentation with flying colors.

*Psychological Strategies*
Effective psychological strategies for treating social phobia can be broken down into three categories:

- Gradual desensitization and unlearning of the fear response is accomplished through exposure-based strategies and will be discussed in the next section. Using this method, you are taught to approach the feared situation in gradual steps until it no longer provokes an anxiety response.

- Cognitive strategies try to identify your anxious thoughts and replace them with more realistic ways of believing and thinking. You have already been exposed to many examples of "false beliefs" and their "true corrections" throughout this chapter.
- Instruction in basic social skills is very helpful to some. This may include the assertiveness training presented earlier and also includes basic communication skills training. Communication skills include how to meet other people, how to give effective presentations, and how to use nonverbal communication effectively.

*Communication Skills*
The lack of communication skills might lead to poor performance in social situations. A series of negative outcomes or even a single event (rejection, humiliation) could then bring on a case of social anxiety in a vulnerable individual. Conversely, having social anxiety prevents an individual from effectively learning communication skills. This is because the avoidance behaviors result in fewer opportunities to learn how to successfully interact with others. Luckily, communication skills can be learned and practiced, greatly improving self-confidence for those with social anxiety. Communication and social skills include what to say, what to wear, body language, and so on. It is also important to realize that most people with social anxiety greatly underestimate their communication skills and assume that they make a much worse impression on others than they really do.

## Social Skills Training
There is no such thing as a perfect set of tools when it comes to social skills. What works well in one situation with a certain person may not work well in a different situation or with another group or culture. For instance, a man's "pick-up line" may win him a date one day and get him rejected the next. A strategy for a job interview might go over well with one boss but work against you with the next. Everyone stumbles, makes mistakes, and has regrets when it comes to their effectiveness in communicating with others. Our negative appraisal of our social skills is often created by our perfectionist ideals that we should always be pleasing and not offend anyone at any time. Being willing to accept mistakes and learn from them is key to learning social skills.

Social skills training involves the following aspects:

- Grooming
- Eye contact
- Body language
- Tone and volume of speech
- Listening skills
- Conversational skills
- Public-speaking skills
- Interview skills
- Dating skills

- Assertiveness skills (already covered)
- Conflict skills
- Listening skills
- Other interpersonal skills

Remember that the strategies given in this section are not hard and fast rules but simply helpful guidelines. You may want to practice certain skills during exposure therapy with a "safe" person (therapist, friend, family member).

### *Grooming and Dress*

First impressions are formed from many things, including our body language, eye contact, and other nonverbal communication. Your grooming and dress also make a powerful nonverbal statement. For some, the disheveled, crazed "bad boy" look may work for them, especially if they are trying to attract fellow rebels or wish to push others away. Many with social phobia adopt strategies of being unapproachable so others won't start conversations they would be uncomfortable with. For instance, they might act grumpy and angry or groom themselves in a scary, bland, or unappealing way. These, of course, are ways of avoiding social interaction. Other times, a person may never have been taught proper grooming habits. They are relatively simple:

- Shower daily and twice if you need to.
- Brush your teeth at least twice a day, floss daily, use a water pick once a day, and see your dental hygienist once or twice a year for teeth cleaning.
- Wear clean clothes.
- Cut and clean your fingernails and toenails regularly.
- Hair can be groomed in an infinite number of ways and styles; the important thing is that it is clean and smells good.
- Dress appropriately for the situation. Get the advice of a friend with good skills in this area if you're not sure.
- If you are going to be in close contact or a restricted space with others, consider avoiding things that would give you bad breath. Tea would be better than coffee; smokers might want to use a breath spray or chewing gum; those with stomach problems such as acid reflux may want to treat with a medication; and go easy on the garlic!

### *Eye Contact*

Making appropriate eye contact with other people is fundamental to good social skills. You might think that continuous eye contact when talking to others is advisable, but it is more subtle than that. For instance, one study showed that men were most attracted to women who made initial eye contact, then averted their gaze (perhaps a show of submission), and then reconnected (perhaps signaling desire).

In the ape world, unrelenting eye contact is a direct challenge and often results in a violent conflict. In the human world, the equivalent might elicit a comment like, "So what're *you* lookin' at?" or, from *Taxi Driver*, "You lookin' at me?"

Appropriate eye contact involves a dance of adjustments that best gets the desired result. If you are trying to persuade others to your point of view, are trying to impress the importance of a point, or want to exude confidence and determination, direct eye contact might be the best strategy. If, on the other hand, you are negotiating a sensitive issue with a spouse or telling a friend he or she is too pushy, a balance of direct contact while asserting your point and then backing off when the other person has a comment may lead to a less defensive or tense confrontation.

Those who clearly try to avoid eye contact are telling others that they are uncomfortable with the conversation. This could be because they don't like that person's company, are insecure about the point they are making, or feel they are not worthy to be in the other's company. Clearly, the chance for misunderstandings and misinterpretations of the interaction are high when weak eye contact sends confusing messages. During exposure exercises with a friend or therapist, get feedback on your eye contact. See if the person feels comfortable with your level of eye contact, and let him or her point out whenever you are avoiding contact so you can correct it right then and there.

### *Body Language*

You can tell from across the room whether a person is comfortable and enjoying social interaction by body language. Good body language involves an "open" posture and the ability to find an appropriately close (but not too close) distance from others during conversations. Closed posture (arms crossed in front of your chest, fists clenched, legs crossed tightly, chin down, maintaining a serious or downcast facial expression) tell others you are in your shell and don't want to come out. Leaning back or standing too far away from others may send the message that you are aloof, dislike them, or even that you feel hostility. The reality is that you may be afraid your breath will offend them or that they will notice your hands are sweating. A constant serious facial expression sends the message that you are tired, bored, unhappy, angry, constipated, or disinterested. That is one reason that Botox does such a big business: many people feel that their frown lines send the wrong signals and are misinterpreted by others. During exposure therapy exercises, get feedback on your body language, such as the space you allow during a normal conversation and your posture. Find out if you tend to stand too close or too far away from the other person and what messages your other nonverbal communication is sending.

### *Tone and Volume of Speech*

Talking too quietly or too loudly may make others uncomfortable with you. Especially when first meeting people, it is important to be aware of the tone and volume of your speech. If you are too talkative and gabby, you may be seen as nervous or insecure. If you don't talk enough, you may be perceived as withdrawn and disinterested. These are things that can be improved during exposure therapy with a coach.

*Listening Skills*

Communication is a two-way street. How well you listen is perhaps more important than what you say in producing a successful social interaction, whether it be a first date, a business meeting, marriage counseling, or a job interview.

When you feel anxious in a social situation, your attention tends to shift away from the conversation itself to your own inner self-talk about how you feel about the situation. Instead of listening to what the other person is saying, you may be thinking more about whether others are judging you negatively, how others are assessing your looks, and whether others are noticing your anxiety symptoms. You may then worry whether your responses are appropriate and cogent, given that you have not really been focusing on the conversation. Below are common examples of pitfalls to effective listening:

- Filtering. Those with social anxiety tend to look for statements of negative or critical judgment from the other person. In a thirty-minute conversation, a single critical comment would likely overshadow anything else that was said, including many supportive and complimentary comments. This is called *filtering*, or hearing only what you expect or fear.
- Comparing. Those with social anxiety will often not listen because their self-talk is comparing themselves in a negative way to whom they're talking to. "I'm not as successful/smart/cute/clever as she is" might be the background noise that keeps you from really enjoying the conversation and bonding socially with the other person.
- Rehearsing. Out of fear of sounding stupid or unsophisticated, those with social anxiety will often rehearse what they want to say in their minds during a conversation. Unfortunately, they may not be aware that the conversation has changed direction and that their comment is now no longer relevant or correctly timed. This may lead to awkwardness and increased anxiety. The old rule, "It is better to stay silent and thought to be stupid than to open your mouth and remove all doubt," may have some validity here. Maybe it is better to concentrate on listening rather than feeling that you automatically need to answer smartly or offer an opinion. If you are actively listening, it is more likely you will feel comfortable with your response and time it appropriately. Often, a nod of the head that you are listening creates a better impression than anything you could have said.
- Agreeing. One way to avoid conflict or active involvement in a conversation is to simply agree with everything the other person says. In reality, however, people don't expect you to agree with every point or have all their views go unchallenged. In fact, that's boring for most people. The other person may also suspect you're not really listening to them if you do nothing but agree. The reason we engage in conversation is to get feedback and alternative ideas and bounce our ideas off others. Disagreeing does not mean you will offend or be rejected by others, unless they have particularly weak egos.
- Derailing. Derailing means abruptly changing the topic away from some topic you are uncomfortable with, pretending as if you didn't hear what the other person was saying. The effect of this strategy is often that the other person believes you were not listening to them. It is better to acknowledge the question or topic and indicate you'd rather not talk about it. For instance, if your relationship isn't going great and someone asks you about it, you can nicely say, "Oh, don't

even go there!" or "Don't even get me started!" and then change the subject. Only a thoughtless or rude person (or a best friend) would pressure you more on the same subject.

Effective listening is something that can be practiced and will take a lot of the work and anxiety out of social interaction. Here are the basic principles:

- Maintain appropriate eye contact. Try not to let your eyes dart all over the room to other people or conversations you are not engaged in.
- Occasionally try to paraphrase what the other person has said to show you were paying attention. For example, you might start by saying, "In other words, what you are telling me is that…" This is especially effective if the conversation has come to a halt and you don't necessarily have an opinion to offer.
- Ask for clarification. If something someone has said was not clear to you, it is OK to ask the person to help you understand the point a little better.
- Provide feedback. Feedback does not have to be an opinion. You may simply say, for instance, that you are interested in reading more on the subject. Feedback should always be honest and done in a friendly and supportive way (not hurtful or judgmental).

## Conversational Skills

My father often said that life balances itself with addition and subtraction, and what is left over is conversation. He meant that the beginning of our life is a process of adding friends, knowledge, experience, success, money, and skills, and then there is a gradual decline as our lives become a process of subtracting many of these things. In the end, we are left with our social interactions with others. This is what gives life meaning and purpose. Conversational skills, then, may be fundamental to a fulfilled life experience.

This section is just to get you started thinking about the importance of conversation. No set method will be effective in all situations, and often factors beyond our control influence the success of any particular encounter. If the other person is shy, distrustful, misunderstands your intentions, or just doesn't want to be bothered, we can't let that influence our assessment of any particular communication strategy. To learn more about being a good conversationalist, read Alan Garner's (1997) book, *Conversationally Speaking: Testing New Ways to Increase Your Personal and Social Effectiveness*. Below are a few basic guidelines for structuring your conversation.

### *Starting a Conversation*

There are many ways to get better at starting a conversation. You may want to start by practicing in low-risk situations—that is, situations that won't bother you too much if it doesn't go well or in which you already know the person and don't fear rejection, like a coworker, family member, or friend. Then branch out into more challenging encounters, like a new classmate, fellow traveler on the train, or someone in line with you at the grocery store.

Conversations start with the nonverbal cues. Do you look relaxed and easy to talk to? Is your eye contact friendly and not overly direct? Are you dressed too formally for the situation, or would it be better to take the tie off? If you are near a group of people who are already talking at an informal party, it is perfectly OK to go up and stand with them and listen for a while, even if you don't know any of them. Again, make sure your body language is friendly and relaxed.

Someone may start a conversation with you by saying something like, "I've never seen you here at Joe's house before. My name is David—what's your connection to Joe?" Even without introducing yourself, it is OK to join in the conversation after a while when you feel comfortable, have a question, or would like to make a contribution to what's being said. Shake hands with those you are meeting for the first time. It is customary for the person who is introducing him or herself to extend a hand in greeting.

In meeting a stranger, the topic of the initial conversation should be genial and not too personal. If you're at the dog park with fellow dog lovers, it would be natural and easy to start a conversation by talking about the dogs; "Boy, your Labrador sure has good manners," "Where did you get that beautiful collar?" or "I recognize you have a willful terrier there!" If you don't know the individual well, here are a few ways to start a conversation:

- Ask a question. Sometimes a question is easy and useful, such as "Do you know what time it is?" "Has the downtown bus come by recently?" "Do you know if the rain will let up? I don't have the weather app," and so on.
- Make a compliment. Especially if it is honest and sincere, a compliment is an excellent way to start a conversation. For example, you could say "I really like your haircut," or "Did you choose that clothing combination? It is totally stylish. Awesome, in fact."
- Make an observation. If the opportunity lends itself, an observation is often a comfortable way to make contact: "I noticed you are wearing rain boots," "Looks like it's going to snow," "The ferry should have been here fifteen minutes ago," and "Were you at the farmer's market last week?" are some examples.
- Introduce yourself. This is very simple and effective: "Hi, I don't think we've met before. My name is…" or "Hi there, my name is Heidi, and I think your son plays soccer on the same team as my son," or "I'm Dave, and I have been wondering where you got that T-shirt; that's my favorite band."
- Discuss a common hobby or interest or experience. Like in the dog park example above, it is helpful to use a shared interest as a springboard to a conversation. Sporting events, a movie, some headline in the morning paper, the sunset, or a problem in the neighborhood could all be reasons to strike up a conversation with the person next to you. Also, if you wear interesting clothes, display provocative slogans on your T-shirt, or have a well-disciplined dog on leash, you are providing a "conversation piece" for others to initiate a conversation about.

Remember to save more personal topics—such as your religious beliefs, relationship problems, medical diagnoses, legal concerns, political affiliations, and sexual orientation issues—until you know the person well.

*Improving the Quality of Your Conversation*

Once you have started a conversation or introduced yourself, where do things go from there? No two conversations are the same because no two people are the same. In one situation, it might be fine for one to do most of the talking while another does most of the listening. Other times, things go more successfully when everyone gets equal time to say what's on their minds. Some people feel comfortable with periods of silence; others feel they need to fill it in with some idle chatter. My father (a Londoner enamored by his own mellifluous voice) used to be amazed at how my mother and her relatives (Mennonite German farmers) could "have long conversations without saying anything." He noticed that they didn't need to be talking to enjoy each other's company. Simple smiles, nods, and listening to the wind outside in quiet communion made them feel very much engaged in a mutual experience.

So, improving the quality of a conversation does not necessarily mean improving the clarity of your grammar or the cleverness of your retorts. It has more to do with a truthful, honest, and real interaction that brings you closer to the other person or allows you to understand him or her better. Improving the quality of a conversation begins by improving the quality of your listening. Next, it involves a willingness to be yourself and to, gradually as appropriate, disclose more about yourself to the other person.

Disclosures about yourself should not be overly personal with a new acquaintance. But if the opportunity arises, discussing your interests, passions, hobbies, where you went on a favorite vacation, or a wonderful experience you'll never forget are excellent ways of opening up to another person. Don't embellish, brag, or try to top another person's story. Don't try to sound more important or accomplished than you are. If anything, underplay your successes so as not to make others feel threatened or self-conscious. Talking about people you admire and why is another way to let someone know who you are without necessarily giving out personal information. What about a book you read or a movie that had a strong effect on you? Try asking the other person about his or her experiences: "Read a good book recently?" "Tried any new restaurants in town?" or "What's your favorite travel destination?"

When asking others a question, try to make it open ended if possible. Open-ended questions allow the person to expound and give more detailed responses, supporting an active and lively conversation. Closed-ended questions make room for only a one- or two-answer response. Here are some examples:

## Closed-Ended Questions
Seen your parents recently?
When were you in New York last?
Who are you going to vote for?
What do you do for a living?

## Open-Ended Questions
How's your relationship with your parents?
What do you miss most about New York?
What election issues are most important to you?
How did you end up choosing your career?

*Ending a Conversation*

Ending a conversation can happen before you are ready because of an unexpected interruption, or it may wind down until you feel the need to move on. All conversations dwindle as you both run out of things to say. This may happen in minutes or after an hour or more. Having little more to say does not mean you are boring; it is a normal feature of all conversations.

In informal gatherings, like a party, people hop in and out of conversations as they get to know who's there and enjoy a wide variety of individuals. Finding a charming and pleasant way to excuse yourself or finish a conversation is a valuable talent. It allows you to enjoy a wider experience while leaving others to wish they could have had more time with you. This is much better than to let a conversation drag on because you are too lazy to start another, with the end result of feeling trapped or disinterested.

At a party, you could excuse yourself to use the bathroom or freshen your drink. If you are with a particularly insecure person who is a little clingy, try to pull over another person to introduce to him or her and then gracefully excuse yourself or turn to speak to someone nearby. You could also simply say, "Thanks for talking to me; it was great to catch up with you. I see Joe is here and I'd like to say hi while the night is young. You take care." Remember that parties are designed for people to move around, starting and ending conversations. That is why they are excellent exposure opportunities to try your skills in these areas.

In the work environment or out on the street, it may be convenient to say, "I have to get back to work" or "It's time for me to get home." If you truly would like to develop a closer friendship or spend more time with the person, let that person know in a way that he or she can either accept or decline without discomfort. "I wish I could spend more time talking to you, but I don't have time right now. Maybe we could get together sometime after work if you're free." If someone is really interested, the person will let you know by making a suggestion as to a time that he or she is available.

## Public-Speaking Skills

Most people feel some apprehension with speaking in front of a group of strangers, whether it's a business meeting, a class presentation, a lecture, or a speech at a wedding or party. Improving public-speaking skills involves both improving your preparation and delivery as well as managing the anxiety that is likely to surface before and during the presentation.

### *Preparation*

Most of our anxiety would be greatly reduced if we felt well prepared. Here are the steps needed to prepare for a presentation:

1. **Determining the purpose of the presentation.**
    Your presentation may have one or more of the following functions:
    a. To persuade: This kind of presentation is made in court by the attorneys and is called a *summation*. It is meant to persuade the jurors that the defendant is guilty or innocent. You may also want to persuade a company during a sales pitch presentation that your marketing idea will successfully target a certain demographic or persuade your constituents to vote for you in an election.

b. To educate: For example, you might be required to provide didactic material to a group seminar or to a college class. This might include an in-depth lecture on new information helpful to colleagues in your field.
c. To instruct: Many consultants repeat a presentation over and over to individuals or small groups around the country on a very specific subject, such as how to run a new software program or explaining current advances in telecommunications technology. Because of the frequency that they cover the material to a wide range of audiences, they are likely to become more confident as they know what to expect and have a strong command of the subject.
d. To brief: Some situations require a brief three- to five-minute update to bring everyone in the room up to date on the current status of a specific topic.
e. To entertain: Speeches at birthday parties, weddings, luncheons, fundraisers, and anniversaries are usually meant to entertain. Theatrical monologues and stand-up comedy are also examples of entertainment presentations.
f. To express emotion or feelings: Speeches given at funerals, as well as rallies for various causes (e.g., animal rights, world hunger, and poverty) may be designed primarily to move the emotions of the audience.

2. **Determining the nature of the audience.**
It is helpful to know as much about your audience as possible. Are they professionals or students? Have they been exposed to the material before or not? What size gathering is expected to show up? What is the average age? Are they coming because they want to or because that have to fulfill some requirement? Many seasoned presenters will ask the audience a few questions at the beginning and may then adjust their style or change the contents of the talk to more effectively meet the needs of that specific group.

3. **Deciding the subject matter.**
Be clear about the points you want to get across, even going so far as to list them or show them on an overhead slide at the beginning of the presentation. An appropriate joke, anecdote, or illustration is often useful in focusing the attention of your audience on your main points. When preparing your presentation, choose only material that directly helps you make one of your points. Exclude information that is off the subject or confuses the issue unnecessarily. There may be two ways to explain a particular point; choose the one that is most direct, forceful, and easiest to understand. Weed out extraneous discourse that might bore or tire your audience. It is better to finish your presentation early and open up for a time of interactive questions and answers than to drag on and on until they have to pull you from the stage!

4. **Organizing the presentation.**
Nearly every presentation, except for a brief, should have an introduction, the main body of the talk, and a conclusion. The introduction should let the audience know what you intend to cover and what points you intend to make. The body of the talk should go through in stepwise fashion the content and important details that allow you to arrive at your conclusions. The conclusion should restate your points, summarize your findings, and draw any interpretations or inferences regarding the content.

A presentation may often be laid out in a historical fashion, starting with what happened in the past and how things have progressed over time, and what the latest advances have accomplished. Another effective organization strategy is to present a series of case studies or problems, showing one or more existing solutions. Then show how your technique or product would impact each of those problems and offer a better outcome.

5. **Making the presentation interesting.**

   There are many ways to spice up a presentation and keep the audience's attention. Sometimes an energetic and enthusiastic energy with facial expressiveness and active body language is all you might need. Other times, an appropriate (not offensive) joke, an amusing personal experience, an example that draws on a story in the news, relevant statistics, or a compelling illustration may be the best way to draw your audience in. Keep a scrap book of cartoons, quotes, anecdotes, illustrations, and jokes that you think might one day be useful in a presentation. Go to the talks and lectures of famous or dynamic speakers to see how they do it. Keeping your audience on their toes by occasionally asking individuals direct questions and using their answers to further the point you were making is effective but requires the ability to think on your feet. Supporting materials, such as visual aids (slide show, overhead projector, video tapes, flip charts, chalk board, cartoons, illustrations, graphics, maps, and handouts) will make your presentation seem better prepared and organized. They will also help your audience assimilate all the information and not get lost. Handouts are especially good if they cover the main points so that your audience does not have to take notes.

6. **Rehearsing the presentation.**

   Rehearsing has a number of benefits. It will give you an idea of the time your presentation will take if you speak at a relaxed rate. Try to practice in front of a friend so you can get feedback on your body language, the volume and clarity of your speaking, and the content of your presentation. If this is not possible, videotape yourself from the audience's perspective and watch for nervous mannerisms, eye contact, and overall poise and confidence. It is also helpful to visit the site where the actual talk will be held to familiarize yourself with the venue and practice the volume of speech that will be most effective.

   Visualization is a very effective way to rehearse your speech. Lay down with your eyes closed and silently see yourself giving your talk with a calm and confident demeanor. Decide at which points you will make eye contact to emphasize a point, when you will allow a pause, and when you will leave the podium to engage the audience more directly. See yourself giving the talk in a dynamic and enthusiastic way. Rehearse the memorized sections of your talk over and over in your mind. Think of possible questions and how you might phrase your response, imagining yourself fielding questions confidently.

7. **Delivery.**

   Successful delivery depends on several factors. Once you have prepared, you must learn to let go of worries or concerns about the outcome or how others might perceive you. Realize that no one in the room is better able than you to present this material, and you are providing a valuable service in getting the information together for the others. Even if you stumble a bit, it will not be a catastrophe. Your audience is not there to scrutinize you and, in fact, wants you to succeed. Here are some pointers on improving your presentation and sounding more confident:

- **Volume and rate of speech.**
  Speak at a comfortable volume for everyone in the room. Make sure the people in the last row will not have to strain to hear you by imagining you are delivering your talk to them only. Don't let your voice trail off at the end of the sentence, but keep it strong and confident right to the punctuation mark. Avoid saying meaningless fillers like "um" and "uhh." It is better to say nothing until you have found the word or phrase you would like to use. Don't apologize if you lose your place. Either say nothing until you've found it, or simply say, "Give me a moment while I find my place." If you are anxious, you will tend to talk too fast. Mindfully slow yourself down, even to the point you think you are talking too slowly. Don't try to present a huge amount of material in a short time so you are forced to speak quickly. Finally, enunciate your words clearly and crisply. Take a cup of water with you to the podium if you tend to get "cotton mouth" when anxious, and take small sips occasionally to give yourself a break and keep your mouth working properly.

- **Nonverbal communication.**
  Don't forget that what your nonverbal communication says is more important than what you actually say when it comes to exuding self-confidence. Those with anxiety will often show it by wringing their hands, playing with their hair, covering their mouths with their hands, hunching their shoulders inward, or keeping their eyes fixed downward on their notes. Watch your favorite politician giving a speech. Politicians have honed their skills at being confident and persuasive. Practice standing tall with your shoulders back and your face up. Memorize much of your talk and use notes only as a framework of key points and the order in which you'd like to make them. Try not to read word by word because you will lose eye contact with your audience. Change the position of your eye contact to include all of your audience over the course of your talk. Keep your hands away from your face, but don't be afraid to use arm and hand gestures to communicate key points. If possible, walk around a bit rather than staying firmly planted behind the podium. Plan to walk in front of the podium during parts of your talk that you have particularly well memorized. When returning to the podium to find your place, take your time—take a sip of water and a deep breath. Your audience needs little points of pause, as well.

- **Speak from an outline.**
  As stated above, it is best to speak from an outline rather than verbatim from your notes. Those who are locked into reading word for word because they are afraid to leave something out will often panic if they lose their place. It's OK to forget some items, and it will be better for the success of your presentation if you force yourself to be somewhat spontaneous during your talk by not strictly following a script. One way to avoid sounding scripted is to occasionally put in a short personal anecdote that illustrates your point. Tell the story as you would to a good friend without notes, with good eye contact, and with relaxed and natural facial expressions and gestures. For peace of mind, you can bring both the outline of your presentation and the fully written version to the podium and switch from one to the other as you feel comfortable.

- **Respect the intelligence of your audience.**

  Don't talk down to your audience (unless they are younger than five years old!). Make sure your tone of voice and the words you choose are not condescending. Just because you are the expert for the day, remember that your audience may be experts in their own fields and know quite a bit about what you are discussing, as well. Arrogance is not a quality of a self-confident person; quite the opposite is true. The more you respect the intelligence of your audience, the more they will respect you.

  You should always leave time for questions and requests for clarification at the end of your talk. Encourage your audience to write down questions or points that "I have failed to make clear" (rather than "you don't understand") so that you can explain them at the end of the talk. In some informal situations, it's OK to invite your audience to stop you at anytime they would like to clarify a point. Only do this if you are not rattled by interruptions. When you are asked a question, repeat it out loud if you feel everyone in the room may not have heard it.

  You may be asked questions that you thought were already clearly explained or show that the questioner was not paying attention. Remember that there is no such thing as a stupid question. If someone asks a silly question, show tact and respect by phrasing your response with something like, "Thank you for bringing up that question because it allows me to reiterate an important point…" or "That's an interesting question." Finally, you will likely be asked questions you don't know the answer to. Don't make something up or try to sound as if you have all the answers. It's perfectly OK to say, "I don't know the answer to that, but it is a very good question." It is also reasonable to open the question up to the audience in general ("Does anyone else have an answer to that question?").

- **Repeat the main points.**

  Make a list of the main points of your talk and formulate them into simple, one-sentence talking points. Repeat them frequently as you go. Even if your audience does not remember everything you say, they should remember these key points. Each point should be a stepping stone to the next and support your final conclusions.

- **Keep it simple.**

  Don't try to discuss more than your time allows. Decide in advance the main points and make sure you get these across in a sequence that is flowing and logical. Don't digress unless it really helps solidify one of your key points. Don't go into an unnecessary level of depth just to prove how much you know; let the audience find this out when they ask you more in-depth questions at the end.

- **Manage your anxiety.**

  Preparing for a presentation also includes preparing yourself to be calm and relaxed when you go on stage. First, you should go over your list of anxious cognitions and false beliefs and read the "true corrections" you have made. Say them until you believe them. Practice the slow and regular breathing that you will use before and during the presentation. Don't fight fear or anxiety symptoms. Recognize the symptoms and just let them happen. Don't be afraid to make a remark about your nervousness and laugh it off. This will put your audience at ease, make you less nervous, and win them over to your side. Remember, it is normal to be anxious before and during a presentation. Your audience expects it. And as you make more presentations, you will find it just gets easier.

Many very good speakers take a medication, such as a mild sedative or beta-blocker, before a presentation. Of course, you should rehearse your speech with the medication on board beforehand to see if it helps. Some will argue that this gets in the way of unlearning anxiety by having experiences that don't involve medication or safety behaviors. I have found that as a phobic person gets more experience under his or her belt, the person can often forego the medication with no problem. You may want to discuss the possibility of taking a medication with your doctor.

Hand out a form to your audience to give you feedback that will help future presentations. One example is below:

## Presentation Evaluation Form

Speaker: _____ Date: _____

Topic: _____

Please circle the number to the right that best describes your opinion about the presentation. On this scale from 1 to 5, circle (1) for a "poor" evaluation, (5) for an "excellent" evaluation, and (3) for a "neutral" or "not applicable" response.

|  | Poor |  | Neutral |  | Excellent |
|---|---|---|---|---|---|
| (a) Format of presentation was easy to follow | 1 | 2 | 3 | 4 | 5 |
| (b) Content was clear and relevant | 1 | 2 | 3 | 4 | 5 |
| (c) Content was interesting | 1 | 2 | 3 | 4 | 5 |
| (d) Content was not too difficult or confusing | 1 | 2 | 3 | 4 | 5 |
| (e) My understanding of the topic improved | 1 | 2 | 3 | 4 | 5 |
| (f) Presentation skills of presenter | 1 | 2 | 3 | 4 | 5 |
| (g) Lecturer seemed knowledgeable | 1 | 2 | 3 | 4 | 5 |
| (h) Concepts were clearly explained | 1 | 2 | 3 | 4 | 5 |
| (i) Location was comfortable (space, lighting) | 1 | 2 | 3 | 4 | 5 |
| (j) Audiovisual resources were helpful | 1 | 2 | 3 | 4 | 5 |
| (k) Handouts were helpful | 1 | 2 | 3 | 4 | 5 |
| (l) Overall rating of presentation | 1 | 2 | 3 | 4 | 5 |

## Comments and Suggestions for Improvement

_____
_____
_____
_____

**NOTE:** If you want to improve the quality of your performance, ask for feedback and suggestions. You are likely to find that you are overly self-critical and are basing your own self-evaluation on how anxious you were or whether your anxiety symptoms showed to others. To get a more balanced view of the effectiveness of your presentation, hand out a list of questions for audience members to anonymously fill out and hand in after the talk. The form above is a commonly used format for evaluating presentations.

## Interview Skills

One of the most nerve-wracking experiences is interviewing for a job, university or graduate school admission, or some other needed or highly desired position. The more emotionally invested you are in the outcome, the more nervous you will likely feel. Of course, the interviewer expects some degree of anxiety on your behalf. Showing no anxiety at all could be interpreted as being overly confident or apathetic. Those with social anxiety may have an extra layer of anxiety because of all the inner dialogue: "Do they think I'm competent?" "Can they see my hands sweating and my face turning red?" "Am I going to throw up right on their desk?"

A good strategy for doing well in an interview is outlined below. As with anything, practice improves skills and confidence. Find ways to expose yourself to interview situations. Role-play the interview with a friend or counselor in a mock simulation, if possible. A more detailed discussion of the topic may be found in the book *Messages: The Communication Skills Book* (McKay, Davis, and Fanning 1995).

### *Preparing for the Interview*

- Don't be overly invested in the outcome. From the beginning of your preparation, keep in mind that this is only an interview. The worst that can happen is that you are not chosen. There will be other, perhaps better opportunities. Have faith that the right situation will work out for you if you keep trying.
- Understand the purpose of the interview. What is the interviewer looking for? What does the school/business need or desire from a prospective applicant? Learn as much as you can about the institution, business, or organization that is interviewing you. Go to its website, if possible, and read up on its mission statement, personnel and staff introductions, products and services, and so on. Being knowledgeable about the organization during an interview provides a strong impression that you are a motivated person who is truly interested in the position.
- Know something about your interviewer. If possible, try to find out in advance who will conduct your interview. Memorize his or her name so that you can use it when answering an interview question or when saying good-bye. Sometimes an organization's website will provide a picture and short biographical sketch.
- Make personal contact with the interviewer without being overly ingratiating. If you notice something on his or her desk or an object in the room that you are interested in, make small

talk about it: "I noticed there is a quarter horse in your family photo! Do any of you ride?" or "Isn't that horse statue from the Han Dynasty? I saw one like it in Beijing."

- Know your strengths. Take some time to write down your personal strengths, training, and talents that make you an attractive applicant. How could you contribute to the success of the organization? You may take these notes to the interview with you if you are afraid you might forget a point and refer to them if necessary.
- Know your limitations. Interviewers often ask you to describe your weaknesses. This is not a therapy session, so don't spend too much time gabbing about your faults. Make sure that any limitation you list will not be viewed as a potential problem, like "I tend to be lazy and drink a lot." Instead, list limitations that might be seen as a positive: "I tend to be a workaholic and not leave enough time for my social life," or "I often forget to take breaks when I get into a project, and if I forget to eat I can get hypoglycemic and need to grab an apple." It may also be helpful to list a *past* limitation and how you overcame it: "In my last job, I felt uncomfortable working with the new computer programs. So I took a night class to get up to speed, and now I teach other new staff how to work the programs and feel very confident about my computer skills." This example gives a previous limitation but also shows that the applicant was self-directed and motivated to do better. Have two examples like these ready in case you are asked.
- Prepare your questions. List at least five questions you would like to ask the interviewer. Again, you can take these questions with you in the form of brief notes. You will almost always be asked if you have any questions, and this provides another opportunity to show your interest and preparation. Try not to ask a question that has already been answered in the body of the interview. Here are some examples:
    o Are there any opportunities for advancement in this firm?
    o Will I be asked to telecommute?
    o Are there any places to eat nearby, or is it better to bring a sack lunch?
    o Who will be my direct supervisor, and how often will I be able to meet with that person?
    o What is the dress code?

Consider not asking questions about salary, paid vacations, health insurance, family/sick leave, or other benefits until after you are being seriously considered for the position. Otherwise, you will come across as someone looking for what they can get from the company rather than expressing what you have to offer. If you are applying to a university program, ask about library hours, where to eat on campus, parking options, campus security, research opportunities, or whatever is pertinent to your interests or areas of study.

*Prepare support materials*
Bring a neat folder or small briefcase to the interview with you. Have any notes carefully arranged where you can reach them easily if you want to refer to them. Have extra copies of your updated résumé and any recommendation letters, certifications, copies of diplomas, CV, or anything else that has been requested that you bring with you to the interview.

*Practice*

Before the interview, write down ten questions you think you might be asked and ask a friend or family member to play the role of interviewer. Get feedback on your eye contact, body language, rate of speech, and the content of your answers. Remember to speak confidently at a relaxed rate and in a calm tone—not too loud or too soft.

*During the Interview*

- Be on time. In fact, be early by fifteen minutes.
- Dress conservatively and in a professional manner. Make sure you are well groomed with neat, clean hair and brushed teeth and that you smell good.
- Follow the interviewers' lead. Let them show you where to sit. Are they behaving in a casual or very formal manner? Adapt your style to be compatible with theirs, but don't get too casual. Don't chew gum. Sit up with good posture, but don't be fixed and rigid. Keep your hands away from your face and in a comfortable and relaxed position (i.e., folded in your lap). Don't fidget, twirl your hair, scratch yourself, wring your hands, or tap your fingers. It is good to shift position in a natural way as you would during a class lecture to relieve muscle tension.
- Listen. Remember the interviewers' names when they introduce themselves. It's OK to say, "I'm sorry, I didn't catch your name," if they did not speak clearly. Stay with the interviewers and respond to their questions. Treat the interview as you would any important conversation, and turn off any self-talk about what is going on.
- Have good manners. Be courteous and polite by saying "thank you," "please," "excuse me," and so on. Don't presume to sit in a chair you're not directed to sit in, fix yourself a cup of coffee if not invited to, or play with something on the interviewer's desk that is his or her personal property. Don't look out the window, except perhaps initially to admire and comment on the view.
- Don't be negative. Avoid saying anything disparaging about the organization, the interview process, or the person interviewing you. Don't complain about your last company or boss, even if you were unhappy there. It's OK to discuss what could have been improved about your previous job experience, if asked, but make sure it is done with a positive and constructive attitude.
- Be flexible. Show that you are willing to compromise and see both sides of any issue. For instance, if the hours will be difficult for you, let them know that you understand their needs and will do everything you can to fit into their schedule and meet their needs. After you are offered the position and they like you, they may be willing to accommodate your schedule and home commitments. But if you say, "Oh, that will never do. I can't get in here any sooner than 9:30," you may have disqualified yourself from the start.
- Ask questions. Remember that the interview is a two-way street for them to learn about you and you to find out whether you want to work or study with that particular organization. Asking questions shows you are serious about your decisions.

- Be yourself (unless, of course, you are a jerk). Answer questions honestly, but don't give unnecessary personal information. If they ask if you are nervous, say simply and with a pleasant expression, "Yes, thanks for noticing. I've never been able to be completely relaxed in an interview situation." But don't provide the details of your difficulty finding parking, previous night on the town, marital problems, panic attacks, depression, or medication regimen.

*After the Interview*

- Ask the interviewers if there is anything more they need from you. Ask what the next step is and when and how you should expect to hear their decision. Find out if there will be another round of interviews for successful applicants.
- Say good-bye with good eye contact and a firm handshake, if they offer to shake your hand. Try to use their names; for example, "I enjoyed meeting you and finding out more about your company, Dr. Birnbaum."
- Send a short follow-up "thank you" by e-mail or a handwritten note to the interviewer thanking them for his or her time. Send it the same day.
- Later in the day, think back on the interview and see areas that went well or could have gone better. Write down what you would have done differently, and comment on the times you felt most nervous and most at ease and confident. This information will help you prepare for future interviews.

## Dating Skills

Below are a few guidelines to consider when entering (or reentering) the dating world. Every situation and combination of individuals is different and calls for a unique interplay of chemistry for success. Sometimes this is beyond your control. A partner may see you more as a short-term diversion than a long-term possibility, and this may or may not change. Go into dating with realistic expectations and eyes open. Give as much of your heart as the other person earns, but at the same time, be generous in sharing yourself and take some risk in letting someone get close enough to decide if he or she likes you. Dating, as with any genuine human interaction, involves risk. Be willing to take some risk without being foolish is the art of dating.

*Be Yourself*

Dating skills start with good communication skills. Again, nonverbal communication is often the first thing that others notice. Working on a relaxed, happy, and confident demeanor with your eye contact, posture, and facial expressions will go a long way in making you attractive and approachable. Of course, it is important that you be true to who you are. You don't have to act like a social butterfly if you're a quiet and private person. The point is to be relaxed and confident and *like* who you are. Simply being yourself will endear you to others more than any other thing you could say or do.

*Recognize the Possibility of Rejection without Fear*
Experiencing some form of rejection is a necessary and normal part of the dating process. Rejection may come in the form of a polite but assertive statement, such as "I'm sorry, but I don't feel we have made a connection. I wish you the best and thanks for your interest." Or it may come in the passive form of ignored calls or standing you up. If this is the case, take the hint. If it is really a match, you won't have to work hard to get the person's attention.

Remember that rejection has nothing to do with you as a person; it merely speaks to the compatibility between you and a specific person. Do not adopt a defeatist attitude over a few rejections, rejecting further attempts at dating as futile or too painful. Have a thicker skin and believe in yourself. Good things happen to those who are patient, have faith, and keep an open heart. Being unselfish also increases your chance of success. It is often true that good things happen when you least expect them and are not looking for them. So relax and take your time; dating is not a process that should be rushed or forced, as this will likely only lead to frustration and stress.

*Keep an Open Mind*
Remember that the belief that there is one special person out there waiting for you who is your soul mate is a myth. There are many people you might meet who would make perfectly wonderful long-term partners. They may have very different qualities, talents, and attributes, but, with the right commitment from both of you, it could work out just fine.

*Know Where to Fish*
A 1994 study that looked at how and where people met their significant others found that 35 percent were introduced by a friend, 32 percent introduced themselves, 15 percent were introduced by a family member, 6 percent by a coworker, 6 percent by a classmate, and 2 percent by someone else or a neighbor. In addition, 23 percent met at school, 15 percent at work, 10 percent at a party, 8 percent at a place of worship, 8 percent at a bar, 4 percent at a gym or social club, 1 percent by way of a personal ad, 1 percent while on a vacation, and 30 percent elsewhere (on the bus, at the store, the opera, through a car accident, etc.). My guess is that if this same study were done today, up to 30 percent would say they met by way of a personal ad on a dating site, rather than 1 percent! The point is that anywhere might be an appropriate place to meet a prospective partner. Realize that *you're* there, and so someone you might be interested in meeting or dating might also be there.

The best place to meet people is in places where you enjoy doing things that you are passionate about. Chances are you will be energized and having fun, which makes drawing others to you very easy. If you appreciate people who are well read, you might take evening classes in literature, go to book signings, attend poetry readings, or spend time at the local library. On the other side of that coin, avoid going to places that attract people you don't have much in common with or where you don't enjoy the activity. If you don't like being around people who drink, avoid going to bars.

## Be What You Are Looking For

Before you start dating, it is helpful to know what you're looking for: A serious relationship? Marriage with children? A sexual partner? Companionship? Then remember that you should have the qualities that you seek in another person. If you're looking for a bad boy or femme fatale, you have to exude the same "wild-side" danger and sensuality. If you are looking for a long-term relationship with someone who is considerate, kind, honest, and has a good sense of humor, start by cultivating these qualities in yourself and living as the person you would like to meet. When you finally do meet the person, he or she is more likely to appreciate in you his or her own standards and values. Living as the person you would like to find is also more likely to put you into places and situations where you might meet such a person.

## Network

One of the best ways to increase your odds of meeting new people is to let your circle of friends know that you're interested and available. Let them know the parameters of what would be an appropriate candidate (age, social status, religious beliefs, basic qualities, etc.). The more people you are in touch with and the more invitations you accept to get out into the world and meet others, the greater your chance of success.

## Take the Plunge

Being in the presence of other interesting people will not be enough. To actually *meet* people, it will be necessary to step up to the plate and take some risk. For starters, you should try to make eye contact, smile from time to time, and make a point of saying hello. To ensure that this casual contact has the chance of going further, you will have to engage in conversation. The other person might have better conversation skills and make you feel at ease right away. Other times, there may be some awkward moments. Relax and go slow. Realize that if someone is attracted to you, that person will find your awkwardness charming. If you feel the other person may be receptive, you will have to take a bigger risk in asking him or her to meet you for a cup of coffee or to go to a movie or to a museum or some other activity. You may know of an event or informal get-together that the person could be meet you at that would not make him or her feel committed to a "date." You might also exchange business cards and then call later to invite the person somewhere. If you are really nervous talking in person, call at a time the person probably won't answer (not two in the morning) and leave a message, "Sorry, I must have missed you."

## The First Date

First dates are more charming and comfortable if they are spontaneous and informal. At the time, it may not be thought of as a date at all. For instance, you could walk the person home, offer to help him or her complete a task (such as moving, painting a room, taking the dog to the groomer), or show some act of heartfelt kindness, concern, or friendship. If there seems to be some chemistry and interest developing, you may feel more relaxed in suggesting a more formal outing such as lunch, dinner, or a movie.

On the first date, pay attention to the details. Make sure your hygiene and appearance are at their best. Be a good listener and share something personal about yourself. Think of ways to make the other person feel at ease. Pay attention to his or her body language and act accordingly. If the person is touchy-feely and seems to enjoy physical contact, let yourself be physical. If the person seems withdrawn and needs space, give him or her the space needed to feel comfortable. Don't force a kiss or hug if it doesn't come naturally and if the feeling does not seem to be mutual. If you had a good time, tell the person so and say that you would like to see him or her again. Maybe even make a suggestion for a second date if things went well.

If you are in charge of planning a first date, make it simple and comfortable. Choose a place that is easy to get to, has no parking problems, and will not be a crowded "zoo" scene. Make sure it is a place that is quiet and intimate and allows for conversation and connection. Go to a place that you think will encourage openness and honesty. Choose a venue that reflects something about your tastes or interests. If you go to a movie, allow time to sit together afterward for drinks or coffee to discuss your impressions and feelings about the film. Or go to a favorite street in the city where you can walk to several places and spontaneously choose among a variety of options: dinner, dessert, a poetry reading, a jazz club, dancing, or window shopping. Above all, be prepared and plan things in advance. Have your money, bridge toll, parking lot, tickets, and any other details all under control. The less stress and hassles that crop up, the more you can focus on your date and enjoy yourself.

## Graded Desensitization and Exposure Therapy
### Sensitization and Avoidance

Three factors tend to perpetuate fears and phobias: (1) negative, distorted self-talk; (2) sensitization; and (3) avoidance. The first factor has already been discussed above in the section Changing Anxious Self-Talk.

Sensitization is a phenomenon in which anxiety becomes a conditioned response to a given object, situation, or event. For instance, a person who is the victim of a frightening experience, such as being robbed at gunpoint in a back alley, may from then on feel a similar anxious emotion when driving by an alley or visiting a friend whose home borders on a back alleyway. Those who experience a panic attack while driving on the freeway may then feel anxious emotions every time they enter the onramp to the freeway.

Being *sensitized* means that the presence of—or even thinking about—the feared stimulus will often be enough to trigger an anxiety reaction. After sensitization occurs, the most natural human response is to *avoid* the situation or object. Avoidance is rewarded by not having to feel the uncomfortable symptoms of anxiety. For this reason, it becomes an ingrained coping mechanism that perpetuates the phobia. Avoidance guarantees that you will not get over your fears and will continue to let phobias control your life. This is because avoidance prevents you from learning that you *can* handle the situation and get through it just fine without triggering anxiety.

Avoidance strategies can be so ingrained and subtle that we fail to recognize them as such. Below are examples of various types of avoidance behaviors often used when an anxious individual must endure a fearful situation.

*Distraction*

To distract themselves while traveling on a plane, they might be sure to bring a suspenseful book or blast the iPod at full volume with their favorite tunes. Those with social anxiety at a party may "busy" themselves helping with the preparation, serving, and cleaning so as not to be required to engage in conversation with other guests.

*Overprotective Behaviors*

Those who fear others will notice their anxiety may wear makeup and a turtleneck sweater to hide blushing or gloves to hide sweaty or shaking hands. An insecure date might wear sunglasses to avoid eye contact or choose a dark restaurant where the signs of anxiety are less likely to be noticed. Someone who fears birds might insist on sitting inside the ferry even on a beautiful day when all the person's friends are sitting out on the deck. Those you fear social interaction at parties might always show up with a friend or call in advance to find out who else will be there. Those who fear having a panic attack or vomiting in public might insist on learning the location of all exits and bathrooms before entering a building.

*Overcompensation*

This involves overpreparation or overcompensation for perceived flaws. Those who worry about looking stupid during a presentation may spend so much time rehearsing the details that they lose track of the basic theme. Those who worry about their looks might take excessive amounts of time deciding what clothes to wear, fixing their hair, or working out in the gym.

*Excessive Reassurance Seeking*

This means excessive need for feedback on your looks, your performance, and how you are being perceived. While some amount of feedback is helpful, especially from a trusted friend, constantly looking for and checking for signs of approval or disapproval is a sign that you don't feel secure about who you are. Having faith and trust in yourself is necessary but should be derived from your self-discipline and betterment, not from the opinions or affirmations of others.

*Substance Abuse*

One way to avoid a feared situation is to self-medicate with alcohol or drugs. This teaches you that the only way you can handle your anxiety is through using some substance. For this reason, exposure exercises must be done sober. Don't drink at a party until *after* you have practiced your exposure exercises and the fear has diminished.

Graded desensitization and exposure therapy are the most successful long-term strategies for overcoming phobias and anxiety triggered by external cues. They can be accomplished with the help of medications and high-tech methods like biofeedback and virtual reality or by low-tech means of gradual unlearning of fear through imagery, visualization, self-hypnosis, and incremental exposure to the feared stimulus.

## Understanding How Exposure Works

Exposure works by creating a semicontrolled environment in which you can test the validity of your anxious thoughts and interpretations regarding a particular feared object or situation. Interoceptive exposure, or exposure to physical sensations that elicit anxiety, such as lightheadedness or nausea, works by showing us we can have uncomfortable sensations without connecting them to the emotion of anxiety.

Of course, you may be skeptical that exposure therapy will work for you, especially if exposures to what you fear in the past, either planned or unplanned, caused an *increase* in your anxiety. Unpredictable and unexpected exposure often makes fear worse. So does someone pushing you into a feared situation when you're not prepared. For instance, if you are afraid of spiders and a friend puts a spider on your neck, you will likely feel even more anxious in the future. If you are afraid of birds, and a group of pigeons feeding on the ground is suddenly startled and flies right at you, you may find your avoidance strategies increasing. On the other hand, if you were exposed to one pigeon at a time in a controlled environment and took your time getting used to it, your fear of birds might decrease.

Below is a list of factors that make exposure exercises different from exposures that might make anxiety worse.

- Exposure exercises are predictable and under your control. You decide when to enter and leave an anxiety-provoking situation.
- Exposure exercises are prolonged. You purposely stay in the presence of the anxiety-provoking situation until you feel your anxiety decreasing, thereby learning that the anxiety eventually comes under control if you put up with it for a while. Real-life unpredictable exposures are often too brief for you to learn this. All you learn is that the situation causes anxiety, and the sooner you get away from it, the better.
- Exposure exercises are frequent. Real-life exposures are often few and far between. Planning your exposures to be a part of daily life is much more likely to diminish anxiety over time.
- Exposure exercises involve actively countering your distorted anxious cognitions and replacing them with a reasonable correction. The anxious thinking that goes with everyday, real-life exposures often goes unchallenged and, therefore, perpetuates the anxiety.
- Exposure exercises require that you pay attention to avoidance and safety behaviors, consciously letting go of these over time. Real-life exposures often encourage us to continue these behaviors because they offer quick, short-term relief.

### *Overview*

No matter what method you decide to use, exposure exercises all have several features in common that make them successful. Below is an overview for designing and implementing a successful exposure or "desensitization" program:

*Initial Assessment*
After filling out the personal anxiety assessment plan, you will have identified the situation(s) or object(s) of your fear, as well as avoidance and safety behaviors. You will also have listed any physical sensations that you fear experiencing. This initial assessment is crucial in determining how to go about your exposure treatment.

*Planning Exposure Therapy*
Exposure therapy should begin with situations and exercises that are less difficult and gradually move up to those that are more difficult. To plan this graded exposure, you must create a hierarchy of the situations that you fear, from least difficult to most difficult. A hierarchy may have as few as three or as many as ten levels of difficulty. Below are some examples of possible hierarchies:

*Example one: Spider Phobia*

a. Make a scrapbook of spider photos, from small and cute advancing to hairy and menacing. Look at the pictures with no emotional reaction, as if you are looking at pictures of something you're not afraid of, like gemstones or orchids.
b. Look at a live spider in the outdoors. Nature stores often sell octagonal spider homes for placing in your yard. You can actually watch as a spider spins its web.
c. Sit next to a trapped spider indoors. Have a friend catch a (nonpoisonous) spider for you and put it in a jar with air holes in the cap or a netted cage. Put it on a table and sit next to it. Start with sitting as long as you feel able (maybe just a few minutes). Each time you sit down with the spider, calm your anxious emotions with deep breathing exercises and progressive relaxation exercises. Try to gradually extend the time you spend and decrease your physical distance from the spider.
d. After feeling comfortable being near the caged spider, practice taking the spider in and out of the jar or cage by letting it climb onto a pencil or rolled piece of paper. Shake the paper or pencil to watch the spider fall off, holding onto to its line of web, and then let it climb back up. If it falls on the ground, scoop it up with the paper or let it climb back onto the pencil and put it back in the container.
e. Touch the spider. First gently touch the spider with the tip of your index finger. It will likely be afraid and try to get away from you. Eventually, perhaps after many days of trying, you may be able to actually let the spider walk up your finger. Shake it gently, like you did with the pencil, to make it dangle from its line and climb back up. Let the spider climb off your finger back into the jar or cage.

*Example two: Social anxiety regarding attending social events alone.*

a. Start with a virtual-reality program that places you at a party. Put on your virtual-reality helmet or glasses and see yourself walking freely around the house and among the party guests. They are talking in groups and seem to be enjoying themselves. As you walk by, notice that they may briefly acknowledge you with a nod or smile. The purpose of a party is for everyone to look around and see who's there to talk to. Remind yourself that nobody is focusing undue attention on you or scrutinizing you; that's not why they're there.

b. Now advance the virtual-reality program to the part where you approach a group of people in a conversation and stand on the edge listening to the conversation. Do this program until you feel quite at ease just hanging out listening, and keep telling yourself that everyone is there to mix and mingle, and no one is overly scrutinizing anyone else.

c. Now it's time to try an actual social situation with real people. Find a convenient casual setting to practice hanging out around people. Look in the newspaper and choose at least one outing a week: the grand opening of a new bookstore, a church reception area after Sunday services, a jazz nightclub, or a local dog park where you take your pooch to socialize. Any number of places contain fun people who are out enjoying themselves and have time to shoot the breeze. Make it a rule to have at least one interaction—even if you just stand next to a group of people, make eye contact, smile, and listen. Even better if you take the initiative to start a conversation, introduce yourself to a stranger, or contribute to the conversation already in progress. Notice that people generally appreciate your friendliness and willingness to make an effort. Notice that nobody thinks poorly of you for trying—in fact, just the opposite.

d. Next, accept an invitation to a party or attend a club or celebration in your area. Mix and mingle, spending enough time in any uncomfortable situation until the anxiety subsides. Notice that nothing terrible happened. In fact, you're doing really well. People respond to your good eye contact and pleasant demeanor. Allow yourself to be drawn into any conversation that presents itself, and move on once you feel comfortable or the conversation has run its course.

Notice that the design of this exposure hierarchy involves the use of high-tech virtual reality. Those who enjoy technology will get a kick out of this form of therapy and are more likely to practice and successfully complete the exercises. The point is to design your exposure exercises in a way that appeals to you and still gets the job done.

**Example three: Social anxiety regarding going out on a date.**

a. You've finally asked a person you're interested in if he or she would like to spend some time with you some Saturday afternoon, and the person said, "Sure, give me a call." But you haven't called because you're afraid you'll screw up and embarrass yourself. Think about what you would like to do, then call and ask if that plan is OK with the person. Agree to a specific time and day you will be together. This example is a man asking a woman out (I'm old school), but obviously it could be same-sex or a woman asking the man.

b. Design in your mind a first date you would like to go on with that person. Your first date should be uncomplicated, low stress, and fun or interesting. There should be time for quality interaction and conversation. There should also be the option of cutting things short or adding on a little extra time together, depending on how things are going. Show that you are flexible and can adjust to anything that makes her comfortable and fits her schedule. Make it close to home. You can meet up at a venue, drive together, or walk there together. Don't pick a movie or some entertainment that leaves you little time to interact. Choose something she has expressed an interest in or you think she might like. If you're driving together, park a few blocks away so you can walk a bit together, assuming it's a nice day. So you decide a colorful neighborhood that has your favorite Italian restaurant and coffee shops is a good place to connect for lunch. You know the area and the restaurant owner or manager. Make all the arrangements and consider each detail in advance. Know where to park and make the reservation in advance—and let the restaurant know you want that table by the window. Get there thirty minutes early so you can walk around, look at some historic buildings, or window shop and soak up the feel of the neighborhood. Don't be racing around late, looking for parking. Know some background information on the area or related personal or family history and share that if there is an opening, but don't bore her with five pages of Wikipedia knowledge. The important thing is that you feel comfortable and confident about the logistics and situation of your first date.

c. Now that you have the basic design, think of the details and make a list of things to do. Being prepared will make exposure to the real situation go more smoothly. Your list might include things such as making sure the car has gas, confirming your reservation and table, thinking of a nearby place for coffee or a glass of wine after the lunch if all is going well, and making sure the clothes you want to wear are clean and ready to go.

d. Once the details have been worked out, go on the date in your mind to see if there is anything else to do in advance to reduce your stress and anxiety.

e. Now stop worrying and start enjoying yourself. See yourself having a relaxed and good time with your date. Imagine the conversation going naturally and effortlessly in many directions. Don't try to rehearse what you will say; just let the moment and mood determine the direction of your discourse. Tell yourself this is only a first date. The only goal is to spend some quality time with that person, not to tell your life story or reveal all your inner secrets.

f. If you still feel very nervous about the date, call a good friend and trace over the plan just as you'd like to see it go. Ask your friend if something might be done differently to make the date more fun.

g. Now just do it. Your date will be very flattered by the thought and care you have put into the outing. Be yourself and behave as if you are with a comfortable old friend. Putting another person at ease is an art that is worth learning and is the first step to a closer relationship. Later dates will not need to be so scripted or so much inside your comfort zone. As you feel more comfortable with the person, you will be able to be more spontaneous and adventurous.

In the example three, the hierarchy is to first design the date in your head, then plan the details, then imagine yourself enjoying a successful outing with your new friend, then go through the date with a friend to increase your confidence that the details are in place, then go on the real date. Each step involves a little more anxiety and risk, but your ability to cope is strengthened by the previous step.

As you can see, each situation is unique and requires a thoughtful and personalized hierarchy plan. You can create one yourself or do it with the help of a friend or therapist.

## Carrying Out the Exposure Exercise

Exposure exercises should be structured and thought out carefully in advance. They should be done as frequently as practical, usually on a daily basis. Known avoidance and safety behaviors should gradually be discarded during exposure exercises. At a later stage, it may be useful to add exposure to feared sensations as will be described later in this section.

If you feel yourself getting more rather than less fearful over time, you are pushing yourself too fast or have not designed a properly graded hierarchy. Go more slowly and design more steps, but keep at it. To maintain your improvement, plan to continue your program at regular intervals even when the fear is much less.

## Preparing for Exposure

Plan your exposure exercises in advance. This includes setting aside some time each day and each week for accomplishing your exposure goals. In addition, use the personal anxiety assessment plan to acknowledge your anxious false beliefs. Go over the corrected belief, saying it to yourself several times before each exposure. Actively challenge your anxious thoughts before entering your exposure experience to help you cope with any fear or discomfort.

## The Importance of Predictability and Control

Exposure works best if there is an element of predictability and you have a sense of control as you progress. This is why you should design the first step of your exposure hierarchy with a situation that is fairly predictable and in which you feel reasonable control. By definition, each step becomes more difficult, meaning it has a lesser degree of predictability and a higher risk because you will not have full control. The fear that comes with letting go of control can sometimes be minimized by thinking through the possible scenarios in advance, considering your response to each.

For instance, suppose you can't even get to that first date we talked about above because you're too afraid of being rejected when asking the person out. You might first, and perhaps with the help of a friend, decide the strategy that is most comfortable for you. Remember, you decide the terms of how to approach your potential date. In this regard, you are in total control. So you determine that asking her on your lunch break on Wednesday is the way to go. During the lunch break, you will be able to get some privacy by going for a walk outdoors where coworkers will not be listening. You predict that she also takes a break at this time and will not be too busy or stressed.

You plan your opening line as follows: "Hi Janice! This is Tim. We met at the convention a few weeks ago. How are you?" She may put you at ease by giving a friendly response that she is surprised and happy you called, or she might abruptly tell you this is not a good time and she has to get off the line. Or she might not answer and you are faced with talking to the answering machine instead. Remember, the worst thing that can happen is that, for whatever reason, she's not up for a date.

Think through what you would do in each circumstance. If the opening line is well received, you will likely be emboldened to ask her out. Be straightforward: "You know, the reason I'm calling is that I'm planning to visit my favorite neighborhood and have lunch in the city this Saturday, and I'd like it better if you could come along." How might she respond? If she says, "Sorry, I'm busy," you could say, "Well, I thought I would at least try! Let me know if you have some weekend free. You can always call or shoot me an e-mail. Take care!" Or if she says, "But I don't have transportation," you could say, "I'd be happy to pick you up and take you home after." If you get her voice mail, plan to say, "Hi, it's Tim from the convention a few weeks ago. I was thinking about you and wondering if you could join me this weekend for lunch in the city. I am really craving the fettuccini at Tony's. Give me a call back if you're free, or let me know if there is another time that is better for you. Hope your day is going well. The best way to reach me is on my cell phone at…"

Thinking it all through gives you more options that are under your control. If she explains she is not available or has a boyfriend or girlfriend, or if she simply declines, accept this and move on. If she changes her mind, she knows where to find you.

### Duration of Exposure

Exposure only works if you stay in the feared situation long enough to experience that your anxiety is decreasing. It does you no good to say, "OK, I feel the anxiety; its time to bail." If you are trying to get used to parties, for instance, try to stay as long as possible. If you are exposing yourself to a fear of approaching people, go to a mall for several hours and repeatedly ask strangers for directions to one of the stores: "I'm sorry, do you have any idea where the bookstore is?"

### Frequency of Exposure

Exposure works best if done on a regular basis. It is reasonable to set aside an hour a day to work on your exposure exercises. Find convenient ways to work exposures into your daily life. If you fear subways, work on taking the subway for at least one stop to work every day rather than the bus. Eventually you may feel comfortable riding the subway a greater distance or for the return trip at night, as well. If you fear starting conversations, make it a habit to stop by the local coffee shop in the morning for thirty minutes to get your latte, read the headlines, and strike up at least one conversation, however brief.

### Vary Your Exposure Situations

Once you feel pretty good about your performance with one exposure exercise, you should go to the next step in your hierarchy and try something more challenging. Another option is to modify your exercise by changing the context and location. For example, if you are trying to learn how to start a conversation, you might start with family and friends, then move up to the mall (asking for directions), then use the same strategy to start a conversation with a stranger in an elevator, a party, a busy street, the train station, the bookstore, and so on. Varying the situation will only strengthen your confidence.

### Challenge Yourself, but Don't Make It Impossible

You are supposed to feel apprehensive and anxious during exposure. In fact, the purpose of exposure is to elicit your anxiety response. A successful exposure is not one that causes no anxiety but one that you complete by staying in the situation long enough to feel the anxiety decrease. If your hierarchy is designed too steep, you may be trying to push yourself to do something too difficult too soon. Create an in-between step to bridge the difficulty.

*Don't Put Yourself at Unnecessary Risk*
If you are trying to feel more comfortable being the focus of attention, try low-risk exposures, such as making sure you're the last to be seated at a concert or play just before the curtain goes up. Or walk around with some crazy and creative hat on at the mall. You don't have to do something that will get you on the evening news.

*Accept Help and Advice*
If you have a trusted friend, family member, or therapist, make sure that person is aware of what you are trying to accomplish through exposure therapy. Ask for suggestions for helpful exercises. See if that person will help you role play or act out a certain situation before moving up to it in real life. Make sure it is a person who is understanding and supportive and lets you go at your own pace.

*Monitor Your Progress*
Use the journal forms in the personal anxiety assessment plan to keep yourself on track and monitor your success toward extinguishing and unlearning your fear response.

## Exposure Checklist
When designing an exposure therapy program for yourself, keep in mind the following guidelines:

- Set aside time to practice your exposure exercises. Make sure there is frequency and consistency in your time commitment, perhaps a short exercise for fifteen minutes every day during the week, then a longer exercise on Saturday and Sunday, around an hour each day.
- Plan your exposure exercises in advance so you can enjoy some degree of control over a fairly predictable situation.
- Keep prolonging your exposures. Allow yourself to be in the presence of the anxiety-provoking stimulus for longer and longer periods of time.
- Before entering the feared situation, use cognitive strategies to challenge your false, anxious beliefs. Use these same challenges during and after the exposure exercise, as well.
- Don't fight anxious feelings. Just experience them and realize that nothing terrible happens.
- Eliminate subtle avoidance strategies as you go, such as keeping an anxiety pill in your purse, having some electronic game or iPod to distract you, or needing to have a drink of alcohol first. Eliminate overprotective behaviors like turning down the lights during a presentation to prevent others from seeing your anxious mannerisms.

- Vary the context and location of your exposure sessions to make them more challenging.
- Start with practices that carry little actual risk, and then gradually make them more challenging and difficult.

***TOOL:** Make your plan of attack using the personal anxiety assessment plan section labeled "My Graded Desensitization and Exposure Plan." Keep track of your progress using the personal anxiety assessment plan tables documenting the weekly assessments of your phobic anxiety.

## Interoceptive Exposure

Interoceptive exposure means the intentional exposure to unpleasant physical sensations to unlearn catastrophic thinking and misinterpretations that accompany these sensations in many anxious individuals. Panic disorder patients are frequently frightened by their physical sensations of nausea, sweating, racing heart, chest pain, dizziness, and so on. They will often feel even worse after searching for information on the Internet. "What do the sensations mean?" "Am I having a having a heart attack or stroke?" Often, a sense of doom or even a strong belief that they are dying will follow these anxious symptoms and cause the panic sufferer to seek emergency medical care.

Interoceptive exposure has been found to be very helpful in convincing the patient with panic that the uncomfortable sensations should not be a focus of concern or worry. By making them experience these same sensations in a controlled exposure environment, they could gradually unlearn their misinterpretations and stop fueling their anxiety with anxious cognitions.

Interoceptive exposure exercises will be helpful to you only if you fear having uncomfortable physical sensations that tend to launch into catastrophic thinking. They will especially be helpful if you fear physical symptoms such as blushing, sweating, trembling, or nausea in front of other people.

Before starting any interoceptive exercise, make sure you get the approval of your personal physician. Below are the basic uncomfortable sensations and the exercises to trigger them:

- Dizziness or lightheadedness: (1) Shake head from side to side for thirty seconds. (2) While sitting, bend over and place your head between your legs for thirty seconds, then sit up quickly. Be near a bed so you can lie down if you feel faint.
- Nausea: Spin around in a swivel chair for sixty seconds.
- Breathlessness, sense of smothering, or racing heart: Hold your breath as long as possible.
- Lightheadedness, dizziness, racing heart, numbness, and tingling: Hyperventilate by taking fast, shallow breaths at rate of 100–120 breaths per minute for up to one minute.
- Chest tightness, dizziness, breathlessness, feeling of smothering, or pounding heart: Breathe through a small, narrow straw (plug your nose if necessary) for two minutes (or longer, if needed).
- Sweating, blushing, or hot flushes: Sit in a hot sauna or small room with a space heater. Drink a hot drink while wearing overly warm clothing.
- Racing heart, sweating, flushing, or breathlessness: Run in place or up and down stairs for one to two minutes.

- Trembling or shaking or numbness and tingling feelings in the arms and hands: Carry heavy weights, loaded grocery bags, or gallon jugs full of water in both hands for as long as is necessary to feel the symptoms.
- Trembling or tense feelings in arms and chest: Put your hands together in front of your chest as if praying and push your hands together as hard as possible in a sustained way until you feel the tenseness through your chest and your arms start trembling.

Perhaps you can design an interoceptive exercise specific to your feared sensation. If you fear nausea, you may know that a certain noxious smell makes you nauseated right away. Exposing yourself in small doses to this smell might be very effective for you.

### *How Interoceptive Exposure Works*

By deliberately causing uncomfortable sensations that fuel your anxiety in a controlled and predictable manner, you will learn that you can exert some control over these sensations, that your catastrophic thinking does not come true (having a heart attack or stroke), and that others are not really bothered by your anxiety symptoms. By allowing others to observe you having these anxiety symptoms, you will gradually become less concerned about having these symptoms in public places.

### *Designing an Interoceptive Exposure Program*

There are four main steps in developing your own personalized interoceptive program.

1. Find out which sensation(s) trigger your anxiety response.
2. Find an exercise that effectively causes the feared sensation(s).
3. Develop an interoceptive exposure hierarchy, gradually increasing the intensity or duration of the sensation exposure and the difficulty of the challenge.
4. Practice the exercises alone until you find they no longer cause anxiety. Then add in exposure exercises in real-life situations once you have mastered them in the controlled home environment. Try combining interoceptive exposure with situational exposure. For instance, if you have a fear of sweating in social situations, run in place in the bathroom for two minutes to work up a small sweat before rejoining a social gathering.

*TOOL: Using the section provided in your personal anxiety assessment plan, create an interoceptive exposure program. Allot specific time slots in your personal daily planner at least three days a week to make sure it gets implemented.

### *Summary*

Exposure exercises are most effective when they are self-designed, especially with the advice and encouragement of a therapist. Each program should be individualized to your unique situation, and only you know what that situation is. In addition, there are many methods of enhancing your exposure experience.

Virtual reality can offer elaborate staging for your experience, such as a theater full of people waiting to hear your presentation or an airplane flight complete with turbulence, at a fraction of the cost. In addition, it makes frequent, daily exposures very convenient.

Biofeedback is very useful to prove to yourself that you have power over anxiety and in gauging your progress. It can also let you know when you have stayed in the presence of the anxiety-provoking stimulus long enough for your anxiety to diminish. Even a simple galvanic skin response device will be effective in letting you actually hear the level of your anxiety (through a buzzing noise that changes in intensity as your sweating reaction increases or diminishes).

Imagery and visualization are ancient tools that allow people to experience the situation in their minds in a graded and controlled way. Hypnotherapy and self-hypnosis actually work by the same principle of letting the mind walk through the experience while in a relaxed and detached state of mind. These techniques are especially helpful to athletes who are trying to improve their concentration and focus in stressful situations.

Feel free to be creative and use whatever methods appeal to you in designing your exposure exercises. Refer back to the sections in this book that may be helpful, and follow the URLs or recommended references for further information or how to obtain necessary equipment (like biofeedback devices).

***TOOL:** Design an exposure hierarchy to overcome your feared situation or sensation. Use the forms provided in the personal anxiety assessment plan, and make time on your personal daily planner to accomplish your plan.

You can learn more about cognitive behavioral therapy by visiting the following websites:
https://psychcentral.com/lib/in-depth-cognitive-behavioral-therapy/
https://www.beckinstitute.org/get-informed/what-is-cognitive-therapy/

# CHAPTER 12

Toolbox Compartment Number Nine: Activity Tools

## The Purpose of Activities

Activities can be effective by distracting us, helping us pass the time, supplying opportunities for social interaction, improving our fitness and self-esteem, or tuning into our passions and giving us an uplifting and inspiring experience. As stated in chapter 1, we often choose activities for their ability to dissipate our nervous energy and allow a period of calm and relaxation to follow. This is particularly true of activities that require persistent concentration or challenge us physically.

Whatever activity we choose, it should celebrate what we find beautiful and life affirming. In essence, we should seek to develop an appreciation for culture. Frank Lloyd Wright, in a 1957 speech dedicating his civic center building in Marin County, explained that "culture consists of the expression by the human spirit of the love of beauty…A civilization without culture is like a man without a soul." We have chosen examples of activities that we believe embrace culture and beauty. Making any of these activities a part of your everyday life will give you more depth and positive sense of self. The more you work on adding cultural activities to your life, the more positive and optimistic you will be about life and the more accepting you will be of your fellow man. Those who are grounded in an appreciation for culture are less vulnerable to anxious emotions.

The activities we choose should bring out the positive attributes and unique characteristics that make us valuable. By selecting activities that complement our character attributes, strengths, and personal skills, we avoid wasting time by losing our true selves in the latest social trend. When we consciously choose our interests and activities, we avoid being passively manipulated. In essence, our choice of activities is part of our "soul work" that involves an active decision to live an authentic, positive, joyful, self-directed life.

Unfortunately, many anxiety sufferers allow themselves to choose only the activity of self-loathing. They decide to do nothing that demands anything of them. The TV or streaming video then become the only viable options. But TV programming often has nothing to do with you; it has to do only with feeding you someone else's thoughts or trying to sell you something. It is not informed by some core value or belief system but by what gets attention and sells product. In this sense, there is a great spiritual cost to be paid for watching too much TV.

Moreover, TV fuels anxiety more than it calms or reassures. Many reality-based shows purposely play on our anxious emotions to appeal to our darker curiosities. TV reporting is, by design, more sensational and hyped up, focusing on the violent, frightful, and bizarre. The evening news is quickly replacing the horror movie as the best way to get your adrenals secreting.

Another thought worth mentioning: in the January 23, 2005, issue of *Parade* magazine, writer and social observer Norman Mailer warned that TV is especially damaging to young minds in that it reduces one's desire (and therefore ability) to read, and the constant interruption of short commercials keeps us from developing a good attention span. Perhaps the epidemic of ADHD can be partially linked to the number of hours we let TV take over our minds and our children's minds.

Instead of taking the path of least resistance by letting TV monopolize your precious time, overcome the inertia of the couch and look into activities that require the full attention and participation of your mind, body, and spirit. One way to choose an activity close to your heart is to think back to your youth. In these simpler, less-stressful times (unless you grew up in an environment of abuse or neglect), you may have enjoyed a particular hobby, sport, or activity. Whether it was hunting for fossils, planting a garden, fishing in a local creek, making model airplanes, playing with pets, or building a tree fort, the activities that first brought you joy often reflect your true inner spirit.

As with exercise, many activities are best enjoyed with the encouragement and company of others. Some people enjoy combining their individual activities with those of their significant others. For example, a husband who enjoys playing piano may place his practice room next to the art studio room where his wife paints. She enjoys her painting more with beautiful music, and he not only has an audience but has decorated the music room with her paintings for inspiration.

Activities may be more enjoyable and meaningful if done with a group you belong to, especially if it serves a purpose you believe in. Working in the church's soup kitchen with fellow parishioners, volunteering to clean up the environment with a local nature group, joining a sports team in a gay or lesbian league, or taking a weekly hike with friends from graduate school are all possibilities.

Any activity that gives you satisfaction is a good way to disperse stress. It does not matter what you do, as long as you find it absorbing or fun. Leave your ego out of it. Don't think about whether your activity is admired or esteemed by others. Chances are there are a lot of other people who share your interests and many websites and clubs to learn more about getting connected. I have a patient who discovered croquet about the time he retired. He found that there are many fun people and very upscale venues at which to play this individual lawn sport. His life is now spent preparing for and looking forward to the next tournament. Another elderly Japanese widower discovered the Italian sport of bocce ball and plays three times a week at a local club. He met almost all his friends through participation in this activity. No time for stress or anxiety!

## Indoor Individual Activities

Individual indoor activities are ideal for those who enjoy doing things by themselves in the peace and quiet of familiar and comfortable surroundings. Within this group are many opportunities for self-expression and creativity, as well as challenging your mind and body. See if any of these activities sound appealing to you.

## Pet Ownership

The therapeutic benefits of pets to reduce anxiety and improve the outcome in patients with physical and emotional illnesses has gained increasing attention in recent years. For people of all ages with all kinds of problems, pets provide a constant source of comfort and focus for attention. Animals bring out our nurturing instinct and make us feel safe and unconditionally accepted. We can just be ourselves without worrying about scrutiny or unrealistic expectations or demands. Pets shift our focus away from ourselves and our problems and help us feel connected to a larger world. The best case in point is Robert Stroud, the hardened murderer serving life in prison whose love for a baby sparrow he found in the exercise yard led to a life of studying canaries. Known as the "Bird Man of Alcatraz," he eventually earned world recognition as a leading authority on diseases and medical treatment of canaries. Surprisingly, it does not matter what type of pet you choose—all pets have similar therapeutic value if the animal is of interest to you. The pet should be selected to fit your temperament, living space, and lifestyle.

Research has shown that exposure to pets can do the following:

- Reduce stress and tension before surgery. One study found that patients who spent a few minutes watching fish before dental surgery were more relaxed, as measured by their blood pressure, muscle tension, and behavior, than those who did not watch the fish. In fact, patients who watched the fish were as calm as another group that had been hypnotized before surgery.
- Reduce blood pressure. One study showed that the simple act of petting a dog can lower blood pressure.
- Boost mood and increase social interaction in the elderly. Bringing a pet into a nursing home or hospital has been shown to effectively improve the emotional well being of elderly and institutionalized individuals.
- Decrease the need for medical care. A study conducted at UCLA found that dog owners required much less medical care for stress-related symptoms than non–dog owners.
- Improve the outcome after a heart attack. A study of ninety-two patients hospitalized in a coronary care unit for angina or heart attack found that those who owned pets were more likely to be alive one year later than those who did not. The study found that only 6 percent of the patients who owned pets died within one year compared with 28 percent of those who did not own pets. In fact, having a pet was found to give a higher boost to the survival rate than having a spouse or a good friend!

## Writing Books or Poetry

One of the most rewarding and therapeutic experiences is to express your feelings, thoughts, and creative energy in the form of a book, short story, essay, or poem. There are many styles and forms to choose from: novels, graphic novels, autobiography/memoirs, and travel logs, to name a few. Poetry allows you to test your powers of expression like no other literary form. As my father often said, "Poetry is the most amount of thought in the least amount of words." If you like to read, you may already have a style in mind that fits your personality. If not, check out a book on writing styles at your local library, or check out an adult class or the possibility of auditing a writing workshop offered at a local college or university.

In an interview to promote his book *My Life*, President Bill Clinton recommended that everyone write their life story down when they reach fifty years old—not necessarily for the purpose of publication, but for future generations of your family to know you better. What would you want to pass on to your grandchildren and their children? What great insight or pleasure would you want them to experience, and what heartbreak or disappointment would you want to warn them about?

A patient of mine retired on the West Coast after many years teaching anthropology at an Ivy League school. One of his many retirement activities was the serious writing of poetry. He took classes, read extensively, and took private tutorials on the art. He was good at it and gained some local acclaim. Then he had a terrible accident. He slipped on the ice during a ski trip and suffered a severe concussion and a hemorrhage in the brain. He was in a coma for several days, and it was more than a month before he knew who he was and many months before he regained strength and balance to walk. But he kept writing as soon as he could. The many months in bed gave him the time, even though he felt his mind was "mush." His teacher thought the writings were remarkable and submitted them to a publisher. A week later, he was offered a contract to publish his work. If he had not had this activity, he might well have lapsed into tedium, boredom, self-pity, anxiety, or depression.

## Playing and Composing Music

It's never too late to learn to play a musical instrument. Maybe you won't be auditioning for the local philharmonic, but you might find a fun outlet in playing with friends or a local community group, or just for your own enjoyment. You may already have musical talents as a singer or musician, but you haven't practiced for many years. You may fear you've forgotten how. You might be surprised to find your talent has been right there all along, waiting for you to rediscover it.

Maybe you've always fancied yourself as a songwriter. You write your own lyrics, and the melodies come in the middle of the night. You sing them into a tape recorder so you can write them down on paper in the morning.

Music has a way of touching our deeper emotions and finding our core selves. Find a way to tap into your musical nature and release stress through the uplifting activity of creating and making music.

## Crafts and Indoor Hobbies

Perhaps you have an interest waiting to be turned into a talent. One favorite patient, a middle-aged Catholic nun, found a diet program on the Internet. In addition to teaching healthy-eating strategies, the program also provided cooking tips for its varied recipes. After several months, she had not only lost twenty-five pounds but also felt very proud of her skills in the kitchen. She had learned to throw a nutritious dinner together in short order using exotic spices and the latest culinary techniques. Another patient spends the year inventing and creating Christmas tree ornaments of people and animals cleverly made from simple household items. Her gifts are highly anticipated and prized by her friends and family.

You don't have to go far to find a craft or hobby that you can enjoy at home. Collecting, woodworking, sewing, knitting, cooking, quilting, painting, and many other activities can be done conveniently and inexpensively in the comforts of home. Indoor hobbies have the advantage of being available to you when you have limited resources and time. Especially when you are depressed, you may not be motivated to venture far from home at first. This is a good time to redirect some nervous energy into a favorite hobby.

## Gym Activities

Most gyms, including, perhaps, your local YMCA or community recreation center, have indoor pools that allow year-round swimming. Stationary exercise bikes, both upright and reclining, are also a common feature. Weights, basketball courts, cross-training aerobic gliders, incline treadmill machines, stretching equipment, tennis courts, and racquet ball courts are also commonly found under one roof in a large gym or recreation center. Gym memberships are a good investment if you use them. Making the gym a regularly scheduled activity will make it easier for you when you are under emotional stress. If you don't miss workouts or make excuses when times are good, you're less likely to break your habit when life stress increases.

## Outdoor Individual Activities
### Gardening

Gardening is a hobby enjoyed by people from toddlers to great-grandparents. Remember putting a bulb in water to get a hyacinth to grow in winter, or the first time you planted those "red devil" radishes in the spring? The child within us never ceases to be in awe of the potential that lies dormant within a seed.

Gardening can be done indoors or outdoors, on a small or large scale, and all year round if you have a greenhouse. Even if you don't have a greenhouse, you will have year-round chores of pruning, fertilizing, spraying, planting, raking, and otherwise cultivating your garden paradise. You can also get involved in related landscaping projects and water features.

Some gardens are in pots—like the art of growing bonsai trees and many herbal and vegetable gardens. English gardens are designed to reflect the random and casual beauty of nature, while French gardens are precise and formal. Finding the style that fits your personality, energy level, yard capabilities, and climate limitations is a key part of choosing your garden project. You will have an endless variety of information (magazines, websites, specialty gardening books, friends/neighbors/the local nursery) to help you and a host of activities to become involved in (community gardening projects, flower and plant exhibitions and shows, classes sponsored by local gardening societies) to make you knowledgeable and keep you busy.

There is nothing more life affirming than caring for and nurturing living things. Your garden will take on the elements of a friend and companion and will provide a familiar and peaceful retreat from the stressful grind. Many studies even encourage you to talk to your plants to improve their growth and health. Just don't let the neighbors catch you arguing with a daisy.

### Hiking

When under stress, take a hike (or tell someone else to!). Hiking is not only good for your fitness, cardiovascular system, and bone density; it is also the perfect way to release emotional and physical tension. Make sure you have proper clothing, shoes, and a map and a compass, and then hit the trails. You may enjoy going alone at your own pace or combining your hike with other activities, such as fossil or gem hunting, bird watching, photography, or, if allowed, collecting specimens for your bonsai garden. Stay away from mushroom hunting unless you're a real expert!

## Fishing and Camping

Especially if you did it as a kid and have fond memories of family trips to the lake, fishing and camping can take you back to the simpler times of your childhood in a hurry. Why only enjoy nature in your visualization exercises? There is probably a stream, reservoir, forest, lake, or mountain nearby with campsites available. Half the fun is getting ready for the trip. Make sure you reserve your campsite in advance, and rehearse pitching the tent in your backyard so you don't embarrass yourself in front of the kids. Make a list of all those Boy Scout items: flashlight, toilet paper, telescopic fishing rod, insect repellent, sunscreen, maps, rope, marshmallows/Hershey bars, graham crackers, etc. Don't forget protective clothing and a warm sleeping bag!

For those who don't have the time or inclination to lay out under the stars and smell like the smoke from a campfire, day trips to the lake are a convenient and pleasant way to redirect your thoughts to the bigger picture of life. Camping and fishing are great ways to spend time alone healing your emotions or to create stronger bonds with your family or good friends.

## Indoor Social Participation Activities

After a particular trauma or loss, especially during times of grief, you may not feel ready to join in group activities. While support groups that bring together people going through similar difficult times are very helpful, groups that don't understand your pain will, ironically, may make you feel even more isolated. You may want to start with individual activities or activities with close friends and family. But once you achieve a reasonable level of healing, you may be ready to expand your horizons and friendships with some of these suggestions.

### Indoor Games

How many times have I heard, "I'm sorry doctor, I won't be able to come in for a recheck next Wednesday; that's my bridge/poker/bowling/bingo day!" Being part of a group that meets regularly to enjoy an indoor game can be a nice midweek stress breaker. Some games take great skill and years of studying strategy to be competitive, like chess, mah-jongg, and bridge. Other games can be learned in a few minutes and are great group fun, like charades, Pictionary, Monopoly, and many simple card games. It might be a group of family members, guys'/girls' evening out, a couples thing, or a group of retirees; the important thing is getting together and sharing your ups and downs with familiar faces doing something you enjoy.

### Book and Dining Clubs

Within a few weeks of moving into our new home, my wife was invited by the neighborhood wives to the twice-monthly book club. If you don't have one in your area, you could start one. You might even open it up to the guys. Or you may live in a singles apartment complex and want to find a way to meet interesting and well-read people in your building. Put up a flyer for a book-sharing discussion at your place on an off night like Tuesday or Wednesday.

If pleasant smells, tastes, ambience, and good company sound appetizing, consider a local dining club. Some clubs are designed to hook up singles, while others are for real aficionados of fine cuisine.

### Dancing

Dancing is truly a timeless activity. If you can move something, no matter your age or infirmities, you can find a style of dance appropriate for you. Dancing can be an individual, group, or couples activity. It can be vigorous and exhausting or artful and exhilarating. Some dance forms are designed to encourage socialization, like square dancing and ballroom dancing, while others are designed to encourage individual expression, like modern, jazz, and freestyle forms.

By combining exercise, social interaction, and a mode of expression and communication, dance is a particularly good activity for those dealing with anxiety and stress. Dance studios, clubs, classes, and community-sponsored dance events are everywhere once you start looking, and there are plenty of people who would be delighted to teach you their favorite steps.

### Indoor Sports

How about an indoor social sport you can enjoy all year long? Consider working on your ping-pong paddle grip, joining a local weekly basketball game, seeing if the community recreation center offers indoor volleyball or badminton, or getting into a squash or racquet ball group at the local club. Another indoor sport that is available in most communities and can be enjoyed individually or with friends is bowling. All of these sports have teams and competitions for every skill level. It's never too late to get started.

### Performing Arts

Maybe you are a ham or natural performer who would like to hone your talents on stage. Fellow performers will often form a club to encourage the performing artist in each member. Whether you are a poet, musician, magician, stand-up comic, or thespian with a one-woman act, you'll find a supportive and appreciative audience to help you develop your art. Be a bohemian and express yourself!

## Outdoor Social Participation Activities

As with indoor social activities, the outdoors offers a wide array of activities for every age, interest, ability, and energy level. If you like photography or wildlife, you might choose to join a kayaking or hiking club; if you like strenuous exercise, try rowing, soccer, tennis, ultimate Frisbee, or rugby; if you like being an elitist snob (as per George Carlin), try golf. Even just being a spectator could be considered an outdoor social participation activity. Most sporting events are casual affairs and encourage you to mingle, be yourself, and state your mind about the pitcher/quarterback/free-throw shooter. It's OK to be friendly with strangers. After all, you have something in common: rooting for or against the same team. Many major-league sports offer special "singles nights" complete with a special section.

## Appreciation/Educational Activities

And now for the highbrows out there, I didn't forget you! There is a world of cultural and educational activities out there to be enjoyed as an individual or as a society or club member.

### Music and Theater Performances

If you feel that life is too short to waste on mindless entertainment available through the mainstream media, remember that talented and dedicated artists are in need of your patronage. Local theater troupes, chamber music ensembles, symphony orchestras, stand-up comedy clubs, jazz clubs, and the opera are a few choices. Consider attending opening night and attend the reception after to meet upscale people like yourself. If you know someone in the cast, try to get invited to the backstage party at the end run of a musical, band performance, or play. If you like to hang with free spirits following their bliss, you'll find it backstage. If you want to be challenged intellectually or inspired emotionally, you'll find it in the performing arts.

### Museum and Academy Exhibits

If you're lucky enough to live near a large metropolitan area, you probably have a wide range of museums and academies to visit. Whether it is Asian art, modern art, the classics of the Renaissance, ancient artifacts, aeronautics and space technology, dinosaur species, or rare botanical specimens, you will probably find a place to cultivate your curious mind. Many will have a calendar of events, including special lectures, exhibits, celebrations, fundraisers, and volunteer recruiting programs. These are great ways to get involved with the social life of your community and keep your calendar filled with worthwhile activities that make you feel connected and involved.

### Foreign Language/Adult Education Classes

Isn't there something you always wanted to learn? Wouldn't it be nice to speak Italian next time you visit Tuscany or French in Provence? Or maybe Mandarin would help you more in the business world. What about the classes you always wanted to take in college, but it wasn't part of your major, such as art history, plant biology, astronomy, anthropology, psychology, comparative religion, or music theory? Most colleges and universities allow you to audit or take night classes on a wide variety of stimulating subjects. And there is no better way to keep yourself fascinating than to stay in school and expand your knowledge base.

### Travel Programs

Do you like to travel and learn at the same time? Many top universities offer field trips and extended travel programs, often led by dynamic and renowned professors. You don't usually have to be an alumnus of the university to attend, and you can go by yourself or with a spouse or friend. Single travelers are usually hooked up with another same-sex singles to share accommodations. You can go fancy and stay in five-star hotels or rough it in the outback with tents and mosquito nets. The academic expert in the area you visit will know the inside story, the behind-the-scenes politics, how history was distorted over time, the reason for different architectural styles, as well as the best restaurants, concerts, shopping areas, and other local attractions. The expert will also often have inside connections to get you special viewings or the ability to go places and see things the average tourist will never find or have access to. Travel is fatal to ignorance and arrogance. It also gives a bigger perspective to your outlook on life and your anxiety challenges.

## Volunteer/Group Activities

Teaming up with other like-minded individuals to help the needy or support a worthy cause is a fulfilling way to spend your time and make close friends. If you've never volunteered before, here are some ways you could contribute and have fun at the same time. Helping others is probably the fastest road to turning our thoughts away from a focus on our own inner problems toward a more balanced and positive world perspective.

### The Red Cross/United Way

Two well-respected organizations that do good works around the world are the Red Cross and United Way. There are many other charities that equally deserve and need dedicated and motivated volunteers. If you can't give money, give time and ideas. You can work for your favorite charity in your community or travel to areas of war, natural disaster, poverty, and epidemics around the world.

### Church/Temple/Synagogue/Mosque

If you have a strong sense of obligation to further the work of your faith, all organized religions have outreach programs to help their communities. Whether you want to help in a soup kitchen to feed the homeless, visit condemned prisoners on death row, help build low-cost housing for needy families, be a mentor to a troubled young person, or minister to those dependent on drugs, you will find an opportunity through your local parish, synagogue, or mosque. Helping others through the power of your religious beliefs will balance some of the negative experiences you may be going through and will do much to build your sense of self-worth.

### Advocacy Groups

Do you have a special empathy for the weaker, less fortunate, downtrodden, or otherwise challenged members of society? A husband and wife who are patients of mine have spent their retirement years volunteering as advocates for children in foster care. They have learned how to spot families who are in it solely for the money and are not providing the healthy environment that a kid needs to have a chance in life. As they put it, "There's no one else protecting and standing up for these kids." Without their efforts, many children would be forced to endure prisonlike situations or even downright abuse. Who or what would you like to stand up for? Orphans? Whales? Abandoned or abused pets? Old-growth trees? The homeless? Teenage runaways? Get involved and put your empathy and concern into action.

## Teams and Activities that Promote a Cause

Often you can combine two activities, such as joining a team that promotes a special cause. Gay and lesbian organizations often sponsor sports teams and tournaments that help give their cause a positive face in the community and provide an enjoyable outlet and social network for their members. Police and fire departments often organize teams to compete or work with kids in the inner city. Many cycling, running, and walking clubs hold events to raise money for a variety of causes, from finding a cure for breast cancer, diabetes, and AIDS to raising awareness of their position on abortion or war. Getting involved allows you to bond with others who support your views and get some exercise at the same time.

***TOOL:** Find an activity that you love or have always wanted to get into. It may be obvious to you, or you may have to sleep on it a few nights. Suddenly, the perfect opportunity to find fulfillment in a regular activity will become apparent. Then, just do it!

To learn more about any particular activity, as well as finding any supplies or equipment you might need to participate, just do a Google search!

***TOOL:** Make an activity scrapbook. Maybe you don't have time to take that dream vacation, go fishing in your favorite lake, or walk that mountain trail during the spring runoff. Or maybe you are ill, injured, or low on resources. That doesn't mean you have to be low on imagination. Collect pictures, postcards, brochures, and other memorabilia from your favorite places or destinations and make your "getaway" book. When you want help visualizing a peaceful and healing place, use your book to take you there.

# CHAPTER 13

## Toolbox Compartment Number Ten: Spiritual Tools

### Religion and Spirituality

The purpose of religion and spiritual teachings is to help the followers find a path to love and truth, which we sometimes call a spiritual journey. Our job as feeling and thinking human beings is to listen and assimilate into our being that which rings true in our hearts and inner consciousness and refute and reject that which we feel is untruth. It is an interactive, emotional experience by which we consciously choose to move closer to truth and away from our own fearful, hateful, arrogant, and selfish natures. Truth and love become powerful forces that can change our behavior and attitude, causing transformation.

Religion and spirituality are therefore subjective and lead to an affirmation of the seed of love and truth that is planted in all of us. All three monotheistic ("one God") religions, as well as Buddhism and Hinduism, equate the divine with love and truth. Joseph Campbell, the author of *The Power of Myth*, after years of studying comparative religion, concluded that truth is one and universal, and it has many voices. Jesus said, "Be still and know I am God." Truth and love come to us when we let ourselves fall silent and allow the voice that is the divine within us guide us. He also said, "I am the way, the truth, and the light," stating the most basic principle of religion: only those who seek the way of truth, light, and love are moving toward a spiritual existence and a relationship with God.

In this section, we will be speaking mostly of the power of spiritual insights, rather than any specific religious frame of reference. Religion is a doctrinal belief system practice by a devotee. The three largest monotheistic religions are Islam, Christianity, and Judaism. All three share a common heritage back to Abraham and Jacob but diverge into distinct religions, each with its own scriptures and teachings. The common thread in these religions is that man comes close to God through the practice of faith and trust. In these Western religions, man has a personal relationship to God, but God is "completely other" and beyond comprehension.

In most Eastern religions (East of the Nile River), religion focuses on moving toward unity with God and the universal and eternal source of love and truth by focusing inward on our divine nature and practicing a disciplined code of conduct and teachings to become more selfless. This may need to be accomplished over many lifetimes. Becoming one with God, or Infinite Truth, does not require a personal relationship in most Eastern religions because God is already considered a part of our nature.

As with love and politics, religion can also be used as a tool for selfish interests. Those who wish to manipulate others quickly recognize the emotional power that religion holds. We see this in the self-appointed spiritual leaders of religious cults such as the Branch Davidians, The Family, the Raeliens, and the Moonies. These leaders use deceit and double-talk to subjugate the will of their followers. We also see individuals who hide behind the cloak of religious leadership to affect their own agenda. There is no intention to listen, learn, and change, only to control those who are impressionable and insecure. Osama bin Laden, Jim Baker (and other TV evangelists), and priests who are sexual predators—all have been exposed for using and twisting religion to further advance their pursuit of hate, greed, or sexual gratification. Political movements, dictators, and organized religion have been guilty of the misuse and abuse of religious sentiment to further the goals of greed, power, and ambition.

Religion is only true when individuals can reconcile what they are told with their own experiences and consciences. This is the inner voice that can be heard only in stillness. It is not a voice that can be heard above the drama and demands of the everyday world.

The truth is it is not heard in literal translations of scripture or in groups who isolate themselves in the narrow-mindedness of the cult experience. Beware of any religion that asks you to leave your mind and conscience on the doorstep or that wants to know everything about you, keeps records of your comings and goings, arrogantly dismisses the validity of the belief systems of others, or teaches hatred for any purpose. God, love, and the truth are nowhere to be found here.

When we speak of spirituality, we are talking about mankind's awareness that we have a divine nature that is inextricably connected to the source of infinite wisdom and truth. This appears to be a commonly accepted ideal, even by those who do not follow the teachings of any particular religious tradition. Spirituality is the development of that part of the heart and mind that understands the true source of peace, love, and inner calmness.

Even those who do not believe in a God or creator who cares about them may feel an interconnectedness of the human spirit and can reap the benefits of spiritual tools. Studies have shown, for instance, that prayer speeds the healing process for those who are being prayed for, even if they have no belief in prayer and no knowledge that they are being prayed for. Studies have also shown that those who use their faith as a tool to lower their anxiety level have a better chance of speedy recovery from illness or surgery with fewer complications and shorter hospital stays. Meditation, whether directed toward the divine or focused solely on silence and peace, has been shown to have profound healing effects on the emotional mind. Thinking outside yourself, letting go of your image of self, letting go of your attachment to outcomes—all are spiritual tools that work independent of your religious beliefs or lack thereof.

The ATP compartments up to this point have been devoted to exploring how our minds and bodies respond to anxiety and fear and how we can counterbalance and find a point of stabilization between mind and body. Ultimately, however, the answer to conquering fear may lie in letting go of our minds and bodies. Majid Ali, MD, gives his definition of spirituality in his book *The Canary and Chronic Fatigue*: "The spiritual is the unknown without any uncertainty. Fear cannot exist without a sense of loss, and there can be no sense of loss in the spiritual where there is no awareness. In the spiritual we do not plead for freedom from fear of suffering, but for the heart to reach a stillness that is beyond any concept of freedom from fear."

Dr. Ali speaks of spiritual health through "practicing gratitude, serving others, and through silence." On this latter point, he writes: "Depression is a serious disorder of neuronal and neurotransmitter function, which is frequently made worse by metabolic roller coasters. In many cases meditative silence initially exaggerates these malfunctions. Here, healing sounds can be of great value during the initial stages. After they are stabilized, I strongly urge my patients with anxiety-panic disorders and depression to learn the profoundly healing practice of silence. Indeed, in my clinical experience, positive long-term results for such disorders cannot be obtained without persistent and prolonged spiritual work."

Without a spiritual answer, we may be doomed to anxiety over the question of the meaning of life. The theologian Paul Tillich wrote in his book *The Courage to Be*: "The anxiety of meaninglessness is the anxiety about the loss of an ultimate concern, of a meaning which gives meaning to all meanings. This anxiety is aroused by the loss of a spiritual center, of an answer, however symbolic and indirect, to the question of the meaning of existence."

In fact, the psychiatrist C. G. Jung felt that those without a sense of meaning often suffered from this alone: "About one third of my cases are not suffering from any clinically definable neurosis, but from the senselessness and aimlessness of their lives. I should not object if this were called the general neurosis of our age."

Many who have studied emotional illness and spirituality have come to the conclusion that, while depression can be a catalyst for spiritual growth—faith and true release from fear require mental and emotional health and balance. To let go of ourselves, we must first be whole. The theologian Wayne Oates believed that those with emotional illness often developed "unhealthy" religious ideas to hide behind in their fears, rather than fearlessly and courageously letting go of the self. In his 1955 book *Religious Factors in Mental Illness*, he wrote: "When religious ideas are used as concealment devices, the resultant unhealthy religion defensively protects the individual from the demands of participation in a real world. Therefore, the clinician can legitimately ask the question: 'Is this a religion of fear or a religion of self-abandon in courageous action and thought?'"

Spirituality is devoid of fear. That is why those who resort to war, racism, and hatred of any kind cannot point to spirituality as the source of their behaviors or feelings. This is because hateful human actions are all based on ignorance and fear. We fear others will attack us first or take away our quality of life. We are ignorant about the truth that genetic differences are just as varied within a given race (say, all Chinese people) as between races (between Northern Europeans and natives of the Congo). This means you may be more closely genetically related to someone outside your race than within your race, because skin color is such a minuscule part of who we are. We are intolerant of the beliefs and behaviors of others because we fear it will erode or change our beliefs or behaviors.

In *Oedipus Rex*, Sophocles gives this assessment of man's relationship to fear through the voice of his character Teiresias, the blind prophet: "Fear? What has a man to do with fear? Chance rules our lives, and the future is all unknown. Best live as we may, from day to day."

The Christian scriptures assure us that fear is not from God: "Wherever you learned you fears, you may be sure you did not learn them from God. For God did not give us a spirit of timidity, but a spirit of power and love and self-control" (2 Timothy 1:7).

The Bhagavad Gita speaks to the futility of fear: "Fear not. What is not real never was and never will be. What is real always was and cannot be destroyed."

It seems we should first strive toward wellness through living a positive and productive life, one that we feel good about. Deepak Chopra explains this dharma, or purpose in life: "Everyone has a purpose in life...a unique gift or special talent to give to others. And when we blend this unique talent with service to others, we experience the ecstasy and exultation of our own spirit."

For the most part, it is our choices in life that lead us to a point of security and strength or vulnerability and weakness. It is from the point of strength and health that we best enter a true spiritual realm.

The many Buddhist traditions agree that one must first strive toward self-perfection and then find the path of letting go of ourselves and our attachments to the outcome as we follow the path that best expresses our true purpose and divine nature.

To deepen the benefits of meditation and relaxation in reducing our anxiety and fear, Dr. Herbert Benson wrote *Beyond the Relaxation Response*, in which he recommends adding what he calls the "faith factor" to our practice of meditation. In doing this, he is really discussing prayer as a more powerful form of meditation. He explains that what we believe or perceive has a more powerful effect on our psychological well being than what we see or feel, and we can all experience this improved sense of well being by tapping into our personal belief systems.

In the end, our goal is to bring homeostasis and balance to our lives through an approach that considers the mind, body, and spirit as an inseparable, integrated, and interdependent whole.

## Seeking a Spiritual Framework

As we develop a spiritual framework to surround our life decisions and goals, we experience a shift in how we feel about ourselves and the meaning of our life experiences. This is because our basic beliefs and assumptions about life necessarily change in light of this new perspective. Our understanding about our own feelings of anxiety is especially likely to be altered by our emerging spiritual experiences. Struggles may now be seen as opportunities and challenges and fear as a test of faith.

In seeking a spiritual framework, there are two great facilitators of and four common roadblocks to spiritual growth. The two facilitators are gratitude and prayer; the roadblocks are materialism, sexual obsessions, addictions, and pride.

- *Gratitude*
  To develop a spiritual frame of mind, the most important attribute is a grateful heart. When my son was thirteen, he had to write an essay for the high schools he was applying to. As you will read, he was influenced by his late grandfather to think about the importance of gratitude in our everyday lives, and he decided to use this as the theme of his essay. It has a lot of good points that are relevant to our discussion, so I thought I would include it here:
  > It was a big event for me when my grandfather started coming to my horseback riding lessons every Friday. I had just turned 12 and had not seen him much before that. Maybe he thought it was a good idea to pass his knowledge on to me before it's too late (he's 96 years old). He is a retired Presbyterian minister so he talks mainly about theology and philosophy, but he also talks about music and poetry.

We go to a Starbucks after my riding lesson to talk about these topics. He usually starts with some challenge along the lines of "I will give you one thousand dollars if you can tell me who Hugo Grotius is" or "Did you know that poetry is simply the greatest amount of thought in the least amount of words?" or "What does 'The crowd is untruth' mean?" His talks about gratitude have changed my view of myself and life.

Grandpa Tom likes to discuss "the human condition." He says that the most important verse in the Bible is "In everything give thanks." He says that if you practice gratitude, your heart and mind will be in the right place. Since some in my family are Buddhist in the Taoist tradition, I did a quick Internet search and found a man by the name of Master Mikel Steenrod who writes: "I'm going to reveal the single most important invocation: gratitude. It is amazingly powerful in getting you to set up an interaction with the Tao. It adjusts you spiritually."

I think that gratitude has certain benefits. No matter what (happy or sad, sick or healthy, rich or poor), if you are grateful, you will feel more balanced and calm. Being a good sport involves gratitude towards failure which will encourage you to get better. You will not take 100 percent of the credit when something good happens but realize that other people helped you succeed. If you choose to be grateful for painful experiences, it will help you not get mad or blame others.

Also, things will go better in life if you are grateful. People will think that you are a more humble and pleasant person which will up the chance of them helping you if you need it. If you thank your customers, maybe your business will do better. It's a win-win situation if you are always grateful. I do enjoy having stuff go my way and go as expected, but that's not always the best thing for you. Maybe there is a lesson in disappointment that will help you evolve and be a better person if you have a good attitude.

I wanted to know more about what grandpa Tom thought about gratitude, so I texted him the question "Why should I be grateful?" A few minutes later, he answered me, "Very good question! Gratitude leads directly to the understanding of contentment. We are never content with today and what we have. We tend to live for something better tomorrow. The Creator expects us to enjoy today. Tomorrow will take care of itself."

I have come to the conclusion that gratitude is important to have in my everyday life because it allows me to enjoy the present no matter what. It helps me realize how lucky I am. Master Steenrod recommended that we take ten or fifteen minutes a day to think about what we are grateful for and why, even if we find it challenging. When I remember to do this, it helps my day get off to a good start. Today I'm grateful that grandpa Tom is still around to teach me new things.

- *Prayer*

In the Bible, we are exhorted to "pray without ceasing." This means we should pray just about anytime, anywhere, about anything. In fact, our lives should be seen as an extended prayer or conversation with our creator. In a few pages, you will get to a more detailed discussion of benefits and studies on the power of prayer.

- *Materialism and Wealth Seeking*
  Those who get on a track of seeing how much they can acquire in a material sense risk ignoring their true selves and failing to find the happiest use and purpose of their lives. Failing to recognize that your life has greater meaning than being a money-making machine will prevent you from developing that deeper connection with your spiritual nature. Instead, we should all strive to be content with what we have. Before we acquire more, we should be grateful for less.
- *Sexual Obsessions and Addictions*
  Allowing yourself to be pulled off course by your sexual curiosities and desire for more wild and crazy experiences is another way people can spend large quantities of their lives and resources seeking fulfillment that is meaningless and activities that are sometimes hurtful to our emotional and physical health, as well as that of others. There are psychiatrists and psychologists whose main focus is to help people overcome their addiction to pornography. Dependence on pornography for sexual gratification can negatively affect our ability to engage in healthy sexual and intimate relationships in the future.

  The late Pope John Paul II taught a course in ethics at the Catholic University in Lubin in the 1950s. The class was remembered by students as being standing-room only, primarily because the young professor was always talking about sex. One day, someone finally asked him, "How come you talk so much about sexuality? There are more important things." He answered, "There's nothing wrong with sexuality itself, but the abuse of sexuality is the main obstacle to spirituality." Although many people disagreed with the pope's stance on homosexuality and protective stance toward those clergy who were accused of molesting children in their parishes, his basic belief on the place of sexuality in a spiritually healthy life is worth reflecting on.

  Addiction also steals our energy, resources, and focus away from a spiritual direction. We put the thing we crave—alcohol, drugs, gambling, sex—above our friends, family, health, and emotional well being.
- **Pride**
  Pride is a barrier that keeps us from being open to spiritual growth or learning the lessons of humility and service that are central to a spiritual mind-set. Wanting to see our name in lights and telling ourselves that our success is self-made turns our focus and direction toward feeding our ego. Everything we do must have the end purpose of drawing attention, envy, and admiration to ourselves. Again, we can lose sight of a bigger plan and deeper purpose. In fact, we can become a negative force in the world by stepping on the dreams, hopes, and rights of those in the way of our plan to elevate ourselves.

The attributes that bring us closer to a spiritual perspective will be discussed as "tools" at the end of this chapter. They are love and kindness, faith and hope, patience, humility, honesty, mercy and compassion, forgiveness, and gratitude. When developing a spiritual framework you feel natural and comfortable with, consider the following common spiritual assumptions. Formulate your own spiritual truths and discuss them with your significant other, trusted friend, minister, priest, rabbi, or cleric. Some of the following thoughts were adapted from the widely popular and helpful book by Edmund J. Bourne, PhD, *The Anxiety & Phobia Workbook, Third Edition*.

## The School of Life

The existentialists believed that, since everything that brings meaning and purpose to our life eventually ceases to exist, and we ourselves ultimately pass away, there is no real meaning to life other than what you experience in the present moment. Since every dream, desire, ambition, and thought eventually is lost, how can there be any point to our existence? To move beyond this existential "angst," spirituality makes the assumption that what we see, feel, and experience in human form is not all there is. Some part of our nature continues after our human life, and so life itself becomes a journey from one state of being to another. Life, then, is understood as a preparation or training for the next existence, which cannot be understood or revealed while still in this human form. Life then becomes a classroom or school where the lessons are taught. Our response to these lessons, which are the challenges and tasks life sends our way, has meaning on an eternal scale. As we complete one lesson, a new one will be prepared for us. The school of life is never out for summer. It continues every moment of every day in each thought, action, and choice. The purpose of our time on earth, then, is to grow in consciousness, developing wisdom and a greater capacity to love.

**Trials and tribulations are by design.** One spiritual assumption is that we are given only difficulties that are within our capacity to overcome. Human learning, it appears, happens only when there is loss, pain, and yearning. Only in these times do we turn to listen to our hearts and seek answers to deeper questions of meaning and purpose. The Christian existentialist Soren Kierkegaard believed that the truth is implanted by God into each individual's heart. We don't have to read about it or ask someone else what is right or wrong. We need only to steer clear of the distortions of crowd consciousness and listen to our own consciences only. By applying this imprinted divine knowledge to our problems, we find that the answers have always existed within us. The lesson of life is to learn to trust and live by the truth that is already in our hearts.

With this insight, we can stop asking, "What did I do to deserve this?" and ask instead, "What is this meant to teach me? What am I supposed to learn from this situation?"

**God made you the way you are for a reason.** You may sometimes blame God for being poor, having less opportunity than others, or having some physical limitation. You may ask, "Why wasn't I born rich like Mary, or cute like Beth, or smart like Samantha, or socially skillful like Jo Ann?" Especially if you are dealing with an emotional disorder like OCD, panic disorder, agoraphobia, or social phobia, life may seem particularly unfair. Maybe you have tried your best with your therapist and have attempted several medical regimens without much success. Why have you been given such difficulties and burdens?

Consider that there may be some valuable growth experience in facing difficult times and personal limitations. Perhaps certain qualities of compassion, empathy, and patience will result, if you have faith and keep a positive attitude. Maybe you need to trust and let go of your futile attempts at control. It is at the moment that you stop struggling for control that you may feel some measure of relief. Spirituality does not mean you turn responsibility for your life over to God. You must first do all you can to help yourself ("God helps those who help themselves"), then turn things over to a higher source of wisdom.

If you are gay, lesbian, bisexual, or transgender, accept that God did this for a reason and that any difficulties or blessings that you experience with a gender-identity journey may have some deeper meaning and carry some special lesson or message. Think how you can use this to gain insight, be a stronger person, and help others. Every challenge and hardship contains gifts of insight, empathy, or character building that is a catalyst for spiritual growth. Or maybe you are beautiful and born into wealth, but you would prefer not to have all the attention and insincerity that results. Consider that this is a challenge made especially for you, and learning to find your true self despite this will give you the skills you will need to find your destiny and purpose. If you were born with or acquired physical limitations or disabilities, think of this as part of your unique gifts that will give you experiences and insights not available to others. Then use these insights to inspire others.

**Your life has a unique purpose and mission.** Your life is not a random, meaningless sequence of accidental and coincidental events but follows a specific plan created before you were born. It is up to you whether you fulfill this plan, and knowing which direction to go requires that you pray and listen to your inner voice and feelings.

Before we are ready to accomplish the tasks that life has provided us, we must first experience the growth in consciousness that allows us to know our true selves in all our potential. We should recognize our unique gifts and talents and be compelled to put them to good use. Your life purpose is something that you will feel you *need* to do to feel whole and fulfilled. It may involve risk and danger. It may affect the world or a single person. It may or may not be recognized or appreciated by others in your lifetime. Your purpose might be to help care for a neighbor, master a musical instrument, raise a child, provide a home, achieve a political position, minister to others about your common experiences, be a mentor, design furniture, create art or music, invent helpful devices, or manufacture lug nuts.

Whatever your purpose is, it is uniquely your own. No one else is in a position to accomplish it. It will either be done by you or it won't get done. Purpose comes purely from within, so don't look for it outside yourself. And until you make time for what it is that you truly feel passionate about and are driven to explore, you will feel a sense of anxiety and incompleteness. This is one of the highest benefits of anxious emotions—to drive us onward toward finding our purpose.

**Letting go of our attachment to the outcome allows us to let go of fear and have faith.** While we should set our sights on particular goals and desires, being attached to the outcome is built on the false assumption that we can control our destiny based on past understanding and conditioning. Detachment, on the other hand, is based on the unquestioning belief in our true inner self. Attachment can lead to frustration, anger, and anxiety when the end result does not meet our expectations.

In *The Seven Spiritual Laws of Success*, Deepak Chopra writes the following:

Attachment is based on fear and insecurity—and the need for security is based on not knowing your true Self. The source of wealth, of abundance, or of anything in the physical world is the Self; it is the consciousness that knows how to fulfill every need. Everything else is a symbol: cars, houses, bank notes, clothes, airplanes. Symbols are transitory; they come and go. Chasing symbols is like settling for the map instead of the territory. It creates anxiety; it ends up making you feel hollow and empty inside, because you exchange your Self for the **symbols** of your Self.

Attachment comes from poverty consciousness, because attachment is always to symbols. Detachment is synonymous with wealth consciousness because only with detachment there is freedom to create. Only from detached involvement can one have joy and laughter. Then the symbols of wealth are created spontaneously and effortlessly. Without detachment we are prisoners of helplessness, hopelessness, mundane needs, trivial concerns, quiet desperation, and seriousness—the distinctive features of everyday mediocre existence and poverty consciousness.

Letting go of our attachments further means that we have faith in ourselves and are willing to accept that our creator ultimately knows best. This does not mean we make God responsible for our successes or failures or that we feel the outcome is predetermined and that our efforts are meaningless. Rather than leave everything up to fate, we should strive toward what we feel is the right direction, all the while asking for guidance and support from a higher power. But the final outcome we must let go of and trust in the wisdom of God. In doing so, we let go of our fears and anxiety of failure, humiliation, and defeat.

**God is always available to those who seek him.** Much of our anxiety comes from the perception that we are separate and alone in the universe. The truth is that we are never alone or disconnected from our higher power.

The Bible points out that we as humans are given the capacity to tolerate and even overcome many things, including illness. But it also says that we need God to help with those things that are emotionally overwhelming, such as grief over the loss of a loved one. Proverbs 18:14 asks the rhetorical question: "The human spirit will endure sickness; but a broken spirit, who can bear?"

Western religions teach that we can enter into a personal relationship with God, just as real as and more lasting than any human friendship. Within this personal relationship, we can experience both support and guidance. This guidance may come in the form of sudden insights or intuitions that point to a certain direction that we should go. This type of inspired realization often seems wiser or more intelligent than anything we could have figured out with our rational mind.

Eastern religions speak of the connectedness of all things. There is no reason to speak of a personal relationship with the creator because that same source of love, wisdom, and truth lives within us and joins us with all other living things. In this sense, God is the intelligence of the universe, the fundamental source of all things, and we cannot be separated from this higher power; we can choose only to ignore it or fail to heed its voice.

We can call on God for inspiration, peace of mind, inner strength, hope, and many other gifts. All we need to do is ask with sincerity and be willing to accept that the answer will come in God's time and in God's way. Jesus said, "Ask and you shall receive." This is true regardless of the particular spiritual tradition you follow. This connection to the eternal truth is a resource that is available to anyone at any time and can be tapped into through inner focus, contemplation, meditation, and prayer.

**That which you intend from the deepest aspects of your being will tend to come true.** What you wish for from your heart, if it is truly what you deeply desire, will eventually manifest itself in your life. That which you strongly believe in and commit to, as long as it is not destructive or harmful to yourself or others, will likely become a reality. Ask anyone who has made a significant accomplishment or risen to a high position, and they will tell you they always knew it would happen or felt it was strongly possible. This is because a deeply held intention focuses on our inner consciousness. This is also the place where we are interconnected with all of creation. Because of this, a remarkable thing happens: events in the outer world tend to come into alignment with our wish or intention. Goethe summed up this belief in the following remarks:

> Concerning all acts of initiative or creation,
> There is one elementary truth;
> The ignorance of which kills countless ideas and splendid plans:
> The moment one definitely commits oneself,
> Then Providence moves too.
> All sorts of things occur to help one
> That would never otherwise have occurred.
>
> A whole stream of events issue from the decision,
> raising in one's favor all manner of unforeseen incidents and assistance,
> which no person could have dreamt
> would have come their way.

**Love is greater than fear.** God is love. This means that pure, unconditional love is at the very center of all beings and the universe. It is the foundation on which we are built. Fear is superficial and can never undermine this foundation or cause us to be separated from our divine nature. This view is held by both Eastern and Western religions.

Once it is fully realized, a great source of "separation fear" is immediately eliminated. Some of our deepest fears involve separation, either from others, our true purpose, or the love of God. Specific fears of abandonment, rejection, humiliation, poverty, illness, confinement, dependency, and death can be explained in terms of the fear of separation and loss.

But the unifying force of love cannot be lost, split, or fractured. This is the only thing in life you can truly take to the bank. This is because God is eternal, infinite, all powerful, and forever the same. God always was and always will be, concepts difficult to grasp through our time-dependent understanding of reality. Every fear we feel, in fact, is just an illusion. It is something that we have created by allowing ourselves to drift away from the inner consciousness that knows the fearlessness of love.

Remember that life is transient and offers each being a brief opportunity to encounter others, to share, and to love. This is the highest expression of our human potential. But how many of us recognize the preciousness of this moment in time that they are alive and have the capacity to love? If we are able to find a way to love, then our time here will have been worthwhile.

**You must give to receive.** The scriptural admonition "it's better to give than receive" is so often quoted that we fail to see its true meaning. In truth, it is *absolutely necessary* to give to receive anything we that want in life. This is what Deepak Chopra calls the "law of giving." If you seek influence, you must be willing to give others influence; if you seek affluence and money, give affluence and money; if you seek love, appreciation, gratitude, or affection, then first give these things to others. Giving activates a law of spirituality known to the mystics as *karma*. Giving creates an energy field of good karma that brings all good things toward us and makes our lives go more smoothly and in a positive direction. People show up to help when we need them, answers to our questions come without asking, and solutions to our problems appear even before those problems arise. The fastest way to change your bad luck, losing streak, or negative life situation is to stop believing that you must force life to give you what you want. Instead, focus only on what you can do for others.

**Death is a transition.** All of the world's major religions share the idea that our essential nature and soul survives physical death. Some religions believe that our physical bodies will one day be resurrected, including our minds and memories. Others believe we are absorbed back to the source of infinite love from whence we came and were never really separated from. For those who believe in the continuance of the soul after death, there is little fear of death. In fact, death may be embraced and anticipated as a long-awaited reward for a life well lived.

Some point to highly publicized accounts of near-death experiences as proof of an afterlife. Because the descriptions of the experience of being near death or even having been officially pronounced dead are surprisingly similar, even among individuals of widely varying cultural and ethnic backgrounds, many feel there is compelling evidence to believe that death is a beautiful and positive event.

Others feel that God, life after death, and heaven are by their nature not provable, nor should we expect or want them to be. How could we worship a finite and explainable God that we can put in a box? What would be the meaning of human freedom if we believed that God controls us through fear and intimidation like an oppressive government or totalitarian regime? Should we really be motivated by promise of reward or threat of punishment? God gives the gift of complete freedom to all people—including freedom from fear. What would be the meaning of life and individual growth without this freedom?


## The Power of Prayer

Prayer comes from the Latin *precarius*, "obtained by begging," and *precari*, "to entreat or ask earnestly for." At its most basic level, prayer is the spiritual manifestation of human hope. It must be entered into with a sense of humility that we do not know all the answers and we need guidance from a larger and wiser source than ourselves. Some believe prayer should reflect a desire to put God's will ahead of our own ("Thy kingdom come, thy will be done").

Mahatma Gandhi described prayer in the following way:

Prayer is the key of the morning and the bolt of the evening. There is no peace without the grace of God, and there is no grace of God without prayer.

Prayer is not an old woman's idle amusement. Properly understood and applied, it is the most potent instrument of action.

Undoubtedly, prayer requires a living faith in God. Heartfelt prayer steadies one's nerves, humbles one and clearly shows one the next step.

There are many styles of prayer that are individual and personal. There are no fixed rules on content or location, whether silent or aloud, in conversational speech or in song, alone or with others, during rest or activity, or recited or unrehearsed and spontaneous. Above all, prayer must be an expression of the needs of our heart.

Gandhi further said of prayer:

Prayer is no mere repetition of empty formula. It is better in prayer to have a heart without words than words without a heart. It must be in clear response to the spirit which hungers for it.

Prayer is the only means of bringing orderliness, peace and repose in our daily acts. Take care of the vital things and the other things will take care of themselves.

Begin your day with prayer. Make it so soulful that it may remain with you until the evening. Close the day with prayer so you may have a peaceful night free from nightmares.

Do not worry about the forms of prayer. Let it be any form; it should be such as can put us into communion with the Divine. Only, whatever the form, let not the spirit wander while the words of prayer run on out of your mouth

A heartfelt prayer is not a recital with the lips. It is a yearning from within which expresses itself in every word, every act, nay, every thought of man.

Prayer has been called the *native language* of the soul. It is a reflection of the universal human desire to make contact and commune with the divine. Prayers seem to have been a part of the human experience all the way back to the caveman, whose prehistoric drawings may have been intended to invoke prehistoric gods for help in the hunt. The earliest recorded prayers are found in 4,500-year-old Sumerian inscriptions from Mesopotamia. Regardless of the precise nature of its origins, prayer has long been an irreducible feature of virtually every living religion.

Christians and Jews understand God as a personal being who hears prayer and responds to his people in his own way. Christians frequently follow Jesus Christ's custom as a devout Jew of praying at meals. Jews are obligated to pray as a point of law, with a threefold structure of praise, petition, and thanksgiving. In Islam, prayer is considered primarily as an instrument of adoration to be incorporated into the daily routines of life through the *salat*, a ritual prayer recited five times a day while facing Mecca. In Hinduism, daily liturgical prayers are encouraged over personal petition and are spelled out in the Vedas, a collection of ancient hymns. And in some forms of Buddhism, monastic prayers are practiced morning, noon, and night to the sounding of a small bell.

Prayer can be thought of simply as a conversation between child and father or mother. There is no special training or specific formula required, and no topic is off limits. As children of God, we can pray anytime, anywhere, anyplace, and about anything. Prayer is most effective when it involves empathy and caring for others, especially when we are asking for the healing of emotional or physical illness.

For most people, the purpose of prayer is not to get answers but to develop a more intimate relationship with God. In a recent *U.S. News and World Report* poll of 5,600 Internet respondents, 73.9 percent said that when their prayers are not answered, the reason is because they did not fit into God's plan. In addition, 65.1 percent said that when their prayers relate to health, they pray about mental health or depression.

It appears that whether we see God as benevolent and responsive or punishing and cruel affects the effectiveness of prayer on the healing process. The latest research on prayer suggests that your perception of your higher power may predict your ability to recover from emotional setbacks like anxiety and depression. Kenneth Pargament, PhD, a psychologist and researcher at Bowling Green State University in Ohio, examined many cases, from patients struggling with serious illnesses to battered women. He found that those who embraced a "collaborative style" of prayer were most successful in coping with their situations.

In the collaborative style of prayer, God and you are copilots together in a bumpy and frightening ride. You talk to God, listen, consult, and then share responsibility for your decisions and actions. Professor Pargament found that collaborators, as opposed to those who left everything up to God to take responsibility for, came away with a strong sense of spiritual support. They saw a crisis as an opportunity to grow spiritually and to learn more about themselves and God.

## How Does Prayer Work?

In his book *Beyond the Relaxation Response*, Dr. Herbert Benson writes of the use of faith to enhance the relaxation response when we are in a meditative state. He showed that if you meditate while invoking faith (which is really the same as prayer), your blood pressure lowers, your anger decreases, and you are more quickly able to tap into your potential for healing.

A long-time patient of mine recently told me of her experience with a form of prayer called *contemplative prayer* practiced by those who follow the religious beliefs of Eckankar (www.eckankar.org). She had been trying to heal a riff between her sister and herself that had gone on for years over family-related quarrels. She wanted to regain a loving relationship with her sibling but could not find a way to change her sister's hardened heart. So my patient spent a full year practicing a daily contemplative prayer focused on forgiveness and unconditional love directed toward her sister. Of course, the sister did not share the same belief system and never knew she was being sent daily packages of love from her sister many miles away. But that sister was suddenly compelled to break the "Cold War" and unexpectedly showed up at my patient's home to reconcile their differences. It was as if nothing had ever come between them, and there was a sudden comfortable connection that seemed impossible just a year before.

Many studies have found that prayer helps emotional and physical healing. The first to establish this took place in the coronary care unit at San Francisco General Hospital in 1988. Researchers found that those who had been prayed for (even though they and their doctors were not aware they were being prayed for) tended to recover with fewer complications and shorter hospital stays. Their need for antibiotics was one-fifth that of the recovering patients who had not been prayed for, and they were one-third as likely to develop pulmonary edema.

Certainly there is much anecdotal evidence that prayer can alleviate conditions of anxiety and depression. Prayer allows you to proactively participate in the healing process. You're not just sitting there; you're doing something about it. The struggle to fight emotional problems becomes easier when you realize that you are not alone. You feel better after sharing your fears with God and feel a lift from knowing that others are praying for you, as well.

In summing up her thoughts on prayer in her *U.S. News and World Report* article of December 20, 2004, Marianne Szegedy-Maszak wrote:

> For those who pray, there are clearly few limits to innovation or forms of expression. Psychologically, prayer can organize anxieties, focus worries, offer a sense of comfort and connection, and solidify communities. It can assist in changing bad behavior, as those who are enrolled in a 12-step program can attest. But in the end, prayer is ultimately about realms of consciousness as yet unexplored—about what believers might call the soul, or the spirit, or some transcendent part of being. Some believe that prayers are actually answered. But it doesn't really matter: For those who believe, that is not where the true power of prayer will ever reside.

Here are some suggestions on the practice of prayer:

- Prayer works best when it is cumulative. As in meditation, daily practice tunes the mind and heart for more effective experience or prayer.
- Pray for others as well as for yourself. By including those you care about in your prayers, you are solidifying the bonds between you.
- After your conscious mind has spoken, let it rest and allow your more personal feelings to express themselves. You may find your prayer moving in a new and unexpected direction.
- After a while, try adding moments of prayer with a change in organization and location throughout the day. This will keep the experience fresh and heartfelt.

**\*TOOL:** Set aside a time each day to pray. It could be morning when you get up, at night when you go to bed, at mealtimes, on the commute train, or any combination of times or locations. It would be natural to combine prayer with meditation. Pray in a manner that is comfortable and natural for you. If you feel so inclined, seek the advice and community of your local parish, temple, or mosque. In addition, try to get in the habit of reading uplifting and inspirational literature of your preference. It may be easiest to keep this material at your bedside and spend a few moments each morning and night to reflect on what it means to you personally.

## Other Spiritual Tools

The tools for building a spiritual foundation are love and kindness, faith and hope, patience, humility, honesty, mercy and compassion, forgiveness, and gratitude.

**\*TOOL:** Love and kindness. Major religions agree that the fundamental nature of God is love. The Bible explains love in this famous verse:

> Love is patient; love is kind
> and envies no one.
> Love is never boastful, nor conceited, nor rude;
> never selfish, not quick to take offense.
> There is nothing love cannot face;
> there is no limit to its faith,
> its hope, and endurance.
> In a word, there are three things
> that last forever: faith, hope, and love;
> but the greatest of these is love.
> —1 Corinthians 13

Memorize these words and use them to inform your words and actions. Practice acts of love and kindness as part of your everyday interaction with others.

***TOOL:** Faith and hope. Faith is an act of trust in God. We cannot possibly know his plan for us and need to trust and believe in that which we cannot see or understand. Having faith means we do not abandon our values and beliefs when life becomes difficult and challenging. God may send all of us trials and tribulations to test our faith. Hope means that we intend for the best and most positive outcome. Hope is tied to faith in that we must trust God that his plan will lead to the best outcome and use of our lives. Those who give their lives to divine will with faith and hope have chosen a spiritual path.

***TOOL:** Patience. Patience, like all the remaining six tools for spiritual health, is just an extension of practicing love and kindness. Patience is also an act of humility and faith in which we show that we do not always have the answer and are willing to let God reveal it in time. Remember to practice patience the next time you are in a situation that is best not rushed, like a big decision that affects your future. Give it time, pray about it, sleep on it, and let the right choice become clear to you in its own time. Also practice patience in situations in which you have no control, like sitting in a traffic jam, waiting for a flight that has been rescheduled, or enduring a setback in the schedule of a project at work. Ask how you could benefit from this "wasted time" by being productive in some other way. For instance, keep a foreign-language CD in your car and learn a few new words if you get stuck in traffic.

***TOOL:** Humility. Acts of humility are one of the fastest ways to connect with our divine nature. When we let go of pretension, arrogance, and pride, we are free to be our authentic selves. We are free to show love, to forgive, to express gratitude, and to practice patience. Being humble means to let go of worrying about how others perceive us. In the office, we once hired a teenage girl to come in on Friday to clean the common areas, including the sinks and bathrooms. Her father is a patient of mine and a successful businessman. One Friday I found him on his hands and knees in the office bathroom cleaning the floor. At first I thought there must have been an accident or spill. He looked up with an expression of satisfaction with his thoroughness and explained that his daughter needed the day off to study for her final exam in school, so he had agreed to do the cleaning for her. He went about the rest of the afternoon doing the office cleaning with such a bright and pleasant attitude that I could not help but respect and admire him.

**\*TOOL:** Honesty. Honesty is not only the best policy; it is a necessary characteristic of a spiritual person. Honesty means you accept your limitations and shortcomings without apology. When you don't know, you say, "I don't know that." It also means you do not wish to deceive or manipulate others for your own advantage. When the woman who sued a fast-food restaurant after planting a human fingertip in a bowl of chili (from a friend who had kept it in formaldehyde after an amputation) was convicted, she was found to have a long pattern of behavior involving dishonest lawsuits and the selling of property she didn't own. Eventually she had to face the consequences with jail time. Less dramatic examples are the everyday lies we tell ourselves and others that keep us from being true to our values and divine nature. Practice honesty with yourself and others regarding who you are and what you want. Let go of any fear of rejection or personal loss, because you will be gaining what is ultimately more important: respect from others, a clean conscience, deep sleep, and a peaceful soul.

**\*TOOL:** Mercy and compassion. Mercy and compassion means to let go of your power and rights for the good of someone else. You may have the ability to put your foot on their heads when they are down, but you give them a hand and help them up instead. As Jesse Jackson said, "Never look down on someone unless you are extending your hand to help them up." You may have the power to destroy, but you choose to heal. You may have the right to sit in a comfortable and safe home, but you go out in a storm to bring a warm blanket to a cold, homeless person in an act of caring. Remember to practice giving up your advantage for the good of someone else—your seat on the bus to a sick person, letting go of the argument you know you are going to win, deciding not to gloat over a success, or letting a coworker "save face" and take the credit at your expense. Every time you show mercy and compassion, you elevate yourself.

**\*TOOL:** Forgiveness. Forgiveness must be heartfelt and sincere to have any meaning. In addition, the person you are forgiving must desire or ask for your forgiveness for it to be valid. God does not forgive those who do not ask for it. My father was once told by a friend, "I'll forgive you, but I won't forget," over a comment he had volunteered about her personal life. He reminded her that he had not asked for her forgiveness and did not want it, because he was not in the least sorry. He saw it as an act of friendship and kindness to tell her the truth she did not want to hear. He pointed out that her offer was insincere, because forgiveness *means* forgetting. When God forgives, the slate is wiped clean, as if it never happened. Never offer forgiveness if you don't intend to forget.

**\*TOOL:** Gratitude. Don't forget to practice gratitude for all the good things in your life. See things in a balanced perspective and realize it could often be worse. Read about the trials and tribulations of persecuted groups throughout human history before you feel sorry for yourself. Choose an attitude of "this is the problem, so let's get going on a solution" rather than an attitude of "bad things are happening to poor victimized me, and someone else should fix it." While you are enjoying a life experience, such as good food and drink, a cold glass of water, a restful nap, the feeling of fresh air filling your lungs, the view of a beautiful sunset, or the sound of the cheerful voice of someone you love, remember that all this can and will be taken away from you someday. Imagine what it would be like to be deprived of these things and how much you would miss them. Then let yourself feel a sense of gratitude that you were able to have that experience. Gratitude goes a long way in putting our minds and hearts in the proper perspective to view our life situations and keep negative impulses like self-pity, irritability, unkindness, and arrogance in check.

## FINAL NOTE AND BEST WISHES

Well! You've come a long way in a short time. Hopefully, you've learned something about yourself and your anxiety condition that you didn't know at the beginning of this book. Healing begins when we recognize and decide to take responsibility for our problems. Now that the issues are more clearly defined, the daily work of transforming and changing lies ahead.

You have examined your goals, values, attitudes, thoughts, beliefs, and spiritual perspective. You have been introduced to a wide variety of tools and helpful strategies to decrease your vulnerability to anxious emotions. Just understanding your anxiety better and the simple technique of deep-breathing exercises may be all you need to feel control. If not, take it to the next level by planning a course of action that is targeted at your specific issues.

After you proceed to take the cast anxiety self test, fill out the personal anxiety assessment plan and develop a personalized program with the personal daily planner, make a commitment to yourself now and every day after that you will attempt to put into action what you have learned and the new tools you have acquired. Consider a morning and evening prayer, asking for the strength and wisdom to grow and evolve into the healthy, happy, and emotionally sound person you were created to be.

You are not alone. Many others are embarking on this journey with you, and we will be with you in spirit all the way. There will be times of discouragement, doubt, apprehension, and disappointment. There will also be times of satisfaction, pride of accomplishment, and the deep peace that comes from knowing you are doing the right thing. Thanks for reading, and my profound hope is for you to find lasting happiness and joy.

—Dr. James Gardner and the many who influenced and contributed to this edition of
*The Anxiety Toolbox Program.*

# T. F. GARDNER'S FAVORITE QUOTES AND BIBLE VERSES

## Quotes:

"The crowd is untruth." —Soren Kierkegaard

"He that can have patience can have what he will." —Benjamin Franklin

"Age does not diminish the extreme disappointment of having a scoop of ice cream fall from the cone." —Jim Feibig

"Education is learning what you didn't even know you didn't know." —Daniel J. Boorstin

"The most important thing in conversation is to hear what isn't being said." —Peter F. Drucker

"Be yourself, everyone else is taken." —Oscar Wilde

"At the touch of love, everyone becomes a poet." —Plato

"I'm always fascinated by the way memory diffuses fact." —Diane Sawyer

"For 'fast-acting' relief, try slowing down." —Lily Tomlin

"When all else fails, read the instructions." —Agnes Allen

"Correction does much, but encouragement does more." —Goethe

"Painting is easy when you don't know how, but very difficult when you do." —Edgar Degas

"Tact is the art of making guests feel at home when that's really where you wish they were." —George E. Bergman

"The greatest gifts you can give your children are the roots of responsibility and the wings independence." —Denis Waitley

"Yes, you can do one thing for me; you can stand out of my light." —Diogenes, in reply to Alexander the Great offering him anything he desired

"Panta gar kairo cala." ("All is made clear in time.") —Sophocles in *Oedipus Rex*.

"Time makes more converts than reason." —Thomas Paine

"The mill won't grind with the waters of the past." —Old English proverb

"Everything is either addition or subtraction; the rest is conversation." —Abraham Polonsky

"Poetry is the most amount of thought in the least amount of words." —T. F. Gardner

**Verses:**
"The prophet is not without honor except in his own country and house" (Matthew 13:57).

"Rejoice Always. Pray without ceasing. In everything give thanks. For this is God's will for you in Jesus Christ" (1 Thessalonians 5: 16, 17, 18).

"Blessed is anyone who takes no offense at me" (Matthew 11:6).

"No one can come to me unless it is granted by the Father" (John 6:65).

"Do not stop him; for whoever is not against me is for me" (Mark 9:41).

"One who puts on Armor should not brag like one who takes it off." King of Israel to Benhadad, King of Arameans (1 Kings 20:11).

## The Anxiety Toolbox Program

© 2017 by James C. Gardner, MD. All rights reserved.

No contents may be copied without express written permission from Dr. Gardner.

## APPENDIX I

# Comprehensive Anxiety Screening Tool Self-Test
## Section I
Check off any letter that applies to you, even if you have only one of the items listed under that letter:

a. _____ Feeling anxious out of proportion with any real threat or current danger
b. _____ Easily fatigued, tired all the time, even when you wake up
c. _____ Constant worrying, anticipating the worst
d. _____ Inability to calm down, unwind, and relax
e. _____ Feeling impatient, irritable, or agitated
f. _____ Feeling nervous, keyed up, restless, jumpy, or on edge; startle easily
g. _____ Depression, lack of interest, unable to feel pleasure, cry easily
h. _____ Pounding, rapid, or irregular heartbeat, throbbing in your blood vessels
i. _____ Breathing too fast of difficulty catching your breath, choking, sighing
j. _____ Chest pressure, pain, or constriction
k. _____ Problems concentrating/staying focused, making decisions, poor memory
l. _____ Family history of anxiety or depression diagnosis
m. _____ Vivid dreams, night terrors
n. _____ Problems falling asleep, waking up too early, broken, unsatisfying sleep
o. _____ Frequent or urgent urination, loss of female period, sexual dysfunction
p. _____ Nausea, upset stomach, belching/gas, difficulty swallowing
q. _____ Irritable bowels (bowel cramps/pain, bloating, or diarrhea/constipation)
r. _____ Headaches, ringing ears, prickly sensations, blurry vision, feeling weak
s. _____ Muscular tension, stiffness, jerking/twitching, aches, grinding teeth
t. _____ Trembling or shaking
u. _____ Sweating, dry mouth, flushing, raising of hair, giddiness, turning pale
v. _____ Dizziness/lightheadedness
w. _____ Feeling needy, requiring more attention and reassurance than usual
x. _____ Fear of losing control, going crazy, doing something uncontrollable
y. _____ Feeling an unreal, dreamlike state
z. _____ Feeling like drinking alcohol or taking a drug to control your anxiety

## Section II
_____ Check here if you checked any of (a) through (f) in section 1 above and any three others from among the list above and if you have felt these symptoms for at least six months. Do not check if you have had panic attacks (unpredictable and random attacks of intense fear) or your symptoms are due to a phobia (fear of a specific object or situation or fear of social performance and interaction.)

## Section III
Check if any of the following apply to you:

a._____ Survived or witnessed a particularly terrifying experience, such as rape, wartime combat, a fire you narrowly escaped, a serious car accident, or other attack or injury that threatened your life or the life of someone else. (Skip this section if the answer is no.)
b._____ Have recurring nightmares about the traumatic incident
c._____ Avoid specific people or places that bring back memories of the trauma
d._____ Have difficulty making plans for the future because of a belief you may not survive "until then"
e._____ Feel distracted throughout the day by flashbacks and memories of the traumatic experience
f._____ Feel irritable, jumpy, or emotionally numb since the traumatic experience
g._____ Have had (a) plus any of the above (b-f) for more than one month
h._____ Have had (a) plus any of the above (b-f) for less than one month
i._____ Suffered a serious head injury from trauma or an explosion causing a concussion

## Section IV
Check below any symptoms that have occurred as sudden, unpredictable, random attacks:

a._____ Sudden onset of intense fear with a sense of impending doom (like you're about to die of a heart attack or stroke)
b._____ Sudden attack in which you fear you are losing your mind, dying, or losing control
c._____ Sudden attack in which you feel a sense of high anxiety and unreality or out-of-body experience
d._____ Sudden attack of intense fear that includes any of the following:
_____ shortness of breath, feelings of choking or smothering
_____ pounding or irregular heartbeat, chest pain or discomfort
_____ dizziness or unsteadiness
_____ trembling/shaking
_____ nausea, vomiting, or diarrhea
_____ cold sweats
e._____ Check if you fear having an attack of anxiety symptoms in a situation in which escape or getting help may be difficult. Check if you are afraid of having an attack in public that will lead to some catastrophe or great embarrassment, causing you to avoid situations and places that might trigger such an attack.
f._____ Check if you are so anxious about having panic attacks that you find it difficult to leave home or familiar surroundings without feeling intense dread, disorientation, or becoming physically ill (nausea/vomiting, fainting, choking, sweating, etc.).

## Section V
a._____ Check if you frequently have obsessive anxious thoughts (there are germs everywhere; someone will break into your house; there will be scarcity and famine; or you feel overly concerned about detail, health, safety, or cleanliness).

b._____ Check here if you have any compulsive behaviors (wash hands over and over; check frequently to see if the doors and windows are locked; check many times to be sure that things are turned off—such as electricity, gas, or water; collect and hoard things you will likely never need; need to do things in a precise and ritualistic way to reduce anxiety). Check if your ritualistic behaviors are embarrassing to you and take a lot of your time every day.

## Section VI

a._____ Check if you have experienced a persistent, irrational fear of a specific object, activity, or situation, such as spiders, birds, needle injections, heights, tunnels, bridges, or airplane travel. Check only if this fear causes a significant disturbance or problem in your life.

b._____ Check if you have difficulty in social situations, like meeting new people, giving a public speech, or being called on in class. Check only if fear of scrutiny by others is a persistent problem that causes you to avoid social situations or endure them with great difficulty.

## Section VII

Check off those symptoms that you have had every day, for most of the day, for at least two weeks:

a._____ Depressed mood (feeling sad, crying spells, hopeless, thoughts of suicide)
b._____ Diminished interest in pleasure (no interest in hobbies, sex, sports, or other things that you used to enjoy)
c._____ Appetite or weight changes (eating more or less than usual, losing or gaining weight)
d._____ Sleep change (sleeping more or less than usual, especially waking up early in the morning)
e._____ Psychomotor agitation or retardation (feeling you are sped up, irritable, and shaky or slowed down and lethargic)
f._____ Fatigue or loss of energy
g._____ Frequent negative, pessimistic thinking
h._____ Feelings of guilt or worthlessness
i._____ Feeling anxious, restless, unable to relax
j._____ Problems with mental concentration, focus, making decisions, or memory
k._____ Check if you have had a depressed mood (letter [a] above) for more than two years and at least two other items among (b) through (j).
l._____ Check if you have experienced depressed mood (letter [a] above) and any other symptoms from the above list during the winter months only.
m._____ Check if you checked (a) or (b) above plus any two items among (b) through (j). Do not check here if your symptoms above are better explained by bereavement (grief).

## Section VIII

Check only if you experienced the symptoms below for at least four days in a row:
a._____ Decreased need for sleep (felt fine after just a few hours of sleep)

b._____ More talkative or feeling a need to keep talking
c._____ Feeling that your thoughts were sped up or racing
d._____ Inflated self-esteem, feeling powerful, infallible, extra smart, extra sexy
e._____ Increased goal-directed activity—feeling an urgent need to achieve social, career, or academic goals
f._____ Excessive involvement in high-pleasure, high-risk activities, like shopping sprees, gambling, sexual indiscretions
g._____ Feeling boundless energy and fearlessness
h._____ Feeling love for the world and a joyful optimism and exuberance about life
i. _____ Feeling increased irritation, anger, and hostility toward others
j._____ Felt elevated, expansive, or excessively irritable and agitated mood for at least one week, with significant impairment in functioning or hospitalization
k._____ Felt elevated, expansive, or excessively irritable and agitated mood for at least four days, with changes observable by those who know you but not greatly affecting functioning or requiring hospitalization
l._____ While experiencing some of the above symptoms, you lost touch with reality, heard voices, thought people were out to get you, thought you were someone you were not (like a CIA agent or Jesus Christ), especially if the episode caused legal problems (arrest) or required hospitalization

## Section IX

Check all that apply:
a._____ Difficulty finishing projects
b._____ Disorganized
c._____ Problems remembering appointments or obligations
d._____ Lack of focus or poor concentration
e._____ Have to work extra hard or take longer than others to finish a task
e._____ Get restless, fidget, or squirm when trying to concentrate
f._____ Symptoms above started in childhood and have caused you to underachieve throughout life.

## Section X

Check any of the following that applies to you:
a._____ Sometimes choke up during a sporting performance (pitching or hitting a baseball, shooting a free-throw shot, connecting solidly with a shot off the tee or a 15-foot putt, or any other sport that requires accuracy and concentration under pressure)
b._____ Get anxious during a big job interview, not answering the questions as smoothly and confidently as you would like
c._____ Worry and lose sleep for several days before a big exam, court appearance, TV interview, or other event that is important to you

d.\_\_\_\_\_ Feel significant discomfort and apprehension whenever experiencing something new (a first date, meeting your significant other's folks for the first time, the first time you asked for a raise or had to fire an employee)

e.\_\_\_\_\_ Experienced a recent stressful event or situation, such as a serious illness in the family; being served with divorce papers; the death of a beloved pet or friend; the rubber broke during sex with a new partner, and you are worried you might have contracted a deadly disease; deciding to file for bankruptcy; or realizing the finality of a broken relationship. Check only if you have been experiencing at least five of the symptoms listed in section 1 for anywhere from a few days to several weeks.

## Section XI

Check if you are anxious and any of the following applies to you:

a.\_\_\_\_\_ Any neurologic diseases, like stroke, concussion (head trauma), Parkinson's disease, multiple sclerosis, chronic pain

b.\_\_\_\_\_ Any endocrine/metabolic diseases, like diabetes, hypothyroidism, Grave's disease, Cushing's disease, Addison's disease

c.\_\_\_\_\_ Any cardiopulmonary diseases, like coronary artery disease, cardiomyopathy, arrhythmia, emphysema, asthma, sleep apnea, pulmonary fibrosis

d.\_\_\_\_\_ Any autoimmune disease, like Lupus, fibromyalgia, rheumatoid arthritis, Sjogren's syndrome

e.\_\_\_\_\_ Any cancer or blood disorders, like anemia; leukemia; cancer of the lung, brain, bone, kidneys, pancreas, or adrenals

f.\_\_\_\_\_ Any gastrointestinal disease, like irritable bowel syndrome, stomach ulcer, gastroesophageal reflux, Crohn's disease, cirrhosis of the liver, hepatitis B or C, chronic pancreatitis

g.\_\_\_\_\_ Any prescription medication that can alter mood or cause anxiety—like diet pills, decongestants, stimulants, steroids, hormones and birth control pills, pain pills, sedatives, or antidepressants

h.\_\_\_\_\_ Any foods/herbs that are stimulants, like caffeine (found in sodas, coffee, tea, and chocolate), excessive vitamins, ginkgo biloba

i.\_\_\_\_\_ Any toxic environmental exposures, like heavy metals, mold spores, paint, stains and lacquers, insecticides

j.\_\_\_\_\_ Overuse of alcohol, especially to help when you feel stressed, anxious, or depressed

k.\_\_\_\_\_ Overuse of marijuana

l.\_\_\_\_\_ Use of any stimulant drug, such as cocaine, ecstasy, amphetamines

m.\_\_\_\_\_ Use of any sedatives or downers, like valium, barbiturates, sleeping pills

o.\_\_\_\_\_ Any eating disorder, such as going without food, occasionally eating large amounts, or forcing yourself to throw up after a meal (binging and purging)

## Section XII

Check any of the below that describes your personality, if any. Only check if most of the description applies to you. Sometimes it's better to have a close friend, parent, sibling, or family member lend an opinion, as most of us are not clued in to our own personality traits.

a._____ Defensive, oversensitive, secretive, suspicious, hyperalert, hypervigilant, blunted emotional response

b._____ Shy, introverted, withdrawn, avoids close relationships

c._____ Perfectionist, egocentric, indecisive, rigid thought patterns, need to be in control

d._____ Dependent, immature, seductive, egocentric, vain, emotionally up and down

e._____ Superstitious, socially isolated, poor interpersonal skills, odd patterns of speech

f._____ Exhibitionist, grandiose, preoccupied with power, not empathetic with the needs of others, excessive demands for attention

g._____ Fearful of rejection, oversensitive to failure, poor self-esteem

h._____ Passive, overaccepting, indecisive, poor confidence, low self-esteem

i._____ Stubborn, procrastinating, argumentative, sulking, helpless, clinging, negative toward authority figures

j._____ Selfish, callous, promiscuous, impulsive, unable to learn from experience, enmeshed in social or legal problems

k._____ Impulsive; full of anger/fear/guilt; see issues as black or white; lacking in self-control and self-fulfillment; involved in unstable, intense interpersonal relationships; have attempted/thought about attempting suicide; aggressive behavior; feelings of emptiness; may have overused or abused drugs/alcohol; needy, demanding attention

l._____ Argumentative, angry, disregard authority, contentious, looking for trouble, involved in high-risk/illegal activities, think you know it all, disregard the rights of others, usually have a juvenile or adult criminal record

Now read the interpretation instructions below and jot down any notes about your diagnoses or diagnostic possibilities or insights that may apply to you. There are almost always several overlapping diagnoses for each person!

## Interpretation Instructions for the Comprehensive Anxiety Screening Tool Self-Test
### Section I

This is the "a-to-z" list of anxiety symptoms. People with true anxiety disorders will experience many of these physical sensations and emotions. The following sections will try to identify these disorders. All people have anxiety, especially if they are challenging themselves and trying new things. We will discuss this in section 9. These people have normal anxiety, not an anxiety disorder. They will feel a few of the symptoms on this list for only a short period of time while they are adjusting to a new experience or performing a particularly nerve-racking task. Letters (a) through (f) are the primary symptoms of an anxious mood. Letter (g) has to do with depressed mood, which is covered more in sections VII and VIII. One cannot really talk about anxiety without considering depression, since one often is a symptom of the other. Letters (h) through (j) are typical cardiopulmonary (heart and lung) symptoms of anxiety; (k) lists the cognitive impairments common with anxiety; (l) reminds us that anxiety often has a genetic component; and (m) and (n) list the sleep disturbances experienced during times of anxiety. Genitourinary complaints are listed in (o). Gastrointestinal symptoms are listed in (p) and (q). Letter (r) gives somatic sensory symptoms, while (s) shows somatic muscular complaints. Letters (t), (u), and (v) are caused by the activation of the autonomic nervous system in anxiety. Common psychological responses to anxiety are listed in (w), (x) and (y). Letter (z) reminds us that a high percentage of anxiety sufferers self-medicate with a variety of substances.

## Section II
If you checked this question, you should be evaluated for generalized anxiety disorder.

## Section III
If you checked (a), any of (b) through (f), and (g), you should be considered for a diagnosis of PTSD. If you checked (a), any of (b) through (f), and (h), you might have acute stress disorder. Those who checked (i) should be evaluated for TBI by a neuropsychologist and tested for emotional and cognitive problems, especially if there was a known loss of consciousness or brain hemorrhage.

## Section IV
If you checked any of (a) through (d), you may have panic disorder. If you checked any of (a) through (d) and also checked (e), you could have panic disorder with agoraphobia. If you checked (f), you most likely have severe agoraphobia.

## Section V
If you checked both (a) and (b) in this section, you should be evaluated for the diagnosis of OCD. In OCD, the ritualistic behaviors often take several hours each day to complete and are thought to be a coping strategy to distract oneself from the obsessive anxious thoughts.

## Section VI
If you checked (a), you may have a specific phobia. If you checked (b), you may have social phobia.

## Section VII
If you checked (k), you will want to be evaluated for dysthymic disorder. If you checked (l), you should be considered for seasonal affective disorder. If you checked (m), you may qualify for the diagnosis of a major depressive episode or major depressive disorder. This section attempts to identify those with depressive mood disorders because of the high incidence of anxiety symptoms that accompany mood disorders. This is probably because depression causes so many difficulties in work, family life, and intimate relationships and friendships that the person begins to experience loss. Once someone has felt the

pain of loss, he or she begins to worry about future loss, and the anxiety symptoms begin. This is also true of normal grief or bereavement from a close, personal loss. Fortunately, anxiety born of depression or grief responds equally well to the tools in the ATP.

## Section VIII

If you checked any three of (a) through (g) and (h), you have likely experienced a euphoric manic episode. If you checked any three of (a) through (g) and (i), you have possibly experienced a dysphoric manic episode. If you checked any three of (a) through (i) and (j), you may carry the diagnosis of a manic episode associated with bipolar II disorder. If you checked any three of (a) through (i) and (k), you meet the criteria of a hypomanic episode. If you checked any three of (a) through (i) plus (l), you should probably have already received the diagnosis of bipolar I disorder with psychotic features. Bipolar patients cycle back and forth between depression (one pole) and mania (the opposite pole). Most people with bipolar illness have episodes of mania that are much shorter than their periods of depression. They often do not have insight into when they are manic, because they feel this is a good and normal level of energy. Bipolar patients will seek help only during their depressive cycles because that is the only time they feel bad. Even people with dysphoric mania do not necessarily feel bad; they just feel they are the only smart and competent person around and everyone else is an idiot and getting in their way. In fact, many bipolar patients resist treatment because they enjoy their mania so much. Unfortunately, whether it's the depressive or manic phase they're in, those with bipolar disorder will likely experience difficulties with financial security, relationships, failed businesses and careers, and poor health. These problems will eventually lead to anxiety, which is why we're talking about this disorder in the first place! In addition, up to 85 percent of bipolar patients carry the additional diagnosis of substance abuse, as they commonly self-medicate with alcohol and drugs.

## Section IX

If you checked any three, especially if you also checked (f), you should be considered for the diagnosis of ADD. This disorder often leads to depression and anxiety because people with ADD have difficulty holding their lives together as adults. Divorce is common because their spouses get frustrated trying to work with husbands or wives who can't stay focused and forget to follow through on things they promised to do. Likewise, bosses and coworkers are dissatisfied, leading to a series of career failures. A person with ADD will often succeed and reach a high level of education due to trying extra hard and getting special tutoring. Sometimes they cover for their deficiencies by relying on their looks or good personalities to get ahead. But, sooner or later, the disorder gets in the way of normal functioning.

## Section X

If you did not qualify for any of the diagnoses in the previous sections but can relate to some of the common anxiety-provoking situations presented here, you are experiencing normal anxiety. If this anxiety keeps you from performing the way you would like, the tools in the ATP will allow you to overcome and conquer it.

If you checked (e), you may be suffering from acute situational anxiety. Even though you may not have all the criteria of an anxiety disorder, symptoms such as sleeplessness, nausea, chest pains, and crying can be overwhelming during episodes of acute situational anxiety. Often, those who don't adjust and improve after a few weeks will go on to develop an anxiety disorder. Many will be found to have underlying stressors and a lack of coping skills that should be recognized and addressed.

## Section XI

If you checked any of (a) through (f) in this section, you likely have anxiety due to a medical condition. If you checked (g), you may have anxiety due to a prescription medication. If you checked (h) or (i), you possibly have anxiety due to a toxic substance or exposure. If you checked any of items (j) through (m), you should seek help for the possibility of anxiety due to substance abuse. Finally, if you checked (o), you should be evaluated for binge eating, anorexia, or bulimia, all thought to be caused by underlying anxiety issues. The purpose of this section is to remind you that there are many medical conditions that cause anxiety. You will need a thorough and thoughtful evaluation by your doctor to determine whether any of these problems could be playing a role or actually be the root cause of your anxiety.

## Section XII

These are typical-yet-incomplete descriptions of personality disorders, so don't take them too seriously. If you are under eighteen years of age, it is too early to determine if you have a personality disorder. People with personality disorders are usually in denial about it, seeing themselves very differently from how others see them. It would take several sessions for a psychiatrist to determine if the diagnosis of a personality disorder is appropriate. But, in case you're curious, here are the disorders that fit the descriptions:

(A) is paranoid personality, (b) is schizoid personality, (c) is compulsive personality, (d) is histrionic (hysterical) personality, (d) is schizotypical personality, (e) is narcissistic personality, (f) is avoidant personality, (g) is dependent personality, (h) is passive-aggressive personality, (i) is antisocial personality, and (j) is borderline personality. Those with borderline personality may experience psychotic breaks with reality under high stress, and they are often codiagnosed with anxiety and depressive mood disorders, PTSD in particular. Some go on to develop bipolar I disorder. Item (l) is not a personality disorder but a description of someone with oppositional defiant disorder. Personality disorders and oppositional defiant disorder lead to vulnerability to anxiety by setting the person up for failure in many areas of life over time.

**NOTE:** Many who take this test will find that they have multiple and overlapping conditions. This is the norm rather than the rare or exceptional case. We recommend that you circle all of the diagnoses above that may apply to you. Then present this to your primary care physician or psychiatrist on your next visit. Have fun with understanding yourself better, and don't take any of it personally because anxiety is not your fault (unless it is)!

—Dr. Gardner and *The Anxiety Toolbox Program* staff, www.anxietytoolbox.com

APPENDIX II

## Quick-Fix Formula Workbook : Getting Anxious Emotions under Control in the First Week

### Disclaimer

The ATP contains information the author believes to be correct. However, this program in no way substitutes for the advice and care of a skilled medical or psychological professional. Although general principles and practices of treatment are described here, no specific recommendation for any individual's therapy or medical care is intended, expressed, or implied.

When it comes to health care, no reader should act on the basis of any printed information, including the contents of this book, without consultation with a health-care professional. Nothing in the ATP should be construed as an attempt to diagnose, prescribe, or recommend a treatment for any health condition. You should not try to treat yourself with any of the methods described in this program without the guidance of a qualified health-care professional who is thoroughly familiar with both the remedies and your medical and psychological status. Some of the herbs and alternative remedies listed are known to be poisonous if taken inappropriately; some can elicit allergic reactions. Do not attempt to self-diagnose or self-treat based on information in this program, including the comprehensive anxiety screening tool self-test and the quick-fix formula.

The ATP also provides various URLs as helpful resources. Although I have chosen sites that I believe are helpful and have reviewed the sites and tested all the provided URLs as of March 1, 2017, I do not take responsibility for their content or any product that you might purchase through them.

### Introduction

The term *quick fix* implies a speedy repair job that will later need to be reinforced with a more permanent solution. This is true in the case of a quick fix for emotional problems. In the case of anxiety, when the "panic" stage is reached and overwhelming waves of anxiety pound at the very foundation of our being, no amount of talk therapy is likely to calm the swirling seas around us.

This is a state of brain chemical imbalance and central nervous system activation that triggers an outpouring of stress hormones from our adrenal glands and influences all aspects of our physical and psychological beings.

All the symptoms of a panic attack can be explained by this nervous system overload and activation, including chest pain, heart palpitations, nausea, dizziness, sweats, shaking, and difficulty breathing. The psychological reactions that accompany these physical symptoms include feelings of unreality, fear of going crazy, fear of doing something uncontrollable, and a sense of doom or dying.

If these symptoms prove to be intolerable or even make you feel suicidal, you belong in the nearest emergency room. It is completely appropriate to dial 911 for emergency attention if you feel you cannot safely drive to the ER or do not trust yourself with your own life.

If you feel reasonable control and stability, you may want to try the quick-fix formula program before delving deeper into the ATP for long-term answers. The quick-fix formula strategy recognizes that the most successful approach to severe anxiety and panic attacks will be a combination of several ingredients working together on the nervous system to calm down the overactivation and restore balance. Read each of the general categories below, and if applicable, choose an option from that category for your quick-fix formula program. You will then plug these choices into the day planner provided at the end.

## Overview of Quick-Fix Formula Contents

**Quick Cognitive Tools to Cope With Anxiety and Panic**

**Quick Ways to Direct Attention Away from Internal Sensations**

**Quick Methods to Induce the Relaxation Response**

**Quick Dietary Strategies to Reduce Anxiety**

**Quick Strategies to Improve Sleep**

**Quick Supplemental and Medical Strategies to Calm Anxiety**

**Quick Positive Affirmations/Spiritual Support**

**Summary Note**

**Quick-Fix Daily Planner**

## Quick Cognitive Tools to Cope with Anxiety and Panic

The first thing to realize when you are feeling high anxiety or panic is that *you can cope*. The tools you will learn here are presented in more detail in *The Anxiety Toolbox Program* and will be your emergency first-aid kit. Just knowing that you will be able to survive and regain control without anything terrible happening is the first step in fixing anxiety. Remind yourself of the following facts and check any statements that make sense to you:

*Fact: There Is No Real Danger!*

Anxiety attacks are normal reactions to stress. Although unpleasant and uncomfortable, they rarely pose any true danger or cause any damage to your body or health. Even though you may feel like you are having a heart attack, stroke, or even dying, this is not the case! Stop any self-talk that tries to explain your panic as being caused by some internal danger. Tell yourself firmly that you are not having a heart attack, suffocating, losing control, or dying. The worst that can happen is you might hyperventilate and faint for a short period of time if you don't slow down your breathing with the technique taught in the next section.

*Fact: This Is Not a Catastrophe!*

People prone to anxiety attacks often misinterpret slightly unusual or uncomfortable body sensations in a catastrophic way. This internalization of the experience causes a magnification of any unusual or sudden change in the body's sensations. Rather than turning your focus inward and making up problems that don't exist, the tools you will learn in this quick-fix section will help you direct your attention away from internal sensations. In addition to those who misinterpret their anxiety as meaning a physical catastrophe, many fear that their anxiety symptoms (e.g., sweating, nausea/vomiting, fainting, blushing, shaking/tremors) will cause a psychological catastrophe they will not be able to recover from or live down. They worry that those witnessing their attack will judge them harshly. They may say to themselves, "How will I ever face them again?" "They will think I'm crazy," "They will never forgive me," or "I'll never be able to show my face around here again." The truth is, no one will remember or care. It's OK to have a panic attack. You don't have to apologize or explain it to anyone. If anything, others will be concerned about helping you feel better, not judging you negatively.

*Fact: I Can't Win by Fighting!*

Resisting or struggling against an anxiety or panic attack will likely make it intensify and last longer. Rather than gritting your teeth, clenching your fists, and tensing muscles, respond to anxiety as a passive observer with no emotional investment in what is happening. Consider adopting the following attitudes toward your anxiety:

- I will face my symptoms and allow them to happen. Rather than fighting or running away, I will adopt a passive attitude and tell myself, "No biggy. My anxiety symptoms are back. I will

just let my body go through its normal anxiety response with all the usual symptoms. I've been through this before, and I will get through this one as well. I can handle this."
- I will observe my anxiety symptoms but not react to them emotionally. There is no benefit to getting all worked up and upset; that will only make things worse. I will let go and allow this unpleasant experience to run its course. All anxiety attacks are activations of the nervous system that will eventually reduce and extinguish without any effort on my part. The adrenalin surge I'm feeling won't last. I will just float along and let the anxiety take me where it wants until it finally leaves.

## Quick Ways to Direct Attention Away from Internal Sensations

- **Retreat**: Especially in the case of phobias, temporarily leaving or exiting a situation that is triggering your anxiety is often helpful. This should be distinguished from avoiding or escaping a situation. *Avoiding* means that you never go near the feared situation in the first place because you think you can't handle it. *Escaping* means that you run away with no intention of coming back. These two means of coping only lead to reinforcing the persistent false belief that you are not capable of surviving the phobic object or situation. Retreating, on the other hand, means you choose to withdraw temporarily from the situation until you feel better. This is especially reasonable if you experience overwhelming anxiety on a bridge or the freeway. If it is safe to do so, pull off to the side of the road or leave at the nearest exit, stop the car, put on your emergency blinkers, and allow the anxiety attack to run its course. In a grocery store, you may leave all your items in the shopping cart and simply walk out—planning to come back later and start over. No explanation or apology is necessary. At a party, you can retreat to a quiet room, balcony, or the outdoors (try not to hide in the bathroom as lines tend to form outside). Once the anxiety attack has passed, it is unlikely to return. You can then go back and prove to yourself you can get through it just fine.
- **Talk to someone**: One of the fastest and most effective means of diverting attention from yourself is to talk to someone. If you have a cell phone, call a friend or relative and ask how his or her day is going. It's OK to admit you are going through a period of anxiety and are trying to ignore it; this will help reduce your nervousness. Try not to talk about yourself too much, though. If you are in line at a store, bank, or the post office, strike up a conversation with someone nearby. If you are on an airplane, bus, train, subway, or boat, look around for someone who looks bored and might enjoy some light conversation.
- **Engage in brisk exercise**: Brisk, vigorous exercise for just a few minutes is an excellent way to burn off nervous energy from anxiety attacks while proving to yourself that your body is strong and can handle it. Run in place for two minutes. Run up and down a flight of stairs a few times. Jump rope for a minute or two (this is harder than you think).
- **Stay focused on the present**: Focus your attention on concrete objects in your immediate environment. Look carefully at your watch or a piece of jewelry, or get out your purse or wallet and contemplate each item carefully. Read the calling cards and carefully observe each credit

card, including the expiration dates. Look at any photographs and think about where that person might be at that moment. If you are driving a car, pay attention to the cars in front of you; what color and types do you see?

- **Find a distracting activity**: Sometimes a simple, repetitive activity will help take your mind off the immediate symptoms of anxiety. Here are some suggestions:
    - Feel the edge of a key or the teeth on a comb with your thumb or finger
    - Snap a rubber band against your wrist
    - Sing or play a musical instrument (carry a harmonica in your pocket)
    - Perform a puzzle or mind game, like counting backward by threes, fives, sevens, and so on
    - Knit or sew
    - Go work in the garden
    - Turn your attention to a hobby or activity you enjoy
    - Record your favorite TV shows to watch when needed
    - Hug someone you love
    - Eat a delicious snack
    - Your idea:

**Quick Methods to Induce the Relaxation Response**

The relaxation response has been widely studied and written about by Dr. Herbert Benson of Harvard University. It is an actual physiologic state of being that triggers alpha brain-wave activation and shuts down anxious background noise in our minds and bodies. Below are simple and very effective ways to induce this response.

*Abdominal Breathing*

To make deep abdominal (diaphragmatic) breathing come naturally, you may need to spend time practicing with proper technique. After a while, you will be able to use this technique to invoke the relaxation response spontaneously and effortlessly. Follow the steps below until you feel you fully understand deep breathing:

- Lie down on the floor on a mat or blanket. Place your back flat against the floor with your legs slightly apart and your arms away from your body with the palms facing up. Your toes should fall outward comfortably.
- Close your eyes and scan your body for any tension. Allow any areas of tension in your face, shoulders, arms, or legs to release.
- Take slow, deep breaths in through your nose. Let the air escape through your mouth as you exhale. Pay attention to which part of your body rises and falls as you breathe. Is it your chest, abdomen, or a combination of the two?
- Place your left hand on your abdomen and your right hand on your chest. As you breathe in, feel your left hand being actively pushed up by your abdomen. Feel your chest moving less actively and only to follow your abdominal movements.

- Take slow, deep breaths in through your nose, filling your entire lungs, and then let the air out through relaxed, slightly open lips. Make a quiet, relaxing sound like an afternoon breeze as you gently exhale. Make sure your jaw, tongue, and mouth are relaxed.
- Continue this method of breathing for five to ten minutes, making sure your abdomen is expanding more actively that your chest and that your chest is just going along for the ride. Continue to scan your body for tension.

*Progressive Relaxation*
Find a comfortable position in a quiet room free from distractions or interruptions. Wear comfortable, loose clothing and take off your shoes. Now follow the following script:

- Begin relaxing by taking in several slow, deep abdominal breaths. Imagine all of your worries and concerns leaving your body as you exhale.
- Let your entire body go completely limp and relaxed as you continue your deep, slow breathing pattern.
- Squeeze your eyes closed tight, and then allow them to relax. Let them remain closed gently and comfortably.
- Alternatively smile and frown using all the muscles of your cheeks, then let go of all the tension. Give it a full twenty seconds.
- Push your tongue into the inside of each cheek and the roof of your mouth, then relax.
- Bring your chin up toward your neck and hold a few seconds. Then lay your head back and gently roll it all the way to each side. Then bring it back to a central position and feel complete relaxation.
- Shrug your shoulders up toward your ears and then pull them downward as if someone is pulling on your hands. Bring them back to a comfortable position and feel all the tension melt away.
- Scan your entire head, neck, and shoulders and upper body. Let go of every last bit of tension in your face, jaw, throat, scalp, forehead, neck, shoulders, and arms.
- Now feel your stomach as you check your abdominal breathing. Your hand should be pushed up by each breath. Breathe in deeply and slowly, feeling the air expanding your lungs, then let the air out by relaxing the entire chest and abdomen.
- Arch your back by putting your feet flat on the ground with bent knees and lifting your hips off the floor. Don't strain. Hold the position for several seconds, feeling the tension in your low back. Bring your hips back down and relax. Do this one or two more times, relaxing more and more. Then let your legs go straight and relaxed with your feet pointing slightly outward.
- Tighten your buttocks and thighs, then relax and feel the difference. Repeat a few more times.
- Straighten and tense your legs with your toes curled downward. Hold and then relax. Now straighten and tense your legs with your toes bent upward. Hold and relax.
- Scan your chest, abdomen, back, hips, thighs, calves, ankles, and feet. Let go of every last bit of tension.

- Feel deeper and deeper relaxation throughout your entire body. As you breathe slowly and deeply, experience the warmth and heaviness of complete relaxation. Everything is loose, heavy, and comfortable. Focus on slow, deep abdominal breathing and notice that your entire body is loose and relaxed, calm and rested.

## *Meditation*

The goal of meditation is to quiet the mind and disconnect it from the constant barrage of external and internal stimulation. In studies on yoga, Zen Buddhism, and Transcendental Meditation, scientists have come to the conclusion that meditation is a "wakeful, hypometabolic state." During meditation, both the heart rate and the rate of perspiration are slowed; the rate of metabolism is slowed as confirmed by decreased oxygen consumption and carbon dioxide output; there is an increase in the calm alpha-rhythm brain waves as seen on EEG recordings; and the skin resistance to electrical stimulation is increased (indicating increased tolerance to external stimuli).

There are four components of the relaxation response that are also common to most practices of meditation and prayer:

1. The first component is a *quiet environment*. Meditation involves both quieting our internal noise as well as external distractions.
2. The second component is an *object on which to focus our thoughts*. It may be a word, the tone of a bell or repeated chant, or gazing at a symbol. These are to help us block out other thoughts that might distract us.
3. The third component is a *passive attitude*. This means you do not care about how well you are doing with your meditation session. Moreover, you should ignore and not try to analyze any thoughts or perceptions; just let them pass in and out of your consciousness.
4. The fourth component is a *comfortable position*. You should find a position you can hold comfortably for at least twenty minutes. A sitting position is recommended. At first it may seem to take effort to maintain this posture, but if you continue to practice on a daily basis, the position will become easier as your body strengthens. Although lying down is most comfortable, it may lead you to fall asleep, which is not the desired state of mind.

Evoking the relaxation response is no mystery. We have already experienced this trancelike state many times, such as when we get into our favorite TV show or an engrossing movie. In this state, we may forget what time it is or fail to hear our spouse calling our name for the tenth time. Two basic steps are necessary:

**Step one.** Focus on a chosen word, phrase, object, or sound. The repeated word could be from nature, humanity, or religion, such as one, ocean, earth, moon, love, peace, calm, and so on. The sound could be a fountain, a gong, or the repetition of a sung tone or chant. The object could be a symbol, a plant, a cross, or some other item of special meaning.

**Step two.** Maintain a passive attitude, ignoring everyday intrusive thoughts without irritability or concern. Recognize them and let them go, turning your attention back to your meditative focus point in step 1.

In performing the above, make sure to relax your muscles, close your eyes, sit quietly in a comfortable position, breath slowly and naturally from the diaphragm, continue ten to twenty minutes, and practice this technique once or twice every day.

Below is a simple meditation technique that can be done just about anywhere:

- First, dedicate a room in your house or a deck or garden in your yard (if the weather is good) to practice your daily meditation. If a room is not available, then a corner of the room; if that is not possible, then at least a special chair or cushion used only for meditation. You may also want to create a meditative space by wrapping yourself in a comfortable cloth garment. Turn off all phones and any possible distractions.
- Choose a specific time of day to meditate, and be consistent with this time.
- Sit in a relaxed position with a straight back to help avoid slouching. This may seem uncomfortable at first, but as your muscles strengthen over time, you'll be able to hold this position longer and longer and avoid back problems.
- Begin your meditation with the awareness of a single breath. Think of nothing but the sensation of the air slowly and completely filling your lungs, then experience your chest wall relaxing as the air is released in a slow and controlled expiration.
- Now take several slow "awareness breaths," letting go of past problems and future worries, moving yourself closer and closer to the present moment. Be aware of how your body feels, and let go of any muscle tension except for that which allows good posture.
- If you find your attention wandering, it may be helpful to focus on a single word, phrase, or name repeated over and over. Choose one word or name for the inhalation and another for the exhalation phase. For those with religious beliefs, it may be helpful to choose words that reflect your faith. Those of the Jewish faith may, for instance, say "Sh'ma" during the inhalation and ""Yisrael" during the exhalation. Similarly, "God" and "love" or "Jesus" and "Savior" may be meaningful to a Christian, "Allah" and "Great" to the Muslim, "Hare" and "Krishna" to the Hindu, and so on. In truth, any name or word that holds meaning for you is equally useful to focus your concentration and attention. Some people prefer a tone during the exhalation, sung softly or hummed, using the utterance: "Ommm."
- Continue this practice over and over, letting your focus shift away from your breathing and body to your tone, word, or name.
- Remember, the purpose of the practice of meditation is to let go of our own thoughts and awareness by letting the conscious mind relax and take a break. It is not a "trying" but an "allowing." As the mind and body are encouraged to relaxed, our greater self is free to experience a natural awakening.
- When you are ready to conclude your meditation session, release your focus on the word, name, or tone and end the process just as you began, by noticing each breath and how your body feels. Then take a deep breath and slowly open your eyes. Take a few moments to gently stretch your arms and legs.

### Visualization and Imagery

You will learn the basics of these tools in *The Anxiety Toolbox Program*. For now, however, you can employ a brief and helpful exercise. The most helpful visualization/imagery exercise is the creation on your own private, safe haven. It could be a place you saw pictures of in a travel magazine and dreamed of visiting, a favorite vacation spot, or a place from far back in childhood that now exists only in your memory. You will now create or re-create this ideal, peaceful refuge and be able to go there whenever you want!

Visualization and imagery work best when used in conjunction with a relaxation technique. When your physical body is relaxed, you can give your mind the freedom to daydream. Meditation, progressive relaxation, and yoga are the most common relaxation techniques used with imagery. Here is the basic format to follow:

Loosen your clothing, take off your shoes, and sit in a comfortable position on a chair or pillow. Dim the lights or close your eyes. Take in a few deep breaths. Picture yourself descending an imaginary staircase. With each step, notice that you feel more and more relaxed.

When you feel relaxed, imagine a place you would like to spend some peaceful quiet time. It could be a beach, a mountain, a monastery, or the shore of a serene lake or waterfall you enjoyed in childhood. Try to go into this scene each time you practice your imagery. Make sure your scene has special meaning to you and that you feel safe and secure here. No one can find you or hurt you. If you feel this way, it will make you more receptive to other images.

Once you feel comfortable in your special place, gradually direct your mind toward the problem or fear that you're concerned about. Let your mind create images as you think about this concern. Try to let the images become more vivid and in focus, but don't worry if they fade in and out at times. If several images come to mind, choose one and stick with it for that session.

Your images may take different forms, sensations, sounds, smells, or colors. Let your mind find the images that reflect your emotions. Don't expect great revelations or insights to strike you; just allow your mind to rest and do its daydreaming. Let yourself loiter in your thoughts.

At the end of each session, spend some time imagining that your problem is completely resolved. Take a few deep breaths and picture yourself reclimbing the imaginary staircase and gradually becoming aware of your surroundings. Open your eyes, stretch, smile, and go on with your day.

### Exercise

Exercise works to induce relaxation by expending nervous energy generated by the body's fight-or-flight response during anxiety, by stretching and relaxing muscle groups to trigger the body-mind relaxation response, and by correcting blood-gas imbalances that arise from anxiety-altered breathing patterns. The three main forms of exercise are discussed below. Choose one that is convenient and fits your personality, health limitations, and energy level.

- Aerobic exercise is sustained activity involving the major muscle groups, such as swimming, running, or brisk walking. Additional aerobic activities include sports such as tennis, volleyball, soccer, yoga, tai chi, and some forms of martial arts. This kind of exercise strengthens your

cardiovascular system and increases overall strength and stamina. The goal of aerobic exercise is for your pulse to reach a training rate that is appropriate for your age. Start out with five minutes three times a week, and try to gradually work up to a twenty- to thirty-minute session. Aerobic activities include running, brisk walking, cycling, exercise machine (bike, treadmill, stair climber, elliptical cross-trainer, etc.), swimming, rowing, aerobic dancing, or any other exercise that requires sustained activity of your large muscle groups. This type of exercise reduces stress and anxiety while building stamina.
- Strength training can be accomplished through isotonic or isometric exercises. Isotonic exercise occurs when your muscles contract against a resistance with movement, as in weight lifting. Weight lifting causes tiny tears in the muscle being exercised that take several days to rebuild and strengthen. This process builds increased muscle mass and causes our body metabolism to increase, thereby burning off fat, even on the days we are not lifting. Isometrics involves contracting your muscles against a resistance without movement. Isometrics increases muscle strength and tone without increasing muscle bulk. Weight lifting, hiking, and rock climbing are examples of strength-building exercise.
- Calisthenics are stretching exercises, such as sit-ups, toe touches, and knee bends. These exercises help increase flexibility and joint mobility.
- Rhythmic exercises, like yoga and tai chi, are extremely helpful but take time to learn. If you already have these skills or can readily start a program in your area, strongly consider these programs, as they offer a healthy long-term tool to make you anxiety resistant.
- HIIT (high-intensity interval training) is considered by many to be the most effective form of exercise for weight loss and cardiovascular fitness. If you are healthy and in good physical shape, HIIT might be for you. This type of exercise involves five to ten minutes of peak performance activity, such as spinning on an Exercycle at full speed, running in place with full effort, or jumping rope briskly. Within minutes, you are short of breath and sweating and feel your heart pounding in your chest. If you feel more release from anxiety and stress with HIIT than with strength training, calisthenics, or rhythmic exercise, then try doing an HIIT activity that agrees with you up to three times a day.

The kind of exercises you choose depends on your personal preferences and your physical ability. Isotonic exercises should be limited to two times a week, as the body needs time to recover. Isometrics, calisthenics, and HIIT can be done every day, if time allows. Always get a complete physical exam from your physician before embarking on a new or vigorous exercise program.

### *Aromatherapy, Hydrotherapy, Music Therapy, and Massage Therapy*
These will be covered more in the program, but consider the above options for inducing the relaxation response if they appeal to you, have been successful in the past, and are convenient or accessible. A hot lavender bath combines aromatherapy with hydrotherapy. One session in a sensory-deprivation flotation tank might calm anxiety for a full week. Relaxation CDs or downloads of the relaxing sounds of nature (rain, waterfalls, the ocean, birds) are readily available online or

at your local music store. The website contimusic.com is discussed in the text of the ATP under "Music Therapy." Massage therapy is readily available in spas and health centers and comes in a large variety of techniques. Tell your massage therapist you want a relaxing and calming style to help destress.

## Quick Dietary Strategies to Reduce Anxiety

You will learn more about healthy dietary choices in the ATP. For purposes of a quick fix, we will focus on the main foods to avoid and foods you should include in your diet, just to make sure your diet is not contributing to your anxiety or counteracting other remedies or medications.

### *Foods to Avoid*

- Caffeinated beverages (if this is hard, substitute black tea for coffee, as it has one-third the caffeine and none of the harmful oils)
- Sugar and other simple carbohydrates, including anything made from flour, white rice, fruit juices, and candy
- Alcohol
- Fatty and fried foods cause fatigue, obesity, and lower immune system functioning. Avoid trans fats in favor of a small amount of poly- and monosaturated fats.
- Sodium: Eat less than 2,300 mg of sodium daily (about one teaspoon of salt!)

### *Foods to Include*

- Lean proteins: Lean meats, nonfat dairy products, eggs, beans, soy/tofu, nuts, seeds, peas, whey protein powder
- Complex carbohydrates: brown rice, wild rice, oats, bran, whole grain cereals/bread
- Limited fresh fruits, no fruit juices. Eat up to two cups of fresh fruit daily.
- Nonstarchy vegetables (peas, carrots, string beans, broccoli, etc.)
- Calcium: Drink three cups of low-fat or fat-free milk daily, or eat an equivalent amount of low-fat yogurt or other dairy foods.
- Potassium: Include foods high in potassium, such as bananas, which can counteract some of sodium's effects on blood pressure.

## Quick Strategies to Improve Sleep

No program to reduce anxiety will work if you are not getting good sleep. A quick visit to your doctor is recommended to make sure you don't have a medical reason (such as hyperthyroidism or a headache disorder) or some other psychological condition (such as mania of bipolar disorder).

### Sleep Hygiene

Before considering a medical treatment or over-the-counter remedy for insomnia, you should first look at your sleep hygiene practices. Basic guidelines for overcoming insomnia that worsens anxiety and for achieving restful, healthy sleep include the following:

- Go to bed at night and get up in the morning at the same times each day.
- Avoid afternoon naps that keep you from falling asleep at night.
- Do your exercise in the morning, not late in the day.
- Avoid alcohol and caffeine.
- Use the bedroom for sleep and sex. Don't read, watch TV, surf the Internet, do paperwork, answer the phone, have arguments, or do anything stressful in the sleep environment.
- Make sure the bedroom is quiet and comfortable. If you live in a noisy area, buy a device to create white noise, such as a fan, or wear earplugs.
- Go to bed in a relaxed mood. If you're not relaxed, consider eating a snack high in carbohydrates, such as grains, legumes, pasta, bread, vegetables, fruits, or a bowl of cereal. You could also take a hot bath or shower with lavender.
- Don't lie in bed awake, thinking and worrying. Get up and leave the bedroom, go to the bathroom, eat a snack, or watch part of a late-night movie. When you feel sleepy and relaxed, go back to the bedroom.

### Sedatives

Remember that the most recent studies on anxiety and sleep have shown that cognitive-behavioral therapy is more effective in restoring good sleep architecture and reducing anxiety long term than any medication or supplement. However, a sedative is often helpful initially to induce sleep and restore normal sleep cycles, especially for those whose sleep patterns have been disrupted by illness, international travel, or anxiety. You should be following all the above advice on proper sleep hygiene before turning to a supplement or medication. You should also not mix alcohol or drugs with any sleep remedy. Those with addictive personalities should stay away from prescription sedative medications unless prescribed by a physician who knows you well. The ATP lists several over-the-counter herbal and proprietary anxiety formulas available at your health food store or through the Internet. Start with any of these that you like.

### Here are some herbal choices:

**kava kava**: Although helpful for anxiety and insomnia, this herb has been associated with liver toxicity and withdrawal side effects. It should not be mixed with alcohol or sedative drugs or taken more than twenty-five weeks straight.

**valerian root**: From the plant Valeriana officinalis, this herb has shown benefit in the treatment of insomnia in some studies. It has been used for thousands of years in India and China as a sleep enhancer.

**chamomile**: This herb is widely used in the Western world as a treatment for anxiety, nervous stomach, and relaxation. It can be found in small amounts in a tea form or more effectively dosed through a standardized extract. The active ingredient, apigenin, works on GABA receptors much like the benzodiazepine medications.

**Ashwagandha:** This is one of the most powerful herbs in Ayurvedic healing, has been used since ancient times for a wide variety of conditions, and is most well known for its restorative benefits. Ashwagandha is commonly used for the symptoms of stress, fatigue, lack of energy, and difficulty concentrating.

*Homeopathic choices include:*
**Ignatia**: For worry, insomnia, anxiety, and emotional stress
    **Pulsatilla**: For insomnia and anxiety
    **Sleep Ease**: Made by Lehning Laboratories in France, it is a nonaddictive sleep aid first available in Europe and now being distributed in the United States.

*Over-the-counter supplements and antihistamines for sedation include:*
**5-HTP**: 5-HTP is created in the body from the amino acids tryptophan. It is then used in the synthesis of serotonin, the brain neurotransmitter most responsible for healthy sleep cycles. Because 5-HTP crosses easily into the brain across a membrane barrier known as the *blood-brain barrier*, it ultimately causes an increase in the brain's serotonin levels. The supplement is considered safe and is generally well tolerated.

**Melatonin**: Marketed as a dietary supplement, melatonin has been shown to improve sleep. It is available in a number of forms (tablets, time-release capsules, under-the tongue lozenges, liquid extract, and tea). Of course, you should cooperate with the melatonin in trying to regulate your circadian rhythms by going to bed at a regular time and following the other sleep hygiene recommendations.

**Antihistamines**: The FDA has approved two over-the-counter antihistamines for use as sleeping aids that do not require a prescription. They are diphenhydramine and doxylamine. These are the drugs most commonly found in "PM" products, such as Tylenol PM, Unisom, and Sominex. Although generally safe and nonaddictive, it is still illegal to drive a motor vehicle while under the influence of these drugs in many states!

**Medical choices:** Your doctor, if it is medically indicated, may prescribe antidepressants, benzodiazepines, or newer sedative hypnotics for sleep, especially if other methods have failed. Antidepressants are usually tried first, as they do not have the habit-forming potential of the other two categories:

**Antidepressants**: These drugs have no potential for abuse/addiction. Some have generic equivalents that are more affordable.

- Tricyclics (Amitriptyline, Nortriptyline, Silenor (low-dose Doxepin))
- Trazodone (Desyrel)
- Mirtazapine (Remeron)

**Benzodiazepines**: These drugs exert their effects on the GABA receptors in the brain. When stimulated, these receptors trigger a decrease in brain cell excitability. With regular use, these drugs are habit forming and cause rebound insomnia if you try to stop them (several days of difficulty sleeping).

- Temazepam (Restoril)
- Dalmane (Flurazepam)
- Halcion (Triazolam)
- Clonazepam (Klonopin)
- Xanax (Alprazolam)
- Valium (Diazepam)

**Newer benzodiazepine receptor agonists**: These drugs bind selectively to one or more of the GABA receptors, improving tolerability and safety.

- Ambien (Zolpidem, Intermezzo)
- Sonata (Zaleplon)
- Lunesta (eszopiclone): The first drug approved for long-term use by the FDA.

*Newer agents take advantage of the melatonin release mechanism of action:*

- Ramelteon: a melatonin 1 and 2 receptor stimulator

One of the fastest ways to reduce your vulnerability to anxiety attacks is to get deep, restorative sleep on a regular basis. If nonmedical options are no help, get to your doctor and discuss the difficulty you are having with your sleep patterns. Get a referral to a cognitive-behavioral therapist who specializes in sleep and anxiety.

## Quick Supplemental and Medical Strategies to Calm Anxiety

The most successful medical drugs for treating uncomplicated anxiety disorders are those that augment the brain's serotonin levels. First, get your sex hormones and thyroid hormones optimized (see my discussion of implanted hormone pellets in the book). Hormones may be the fastest way to restore good sleep cycles, stop irritability and anxiety, and regain normal sexual functioning. Go ahead and take the comprehensive anxiety-screening tool self-test above to see if your case is more complicated (like bipolar disorder), for which mood stabilizers must be on board first before considering other medical strategies for anxiety. Some people find that they feel better after eating certain foods high in the amino acid tryptophan. This is because tryptophan is a building block for serotonin and helps the brain make more of this helpful neurochemical. Here are the supplements and medical treatments that are known to successfully increase brain serotonin levels.

*Supplements that help serotonin levels:*
**SAM-e**: A dietary supplement whose antidepressant effects were first reported in 1973. Used for many years in Europe and especially Italy, SAM-e is now finding increasing popularity in the United States. The three monoamine brain neurotransmitters (serotonin, norepinephrine, and dopamine) are synthesized with the help of SAM-e by its donation of a methyl group to these brain chemicals. The daily dose range is from two hundred to eight hundred milligrams per day for anxiety and depression.

**5-HTP**: 5-HTP is formed in the body from the amino acid tryptophan. 5-HTP is then used to create the neurotransmitter serotonin. Because it can readily cross over the blood-brain barrier and enter the brain from the bloodstream, taking supplemental doses of 5-HTP ultimately works by increasing brain serotonin levels. The 5-HTP that is available in stores comes from the Griffonia seed, the product of an African tree grown mostly in Ghana and the Ivory Coast. Like many of the SSRIs, the list of disorders and ailments helped by 5-HTP is long and includes eating disorders, depression, anxiety, insomnia, fibromyalgia, premenstrual syndrome, and migraine headaches. The supplement is considered safe and generally well tolerated.

*Supplements for anxiety, irritability, and insomnia:*
Niacin (vitamin B3), vitamin B6, vitamin B15, folic acid, choline, L-tryptophan, vitamin A, beta-carotene, chromium, inositol, B-complex, calcium, selenium, magnesium, silicon, and manganese

*Supplements for depression and fatigue:*
Vitamin B12 (injection or under-the-tongue formula), B complex, selenium, calcium and magnesium, flower essence, pyridoxine (B6), thiamine (B1), niacin (B3), choline, chromium, vanadium, zinc, potassium, lecithin, iodine, essential fatty acids, vitamin C, L-tyrosine, folic acid, and inositol

*Supplements for Stress:*
B-complex (especially B2, B5, B6, and B15), folic acid, vitamin C, bioflavonoids, vitamin E, calcium, magnesium, lecithin, phosphorous, Bach flower remedy, zinc, potassium, selenium, and L-tyrosine

*Medical Options*
Besides hormone optimization of estrogen and testosterone in women, testosterone in men, and thyroid hormone in both sexes, the primary medications used to quickly improve anxiety are antidepressants, sedatives, and atypical antipsychotics. Of course, a thorough evaluation by your doctor and psychiatrist is necessary before embarking on any medical regimen, as these drugs require a doctor's prescription. As far as hormone replacement, do not believe that this applies only to women in menopause or men in andropause. If you are older than thirty years old, male or female, you may have testosterone deficiency that is at the root of your emotional instability. And don't let your doctor tell you testosterone is only for men; ask to have it checked. Under 42 ng/dL is a postmenopausal level, and you may be only thirty-five years old!

*Antidepressants*
Antidepressants, primarily the SSRIs, are the mainstay of medical treatment of anxiety disorders. They work by increasing the serotonin levels between nerve cells in the brain, thereby enhancing transmission along nerve pathways. Prozac was the first of these and still is the best choice for some people. It has the longest half life of any of the SSRIs, which means you can stop it anytime with no withdrawal symptoms because it wears off so slowly. It is also great on an as-needed basis for premenstrual syndrome, taken each morning for just a few days before the menstrual period when premenstrual syndrome irritability is the worst. The difficulty with sexual climax (orgasm) with SSRIs in general and Prozac in particular has led to it being used for premature ejaculation in men. Lexapro, which is a modified form of Celexa, has fewer sexual side effects and works faster, in some cases. For some people, the more sedating Zoloft or Paxil at night are better choices, especially for those with panic attacks. I think Luvox is the most powerful for OCD, but others also work well for this. Remember, SSRIs and SNRIs are not appropriate for initial therapy in patients with bipolar "manic-depression."

*Sedatives*
These work within minutes and are often given in the emergency room to stop a panic attack. Some have already been discussed in the section on sleep above. They include Xanax, Ativan (Lorazepam), Clonazepam, and Valium.

*Mood Stabilizers and Atypical Antipsychotics*
These drugs were developed to treat psychosis with irrational thinking, hallucinations, and paranoia and to stabilize the cycling moods of patients with bipolar disorder "manic-depression." In small doses, however, they can be extremely effective in treating an overactive mind that won't relax and fall asleep and can block night and early-morning anxiety with the first dose. These drugs include Risperdal, Zyprexa, Seroquel, Abilify, Neurontin, Topamax, Lamictal, and Depakote. Their use for anxiety is considered off label, meaning the FDA has not approved the drugs for this use. Your doctor can prescribe them for anxiety, however, if he or she feels it is indicated.

## Quick Positive Affirmations/Spiritual Support

Before getting out of bed in the morning and falling asleep at night, focus on a positive intention or affirmation. This can be in the form of a prayer, meditation, or affirmation exercise as outlined below.

The power of positive thinking is well established. Affirmations are an attempt to reprogram the mind. They are not lies that we tell ourselves to cover the truth but are corrections to an overly critical and judgmental negative attitude. Negative thinking always stems from a deep wound in our psyche. The only way to truly heal this wound is to look at it unflinchingly and accept it—no, embrace it. When we treat our wounds and shortcomings with love and acceptance and see the wisdom of our pain and suffering as part of a grand design beyond our comprehension, then the healing process has begun.

Rather than repeating meaningless affirmations or prayers that you don't truly feel on an emotional level, I recommend you seek a life-affirming mind-set in combination with any number of relaxation techniques. Below is a simple, five-step exercise for developing a positive mind-set:

1. **Relax.** First off, invoke the relaxation response by any number of methods: deep breathing, yoga, rhythmic exercise, meditation, self-hypnosis, etc. Be silent and completely relaxed. Be your natural self and let your mind float freely.
2. **Be grateful.** Say a simple prayer of gratitude. Give thanks for all of life, including your disappointments and failures, for they may be your greatest gifts in the larger scheme of things. Have faith that there is meaning in your suffering, illness, and pain, and be thankful for it.
3. **Affirm the truth.** Admit the truth to yourself. See yourself as you truly are. Acknowledge your weaknesses, mistakes, flaws, and your dark and ugly sides. Then throw away any judgment or feelings of guilt or regret. Look at your strengths and think of what you can do to build on them. Accept all aspects of yourself as a necessary part of the growing process. Affirm that you have a desire to find purpose, meaning, and happiness in your life and that you seek a positive, life-affirming road to this end. Acknowledge that you can achieve this without harming the rights or happiness of others. Affirm that your anxiety is a temporary condition that does not have anything to do with who you are but is a hindrance to who you want to be.
4. **Set your goals.** Focus on your intention. See clearly what you would like your life to be. See the financial success you would like to have. See the healthy and fit body in the mirror. See yourself having the right person in your life and being happy with your career the way you want it. If you cannot visualize your goals and intentions, they cannot happen. No one will walk up and give you your dream; you have to see it first and then move in that direction.
5. **Take action.** "Moving in that direction" means to take action. Nothing happens if we stay in a relaxed, dreamlike state. Put in the energy and be persistent. Face your problems and find solutions to the obstacles that stand in your way. Don't let negative thinking or doubts deter or discourage you.
6. **Prayer.** Also, if you have strong spiritual beliefs or a supportive spiritual friend, counselor, adviser, or community group, times like these are when you need them the most. Seek out the comfort, empathy, and support of your spiritual foundation. In addition, write down a prayer that reflects your deepest beliefs, wishes, and concerns. Make it a personal letter to your creator. Admit your faults and shortcomings. Ask for forgiveness. Ask for wisdom and guidance. Ask for insight and lessons that will help you find your true purpose and joy. Be prepared for tough lessons and difficult adjustments, and pray for the strength to persevere.

## Summary Note

We sincerely wish for you a quick recovery and complete control of your anxiety, both short term with the quick-fix formula and long term with the tools in the ATP. Check off the tools you intend to try or use in the sections above and then fill in the daily schedule provided below. Note that each day should be repeated the same, except for some strengthening exercises that should be done less frequently. We recommend that everybody include the following elements in his or her quick-fix formula program:

- Repeat the cognitive facts on a daily basis
- Engage in an exercise program, be it brief bursts of activity a few times a day, daily calisthenics or aerobics, or a rhythmic exercise like tai chi. Weight lifting should be kept to two to three times per week.
- Ten minutes of deep breathing at least twice a day
- Meditation or visualization/imagery once or twice a day
- Sleep hygiene
- Sedative (over-the-counter or prescription) for sleep, if needed
- Serotonin augmentation with supplements or medical treatment
- Anxiolytic drug for acute panic attacks if needed (requires a prescription)

Get into a rhythm with your quick-fix formula program and you should feel significantly better by one to seven days. Then keep this program going while you embark on adding more tools from the ATP. Review the example below and then fill in your own daily plan!

Remember, this example is not a recommendation for you specifically. Also, there is no shame in going to the emergency room and telling the doctors and nurses you are having out-of-control anxiety or panic attacks. They are very familiar with this and will get you relief quickly so you can get back home and start on a long-term program. And always get the advice of a medical professional before trying the strategies in this or any anxiety-treatment program.

—Dr. Gardner and *The Anxiety Toolbox Program* staff
www.anxietytoolbox.com

## Quick-Fix Daily Planner—Example

| DAY: | FIRST HALF HOUR | SECOND HALF HOUR |
|---|---|---|
| 7:00 a.m. | Morning prayer/ten minutes deep breathing/five-minute brisk run in place/shower | Dress and eat breakfast<br>Take SAM-e supplement or SSRI (from doctor) |
| 8:00 a.m. | Review cognitive facts/ten-minute meditation | Drive to work |
| 9:00 a.m. | Work | Work |
| 10:00 a.m. | Work | Work |
| 11:00 a.m. | Five minutes deep breathing/work | Work |
| Noon | Work | Work |
| 1:00 p.m. | Lunch break/ten-minute visualization | Work |
| 2:00 p.m. | Work | Work |
| 3:00 p.m. | Five-minute run up and down stairs/work | Work |
| 4:00 p.m. | Work | Work |
| 5:00 p.m. | Drive to gym | Twenty minutes of aerobic exercise on bike |
| 6:00 p.m. | Steam room and shower | Drive home |
| 7:00 p.m. | Prepare dinner | Eat |
| 8:00 p.m. | Read | Read |
| 9:00 p.m. | Write reminder notes/ten-minute deep breathing | Chamomile tea/valerian extract |
| 10:00 p.m. | Hot water foot soak with lavender/fifteen-minute meditation | Positive affirmation and bedtime prayer/Restoril (sedative from doctor) or Tylenol PM |

## Quick-Fix Daily Planner Template

| Sunday | FIRST HALF HOUR | SECOND HALF HOUR |
|---|---|---|
| 6:00 a.m. | | |
| 7:00 a.m. | | |
| 8:00 a.m. | | |
| 9:00 a.m. | | |
| 10:00 a.m. | | |
| 11:00 a.m. | | |
| 12:00 noon | | |
| 1:00 p.m. | | |
| 2:00 p.m. | | |
| 3:00 p.m. | | |
| 4:00 p.m. | | |
| 5:00 p.m. | | |
| 6:00 p.m. | | |
| 7:00 p.m. | | |
| 8:00 p.m. | | |
| 9:00 p.m. | | |
| 10:00 p.m. | | |
| 11:00 p.m. | | |
| 11:30 p.m. | | |
| NOTES: | | |

Quick Fix Planner

# APPENDIX III

## Combat Relief Brief: What Returning Veterans and Athletes with TBI and Postconcussion Syndrome Should Know about PTSD

TBI and PTSD have gotten a lot of press lately. There are two areas that are most in news: TBI caused by contact sports at all levels and TBI in returning veterans exposed to combat, especially the repetitive percussive effects of loud explosions on the brain. In the case of combat-related TBI, there is nearly always some overlap with the symptoms of PTSD, as they are nearly identical: fatigue, mental fog, anxiety, depression, headaches, insomnia, and so on. I often see young athletes in my clinical practice who have suffered concussions or adult bicycle- or car-accident victims with TBI. Postconcussion symptoms in athletic injuries are followed carefully by the school athletic program, and the athlete is not released to competitive action until all symptoms have cleared—at least two weeks later. A neurologist is almost always involved in these cases. Car- and cycling-accident cases are usually followed by a primary care doctor, often with the input of a TBI/PTSD neurology specialist. In the San Francisco Bay Area, I work with Fernando Miranda, MD. Much of the clinical information on TBI and PTSD in this section is derived from a lecture by Dr. Miranda on the subject.

My experience with understanding TBI and PTSD in combat veterans started when I served on the board of the Grant Humanitarian Foundation from 2010 to 2013 and as the medical adviser to a program funded by the Grant Foundation known as "Combat Relief." We assessed the gaps in needed services and the locations where returning veterans were underserved. This was done with direct input from the Department of Defense. Our main focus was in helping returning veterans with TBI and PTSD get an immediate evaluation of risk factors, degree of impairment, and early intervention and support to reduce substance abuse, suicide, homelessness, unemployment, and family trauma in this population. We provided financial support to existing nonprofits and individual service providers, giving vital care and support to those who might otherwise be unable to continue operations.

Returning veterans face challenges unique to their experiences in combat areas. They often have sustained concussion-type injuries, which require extended periods of healing to recover from. They have seen friends killed and the suffering inflicted by war on innocent civilians and children. They have often been under extreme duress while fearing for their own safety and survival. These experiences profoundly affect them at the core of their beings. PTSD is an anxiety disorder that is a normal human response to stressful and horrific life events and requires special understanding and therapy to overcome.

My interest in TBI and PTSD is also related to my role as a BioTE hormone replacement practitioner. BioTE, in partnership with Veterans Advocacy Center, is conducting a large study across the country on combat veterans with TBI and PTSD. BioTE is a Dallas-based company that developed a very popular nationwide bioidentical testosterone and estrogen-pellet implant program in 2008. It has recruited hundreds of veterans with TBI to be given implanted hormones to help overcome the brain deficits, both emotional and cognitive, caused by TBI. Many studies over fifty years have shown the benefits and protective effects of estrogen and testosterone on neurodegenerative disease. We have seen for a long time that patients who avoid (female) menopause or (male) andropause by optimizing their levels through pellet implants have the benefit of improved mental cognition, alertness, focus, and memory; a better mood with improved motivation and confidence and reduced social anxiety; deeper restorative sleep cycles; reduced headaches; and so on. BioTE believes its treatment will have a dramatic benefit for those with combat-related TBI and PTSD.

It is a shame that professional athletes are not allowed to seek testosterone optimization throughout their careers, especially those who have suffered TBI. They would be protecting themselves from degenerative brain diseases while maintaining better strength and resistance to injury, and would also recover faster after an injury. To penalize a professional athlete (male or female) for supporting themselves with their youthful and optimal levels of natural, bioidentical testosterone is dangerous and is a contributing factor in the plethora of injuries and early retirements that we are seeing in all professional sports.

Mesenchymal stem cell IV infusions are being studied for a number of degenerative neurological conditions, such as multiple sclerosis, Lou Gehrig's disease, Parkinson's disease, Alzheimer's disease, peripheral neuropathy, postconcussion syndrome, and TBI. I believe stem cell infusions right after severe concussions and any TBI, combined with hyperbaric hydrogen therapy, will prove helpful and be the standard of care in the future.

Right now, we are making do with limited options to treat TBI, including optimizing nutrition (high fat, fiber, and protein with low carbs), certain dietary supplements (vitamins D3, B complex, B12, A, K2, fish oil, and probiotics), as well as medical treatment of anxiety, depression, addiction, ADD, and general medical support with psychological counseling, cognitive-behavioral therapy, and group therapy in the returning veteran group. Student athletes are usually under the care of a neuropsychologist. I work closely with Edgar Angelone, PhD, an assistant professor at UCSF who also runs the Marin Neuropsychological Institute in San Rafael, California. He does all the cognitive evaluations and offers programs to speed recovery after TBI using various cognitive exercises, often using computer programs.

As Hippocrates (460–377 BC) said, "No head injury is too trivial to ignore." The most worrisome cases are back-to-back concussions or TBIs, especially within six months of each other, which can cause an increased risk of long-term damage and even sudden death. As there is more awareness, more cases are being reported, both by athletes and their coaches, than ever before. Helen Irlen wrote a very useful book (available on amazon.com) for student athletes and their parents: *Sports Concussions and Getting Back in the Game...of Life: A solution for concussion symptoms including headaches, light sensitivity, poor academic performance, anxiety, and others....* As an expert in visual-perceptual problems, she developed the use of spectral filters for treating concussions and TBI, and this method is called the "Irlen Method." It will no doubt be of special interest to the Veterans Administration, since Ms. Irlen discusses the significant research conducted with veterans with TBI and the use of spectral filters.

The Japanese Ministry of Health is looking at inhaled hydrogen (H2) gas mixed with air for brain-regenerative effects for TBI, and NAD infusions have been used since the 1940s, with some TBI patients feeling immediate brain-fog clearing effects. I'm hoping there are some real breakthroughs in the regenerative medicine and functional medicine fields, but for now, we follow pretty standard protocols for evaluating and treating TBI. It's not surprising that many students and their parents opt-out of contact sports after a single concussion, given all the new information on long-term cognitive and learning issues following concussions. This concern and awareness was rare a decade ago.

The symptoms of TBI and concussion generally fall into four categories. The first concerns the prefrontal cortex of the brain involved in supervising, planning, decision making, alertness, and focus. Symptoms of injury here will manifest as difficulty concentrating, difficulty remembering new information, not thinking clearly, and feeling "slowed down." The emotional centers of the amygdala and brain stem will show several common symptoms if injured, including irritability, sadness, emotional lability, anger, anxiety, and nervousness. Physical or somatic symptoms of brain injury might include headaches, nausea, vomiting, dizziness, blurry vision, balance problems, feeling sensitive to noise and bright lights, or just feeling tired. Sleep cycles also suffer with brain injury—either sleeping too much, sleeping too little, not being able to initiate sleep (fall asleep at the beginning of the night), or not being able to maintain sleep (early-morning awakening).

The ATP has many suggestions and tools for restoring deep sleep. Often, a stimulant to stay alert and focused during the day is also necessary, along with a medication to improve brain chemistry in the synapse between brain neurons. Anything that improves chemistry will improve neuronal regeneration and brain neuron connectivity. In TBI, shearing forces of a head injury cause brain neurons to be torn in the area of atonal connections between neurons. This can lead to neuronal deterioration and atrophy over time, causing all the symptoms and dysfunctions attributed to TBI.

The anxiety component of brain injury, called *PTSD*, is caused by both the emotional trauma of the injury, especially if deep fear was experienced, as well as the physical injury to the brain itself. The anxiety of PTSD must be treated for the brain to heal faster from the brain injury. Too often, the cognitive aspects of TBI are addressed with therapy, but the emotional ups and downs and poor sleep patterns are less aggressively documented and addressed at the same time. That's why a team approach of neurologist, psychologist, and psychiatrist are necessary to get the fastest and most complete recovery from TBI with PTSD.

Here are some resources for our servicemen and servicewomen:

Veteran's Support Foundation: http://vsf-usa.org

Veteran's Crisis Line: https://www.veteranscrisisline.net

Wounded Warriors Programs: https://www.woundedwarriorproject.org/programs

Swords to Plowshares (San Francisco Bay Area): https://www.swords-to-plowshares.org

APPENDIX IV

# Personal Anxiety Assessment List Workbook

Copyright © 2017 by James C. Gardner, M.D. All rights reserved.
No contents may be copied in part or full without express written permission from Dr. Gardner.

The Personal Anxiety Assessment List Workbook (PAAL) is list of experiences, symptoms, emotions, thoughts, beliefs, attitudes, diagnostic possibilities, and other data that help you assess your emotional balance. Some of this information will be utilized in your Personal Daily Planner Workbook (PDP) in helping you chose the tools that will be most helpful for your condition(s). The PAAL also provides graphs to help you follow your progress from week to week. Your personal lists should be reviewed from time to time while designing your Anxiety Toolbox Program to get a sense of your progress.

I realize there is some overlap to my questions below, so some will seem redundant.

Sometimes, however, being asked the same question may lead to different thoughts, insights, and answers the next time around, so please bear with me. Be as complete and detailed as possible in your answers. Yes, you can use an extra sheet of paper!

## MY ANXIETY SYMPTOMS

Each week of the Anxiety Toolbox Program, spend a few minutes filling in the following symptom graph. Give each item that applies to you a score between 1-10; 1 being no problem (symptom gone) and 10 meaning the symptom is the worst it has ever been or is at its peak intensity.

| MY ANXIETY SYMPTOMS | Week 1 | Week 2 | Week 3 | Week 4 | Week 5 | Week 6 | Week 7 | Week 8 |
|---|---|---|---|---|---|---|---|---|
| Anxious emotions. Nervous and worrying | | | | | | | | |
| Feeling fatigued and exhausted | | | | | | | | |
| Feeling impatient, irritable, or agitated | | | | | | | | |
| Feeling depressed, sad, or crying easily | | | | | | | | |
| Unable to enjoy pleasurable activities. hobbies | | | | | | | | |
| Heavy, pounding or irregular heartbeat | | | | | | | | |
| Chest pain, pressure, or constriction | | | | | | | | |
| Short of breath, sighing, and difficulty getting air. enough air | | | | | | | | |
| Feeling in an unreal, dream-like state | | | | | | | | |
| Feel needy; needing more attention and reassurance. | | | | | | | | |
| Fear of losing control or going crazy | | | | | | | | |
| Problems with memory, focus, or concentration | | | | | | | | |
| Problems with decision making | | | | | | | | |

| | | | | | | | | |
|---|---|---|---|---|---|---|---|---|
| Vivid dreams, night terrors | | | | | | | | |
| Problems falling asleep | | | | | | | | |
| Waking up too early, restless sleep | | | | | | | | |
| Frequent or urgent urination | | | | | | | | |
| Loss of sex drive | | | | | | | | |
| Loss of female orgasm or male erection/orgasm | | | | | | | | |
| Nausea, loss of appetite, or difficulty swallowing | | | | | | | | |
| Heartburn, belching, acid reflux or over-eating | | | | | | | | |
| Diarrhea, constipation, bloating, stomach cramps | | | | | | | | |
| Headaches, ringing ears, blurry vision | | | | | | | | |
| Rashes, hives, acne, prickly sensations, itchy skin | | | | | | | | |
| Muscular stiffness, aches, twitching, or grinding teeth | | | | | | | | |
| Trembling or shaking | | | | | | | | |
| Dizziness/lightheadedness | | | | | | | | |
| Sweating, dry mouth, flushing, turning pale | | | | | | | | |
| Self-medicating with alcohol, drugs, gambling or self-destructive behaviors | | | | | | | | |

## MY PSYCHOLOGICAL WORRIES AND PHOBIAS

Throughout the Anxiety Toolbox Program, you have read about catastrophic thinking, worrying about things that you have little control over, and irrational concerns over things that are unlikely to happen. For instance, you may have a constant fear of having a heart attack, getting cancer, or getting old and being alone. Maybe you worry about going crazy or committing suicide, or perhaps you experience an intrusive phobia, such as fear of birds, heights, or spiders. Write in your worries and phobias in the left column of the graph below. Then rate the level of discomfort and intensity of each item each week for the first eight weeks. Again, 1 means no problem (didn't bother you at all), and 10 means you had a severe anxiety attack because of exposure to the phobia.

| My Worries and Phobias | Week 1 | Week 2 | Week 3 | Week 4 | Week 5 | Week 6 | Week 7 | Week 8 |
|---|---|---|---|---|---|---|---|---|
| 1. | | | | | | | | |
| 2. | | | | | | | | |
| 3. | | | | | | | | |
| 4. | | | | | | | | |
| 5. | | | | | | | | |
| 6. | | | | | | | | |
| 7. | | | | | | | | |
| 8. | | | | | | | | |
| 9. | | | | | | | | |
| 10. | | | | | | | | |

## MY PERFORMANCE IN SPORTS, SOCIAL INTERACTIONS, AND IN OVERCOMING MY PHOBIAS

The main reason for participating in this program is to overcome anxiety roadblocks that keep you from performing well in sports, relationships, career, and other personal goals. By learning the relaxation response through breathing techniques, biofeedback, guided imagery, hypnosis, alternative strategies, and many other techniques presented in the Anxiety Toolbox Program, as well as taking medication that may be prescribed by your doctor, you may experience anything from sudden, dramatic resolution to gradual improvement in your anxiety. The graph below is to document your progress in these areas. In the far left column, write your goal. Then in each of the next eight weeks, give yourself a score from 1 to 10 on how you would rate your performance. In this case, because it is the usual convention, give yourself a 1 if you failed miserably and a 10 if you performed the task perfectly.

For instance, if you're a golfer, the left column might include: 1) GOLF; a) Relaxed focus and concentration on the ball without influence from external stimuli (the gallery or obnoxious buddies), b) Effortlessly smooth and relaxed swing and follow through, and c) improved score. If you have social phobia, the left column may list: 1) MEETING PEOPLE; a) Ability to make eye contact and introduce myself comfortably, b) Ability to mingle with others comfortably, and c) Ability to make a personal connection with someone I find interesting. Someone who is housebound with agoraphobia might list: 1) LEAVING HOME; a) Ability to walk to the mailbox without anxiety symptoms, b) Ability to walk around the block without a symptom attack, and c) Ability to walk to the store and back. If you have a specific phobia to spiders, you might list: 1) SPIDERS; a) Ability to watch a spider from a distance without feeling anxiety symptoms, and b) Ability to touch a (nonpoisonous) spider or let one sit on my hand without getting freaked out (I recommend the gentle "Daddy Longlegs" variety).

| Activity or Task | Week 1 | Week 2 | Week 3 | Week 4 | Week 5 | Week 6 | Week 7 | Week 8 |
|---|---|---|---|---|---|---|---|---|
| 1. | | | | | | | | |
| a. | | | | | | | | |
| b. | | | | | | | | |
| c. | | | | | | | | |
| 2. | | | | | | | | |
| a. | | | | | | | | |
| b. | | | | | | | | |
| c. | | | | | | | | |
| 3. | | | | | | | | |
| a. | | | | | | | | |
| b. | | | | | | | | |
| c. | | | | | | | | |
| 4. | | | | | | | | |
| a. | | | | | | | | |
| b. | | | | | | | | |
| c. | | | | | | | | |
| 5. | | | | | | | | |
| a. | | | | | | | | |
| b. | | | | | | | | |
| c. | | | | | | | | |

## MY ANXIETY DISORDERS

First, look at the results of your CAST test, sections II-XI. List only those disorders that are suspected by you based on what you have read. Explain why and how you meet the criteria for each disorder. In the case of Social Phobia, Specific Phobia, and Agoraphobia, list the object(s) of your phobia, as well as your safety and avoidance behaviors (see Chapter Eleven). In the case of Agoraphobia, list your external and internal danger signals, your feared symptom attack, and your feared catastrophe. Then have your doctor review your findings and confirm any diagnoses.

1. **GAD:**

   _____

   _____

   _____

   _____

2. **PTSD:**

   _____

   _____

   _____

   _____

3. *Grief or Situational Anxiety:*

   _____

   _____

   _____

   _____

4. **Panic Disorder:**

5. **OCD:**

6. **Specific Phobia:**

7. **Social Phobia**

a) *physical feelings and sensations related to my social anxiety*

b) *anxious thoughts, expectations, and predictions about social situations*

c) *avoidance or safety behaviors involving social situations*

8. *Agoraphobia:*

    a) *external danger signals*

    b) *internal danger signals*

    c) *feared symptom attack*

*d) feared catastrophe*

## MY DEPRESSIVE MOOD DISORDERS

See Sections VII and VIII of the CAST test, and then fill any potential diagnosis below if it is suspected by you based on what you have read. Explain why and how you meet the criteria for each disorder. Then discuss your thoughts with your psychiatrist for confirmation of the diagnosis.

1. *Dysthymic Disorder*

2. *SAD*

3. *Major Depressive Disorder*

4. *Bipolar I Disorder*

5. *Bipolar II Disorder*

## MY OTHER CONDITIONS

Explain why you feel you may have any of these other conditions.

1. *ADD/ADHD*

   _____
   _____
   _____
   _____
   _____

2. *Normal Situational Anxiety With or Without Any Anxiety Disorder*

   _____
   _____
   _____
   _____
   _____

3. *Grief or Bereavement Without Any Anxiety or Depression Disorder*

   _____
   _____
   _____
   _____
   _____

## HOW ANXIETY HAS AFFECTED MY LIFE

Think how Anxiety has affected your life. Then complete the following statements as fully as possible (if they apply to you):

1. My anxiety has affected my relationship with my spouse/significant other in the following ways (include X-spouses and previous intimate relationships, if applicable):

   _____
   _____
   _____
   _____
   _____
   _____

2. My anxiety has affected other family members (parents, kids, siblings) in the following ways:

   _____
   _____
   _____
   _____
   _____
   _____

3. My anxiety has affected my career in the following ways (think of whether or not your career choices have been limited, or relationships with bosses/coworkers or your productivity/reliability has been affected):

   _____
   _____

4. My anxiety has affected my performance in sports, job interviews, school exams, presentations/speeches, and/or dating/meeting new people in the following ways:

## FACTORS THAT HAVE CONTRIBUTED TO MY VULNERABILITY TO ANXIETY

1. List any genetic vulnerabilities, including your basic temperament (especially if timid or melancholy, rather than bold or cheerful), any family history of emotional problems:

2. List any childhood or young adulthood experiences that may have been a factor, such as abusive, neglectful or overly protective/neurotic parents, childhood sibling/peer influences, embarrassing, frightening, humiliating, or traumatic experiences:

_____

_____

_____

_____

_____

_____

3. List overwhelmingly difficult situations or circumstances you are in. Do you have a heavy responsibility that there is no escape from or easy answer to? Are you a single working parent, a full-time care-giver to an ill family member, or are you dealing with impossible legal problems?

_____

_____

_____

_____

_____

_____

4. List your other greatest stressors. Include destructive or stagnant relationships, work- related stress, family stress, financial difficulties, health problems, bad habits/unhealthy lifestyle choices (gambling, drinking, overeating, overworking, sexual exploits), stress related to your living situation, or some recent or upcoming change in your life (such as moving, starting a new job, entering a new relationship or leaving and old one):

_____

_____

5. List any personality disorders (from the CAST test):

6. List any medical problems, medications, toxic exposures, or substance abuse problems (from the CAST test):

7. Discuss the failures of your support system and your own lack of coping strategies, personal skills, or belief system that make you more vulnerable to anxiety (such as minimal or no emotional support from others, disconnectedness from family/friends/community, poor

interpersonal/social skills, poor time management/organizational skills, lack of belief/value system or spiritual frame of reference).

_____

_____

_____

_____

_____

## TOOLS THAT I ALREADY POSSESS TO HELP ANXIETY

1. List your talents, career training/education, personal skills (social/organizational/good heart/ positive attitude):

   _____

   _____

   _____

   _____

   _____

2. List your activities/hobbies/interests. Include those things you are or have been passionate about or found great enjoyment in:

   _____

   _____

   _____

_____

_____

_____

3. List any positive role models, friends, family, neighbors, or clergy who have helped you or are there for you with friendship, advice, monetary or other support:

_____

_____

_____

_____

_____

_____

4. Count your blessings (good health, safe living environment, food to eat, intelligence, a job, access to medical care):

_____

_____

_____

_____

_____

_____

5. List any doctors, counselors or medical treatments that have been helpful now or in the past:

_____

_____

6. List any positive habits/lifestyle routines (yoga, exercise, meditation, healthy diet, saying no to drugs/alcohol):

7. List any alternative treatments (herbal/supplements, acupuncture, homeopathic, Chinese Medicine):

8. Write down your value system/belief system. What are your priorities in life--- what matters to you? What gives your life purpose and meaning?

_____

_____

_____

_____

_____

_____

_____

_____

_____

_____

_____

_____

_____

_____

_____

_____

_____

## MY MEDICAL TREATMENT REGIMEN

List all medications you have ever been prescribed in the past for anxiety or depression. Try to remember the name, dosage, how long (duration) you took the medication, and what the positive benefits and negative side effects were. Why did you stop or change to another medication? (e.g., not effective or too many side effects). Who prescribed this medication?

**Medication:**_____dosage: _____
Side effects: _____
Beneficial effects: _____
Why discontinued? _____
Who prescribed? _____

**Medication:**_____dosage: _____
Side effects: _____
Beneficial effects: _____
Why discontinued? _____
Who prescribed? _____

**Medication:**_____dosage: _____
Side effects: _____
Beneficial effects: _____
Why discontinued? _____
Who prescribed? _____

**Medication:**_____dosage: _____
Side effects: _____
Beneficial effects: _____
Why discontinued? _____
Who prescribed? _____

**Medication:**_____dosage: _____
Side effects: _____
Beneficial effects: _____
Why discontinued? _____
Who prescribed? _____

**Medication:**_____dosage: _____
Side effects: _____
Beneficial effects: _____

Why discontinued? _____
Who prescribed? _____

**Medication**:_____dosage: _____
Side effects: _____
Beneficial effects: _____
Why discontinued? _____
Who prescribed? _____

## MY GOALS AND VALUES

After reading and doing the exercises in Chapter Eight of the Anxiety Toolbox Program, write in your primary goals and values below.

*Goals:*

_____
_____
_____
_____
_____
_____

*Values:*

_____
_____
_____
_____
_____
_____

## MY ATTITUDES AND BELIEFS
After reading about attitudes and beliefs in Chapter Eight, formulate your own thoughts below:

*About Life:*

*About Success:*

*About Love, Relationships:*

## MY COGNITIVE DISTORTIONS

After reading the section in Chapter Eleven of the Anxiety Toolbox Program about "Cognitive Distortions," fill out your own distortions and write in the corrections in your own words:

### Cognitive Distortions in Specific Phobia

*1. Distortion:*

_____

_____

*Correction:*

_____

_____

*2. Distortion:*

_____

_____

*Correction:*

_____

_____

*3. Distortion:*

_____

_____

*Correction:*

_____

**4. Distortion:**

*Correction:*

# Cognitive Distortions in Social Phobia

**1. Distortion:**

*Correction:*

**2. Distortion:**

*Correction:*

*3. Distortion:*

*Correction:*

*4. Distortion:*

*Correction:*

## Cognitive Distortions in Agoraphobia

*1. Distortion:*

*Correction:*

*2. Distortion:*

_____

_____

*Correction:*

_____

_____

*3. Distortion:*

_____

_____

*Correction:*

_____

_____

## STOPPING NEGATIVE THOUGHTS
***Negative Self-Talk Causes an Emotional Response.*** List any negative thoughts that lead you to have an emotional response, such as anger, frustration, or anxiety. Place your responses under the appropriate type of negative self talk listed below. Read the section on "Stopping Automatic Negative Thoughts" in Chapter Nine first. Then write a counter statement:

### Perfectionist
**1. Thought:**

_____

_____

**Counter-statement:**
_____
_____

**2. Thought:**
_____
_____

**Counter-statement:**
_____
_____

**3. Thought:**
_____
_____

**Counter-statement:**
_____
_____

## Worrier
**1. Thought:**
_____
_____

**Counter-statement:**

_____
_____

**2. Thought:**

_____
_____

**Counter-statement:**

_____
_____

**3. Thought:**

_____
_____

**Counter-statement:**

_____
_____

## Critic
**1. Thought:**

_____
_____

**Counter-statement:**

_____

_____

**2. Thought:**

_____

_____

**Counter-statement:**

_____

_____

**3. Thought:**

_____

_____

**Counter-statement:**

_____

_____

## Victim
**1. Thought:**

_____

_____

**Counter-statement:**

_____
_____

**2. Thought:**

_____
_____

**Counter-statement:**

_____
_____

**3. Thought:**

_____
_____

**Counter-statement:**

_____
_____

## MY STRESSFUL THINKING PATTERNS

After reading the section on "Stress-Resistant Thinking Tips," identify the following stressful ways of thinking and then write a correction in your own words.

**My Catastrophizing:**

_____

_____

_____

_____

**Correction:**

_____

_____

_____

**My Exaggerations and Over-generalizations:**

_____

_____

_____

**Correction:**

_____

_____

_____

**My "What If-ing":**

_____

_____

_____

**Correction:**

_____

JAMES CONRAD GARDNER, MD

**My Jumping to Conclusions:**

**Correction:**

**My Unreasonable Expectations:**

**Correction:**

**My Self-Rating:**

**Correction:**

## My Feelings
Identify feelings that you hold inside and have difficulty expressing or admitting to others:

## WHAT MAKES ME ANGRY

Identify those things in life that make you most angry. Then think about how you would implement the "Three Rs" from the section on "Anger Management." Imagine yourself actually using this strategy the next time you are angry.

1.

2.

3.

4.

## MY ASSERTIVENESS ISSUES

After reading the section on Assertiveness Training in the Anxiety Toolbox Program, fill in your responses below:

*My Behavior Style (and Why):*

_____
_____
_____
_____
_____
_____

*My Rights:*

_____
_____
_____
_____
_____
_____

*Things I should Say No To:*

_____
_____
_____
_____
_____
_____

*Ways I am Manipulated:*

_____

_____

_____

_____

_____

*New Ways to Show an Assertive Style:*

_____

_____

_____

_____

_____

## MY GRADED DESENSITIZATION AND EXPOSURE PLAN
*My Feared Object or Situation:*

_____

_____

_____

***Providing Initial Predictability and Control:*** By planning your exposure exercises in advance, you can enjoy some degree of control over a fairly predictable situation. Create a situation that is not too risky and that you could escape from if needed.

___

***Duration and Frequency Plan:*** Keep prolonging your exposures by staying in the presence of the anxiety provoking stimulus for longer and longer periods of time. Make sure to practice exposure exercises at least three days a week. Write down how often you plan to do your exposure program and your plan for gradually increasing the duration of exposure.

___

***Varying the Exposure Experience:*** How do you plan to vary the context and location of your exposure sessions to make them more challenging?

___

***Eliminating Safety, Avoidance, and Overprotective Behaviors:*** What subtle avoidance strategies should be gradually eliminated, and in which order do you want to let them go? (Such as keeping an anxiety pill in your purse, having some electronic game or smart phone to distract you, or needing to have a drink of alcohol first). Include overprotective behaviors like turning down the lights during a presentation to prevent others from seeing your anxious mannerisms.

***Gradually Increasing Challenge and Risk:*** Starting with practices that carry little actual risk, show how you will gradually make them more challenging and difficult.

___

___

___

___

___

## MY INTEROCEPTIVE EXPOSURE PLAN

Before starting any interoceptive exercise, make sure you get the approval of your personal physician.

***Physical Sensations that Trigger Catastrophic Thinking:*** List any unpleasant physical sensations that trigger catastrophic thinking and misinterpretations. Include sensations like nausea, sweating, racing heart, chest pain, dizziness, and so on. What catastrophic though accompanies each sensation (e.g.; "Chest pain makes me think I must be having a heart attack").

___

___

___

___

___

***What Method Will I Use to Trigger My Feared Physical Sensation?*** Read the section on Interoceptive Exposure in the anxiety Toolbox Program for suggestions on how you can make your feared sensation happen.

***My Interoceptive Exposure Hierarchy:*** Develop an interoceptive exposure hierarchy, gradually increasing the intensity or duration of the sensation exposure and the difficulty of the challenge. Practice the exercises alone until you find they no longer cause anxiety. Then add in exposure exercises in real-life situations once you have mastered them in the controlled home environment. Try combining interoceptive exposure with situational exposure. For instance, if you have a fear of sweating in social situations, run in place in the bathroom for two minutes to work up a small sweat before rejoining a social gathering.

## MY ALTERNATIVE STRATEGIES
***My Vitamins and Supplements:***

***My Homeopathic Remedies:***

_____

_____

_____

_____

_____

***My Herbal Remedies:***

_____

_____

_____

_____

_____

***My Ayruvedic Program:*** Find an Ayurvedic program in your area that provides insights into how to live one's life in harmony with nature and natural laws and rhythms. It should give guidelines for an intelligently regulated diet and daily routine, as well as stress management and exercises for increased fitness and alertness.

_____

_____

_____

_____

_____

## MY ACTIVITIES
List any activities that appeal to you and would help reduce anxiety and stress while increasing social interaction or bring self-esteem and satisfaction.

_____

_____

_____

_____

_____

## MY SPIRITUAL INSIGHTS AND THOUGHTS
*My Religious and Spiritual Beliefs*

_____

_____

_____

_____

_____

_____

_____

*What is the Greater Meaning and Purpose of My Life?*

_____

_____

## What Style of Prayer Feels Best to Me?

## How Can I Increase These Things in My Life?
*Love and Kindness:*

*Faith and Hope:*

*Patience:*

*Humility:*

*Honesty:*

*Mercy and Compassion:*

*Forgiveness:*

*Gratitude:*

## MY PERSONAL REASONS FOR WANTING TO OVERCOME ANXIETY
Write down how your life, and the lives of those around you, will be made happier, fuller, and more positive by your decision to conquer anxiety.

# THE ANXIETY TOOLBOX PROGRAM

APPENDIX V

## Personal Daily Planner Workbook

Copyright © 2017 by James C. Gardner, M.D. All rights reserved.
No contents may be copied in part or full without express written permission from Dr. Gardner.

## Disclaimer

The Anxiety Toolbox Program contains information the author believes to be correct. However, this program in no way substitutes for the advice and care of a skilled medical or psychological professional. Although general principles and practices of treatment are described here, no specific recommendation for any individual's therapy or medical care is intended, expressed, or implied.

When it comes to healthcare, no reader should act on the basis of any printed information, including the contents of this book, without consultation with a health care professional. Nothing in the Anxiety Toolbox Program should be construed as an attempt to diagnose, prescribe, or recommend a treatment for any health condition. You should not try to treat yourself with any of the methods described in this program without the guidance of a qualified healthcare professional who is thoroughly familiar with both the remedies and your medical and psychological status. Some of the herbs and alternative remedies listed are known to be poisonous if taken inappropriately; some can elicit allergic reactions. Do not attempt to self-diagnose or self-treat based on information in this program, including the Comprehensive Anxiety Screening Tool (CAST) self-test and the Quick Fix Formula (QFF).

The Anxiety Toolbox Program provides various website links as a helpful resource. Although we have chosen sites that reflect our standards and ideals, we take no responsibility for their content or any product that you might purchase from them.

## Introduction

You've made it to the Personal Daily Planner (PDP)! This means you've already taken the CAST self-test and have filled out the Personal Anxiety Assessment List. After that, you read through the Anxiety Toolbox Program and checked off tools that you might be interested in incorporating into your PDP. Maybe you have already finished the one week Quick Fix Formula and are ready for long-term solutions. In any case, congratulations for doing your homework and getting to the point where you are ready to put what you have learned into action. This is where the rubber meets the road. The PDP is where knowledge is turned into action; it is the vehicle for your transformation to an anxiety-controlled and emotionally balanced individual. Without this last step, the efforts you have made getting this far will fall short of the ultimate goal. As with all other aspects of the Anxiety Toolbox Program, I recommend you proceed with the guidance and help of your physician or a trusted emotional health professional.

The PDP is a 14-day repeating plan that should be designed by you to fit your schedule and needs. Overtime, it will need to be updated and redesigned, as your needs and schedule may change. Some tools are mandatory and should be included by everybody; others are optional and can be included or discarded at your discretion. Some tools will be utilized every day, some once a week, and others every-other week. The importance is that you follow the rules listed below for choosing your tools and create a program that is both effective and personalized.

The two-week program may be repeated indefinitely, but can be adjusted as your need for structure decreases. Over time, some tools may be dropped and your program simplified to be more convenient while maintaining efficacy. Other tools may be "tapered," that is, performed less frequently. This is all appropriate if you feel good solid emotional control.

In essence, the PDP is and should be a work in progress that changes as you change--- melding into your daily schedule and becoming an integral and enjoyable guiding structure and stabilizing force in your life.

## Rules For Creating Your PDP
### Simplify Your Life
Before you start to fill in the PDP, think of how you might slow down and simplify your life in order to make room for one to two hours a day dedicated to your emotional and physical health. Would you be willing to give up T.V. for the first 14 days? Can you cancel unnecessary activities or meetings? Can you say, "No, thank you," to someone who is hounding you for a date or outing? Can you go to bed at a reasonable hour and at a consistent time each night? Identify areas of wasted or misspent time and recover this valuable commodity to be used for a very good purpose that will provide lifetime benefits.

### Enter Your Appointments
Throughout this program, you may be inspired to make any number of appointments with a trusted and caring professional. It might be for legal advice, financial advice, or advice from a "life coach" in managing your time. It could be for spiritual counseling from a theologian, minister, rabbi, cleric, monk, or priest. It could be with a biofeedback specialist, body work practitioner, herbalist, homeopathic physician, nutritionist, hypnotherapist, yoga or aerobic exercise instructor, acupuncturist, or a music teacher to get you back on the piano. Any number of people might prove very helpful in reducing stress and calming your anxious thoughts and feelings. First and foremost on this list should be an appointment with your doctor for a full physical focusing on hormone deficiency and sleep/anxiety-attack management, a psychiatrist if recommended by your primary care doctor, and a therapist for possible cognitive behavioral therapy (CBT), guided imagery, visualization, or other forms of psychotherapy. Many psychiatrists handle this "talk therapy" as well as any medical treatment; others will refer you to a specific therapist for this. Start working on this today, and ask yourself every day if you can do anything to make progress on filling out these appointment slots.

### Doctors Appointments:
1. Name:_____Date:_____Time:_____
Location:_____Phone_____

2. Name:_____ Date:_____ Time:_____
Location:_____Phone_____

3. Name:_____ Date:_____ Time:_____
Location:_____Phone_____

**Psychiatrist Appointments:**
1. Name:_____ Date:_____ Time:_____
Location:_____Phone_____

2. Name:_____ Date:_____ Time:_____
Location:_____Phone_____

3. Name:_____ Date:_____ Time:_____
Location:_____Phone_____

4. Name:_____ Date:_____ Time:_____
Location:_____Phone_____

**Therapist/Counselor Appointments:**
1. Name:_____ Date:_____ Time:_____
Location:_____Phone_____

2. Name:_____ Date:_____ Time:_____
Location:_____Phone_____

3. Name:_____ Date:_____ Time:_____
Location:_____Phone_____

4. Name:_____ Date:_____ Time:_____
Location:_____Phone_____

**Other Therapists, Practitioners, Spiritual Advisors, Exercise Instructors, Music Teacher, or Other Activities:**
1. Name:_____ Date:_____ Time:_____
Location:_____Phone_____

2. Name:_____ Date:_____ Time:_____
Location:_____Phone_____

3. Name:_____ Date:_____ Time:_____
Location:_____Phone_____

4. Name:_____ Date:_____ Time:_____
Location:_____Phone_____

5. Name:_____ Date:_____ Time:_____
Location:_____Phone_____

6. Name:_____ Date:_____ Time:_____
Location:_____Phone_____

7. Name:_____ Date:_____ Time:_____
Location:_____Phone_____

After scheduling your important appointments and filling out the detailed information in the spaces provided above, enter a reminder of the visit in the proper time slot in the PDP (see example PDP page).

## Toolbox Compartment Number One: The Medical Treatment of Anxiety; Using the "Somatic Symptom" and "Brain Function" Models to Determine Your Medical Therapy Options

Read Chapter Four in the Anxiety Toolbox Program on the medical treatment of anxiety. I feel medical treatment is often crucial for many in getting an initial hold on emotional turmoil. Do not hesitate to seek professional care for prescription medication with your physician or psychiatrist. Follow their instructions carefully and consistently, and report any unexpected side effects. Write down in your PDP any medical regimen you have been prescribed, including dose and time you're supposed to take each medication.

## Toolbox Compartment Number Two: Alternative Medical Therapy Tools for Anxiety

Review Chapter Five on vitamins and supplements, and alternative medicine strategies. Follow the recommended guidelines and decide if any of these are for you. These can be taken in the morning if activating or at night if calming and sedating. Put a note in your PDP so you won't forget to take them.

Review the sections on homeopathic, herbal, and ayurvedic strategies. If any of these appeal to you, we recommend you seek out a practitioner in your area to learn more. Use the PDP to make sure you are consistent with taking your remedy and making your appointments.

## Toolbox Compartment Number Three: Anxiety Caused by Pain Management and Addiction Problems

If you are challenged with pain or addiction to pain medications, read this section and decide if an alternative treatment for pain is worth looking into. Check out some of the suggestions on neurostimulation devices, regenerative medicine technologies, and non-addictive medication alternatives. Consider an addiction medicine or pain management specialist to help you overcome your dependence on controlled substances. Read the section on IV NAD detox if you don't have time for a traditional program.

## Toolbox Compartment Number Four: Healthy Lifestyle, Self-Care, and Personal Organization Tools

1. Write in the times you plan to eat each day and where you plan to eat.
2. Enter your exercise schedule; the time and days you plan to exercise, the type of exercise, and how much time you are allotting for each session. For instance, you may decide to weight lift two times a week for 30 minutes and perform yoga three times a week for 1 hour. Write down your sleep and waking times.
3. List any supplements or sleep aids you will be taking at the time you will be taking them. Try to be consistent from day-to-day.
4. Use the PDP to promote your personal organization and time management skills. Make your schedule as efficient and well-planned as possible. Try to batch tasks at specific time slots. For instance, you may decide to pay your bills every two weeks at 6:00 p.m. on Wednesday evenings. Or you may want to take care of your laundry and dry cleaning every other Friday at 5:00 p.m. List all your chores and tasks first, then find a way to integrate them into your PDP with the least amount of strain and stress.

## Toolbox Compartment Number Five: Goals and Values; Attitudes and Beliefs

1. Complete the exercises on defining and understanding your goals and values in the Anxiety Toolbox Program book and enter your responses in your Personal Anxiety Assessment List (PAAL). Chose a time each day to review and acknowledge your personal goals and values.
2. In the Anxiety Toolbox Program book, check the Attitudes and Beliefs that you feel you may wrongfully hold and want to correct. Write your own corrected statement (or the one provided in the book, if it is acceptable) in the section provided in the PAAL. Spend time each day reviewing your corrected attitudes and beliefs about life, success, work, money, love and relationships.

## Toolbox Compartment Number Six: Mind-Body Tools

1. Everyone should learn the basics of meditation, with or without imagery, visualization, or self-hypnosis. Meditation starts with deep abdominal breathing techniques taught in compartment
2. It may stand alone as a simple exercise, or grow to include other dimensions, including spirituality and prayer. Make time once or twice a day for 10 to 30 minutes each for meditation.
3. Consider formal training in biofeedback to learn the relaxation response. You may want to purchase a home biofeedback device (see links provided) to continue your practice of invoking a state of alpha brain wave relaxation whenever needed, especially during times of high anxiety, panic, or exposure to phobic stimuli.
4. Consider a simple program of Aromatherapy, Hydrotherapy, Light Therapy, Music therapy, or Humor Therapy as described in the book.

## Toolbox Compartment Number Seven: Body-Mind Tools

1. Learn the deep breathing and progressive relaxation exercises. These can be incorporated into your daily meditation sessions.
2. Yoga and T'ai Chi are considered by some to be forms of meditation, as they involve the practice of meditative deep breathing and a relaxed mental state during the exercise. You can often combine your exercise and meditation into one activity if you are willing to learn these ancient practices. Find a class that meets near you and write in your PDP the class schedule.
3. You may find benefit from once-a-week sessions of EMDR, sensory-deprivation floatation, reflexology, massage, acupuncture, or Chi-gong. Put these appointments in your PDP.

## Toolbox Compartment Number Eight: Cognitive Behavioral Tools

1. Go through the section on "Cognitive Distortions" in your PAAL. Write down the correction in your own words and spend time each day reviewing these insights that you have made.
2. Practice your communication skills, stress and anger management skills, and your assertiveness skills on a daily basis during times that are not dedicated to any particular task. Practice these skills every day at work with your co-workers and boss. Practice every day on the bus, taxi, subway, or any other place that gives you the opportunity to interact with others.
3. If you have social anxiety, read the section on "Social Anxiety and Social Skills" training. Practice these skills whenever possible: a new date; a presentation at work, a job interview, and so on. Try to spend time perhaps three days a week reviewing this section in the book. At the end of each twenty-minute session, spend ten minutes visualizing yourself performing well in various social situations.

4. If you have a phobia, create a desensitization hierarchy as described in compartment 5. Spend time regularly, several times a week, exposing yourself to the feared objects or sensations that trigger your phobia. You may use any number of relaxation techniques while confronting your fear. This will help you endure the discomfort longer and make you feel confident of your ability to turn the anxiety off when you want to. We recommend getting a biofeedback device to learn the relaxation response and monitor yourself in phobic situations.

## Toolbox Compartment Number Nine: Activity Tools

1. Choose one or more activities that appeal to you, are reasonably easy and convenient to initiate, and fit your budget. Decide how much time you have to devote to each activity and carve out that time in your PDP. Start out by making a small commitment of time. You can always increase the time spend in any activity if you really feel the benefits.
2. Consider volunteer activities. Any help you can give others that is meaningful and appreciated will help you see your life and problems in better perspective.

## Toolbox Compartment Number Ten: Spiritual Tools

1. Read the sections on religion, spirituality, and seeking a spiritual framework. Then write down in your PAAL how you personally feel about your own spirituality and the role you want it to play in your life. Will it be a guiding force that informs your actions and decisions, or something you keep on a shelf to bring out and dust off for special occasions? How will you devote more time to spiritual growth? Consider joining a like-minded group or your local church, synagogue, temple, or mosque to learn more and get the support and encouragement you need. Make time on your PDP for contemplating and pursuing your spiritual side.
2. Consider the power of prayer. Decide if daily prayer is right for you, then write the time you will spend praying in your PDP.
3. Look at the "Other Spiritual Tools" and think of ways you could incorporate these attributes into your life and way of thinking. Review any entries you may have made in your PAAL on these subjects and add to or change them as new insights come to you.

## Creating Your PDP

Remember, your PDP is always a work in progress. You will be re-creating it every two weeks, continuing strategies that are helpful, eliminating things that didn't work or were too difficult to fit into your schedule. You are trying to achieve a balance of simplifying your life and reducing stress while at the same time *increasing* your expectations of yourself: taking more responsibility for your thoughts and actions; challenging yourself to face your fears and overcome them to grow emotionally and spiritually. We recommend you fill out your PDP in pencil so that it can easily be adjusted and changed, if needed.

Print out a copy of the 14-day daily planner and write in the day and date at the top corner of each page. Decide when you will wake up and when you will go to bed. Try to be consistent, if possible. Then follow the suggestions above for filling in the tools from the various toolbox compartments in a way that seems natural to you. Again, you may change your mind and do things differently as you progress. Eventually, your PDP will have fewer appointments, and you will need less and less time reviewing your thoughts, beliefs, goal, values, and attitudes.

As you progress you will be able to drop much of the structure and discipline that is necessary in the beginning. Please take a look at the sample PDP below. I have chosen to present just two pages, day 1 and day 7 (Monday and Sunday) from this fictitious person's PDP. Remember, this example is not meant to promote any particular course of treatment and is not intended as a specific recommendation for any individual's therapy or medical care. Always consult with a health care professional before beginning a course of treatment.

Thanks for taking this journey and let me know your thoughts and comments online!

Dr. Gardner
www.anxietytoolbox.com

# PERSONAL DAILY PLANNER: EXAMPLE 1

| Monday | FIRST HALF HOUR | SECOND HALF HOUR |
|---|---|---|
| 6:00 a.m. | Snoozing | Wake up 6:30 am. 15 minutes of deep breathing and meditation. 15 minutes of T'ai Chi. |
| 7:00 a.m. | Take morning vitamins and medication X, 0.5mg. shower/dress/eat breakfast | Commute to work with favorite music |
| 8:00 a.m. | Start work | work |
| 9:00 a.m. | work | work |
| 10:00 a.m. | work | work |
| 11:00 a.m. | 5 minutes or progressive relaxation and deep breathing. Back to work | work |
| 12:00 noon | work | 3 minutes of brisk exercise. Lunch. Short walk outside. |
| 1:00 p.m. | work | work |
| 2:00 p.m. | work | work |
| 3:00 p.m. | 5 minutes meditation, deep breathing Back to work | work |
| 4:00 p.m. | work | Drive to the gym |
| 5:00 p.m. | 30-minute aerobics class | 15-minute hot shower, steam room Dress and drive home |
| 6:00 p.m. | Prepare dinner while watching the news | Eat dinner. 15 minutes progressive relaxation exercises |
| 7:00 p.m. | Review PAAL section on Goals/Values; Attitudes and Beliefs | Review PAAL section on Mistaken Beliefs and Wrong Thinking |
| 8:00 p.m. | Follow exposure hierarchy plan as outlined in the PAAL | Practice biofeedback to reduce anxious emotions during exposure |
| 9:00 p.m. | 15 minutes deep breathing, visualization and imagery. 15 minutes prayer. | 30 minutes foot hydrotherapy with lavender oil aromatherapy while reading favorite magazine |
| 10:00 p.m. | Take Medication Y, 50mg and Supplement Z, 300mg and go to sleep. | sleep |
| 11:00 p.m. | sleep | sleep |
| NOTES: | | |

## PERSONAL DAILY PLANNER: <u>EXAMPLE 2</u>

| Sunday 3/8 | FIRST HALF HOUR | SECOND HALF HOUR |
|---|---|---|
| 6:00 a.m. | sleep | sleep |
| 7:00 a.m. | Wake up. Take medication X. 10-minute prayer, 20 minutes T'ai Chi exercises. | Shower, dress and eat breakfast |
| 8:00 a.m. | Read morning paper | Drive to place of worship |
| 9:00 a.m. | Worship service | Worship service |
| 10:00 a.m. | Mingle with people, practice social skills In supportive environment. | Drive to park and take a walk |
| 11:00 a.m. | Go to the mall to practice exposure to Social situations | At the mall |
| 12:00 noon | At the mall | Eat lunch |
| 1:00 p.m. | Drive home. Pay bills that have come in over the last 2 weeks. | Bills and household paperwork |
| 2:00 p.m. | Clean house/apartment, do laundry | Clean house/apartment, do laundry |
| 3:00 p.m. | Midafternoon meditation while the clothes are drying | Call friends/family who are supportive and concerne |
| 4:00 p.m. | Clean the clutter and organize personal possessions. | Clean clutter and organize. Throw stuff out that's not needed or give it to charity. |
| 5:00 p.m. | Work in garden | Work in garden |
| 6:00 p.m. | Shower. Prepare dinner. | Eat dinner. |
| 7:00 p.m. | Go to library to read, meet friends | At the library. |
| 8:00 p.m. | Evening walk. | Review PAAL section on spiritual thoughts, beliefs Evening prayer |
| 9:00 p.m. | 30 minute hydrotherapy/aromatherapy while watching T.V. | Progressive relaxation. Visualize success in endeavor of upcoming week. |
| 10:00 p.m. | Take Medication Y 50mg and supplement Z, 300mg and go to sleep | sleep |
| 11:00 p.m. | sleep | sleep |
| NOTES: | | |

Personal Daily Planner

# FOURTEEN-DAY PERSONAL DAILY PLANNER TEMPLATE
**Personal Daily Planner: Day 1**

| Monday | FIRST HALF HOUR | SECOND HALF HOUR |
|---|---|---|
| 6:00 a.m. | | |
| 7:00 a.m. | | |
| 8:00 a.m. | | |
| 9:00 a.m. | | |
| 10:00 a.m. | | |
| 11:00 a.m. | | |
| 12:00 noon | | |
| 1:00 p.m. | | |
| 2:00 p.m. | | |
| 3:00 p.m. | | |
| 4:00 p.m. | | |
| 5:00 p.m. | | |
| 6:00 p.m. | | |
| 7:00 p.m. | | |
| 8:00 p.m. | | |
| 9:00 p.m. | | |
| 10:00 p.m. | | |
| 11:00 p.m. | | |
| 11:30 p.m. | | |
| NOTES: | | |

Personal Daily Planner

# Personal Daily Planner: Day 2

| Tuesday | FIRST HALF HOUR | SECOND HALF HOUR |
|---|---|---|
| 6:00 a.m. | | |
| 7:00 a.m. | | |
| 8:00 a.m. | | |
| 9:00 a.m. | | |
| 10:00 a.m. | | |
| 11:00 a.m. | | |
| 12:00 noon | | |
| 1:00 p.m. | | |
| 2:00 p.m. | | |
| 3:00 p.m. | | |
| 4:00 p.m. | | |
| 5:00 p.m. | | |
| 6:00 p.m. | | |
| 7:00 p.m. | | |
| 8:00 p.m. | | |
| 9:00 p.m. | | |
| 10:00 p.m. | | |
| 11:00 p.m. | | |
| 11:30 p.m. | | |
| NOTES: | | |

Personal Daily Planner

## Personal Daily Planner: Day 3

| Wednesday | FIRST HALF HOUR | SECOND HALF HOUR |
|---|---|---|
| 6:00 a.m. | | |
| 7:00 a.m. | | |
| 8:00 a.m. | | |
| 9:00 a.m. | | |
| 10:00 a.m. | | |
| 11:00 a.m. | | |
| 12:00 noon | | |
| 1:00 p.m. | | |
| 2:00 p.m. | | |
| 3:00 p.m. | | |
| 4:00 p.m. | | |
| 5:00 p.m. | | |
| 6:00 p.m. | | |
| 7:00 p.m. | | |
| 8:00 p.m. | | |
| 9:00 p.m. | | |
| 10:00 p.m. | | |
| 11:00 p.m. | | |
| 11:30 p.m. | | |
| NOTES: | | |

Personal Daily Planner

## Personal Daily Planner: Day 4

| Thursday | FIRST HALF HOUR | SECOND HALF HOUR |
|---|---|---|
| 6:00 a.m. | | |
| 7:00 a.m. | | |
| 8:00 a.m. | | |
| 9:00 a.m. | | |
| 10:00 a.m. | | |
| 11:00 a.m. | | |
| 12:00 noon | | |
| 1:00 p.m. | | |
| 2:00 p.m. | | |
| 3:00 p.m. | | |
| 4:00 p.m. | | |
| 5:00 p.m. | | |
| 6:00 p.m. | | |
| 7:00 p.m. | | |
| 8:00 p.m. | | |
| 9:00 p.m. | | |
| 10:00 p.m. | | |
| 11:00 p.m. | | |
| 11:30 p.m. | | |
| NOTES: | | |

Personal Daily Planner

# THE ANXIETY TOOLBOX PROGRAM

## Personal Daily Planner: Day 5

| Friday | FIRST HALF HOUR | SECOND HALF HOUR |
|---|---|---|
| 6:00 a.m. | | |
| 7:00 a.m. | | |
| 8:00 a.m. | | |
| 9:00 a.m. | | |
| 10:00 a.m. | | |
| 11:00 a.m. | | |
| 12:00 noon | | |
| 1:00 p.m. | | |
| 2:00 p.m. | | |
| 3:00 p.m. | | |
| 4:00 p.m. | | |
| 5:00 p.m. | | |
| 6:00 p.m. | | |
| 7:00 p.m. | | |
| 8:00 p.m. | | |
| 9:00 p.m. | | |
| 10:00 p.m. | | |
| 11:00 p.m. | | |
| 11:30 p.m. | | |
| NOTES: | | |

Personal Daily Planner

JAMES CONRAD GARDNER, MD

## Personal Daily Planner: Day 6

| Saturday | FIRST HALF HOUR | SECOND HALF HOUR |
|---|---|---|
| 6:00 a.m. | | |
| 7:00 a.m. | | |
| 8:00 a.m. | | |
| 9:00 a.m. | | |
| 10:00 a.m. | | |
| 11:00 a.m. | | |
| 12:00 noon | | |
| 1:00 p.m. | | |
| 2:00 p.m. | | |
| 3:00 p.m. | | |
| 4:00 p.m. | | |
| 5:00 p.m. | | |
| 6:00 p.m. | | |
| 7:00 p.m. | | |
| 8:00 p.m. | | |
| 9:00 p.m. | | |
| 10:00 p.m. | | |
| 11:00 p.m. | | |
| 11:30 p.m. | | |
| NOTES: | | |

Personal Daily Planner

## Personal Daily Planner: Day 7

| Sunday | FIRST HALF HOUR | SECOND HALF HOUR |
|---|---|---|
| 6:00 a.m. | | |
| 7:00 a.m. | | |
| 8:00 a.m. | | |
| 9:00 a.m. | | |
| 10:00 a.m. | | |
| 11:00 a.m. | | |
| 12:00 noon | | |
| 1:00 p.m. | | |
| 2:00 p.m. | | |
| 3:00 p.m. | | |
| 4:00 p.m. | | |
| 5:00 p.m. | | |
| 6:00 p.m. | | |
| 7:00 p.m. | | |
| 8:00 p.m. | | |
| 9:00 p.m. | | |
| 10:00 p.m. | | |
| 11:00 p.m. | | |
| 11:30 p.m. | | |
| NOTES: | | |

Personal Daily Planner

## Personal Daily Planner: Day 8

| Monday | FIRST HALF HOUR | SECOND HALF HOUR |
|---|---|---|
| 6:00 a.m. | | |
| 7:00 a.m. | | |
| 8:00 a.m. | | |
| 9:00 a.m. | | |
| 10:00 a.m. | | |
| 11:00 a.m. | | |
| 12:00 noon | | |
| 1:00 p.m. | | |
| 2:00 p.m. | | |
| 3:00 p.m. | | |
| 4:00 p.m. | | |
| 5:00 p.m. | | |
| 6:00 p.m. | | |
| 7:00 p.m. | | |
| 8:00 p.m. | | |
| 9:00 p.m. | | |
| 10:00 p.m. | | |
| 11:00 p.m. | | |
| 11:30 p.m. | | |
| NOTES: | | |

Personal Daily Planner

## Personal Daily Planner: Day 9

| Tuesday | FIRST HALF HOUR | SECOND HALF HOUR |
|---|---|---|
| 6:00 a.m. | | |
| 7:00 a.m. | | |
| 8:00 a.m. | | |
| 9:00 a.m. | | |
| 10:00 a.m. | | |
| 11:00 a.m. | | |
| 12:00 noon | | |
| 1:00 p.m. | | |
| 2:00 p.m. | | |
| 3:00 p.m. | | |
| 4:00 p.m. | | |
| 5:00 p.m. | | |
| 6:00 p.m. | | |
| 7:00 p.m. | | |
| 8:00 p.m. | | |
| 9:00 p.m. | | |
| 10:00 p.m. | | |
| 11:00 p.m. | | |
| 11:30 p.m. | | |
| NOTES: | | |

Personal Daily Planner

JAMES CONRAD GARDNER, MD

**Personal Daily Planner: Day 10**

| Wednesday | FIRST HALF HOUR | SECOND HALF HOUR |
|---|---|---|
| 6:00 a.m. | | |
| 7:00 a.m. | | |
| 8:00 a.m. | | |
| 9:00 a.m. | | |
| 10:00 a.m. | | |
| 11:00 a.m. | | |
| 12:00 noon | | |
| 1:00 p.m. | | |
| 2:00 p.m. | | |
| 3:00 p.m. | | |
| 4:00 p.m. | | |
| 5:00 p.m. | | |
| 6:00 p.m. | | |
| 7:00 p.m. | | |
| 8:00 p.m. | | |
| 9:00 p.m. | | |
| 10:00 p.m. | | |
| 11:00 p.m. | | |
| 11:30 p.m. | | |
| NOTES: | | |

Personal Daily Planner

## Personal Daily Planner: Day 11

| Thursday | FIRST HALF HOUR | SECOND HALF HOUR |
|---|---|---|
| 6:00 a.m. | | |
| 7:00 a.m. | | |
| 8:00 a.m. | | |
| 9:00 a.m. | | |
| 10:00 a.m. | | |
| 11:00 a.m. | | |
| 12:00 noon | | |
| 1:00 p.m. | | |
| 2:00 p.m. | | |
| 3:00 p.m. | | |
| 4:00 p.m. | | |
| 5:00 p.m. | | |
| 6:00 p.m. | | |
| 7:00 p.m. | | |
| 8:00 p.m. | | |
| 9:00 p.m. | | |
| 10:00 p.m. | | |
| 11:00 p.m. | | |
| 11:30 p.m. | | |
| NOTES: | | |

Personal Daily Planner

## Personal Daily Planner: Day 12

| Friday | FIRST HALF HOUR | SECOND HALF HOUR |
|---|---|---|
| 6:00 a.m. | | |
| 7:00 a.m. | | |
| 8:00 a.m. | | |
| 9:00 a.m. | | |
| 10:00 a.m. | | |
| 11:00 a.m. | | |
| 12:00 noon | | |
| 1:00 p.m. | | |
| 2:00 p.m. | | |
| 3:00 p.m. | | |
| 4:00 p.m. | | |
| 5:00 p.m. | | |
| 6:00 p.m. | | |
| 7:00 p.m. | | |
| 8:00 p.m. | | |
| 9:00 p.m. | | |
| 10:00 p.m. | | |
| 11:00 p.m. | | |
| 11:30 p.m. | | |
| NOTES: | | |

Personal Daily Planner

## Personal Daily Planner: Day 13

| Saturday | FIRST HALF HOUR | SECOND HALF HOUR |
|---|---|---|
| 6:00 a.m. | | |
| 7:00 a.m. | | |
| 8:00 a.m. | | |
| 9:00 a.m. | | |
| 10:00 a.m. | | |
| 11:00 a.m. | | |
| 12:00 noon | | |
| 1:00 p.m. | | |
| 2:00 p.m. | | |
| 3:00 p.m. | | |
| 4:00 p.m. | | |
| 5:00 p.m. | | |
| 6:00 p.m. | | |
| 7:00 p.m. | | |
| 8:00 p.m. | | |
| 9:00 p.m. | | |
| 10:00 p.m. | | |
| 11:00 p.m. | | |
| 11:30 p.m. | | |
| NOTES: | | |

Personal Daily Planner

## Personal Daily Planner: Day 14

| Sunday | FIRST HALF HOUR | SECOND HALF HOUR |
|---|---|---|
| 6:00 a.m. | | |
| 7:00 a.m. | | |
| 8:00 a.m. | | |
| 9:00 a.m. | | |
| 10:00 a.m. | | |
| 11:00 a.m. | | |
| 12:00 noon | | |
| 1:00 p.m. | | |
| 2:00 p.m. | | |
| 3:00 p.m. | | |
| 4:00 p.m. | | |
| 5:00 p.m. | | |
| 6:00 p.m. | | |
| 7:00 p.m. | | |
| 8:00 p.m. | | |
| 9:00 p.m. | | |
| 10:00 p.m. | | |
| 11:00 p.m. | | |
| 11:30 p.m. | | |
| NOTES: | | |

Personal Daily Planner

www.ingramcontent.com/pod-product-compliance
Lightning Source LLC
Chambersburg PA
CBHW080027180426
43195CB00053B/2805